THE BRONZE AGE ROUND BARROW IN BRITAIN

Sir Richard Colt Hoare of Stourhead, Wiltshire.

Mr William Cunnington, F.S.A., of Heytesbury, Wiltshire.

THE BRONZE AGE ROUND BARROW IN BRITAIN

An introduction to the study of the funerary practice and culture of the British and Irish Single-Grave People of the second millennium B.C.

PAUL ASHBEE

PHOENIX HOUSE LTD
LONDON

In Memoriam
V. GORDON CHILDE
1892–1957

Made in Great Britain
at the
Aldine Press · Letchworth · Herts
for
Phoenix House Ltd
10–13 Bedford Street
Strand, London, W.C.2
First published 1960

CONTENTS

ILLUSTRATIONS

PLATES

TEXT FIGURES

PREFACE

A CENTURY ago England was unique as the first industrial state. Into and out of our geographically nodal islands, an entity but at once a part of Western Europe, flowed the vital knowledge of practice, process, and appliance. Today, in but a life-span, technology's ever-quickening tempo can be seen to have made even more complex the interrelationships of class, community, and nation-state. Appreciation and wider understanding of this pervasive process are only possible when it is seen against the backcloth of history and beyond that the ultimate perspective of the prehistoric past.

It is sometimes said that the roots of our achievement lie in the splendid remains of the static Middle Eastern riverine urbanization, via Greece and Rome which were its European progeny. Indeed, questing youth has been adjured to quit the clinging mire of our island and to set his feet upon the desert highways. Yet they passed away, their monolithic social and economic structure being presumably unable to counter changing environmental circumstance. The formidable edifice which is our modern technological and scientific knowledge rests, ultimately, upon the progressive skills of unnamed artificers in bronze who were active and inventive in the second millennium B.C. For modern Western European society must be viewed against the perspective of its own Western European prehistoric past; such malformed fragments as have come to us from oriental sources have been adapted and assimilated into our own distinctive mainstream. In the measure of this lies the vital importance of the study of our Western and insular prehistory in its each and every aspect.

A decade of excavation, in which I have played a part, has resulted in the careful examination and record of greater numbers of Britain's round barrows, and their associate monuments, than ever before. These mounds, and the burials beneath them, embody the social traditions of those who, if they were not our first practising metallurgists, were the first to gear a society to the products of that craft. Nowadays the extreme complexity of the components of our prehistoric past, which were broadly delineated by pre-war research, is being realized. Thus the present time is particularly apt for this personal assessment of what is known of our round barrows and their builders.

To be valid such an account must view the particular period of our prehistory defined in the archaeological record by round barrows and their contents as part of the wider European entity. Even though we are conditioned by our relative knowledge of the musters of barrows in the different regions of our islands, the primacy of the Wessex region emerges with clarity and substance. Inevitably, the structure of much of the narrative about this is, at this stage, unavoidable. Much of the evidence is fragmentary and even ambiguous but, notwithstanding, a general if incomplete picture emerges. Among other things it poses pointedly the problems and difficulties inherent in convincing identification of the primary diffusive factors which must lie beneath the palimpsest of prehistory. Furthermore, when excavating or writing, I have been continually conscious that like my material I am inescapably an expression of a distinct society. I cannot but be subject to the pressures and prejudices inherent in my own society when I present my view of a period of prehistory. For it should be realized that dedicated objectivity is all but a myth; the mere mechanics of excavation, examination, and synthesis impose unavoidable subjectivity.

Before all else my personal debt to my Professor, Gordon Childe, is overwhelming. For a number of the immediate post-war years I was privileged to study Western European Prehistoric Archaeology under his tutelage. I was stimulated by his ideas, moved by his kindness, and honoured by his friendship, interest, and encouragement. My deep and lasting gratitude is expressed by this book's dedication.

PAUL ASHBEE.

Chelsfield, Kent.
4th October 1959.

ACKNOWLEDGMENTS

DOWN THE years while writing this book I have been encouraged and criticized to its considerable advantage by the penetrating, frequently pungent, and stimulating observations of my wife and her friend Miss Jane Osborn. Their reading of the text removed many blemishes and thus was the rough made smooth. I thank them.

It must be recorded that a memorable and strenuous correspondence, following no less memorable meetings in 1956 and 1957, with the late O. G. S. Crawford, brought the concept of a consideration of Bronze Age Round Barrows to maturity, and that L. V. Grinsell's exhaustive lists have guided my faltering steps at all stages. Discussion, which has involved much dissection and reassembly, with Dr Isobel Smith at Avebury, who has been good enough to read the text in typescript, has strengthened my confidence in my ideas and interpretations. Graham Connah, who has worked with me in the field both hard and often, must be thanked for preparation of the index.

To those whose books and reports I have perused, whose excavations I have scrutinized, or who have favoured me with facts and ideas in converse and correspondence, my debt is considerable. I can but trust that acknowledgment, reflecting my consciousness of indebtedness, will in some small measure express my thanks to them all.

Many individuals and institutions have most kindly allowed me to use their line-drawings and photographs, all of material vital to the theme, for illustrative purposes. It is with gratitude and pleasure that I acknowledge below these contributions and the patient, tireless, and obliging friends who have so generously and skilfully piloted the resources in their charge to my purposes.

Individuals: K. Annable, D. Brothwell, Professor J. G. D. Clark, G. C. Dunning, R. Farrar, Prof. W. F. Grimes, L. V. Grinsell, Mrs M. Guido, J. R. C. Hamilton, B. Hope-Taylor, John Hopkins, Sir Thomas Kendrick, C. P. Lloyd, W. Phillips, Professor Stuart Piggott, R. Rainbird Clarke, Alan Sorrell, G. de G. Sievéking.

Institutions: The Society of Antiquaries of London, the Bodleian Library, the British Museum, the Cambridge Museum of Air Photography, the Central Office of Information, Devizes Museum, Dorchester Museum, Exeter Museum, the Institute of Archaeology of the University of London, the Ancient Monuments Department of the Ministry of Works, the Ordnance Survey, the Prehistoric Society, the National Museum of Antiquities of Scotland, the National Museum of Ireland, Dublin, the National Museum of Wales, the Rheinisches Landesmuseum, Bonn.

'Every man naturally is desirous of knowledge, and therefore man without learninge, and the remembrance of things past, falls into a beastlye sottishnesse and his life is noe better to be accounted of than to be buryed alive.' William Dugdale, 1655.

INTRODUCTION

DURING the early part of the second millennium B.C. a new people came into Britain from the mainland of Europe. Their dead were buried as individual inhumations beneath round barrows. They used battle-axes and bronze daggers, and deposited them in their graves. Down the years there was fusion with indigenous Neolithic stock and with Bell-beaker folk, who had come from the continent a few generations before. The resultant Bronze Age Cultures were thus an amalgam with markedly insular characteristics. Inhumation, generally contracted or flexed, gave way to cremation, but round barrows covered burials throughout the period. Grave-furniture was not provided in the later graves. A distinctive and rather uniform bronze technology developed, which was based upon the skills of Britannico-Hibernian smiths using Irish ores. Ceramics were equally distinctive and also had a marked degree of ubiquity and uniformity throughout the British Isles. There was a mixed-farming economy which involved the cultivation of barley, and probably transhumance. Both food-gathering and hunting continued to supplement the food supply. For part of the year these people lived close by or even in tribal centres (called by us henges), which were set about with the round barrows of their dead. The economy supported chieftains and a warrior class and society was most probably of an 'heroic' character. It is probable that at one particular time political control over at least a greater part of southern England was exercised by the Wessex chieftains, surely from Stonehenge. They probably spoke a dialect of the widespread Indo-European language group.

This brief summary of the British Bronze Age is the product of the application of archaeological techniques to round barrows, to the relics dug from them, and in some part to the circles and henges about which they often cluster. Our knowledge of living Bronze Age society is, and can only be, based almost entirely upon the last century and a half's digging into these monuments to the dead. They are thus of primary importance in any study of the period. At the present time they are being excavated and destroyed wholesale, and in spite of their numbers may in a few decades almost cease to exist. Knowledge of the period cannot go forward without ordered study of their problems, structure, and contents.

When these round barrows were first thrown up, Western Europe would have been an outer barbarian slum compared with the splendid and sophisticated civilizations of the middle-eastern 'Fertile Crescent'. Yet within the millennium and a half which comprises the European Bronze Age, the native technologists outstripped those of the Ancient Orient.[1] Partly because of the proximity of ores, this process took place in two distinctive provinces, the British Isles and Central Europe. In northern Europe the foundations of a further distinctive industry, distant from raw materials, were laid by British and Central European smiths, the effective demand presumably being the

[1] V. G. Childe, *The Aryans*, Routledge & Kegan Paul, 1926, 3; *The Prehistory of European Society*, Penguin Books, 1958.

precious amber and, perhaps, flint. Until comparatively recently Europe's technology continued to lead the world. It is in the Bronze Age that the first clear signs of its amazingly rapid development became manifest. At this time, because of their geographical circumscription, the British Isles housed a more clearly demarcated, and relatively uniform, characteristic bronze technology than elsewhere. This seems to foreshadow the unity and insular nature of our succeeding achievements and institutions, which, although a part of the common European heritage, are of their own kind. It is the intent of this book to examine, by the methods of archaeology, vital and basic aspects of our prehistoric island peoples. These are the beginnings of the intricate processes of material progress, immigration, and development which have produced the comparatively stable alloy which is our present-day society.

Prehistory can only be relived as an inferential intellectual construct based upon evidence recovered by archaeology. Contact with the prehistoric past must be made via the prehistorian's mind.

Concepts of the past are ideally based upon conclusions reached from the ordering, by function and in time and space, of the relics and monuments. However, the mental processes which construct these concepts, which can be at the most only provisional, may consciously or unconsciously be coloured, conditioned, and modulated by numerous wholly extraneous factors. Many aspects of archaeology are only too subjective.

The process of excavation probably affords the most direct contact possible with prehistoric times. Indeed, an account, based upon a comprehensive, meticulously recorded excavation of a favourable site, by a practised modern worker, is probably very close to actuality, particularly as far as habitat and biome at that particular place are concerned. It is not, however, generally possible for concepts of a prehistoric period to be based upon either a single site or personal excavation, observation, and record. *Direct* and personal excavation of monuments and relics in the field, supplemented by a no less direct and personal study of relics in museums and also of unexcavated field monuments, must be supported by *indirect* knowledge of these obtained by the critical study of the descriptions and reports prepared by others.

An historical factor must, then, be paramount in all archaeological reasoning and knowledge. Almost all our general archaeological problems have a history and are largely unintelligible without some knowledge of that history. Thus the resolution of any such problem of prehistory involves, besides the ordering of the actual fragments remaining from the prehistoric past, a consideration of the history of archaeological approach to it. There must be evidence of what has been thought or done before (in the form of publications, letters, or even oral communications) about that problem at various times. Anyone embarking upon a fresh evaluation must consider that evidence, if only to reject it, before propounding another solution.

Lastly, let it be remembered that archaeological evidence is essentially our creation, that is, the objects that we study only acquire their specific character because we apply the techniques of archaeology to them. The men who raised barrows, wielded battle-axes and long daggers, travelled the trade routes with gold and bronze, followed the hunting- and war-trails, and who saw the raw-dressed newly reared sarsen trilithons at Stonehenge, did not think of their tools and weapons, that structure, or any other, as potential archaeological evidence. These things are only such because we record, classify, and analyse them in order to extract from them knowledge of the prehistoric past.

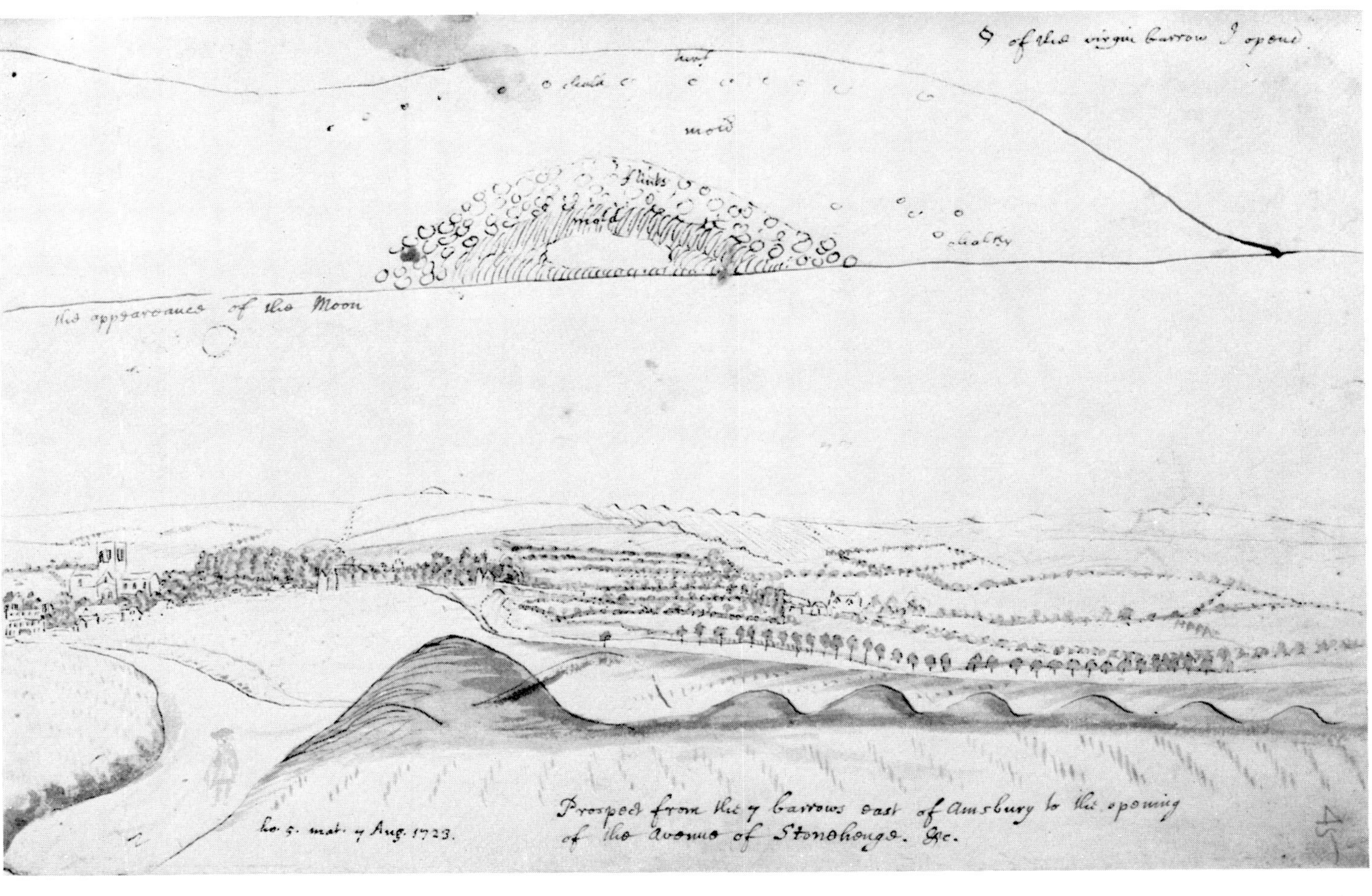

I. Stukeley's section (above) and a prospect of the end of Stonehenge's Avenue.

IIa. Plaques interred in excavated barrows by Sir Richard Colt Hoare and William Cunnington.

IIb. The stone urn surmounting the tomb of Thomas Bateman and his wife. It is in a field near Middleton-by-Youlgrave, Derbyshire.

CHAPTER I

THE BEGINNING OF BARROW STUDY

MEDIEVAL MEN minded little about the barrows of their prehistoric forbears, except to take from them gold to replenish royal coffers,[1] or relics to stimulate the piety of the faithful.[2] As the mists of medievalism dispersed in the bright dawning light of the Renaissance some attention began to be paid to the need for national history.[3] Thus, besides delving into the origins of ecclesiastical and political institutions, abbeys, and castles, the early empiricists observed and commented upon the then frequently prominent earthworks and numerous barrows.

John Leland, that medieval but methodical Tudor, refers to the 'sepultures of men of warre ... in dyvers places of the playne [Salisbury Plain]'.[4] William Camden, Westminster's magistral topographer-antiquary, noted how 'many such artificial hills both round and pointed are to be seen in those parts, and are called burrowes or barrowes, probably thrown up in memory of soldiers slain thereabouts. Bones are found in them'.[5] These remarks appear to record inhumed burials. Some cremation burials in Anglesey were brought to Leland's notice by one of his correspondents and he wrote of them thus: 'Mr Roulande Griffith tolde me that ... in tyme of myned menne usid not in Termone [i.e. Anglesey] to separate thyr grounds, but now stille more and more they digge stony hillokkes yn theyre groundes, and with the stones of them rudely congestid they devide theyre groundes after Devonshire fascion. In digging of these [they] digge up yn many places yerthen pottes with the mouthes turnid douneward, conteyning (cineres et ossa mortuorum).'

The laconic comments and militaristic attributions, normal for their time, of the King's Antiquary and the author of the *Britannia* were called into question by the egregious and whimsical John Aubrey. In his *Monumenta Britannica*[6] he dwells at some length upon barrows, remarking that 'they were the mausolea or burying-places for the great persons and rulers of those times' whom, he says, 'they chose to let lye drye upon such hilly ground; and those of the same familie would desire to lye near one another'. Aubrey also observed that 'some [barrows] about Stonehenge ... have circular trenches about them, and the trench is distant from the barrow'. Indeed, in Aubrey's work, which was ordered by Thomas Tanner and incorporated in the first

[1] Close Rolls, 1234–7, 433, 434, trans. in *PIOWNHAS*, III, 185–6; Grinsell, 1953, 110.

[2] *VCH Herts.*, I, 256–8.

[3] Kendrick, 1950.

[4] *The Itinerary of John Leland*, ed. L. Toulmin Smith, 1907–10, Part X, 81.

[5] *Arch.*, XLII, 162; *PBA*, XXXVI, 199–217.

[6] Aubrey MSS., Bodleian Library, Oxford. For details of John Aubrey: A. Powell, *John Aubrey and his Friends*, Eyre & Spottiswoode, 1948; Aubrey, *Brief Lives*, etc. (ed. Powell).

edition in English of Camden's *Britannia*,[7] one can see the genesis of round barrow classification based upon external form.

Aubrey's *Monumenta Britannica* was written mainly in the 1670's. One of his close friends was Robert Hooke (1635–1703) who, in 1665, became perpetual curator of the Royal Society, and was the son of the Reverend John Hooke, an incumbent of Freshwater in the Isle of Wight. Aubrey's confident diagnosis of the nature and purpose of round barrows may well have been due, in part, to information gleaned from him, as certain barrows on the Isle of Wight had been dug into with scientific intent half a century before. Indeed, this is perhaps one of the first recorded instances of definite digging for knowledge as distinct from the earlier unashamed searches for treasure. Sir John Oglander of Nunwell, the author of historical and antiquarian notes on his own and neighbouring parishes, wrote regarding his excavations which were undertaken at the beginning of the seventeenth century that: 'You may see divors buries on ye topp of owre Island hills whose name in ye Danische tounge signifieth theyr nature, as being places onlie weare men were buryed. . . . I have digged for my experience in soome of ye moore awntientest, and haue found manie bones of men formerlye consumed by fyor, accordinge to ye Romane custome. . . . Wheresoever you see a burie in any eminent place, most commonlye on ye topp of hilles, you may presume that there hathe been soome buryed; according to ye etimoligie of ye woord,—digge, and you shall find theyre bones.' It is perhaps fortunate for us today that Sir John's exhortation to dig for experience was not acted upon, in any measure, until two centuries later!

In the early part of the century succeeding Aubrey's, the engaging Stukeley[8] amassed from the length and breadth of England a store of material which comprised accurate and detailed sketches and notes frequently upon prehistoric monuments, many of which had lain undisturbed since their builders quitted them. William Stukeley's field notes, many of which, in his later life, he turned into theological tracts designed 'to combat the deists from an unexpected quarter', and his ideas contain, as does the manuscript of Aubrey's earlier and famous *Miscellanie of British Antiquities*, that perception of archaeological principle as befits such a pioneer.

Besides drawing attention to various forms of barrows in the Stonehenge region, which he tabulates under a series of peculiar labels, he observes, quite sensibly, that 'In general, they are always upon elevated ground, and in sight of Stonehenge'. Thus he introduces the great barrow cemeteries which are recognized as an integral part of the Stonehenge complex. At Avebury, in north Wiltshire, he made an observation about the 'false crest' siting of barrows which was not made again until recently, when Sir Cyril Fox was investigating a barrow in Wales.[9] Stukeley writes: 'I observe the barrows upon the Hakpen Hill and others are set with great art not upon the very highest part of the hills but upon so much of the declevity or edge as that they make app[earance] as above to those in the valley.'[10] After a scrutiny of Vespasian's Camp at Amesbury, and Poundbury near Dorchester, Stukeley notes that certain round barrows are earlier than these 'camps', which he regards as Roman.[11] Near Beckhampton, again in north

[7] William Camden, *Britannia*, ed. Gibson, 1695. For a general account of antiquarian thought at this time see *English Historical Scholarship in the Sixteenth and Seventeenth Centuries*, ed. L. Fox, Dugdale Society, 1959, 93–114.

[8] S. Piggott, *William Stukeley*, Oxford University Press, 1950.

[9] *Arch. J.*, XCIX, 22.

[10] S. Piggott, *William Stukeley*, 71.

[11] Stukeley, 1723, 138, 188.

Wiltshire near Avebury, and on Oakley Down[12] in Cranborne Chase, he drew attention to the cutting through of disc barrows by Roman roads.

In addition to the observation and recording of barrows, Stukeley, with labour, finance, and persuasion provided by the Lord Pembroke, undertook excavations, the descriptions of which have a most modern ring and are, indeed, probably the first objective account of a barrow's structure on record. He wrote: 'The manner of composition of the barrow was good earth, quite thro', covering it quite over, under the turf. Hence it appears, that the method of making these barrows was to dig up the turf for a great space round till the barrow was brought to its intended bulk. Then with the chalk, dug out of the environing ditch, they powdered it all over', then 'After the turf taken off, we came to the layer of chalk, as before, then fine garden mould. About three feet below the surface a layer of flints humouring the convexity of the barrow. . . . This being about a foot thick, rested on a layer of soft mould another foot; in which was inclos'd an urn full of bones.'[13] To supplement this verbal picture there survives, among Stukeley's Stonehenge manuscripts, a drawing of the composition of the barrow mound (Pl. I). This must be the first 'section' known to British prehistory.[14]

Stukeley's 'Stonehenge' appeared in 1740 and his 'Abury' in 1743. By the middle of the eighteenth century the intellectual climate of England was wrapped in the miasmic folds of the 'Gothick' cult.[15] A barrow on a blasted heath became an object of aesthetic satisfaction and intellectual speculation for many, while 'Gothick' crenellations were to embellish the country's archaeology for a century. Outstanding in this laden atmosphere is William Borlase's *Antiquities of Cornwall* (1754), which describes barrows and was written in all sanity as a substitute for the opportunities of classical study which had, early in life, eluded its writer.[16]

In 1765 Stukeley, who is perhaps the greatest of our pioneer prehistorians, died, and for half a century the field of British prehistory lay practically untilled. It was to the archaeological inheritance of Stukeley that Sir Richard Colt Hoare and William Cunnington[17] (see Frontispiece) succeeded. Not only did they observe and describe barrows and other field monuments but they explored by digging 379 barrows, almost all on Salisbury Plain in the vicinity of Stonehenge. The results of this work, embodied in the notes of Cunnington, who supervised most of the digging, were published by Colt Hoare in 1812 and 1819, in the two elegant folios of 'Auncient Wiltescire'.

Colt Hoare and Cunnington may be justly considered the fathers of the exploration of barrows by digging (Pl. II a) or 'excavation', just as Aubrey was the father of the peculiarly British tradition of 'field archaeology',[18] although why they began their systematic approach to their object is far from clear. 'We speak from facts not theory', writes Sir Richard before describing his work. Again, he gives advice on how to look for signs of occupation in the field, couched in concise and almost modern terms, while inveighing against 'those who arrange Roman Iters [itineraries] in their

[12] Stukeley, 1723, 141, 188.
[13] Stukeley, 1740, 44.
[14] S. Piggott, *William Stukeley*, 111.
[15] T. D. Kendrick, *The Druids*, Methuen, 1927, Chap. I; S. Piggott, 'Prehistory and the Romantic Movement', *Antiq.*, XI, 31; Kenneth Clark, *The Gothic Revival*, Constable, r.e. 1950.
[16] G. Daniel, *A Hundred Years of Archaeology*, Duckworth, 1950, 22.
[17] *WAM*, LII, 213–18.
[18] Atkinson, 1953, 1; Crawford, 1953, 21–50.

closets'. Cunnington writing in the same vein describes himself digging barrows in 1803 'in the hopes of meeting something which might supersede conjecture'. Yet for all their practicality and stern declarations of purpose, 'Gothick' furbished the title-pages, and tempered the text, of the accounts of barrow-digging contained within the stately folios. Indeed, the cult may well have motivated Hoare's contribution to the joint enterprise. Beads and arrow-heads garlanded the title-pages, while the archaistic spelling proclaims 'Auncient Wiltescire'. Colt Hoare recalls a thunderstorm which occurred while a barrow was being dug on Oakley Down as one which would 'ever be remembered both with horror and pleasure by those who were present'. When he uncovered a skeleton in a barrow on Whitesheet Hill, he remarked that the skull 'grinned horribly a ghastly smile a singularity that I have never before noticed'.[19] Later in the century, the portentous probity of Pitt-Rivers was to cause him to comment, drily, that 'no doubt the skeleton must have been laughing at him for his unscientific method of dealing with it'.[20]

In spite of what, from the vantage point of our day and age, seem 'Gothick' lapses, the importance of 'Ancient Wiltshire' cannot be called into question. The great books (small paper copies are rare) are a primary source of much that is vital in our prehistory. They are essentially open-air books, books to be taken into the field—a measure that their size prohibits.

The pattern and development of nineteenth-century archaeology shows as its main theme the collectors preoccupied with objects to fill their cases, and incidentally borrowing systems from geology and palaeontology to classify them. They were concerned with urn and dagger, and descriptions of the barrows whence the relics came occupy a subordinate place in their writings. Thus as the century grew older there was an extension of the methods and practices of Colt Hoare and Cunnington in Wiltshire into other parts of the country where barrows are, or were, nearly as numerous as in that county.

Thus in Derbyshire, Staffordshire, and Yorkshire, the Batemans,[21] William and Thomas, father and son, together with their accomplices Samuel Carrington and James Ruddock, opened well over four hundred barrows. To some extent they defer to the opinions of 'Sir R. C. Hoare',[22] although, presumably with pride in a local and more portable product, Thomas Bateman says in the preface of *Ten Years' Diggings*, 1861, that his earlier volume, *Vestiges of the Antiquities of Derbyshire*, 1848, contains 'a greater amount of information respecting the primaeval sepulchres of Britain, derived from actual excavations than has ever appeared in a single work, except, perhaps, in the costly folios of Sir Richard Hoare's "Ancient Wiltshire"'.[23] However, with the spirit of a progressive era, the Great Exhibition being but ten years past, the costly folios are dismissed as being 'in a great measure useless to the scientific student, from the absence of any Craniological Notices or measurement'.[24] It is worthy of record that the final resting place of Thomas Bateman was well in keeping with such an adventurous age. He was buried in a field, near the village of Middleton-by-Youlgrave, Derbyshire, not far distant from his home at Lomberdale Hall. His tomb, with iron-railing surround,

[19] Extracts from Hoare, 1812–19.
[20] *WAM*, XXIV, 10.
[21] *Dictionary of National Biography*, III.
[22] Bateman, 1848, 29.
[23] Bateman, 1861, v.
[24] Bateman, 1861, v. But see *Berks. AJ*, LV, 27–8. The neglect of accurate record appears to have been their principal failing.

surmounted by a realistic, lichened stone rendering of a Bronze Age cinerary urn (Pl. II b), stands as an object of curiosity and admiration to modern archaeologists.

Contemporary with the Batemans was Charles Warne of Dorset. He produced, in 1866, his book entitled *The Celtic Tumuli of Dorset*, which was the result of his excavation of about forty-six barrows in that county, though it is to a large extent an account of digging by others.

The nineteenth-century landmark of our studies is the monograph 'Ancient British Barrows'[25] by John Thurnam, archaeologist, doctor, craniologist, and medical superintendent of the Wiltshire county asylum at Devizes from 1851 to his death in 1873. Here on fine paper, and illustrated by the detailed engravings that distinguish the contemporary *Archaeologia*, is for the first time a systematic study, untainted by extraneous factors, of the external characteristics of long and round barrows in relation to the relics recovered from them, based upon almost all the work undertaken up to the time of writing. These syntheses are repositories of basic information interpreted with great perception and scholarship, which today, after ninety years, are still of great value.

The year 1877 saw the publication of *British Barrows*, a record of the opening of a great number of barrows, chiefly of the Bronze Age, in Yorkshire, Cumberland, Westmorland, Northumberland, Durham, and Gloucestershire. A paper in *Archaeologia* gives details of the further digging into more barrows, not only in Yorkshire, but in Berkshire and Wiltshire. Canon William Greenwell,[26] the perpetrator of these works, was a Durham cleric who lived to the great age of ninety-seven. He was devoted to fishing as well as barrow-digging, and devised a fly which bears his name—the Greenwell's Glory. It is said, apocryphally, that he once dug into a barrow and discovered a copy of the previous day's London *Times* beneath an urn.[27] It is therefore, perhaps, of some significance that while his book and barrow paper contain much tantalizing information, they do not contain a single plan or section of a barrow; apart from drawings of crania, only artefacts adorn the records of his excoriations.

During the years of Canon Greenwell's activities Lieut.-General Pitt-Rivers[28] studied barrows in his company.[29] When he worked in Cranborne Chase he undertook, for the first time in history, the total excavation of a few round barrows (Pl. III a). These barrows were examined by the general's almost irreproachable system, which was unparalleled until modern times.

The end of the nineteenth century saw, besides the continued extension into all parts of the country of the practice of barrow excavation, a mild renaissance of the 'field tradition' of an earlier age. In Gloucestershire G. B. Witts listed 126 round barrows, nearly all on the Cotswolds.[30] Early in the present century Wiltshire prehistory was further aided by the compilation, for a Victoria County History, only recently realized, of detailed lists and descriptions[31] of great numbers of round barrows, and other antiquities, together with a note of the relics taken from them by Hoare and others. Hadrian Allcroft noted a number of barrows when he compiled his earthwork corpus[32]

[25] *Arch.*, XLII, 161–244; XLIII, 285–552.

[26] *Arch. Ael.*, 3rd Ser., XV, 1–21.

[27] Wheeler, 1954, 7–8.

[28] H. St George Gray, *Index to Excavations in Cranbourne Chase and King John's House, Tollard Royal, also a Memoir of General Pitt-Rivers, D.C.L., F.R.S., and a Bibliographical List of his Works*, 1905.

[29] Pitt-Rivers, 1887–98, IV, 28.

[30] G. B. Witts, *Archaeological Handbook of Gloucestershire*, 1883.

[31] E. H. Goddard, *WAM*, XXXVIII, 153–378. Lists have been compiled for Devon also, *TDA*, XXXIV, LXIX.

[32] Allcroft, 1908, s.v. barrows.

issued in 1908, and J. P. Williams-Freeman discussed barrows in his book on field archaeology, published at the outbreak of the first world war.[33]

While Greenwell was 'turning over' Yorkshire barrows, a Driffield corn-chandler, John Robert Mortimer, was digging into barrows and collecting antiquities in that area also. So great was his prestige in the Wold country that the flint implements found upon the fields by agricultural workers were known as 'Mortimers'. His work had some system, he prepared sections and plans of the barrows that he excavated, and indeed it is possible from his work to identify each barrow. He methodically noted barrow cemeteries, rightly treating his individual barrows as units of such cemeteries. The title of his work—*Forty Years' Researches* . . .[34]—echoes an earlier fashion, as it emphasizes the length of the time taken to amass his collection.

Seven years later John Abercromby published the two volumes of his *Bronze Age Pottery*,[35] following earlier work upon Bronze Age ceramics.[36] His books are, above all, a corpus, but the text, apparently read by few, is a shrewd and scholarly analysis of the Bronze Age much of which has been confirmed by subsequent assessments.

The modern period of barrow study began in the third decade of this century when both field study and excavation began to be seriously and systematically used as avenues of research. The pioneer work in the new field study was an article on barrows by the founder of *Antiquity*, O. G. S. Crawford, which appeared in the first volume of that journal, whose foundation gave a notable impetus to British archaeology.[37] This article he followed with notes upon the barrows of 'Wessex' in his book *Wessex from the Air* and other publications.[38] In the realm of excavation, the fact that a barrow is a complex structure, explainable in terms of human activity, was emphasized and demonstrated by Sir Cyril Fox when he dug barrows at Barton Mills in Cambridgeshire and Ysceifiog in Flintshire[39]—indeed, he almost resuscitated the living ritual and procedures of burial. In the fourth decade of the century came the advance in study, synthesis, and interpretation of barrow contents, signalized by the isolation and ordering of the 'Wessex' culture,[40] which followed upon Abercromby's marshalling of the Bronze Age ceramics a quarter-century before.

The field tradition has been perpetuated by L. V. Grinsell, whose twenty-five years of field observation and record are an enduring monument of our age.[41] Excavation was continued by Sir Cyril Fox and others,[42] before and during the last war. Much of the work was sponsored by the Inspectorate of Ancient Monuments of the Ministry of Works, which right up to the present time frequently provides facilities for the total excavation of barrows. Apart from classificatory refinements[43] and the amplification of

[33] Williams-Freeman, 1915, s.v. barrows.

[34] Mortimer, 1905.

[35] Abercromby, 1912.

[36] *PSAS*, XXXVIII, 323–410.

[37] *Antiq.*, I, 419–34.

[38] Crawford and Keiller, 1928, 13; O. G. S. Crawford: *Air Survey and Archaeology*, and *Air-Photography for Archaeologists*, Ordnance Survey Professional Papers, New Series, No. 7, 1928, No. 12, 1929, respectively, H.M.S.O.; *Luftbild und Vorgeschichte*, Berlin, 1939.

[39] *PCAS*, XXVI, 19; *Arch. Camb.*, LXXXI, 48; Fox and Dickens, 1950, 53. The Dutch influence upon British barrow digging was considerable, cf. van Giffen, 1930. See also Fox, 1959.

[40] *PPS*, IV, 52–106.

[41] Grinsell, 1953; *PPSEA*, VII, 203–30; *PPS*, VII, 73; *Berks. AJ*, XXXIX–XLIII; *PSANHS*, LXXXV, 151–66; *Surrey AC*, XL, XLII; *SAC*, LXXV, LXXXI, LXXXII; *PIOWNHAS*, III, 179–222; *PHFCAS*, XIV.

[42] *Ant. J.*, XXVIII, 25–28.

[43] *ULIAA Rpt*, XI, 37–61.

our knowledge of local facets of the 'Wessex' culture, little more has been done in this field,[44] except the identification of certain ceramic groups.[45]

At the present time research is proceeding, broadly speaking, along these general lines. As will be seen in more detail in Chapter XV, the impedimenta of physical science have been quite recently brought forward to aid the excavator. The information that these methods can provide is chiefly environmental [46] and chronological.[47]

It is apposite at the end of an historical chapter to touch on two dangerous trends, discussed in detail in Chapter XV, which are all too evident at the time of writing. In excavation there has been a dangerous retrograde step in the name of emergency expediency, back to aspects of the discredited and un-understanding 'partial excavation' approach of bygone years. Furthermore, such work is being all too often undertaken by untrained persons with little knowledge of the period or of the informative potentialities of a barrow's structures and contents. We live in an age of totalitarian land usage for agricultural and industrial purposes by persons possessed of powers of destruction, against which the official bodies responsible for the record and preservation of our national historical heritage enshrined in barrows and other field monuments are largely emasculate. Unless, before all else, Grinsell's methods of field recording are applied without delay in certain areas, little knowledge will remain for future generations of the barrows of our Bronze Age forbears.

[44] *PDAES*, IV, 13; *Ant. J.*, XXXI, 29.
[45] *Ant. J.*, XVIII, 169–71; *Arch. J.*, CVIII, 22–4.
[46] *PPS*, XIX, 128–47; 'Techniques in Archaeology', *BA*, 1954, 11–16.
[47] *SP*, CLIV, 225–38; *PPS*, XX, 231–36.

CHAPTER II

THE EXTERNAL FORMS OF ROUND BARROWS

ROUND BARROWS (Pl. IV a, b) are the commonest and often the most noticeable of the monuments that survive from Britain's prehistoric past. In the area termed 'Wessex',[1] which is well explored, some six thousand round barrows have been recorded,[2] while probably about eighteen thousand exist in the British Isles as a whole.

Two principal categories of round barrows are readily recognizable. First, and most numerous, are *bowl barrows*, which are the ubiquitous form, being found all over Britain. In certain circumstances, when built of lumps of rock, they are called *cairns*. (Surface appearance often gives only limited indications of a barrow's structure. A cairn over which a humus has formed and vegetation grown may look like an earthen mound.) The second category comprises a small, distinctive group termed *Wessex barrows*.[3] They are only a fraction of the sum total of round barrows to be found in the country.

Bowl barrows (Fig. 1), the ubiquitous form, consist of a pudding-shaped, often near-hemispherical, mound, or cairn, which may or may not have a surrounding ditch. They range from small mounds, about 30 feet in diameter, to giants of 150 feet or more, with, if ditched, proportionate ditches. If undenuded, they may be as little as 3 feet or 4 feet in height, or as much, in the case of the giants, as 20 feet.[4]

The Wessex barrows (Pl. IV a, b) number about five hundred. Five categories, excluding bowl barrows, have been proposed,[5] but these can conveniently be reduced to three. These are *bermed barrows* (Fig. 2), *saucer barrows*, and *pond barrows* (Fig. 3).

The term 'bermed barrows' embraces *bell*, *bell-disc*, and *disc* barrows. Bell and disc barrows are the extreme forms of the common principle of a circular mound, separated by a wide berm from a surrounding ditch, which often has or had an outer bank.[6] The berm of many bell barrows has weathered over the centuries, and thus slopes towards the ditch from the base of the mound. The final result, when seen unmutilated, is an elegant 'campanile'[7] form. This weathering phenomenon is less noticeable in extremely wide-bermed barrows. Disc barrows, in instances oval not round, have the widest berm of all, as they have a central mound, or mounds, frequently no higher than

[1] *PPS*, VII, 73.
[2] *PPS*, VII, 76.
[3] *Arch.*, XLIII, 290–301; *Antiq.*, I, 419–34; Crawford and Keiller, 1928, 13; *PPSEA*, VII, 203–30; *PPS*, VII, 73–90; Grinsell, 1953, 17–25.
[4] *BBCS*, I, 353–70.
[5] *PPS*, VII, 79–90; Grinsell, 1953, 19–23.
[6] *PPSEA*, VII, 203–30. In instances bell-barrow ditches have been causewayed, *PPS*, XVIII, 148–59. Note also *PCAS*, XXXVI, 134.
[7] Stukeley, 1743, 44.

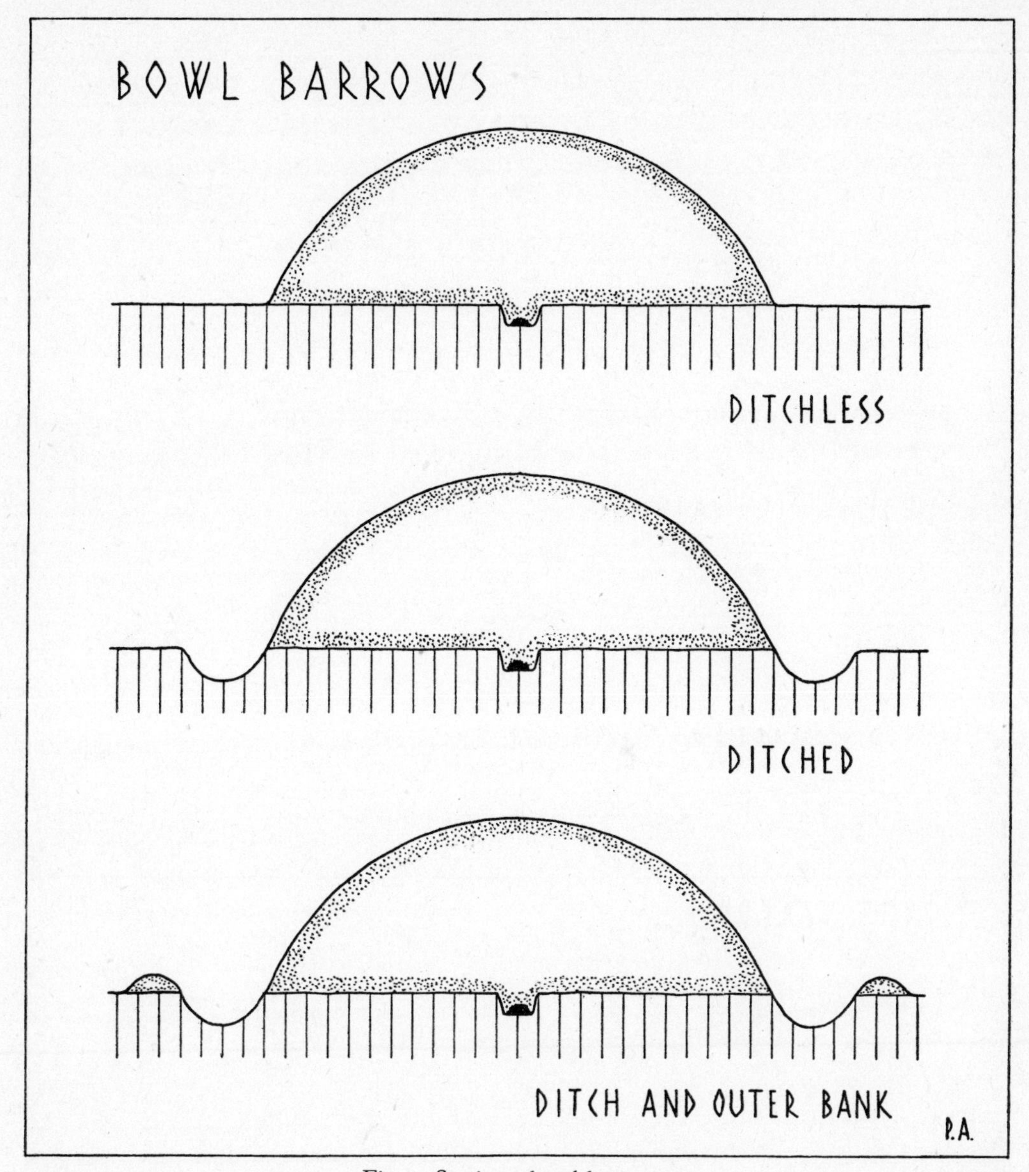

Fig. 1. Sections, bowl barrows.

the external surrounding bank.[8] Bell-disc barrows, as the name suggests, are an intermediate form embodying features of both bell and disc barrows.[9] Although the three bermed-barrow forms shade one into another when considered upon a basis of relative dimension, these three variants are outstanding. Thus the triple terminology should be retained within the omnibus term.

Pond barrows, which are not truly 'barrows'—barrow means literally 'a hill'—,

[8] *Arch.*, XLIII, 293–5; *PPS*, VII, 82–8; Grinsell, 1953, 21–3.

[9] *PPS*, VII, 82; Grinsell, 1953, 21.

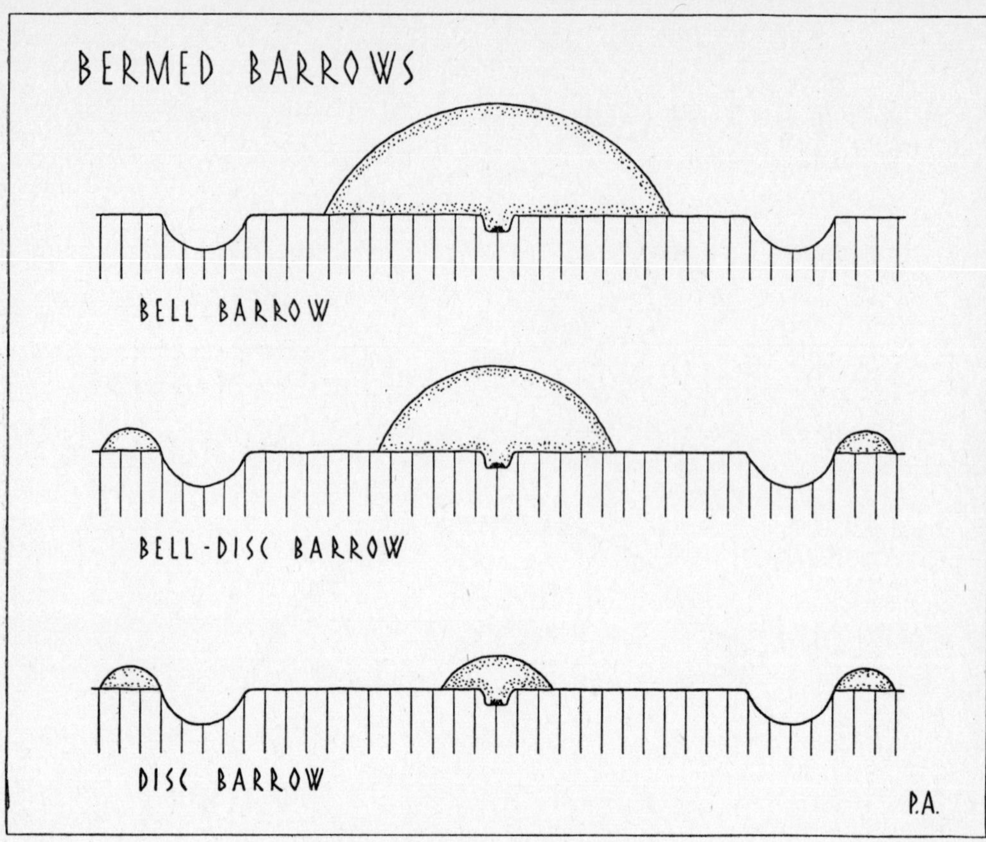

Fig. 2. Sections, bermed barrows.

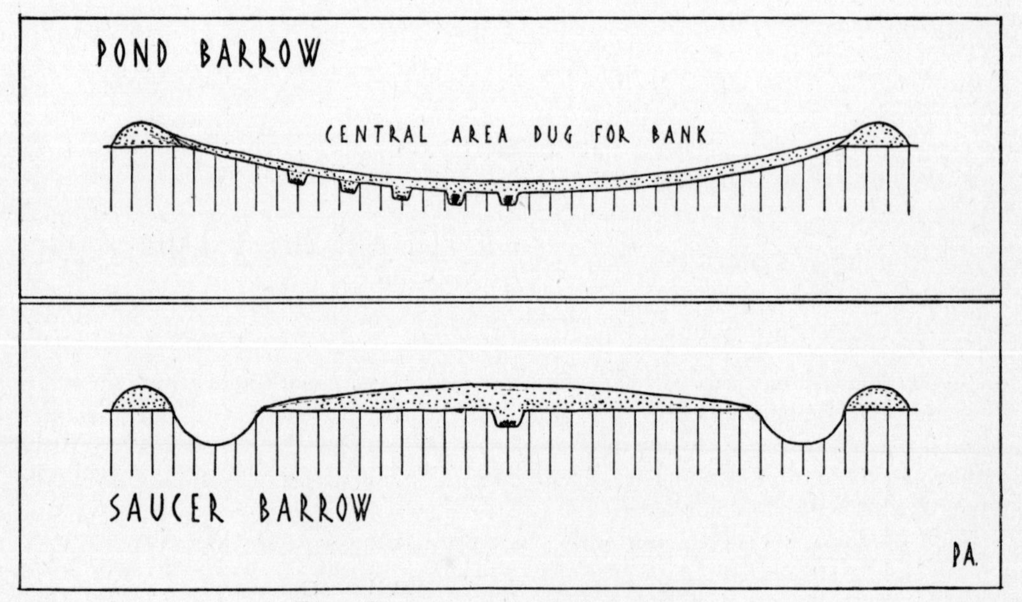

Fig. 3. Sections, pond and saucer barrows.

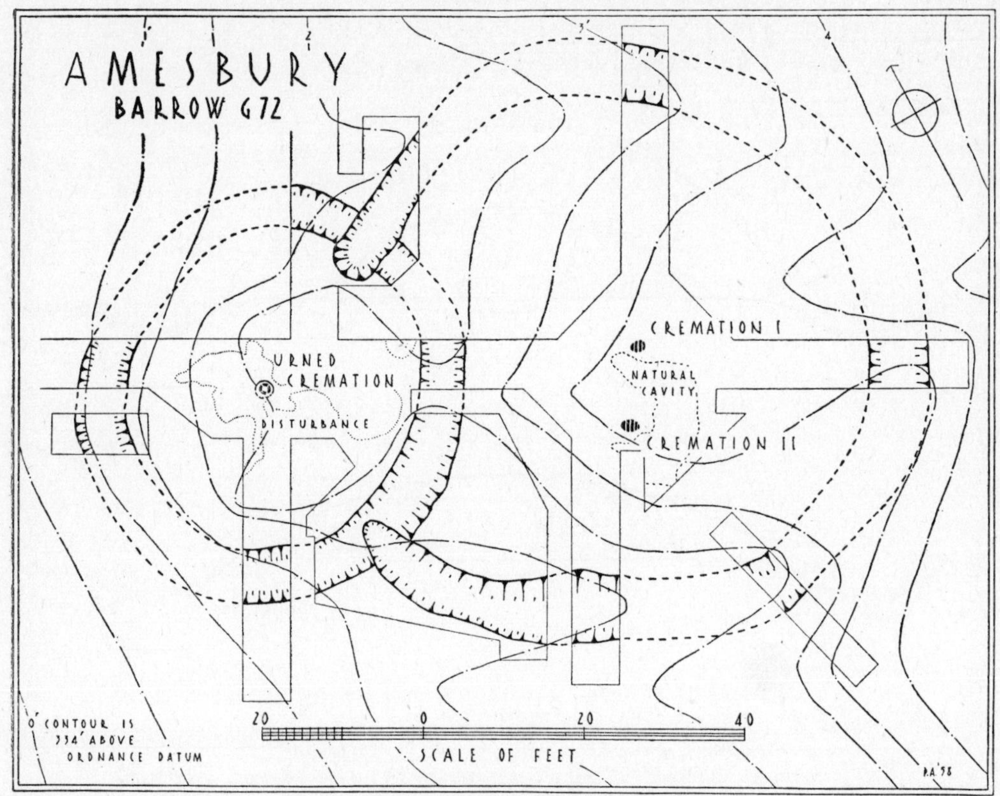

Fig. 4. Plan, confluent barrows excavated.

appear as a marked depression, well and regularly formed, with a bank around the circumference. They range from 30 feet to about 120 feet in diameter.[10]

Saucer barrows consist of a low mound, generally 1 foot or 2 feet in height, and from about 60 feet to 90 feet in diameter, enclosed by a ditch and outer bank.[11] They are difficult to distinguish from outer-banked bowl barrows.

In the Wessex region there exist a number of what are clearly bowl barrows which have an external bank to their ditch. Whether or not these outer-banked bowl barrows are to be regarded as a Wessex form is uncertain in view of their probable occurrence in other areas where the other distinctive forms are absent.[12]

A common factor of many of the Wessex barrows is an external bank and, indeed, the term 'banked barrows' might well be descriptive of the series.[13] However, many bell barrows lack this feature, though whether by original intent or as a result of ploughing is in many cases uncertain.

Occasionally bowl barrows and the localized distinctive forms seemingly overlap one another (Pl. IV b), the implication being that one is of more recent construction than the other (Fig. 4). To this occurrence the term 'confluent barrows' has been given.

[10] *PPS*, VII, 89–90; Grinsell, 1953, 23.

[11] *PPS*, VII, 88–9; Grinsell, 1953, 23; a group of similar mounds in Ireland have been termed 'Ring barrows', *JRSAI*, LXXXVI, 218–25.

[12] *SAC*, 221; Bateman, 1861, 87.

[13] The term 'circle barrows' has been proposed on account of similarities to certain henge monuments, Atkinson, 1956, 160.

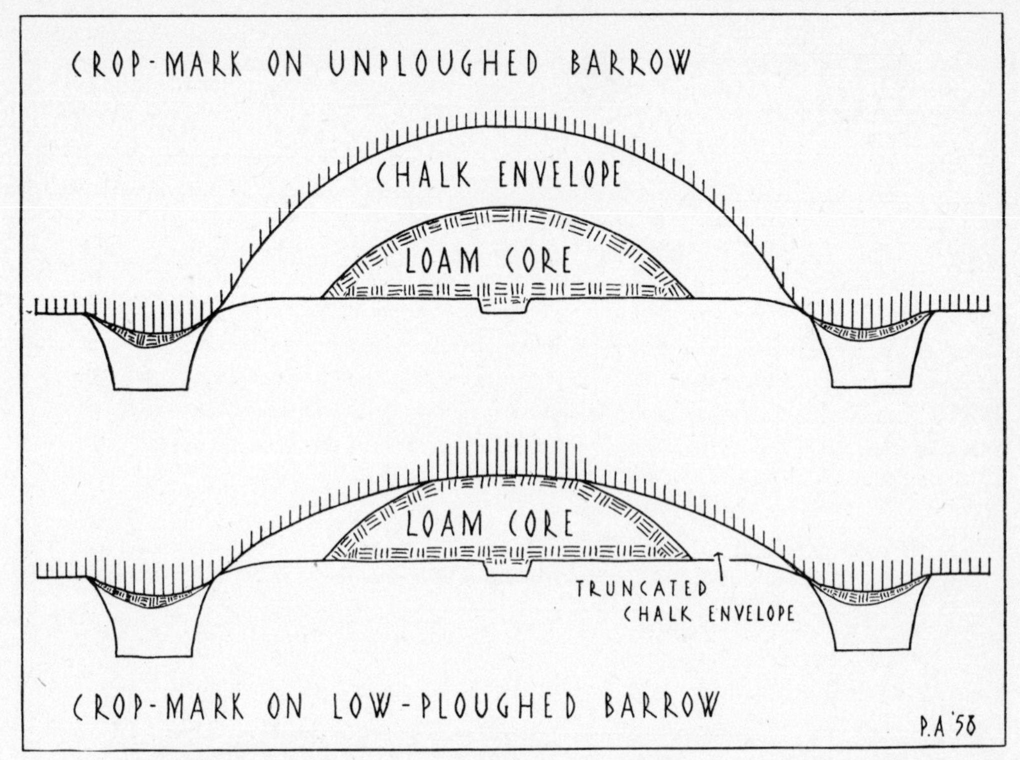

Fig. 5. Sections, unploughed and ploughed barrows: the crop-mark produced.

Barrows of differing forms, besides like barrows, have been found to be confluent. In certain, rather rare, cases a smaller barrow appears to link two larger mounds. Besides these there are, chiefly in Wessex, double (Pl. IV d), treble, and quadruple bell barrows surrounded, apparently, by single ditches.[14]

Five types of round barrow, namely bowl, ring, bell, disc, and saucer, are claimed to exist in Ireland.[15] Bowl barrows, both ditched and unditched, and ring barrows, are well attested, but bermed barrows seem rare. Two in the Boyne valley would appear to belong to this class. A classification evolved upon the chalk downs of Wessex should be applied only with caution in a distant area, and on differing soil.

On downs and moors, beyond the ever-expanding margins of existing cultivations, barrows of all forms preserve their original contours, being moulded only by the processes of weathering and denudation. In such places only burrowing animals or the craters marking the depredations of bygone barrow-diggers mar the bold, sinuous, but strangely satisfying forms often seen silhouetted against the sky. One can only envisage, with faint awe, the lines of unblemished barrows which, before enclosures parcelled, and the voracious plough devoured, our land, met the eyes of early archaeologists.

The solid geology of a particular region may limit the degree of natural denudation that a barrow mound may undergo. Thus on chalk, certain gravels, and rock formations, barrow forms are often readily recognizable and definable, as they have been relatively

[14] *VCH Wilts.*, I (Part I), ix.

[15] Ó Ríordáin, 1953, 75.

little affected by nature on account of their composition. On the other hand, on sands and some clays natural weathering may well, in a brief while, have laid a considerable mound low,[16] leaving only a mild undulation.

Ploughing has blurred the contours and has lowered and spread a great number of barrows and cairns in all parts of the country.[17] In as many cases all surface traces have been eradicated. Yet observation and photography from the air detects many barrows by noting spread banks and mounds, or the remaining subterranean features of erstwhile barrows, ditches, and graves which are clearly seen by reason of multi-coloured soils[18] (Pl. V a) or extra-copious crop-growths (Pl. V b).[19]

In addition to all the barrows and their various appearances described above, it must be remembered that there are, in certain parts of the country, chiefly in the north, 'barrows' that appear to depart from the usual principles in so much as they have eccentric outer banks, or are within enclosures.[20] Again there are numerous structures which are not strictly barrows, but which appear to have been used for burial during the Bronze Age.[21]

A final word regarding low-ploughed barrows in chalk country must be said. When cropped, by reason of the heavier growths on their summits they frequently appear to have been disturbed. On account of this many barrows have been destroyed uninvestigated or have been incorrectly described. What has happened is that ploughing has broken the chalk-rubble envelope and has exposed the loam or sod core (Fig. 5). The crop has taken deep root in this and an extra-luxuriant growth and thus a positive crop-mark has resulted. The similarity to a disturbed barrow on an air-photograph is most marked.

[16] *PPS*, XXIII, 137–66.

[17] e.g. Barnby Howes (Yorks.) barrow group; *YAJ*, XXXIX, 31.

[18] Crawford, 1939, 35 (near Stonehenge), 36 (Everley, Wilts.).

[19] Crawford, 1939, 35 (Beard Mill, Oxon.), 36 (Everley, Wilts.), 37 (Foxley Farm, Oxon.), 37 (North Stoke, Oxon.); *Guide to an Exhibition of Air-Photographs of Archaeological Sites*, Oxford, Ashmolean Museum, 1948, Pl. III; general statement: Crawford and Keiller, 1928; *Arch. J.*, CI, 1–16.

[20] *YAJ*, XXIX, 354; Bateman, 1861, 87.

[21] *YAJ*, XXIX, 363.

CHAPTER III

TOPOGRAPHICAL AND ENVIRONMENTAL

THERE is as yet no overall, definitive distribution map of the bewildering galaxy of round barrows that bedeck the downs and plateaux of the lowlands, and the shoulders or crests of the higher hills of our land. A map [1] recently produced by the Royal Commission on Historical Monuments is not claimed as definitive, since its main purpose is to show how the river gravel crop and soil marks match to the general picture of round barrow distribution; none the less it is a most important contribution to the problem. In addition, since the days when Philip Crocker, Colt Hoare's surveyor, recorded on his maps the barrows of Wiltshire (Pl. III b), there has been a succession of regional maps recording them.[2]

Some knowledge of the distribution of round barrows over a great part of the British Isles can be obtained by the study of the distribution maps of specific Bronze Age relics, many of which have been obtained from barrows. Thus scrutiny of a distribution map of beakers [3] discovers marked concentration in Wessex, East Anglia, the Peak District, the Yorkshire Wolds and Moors, and Northumberland. A similar map of food-vessels [4] confirms, to some extent, this mainly English distribution, and shows concentrations in Scotland and Ireland. It should be remembered that many beakers and food-vessels were, most probably, buried in flat graves. A map of all the antiquities of the Bronze Age,[5] which includes barrows from which relics have been recovered, provides some additional information and confirms the general picture provided by maps of beakers and food-vessels. A number of maps depicting distributions of certain other (mainly English) pottery types are extant,[6] but these add little to the information to be gleaned from the beaker and food-vessel maps. All these maps should be used in conjunction with the maps [7] and lists [8] of beakers, food-vessels, cinerary urns, and extended burials in Scotland, many of which, and all of which in the case of the extended burials, were obtained from cairns and barrows. As far as can be seen flat graves predominate in Scotland. Unfortunately, similar lists and maps do not exist for Ireland.[9]

A further appreciation of the areas other than Wiltshire in which great numbers of barrows are to be found can be obtained from archaeological literature. As mentioned

[1] *Field Archaeology of the River Gravels*, RCHM (England), 1959, Fig. 5.

[2] Hoare, 1812–19; Charles Warne, *Illustrated Map of Dorsetshire, its Vestiges, Celtic, Roman, Saxon, and Danish*, 1865; G. B. Witts, *Archaeological Handbook of Gloucestershire*, 1883; Mortimer, 1905; Sumner, 1931 are the principal ones. See also *Arch. J.*, CI, 20, map.

[3] Fox, 1952, Pl. 3.

[4] Fox, 1952.

[5] Fox, 1952, Map C.

[6] *Ant. J.*, XVIII, 164, Fig. 8 (Pennine Urns); *Arch. J.*, CVIII, 20, Fig. 6 (Sheep Down Urns).

[7] *PSAS*, LXVIII, 188, Pl. I; Childe, 1935, 270–3; Childe, 1946, 53, 67; Childe, 1947b, 115.

[8] *PSAS*, LXVIII, 174–88; Childe, 1946, 101–28.

[9] Ó Ríordáin, 1953, 101–2.

in Chapter I, Cornwall,[10] the Peak District,[11] and the Yorkshire Wolds, and other districts [12] all had insatiable diggers and describers of their barrows. In addition to his work on the distinctive Wessex barrows, Mr L. V. Grinsell has, during the past two decades, undertaken detailed surveys of the barrows of no fewer than six southern English counties [13] besides the Isle of Wight. In his well-known book, *The Ancient Burial Mounds of England*, he has given us an account of most of the English round barrows in a series of chapters, each devoted to a specific region.[14]

Mr Grinsell's approach to the topographical problems relating to round barrows has involved the scrutiny of every barrow on the Ordnance Survey Map sheets of given areas, besides unmapped barrows that he and local workers have discovered. He has noted the dimensions and external characteristics of the barrows that he has recorded, has classified his results into types, and has given indications of the solid and drift geology of the localities in which barrows are found. Furthermore, he has carried out an often most difficult task, and has successfully identified barrows dug into by early antiquaries and has recorded the relics obtained from them. It should be noted in passing that the excavation of a given barrow, recorded thus, would, if the grave-goods were extant, be almost the equivalent of a modern excavation of an undisturbed barrow. Details of Grinsell's approach to the field study of barrows are contained in a proselytizing chapter in his book, which is intended not only to aid the beginner but to encourage an extension, by others, of this essential task before all is destroyed.

Except in areas where detailed surveys have been undertaken along the lines of those described in the preceding paragraphs, there is much to be done in assessing round barrow distributions in relation to specific soils and geological solids. In Wiltshire and the southern counties barrows lie for the great part on chalk downs or sand and gravel heathlands.[15] Heavy loams, clay soils, and the chalk where covered by clay-with-flints have been avoided. Elsewhere in the country, the concentrations of barrows on the limestone of the Peak District of Derbyshire and the chalk of the Yorkshire Wolds should be noted. The poor, podsolized soils of high moorlands in all regions of the west and the north carry great numbers of barrows.[16]

An outstanding problem of our Bronze Age studies is whether or not the presence of the great numbers of round barrows mostly in the high, and today often inhospitable, places of our land is evidence of settlement in these areas. That is, does the distribution pattern of barrows represent the distribution pattern of the Bronze Age settlement, of which we know little? It is possible that the 'ritual' sites, with which we are overburdened, are round houses,[17] and that their occupants lived on the high places amongst the tombs of their ancestors. On the other hand, there are perhaps some grounds, albeit slight, for the belief that the choice of the sites of early settlements was dictated by the same inescapable factors which brought about later settlements that have obliterated the former patterns. Recent pollen evidence from barrows has demonstrated, however, that on what are today high, bleak moorlands, cultivated areas were not far distant

[10] Borlase, 1872.

[11] Bateman, 1848, 1861.

[12] Greenwell, 1877; Mortimer, 1905. See also for Cambridge region, Fox, 1923; for Norfolk, W. G. Clarke, *The Antiquary*, XLIX.

[13] Berkshire, Dorset, Hampshire, Isle of Wight, Surrey, Sussex, Wiltshire. See also Appendix II.

[14] Grinsell, 1953, 121–255.

[15] Fox, 1952, 55, fn. 6.

[16] Fox, 1952, 76, fn. 2.

[17] Atkinson, Piggott, and Sandars, 1951, 81–107; *Arch. J.*, XCVI, 193–222; *Antiq.*, XI, 87–92.

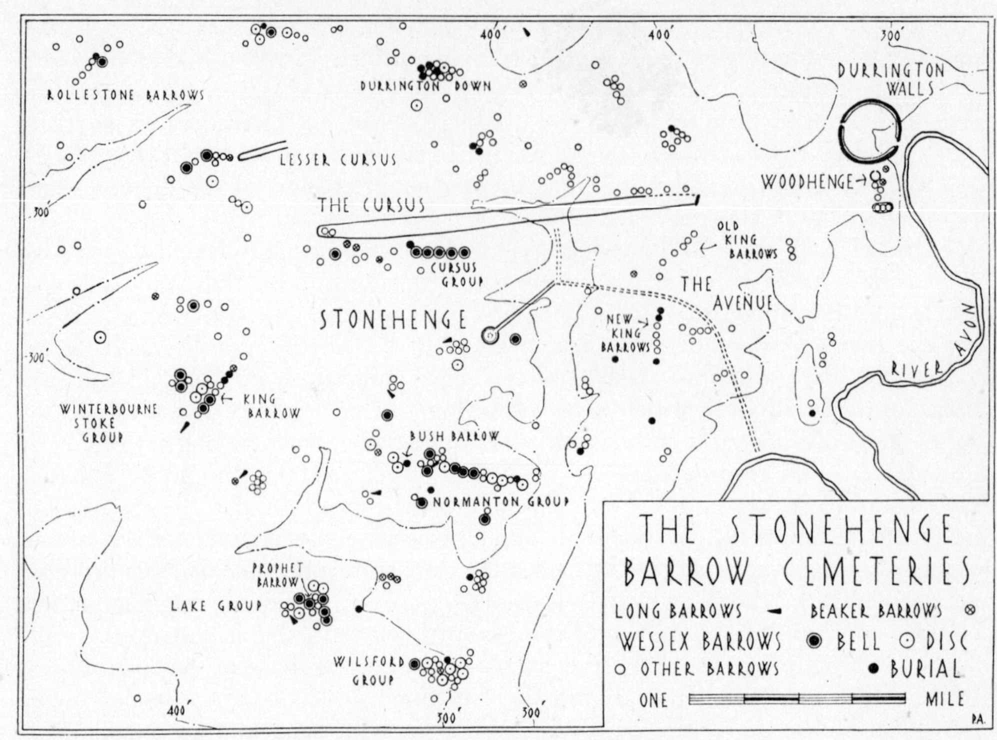

Fig. 6. The barrows around Stonehenge.

when barrows were built.[18] The chalk uplands of the south bear ample traces of intensive cultivation in Iron Age and Roman times, while traces of even earlier farming have also been noticed.[19] It has been suggested that by the Bronze Age such inroads had been made into the primeval forest [20] in these areas and that the downs were parklands.[21] As evidence of this the careful siting of Bronze Age barrows on 'false crests', [22] which appear as horizons from certain viewpoints, had been pointed out.[23]

The restricted distributions of the distinctive Wessex barrow forms have been briefly noted above. Their areas of concentration are almost exclusively round about Stonehenge (Fig. 6) and, to a lesser extent, Avebury.[24] This phenomenon was noted, in great part, by Thurnam.[25] The concentration of barrows in the vicinities of these unique monuments can hardly be accidental and unconnected with them.[26] Indeed, concentrations of barrows in the vicinities of henges is most marked both here and in other areas.[27] Sometimes round barrows have been placed upon the banks of henges.[28] In

[18] *YAJ*, XXXIX, 27. (The effects of prevailing winds upon pollen rain must be taken into consideration.)

[19] *PPS*, VII, 114–33.

[20] *Antiq.*, XIX, 57–71.

[21] Fox, 1952, 55.

[22] *Arch. J.*, XCIX, 22; S. Piggott, *William Stukeley*, Oxford University Press, 1950, 71.

[23] Fox, 1952, 55.

[24] *PPS*, VII, 73–113.

[25] *Arch.*, XLIII, 307.

[26] *Arch.*, XLIII, 307; 'Stonehenge Reviewed' in Grimes, 1951.

[27] Knowlton: Sumner, 1931, 28–31; Arbor Low: *Arch.*, LVIII, 461–98; Hutton Moor: *YAJ*, XXXVIII, 426.

[28] Arbor Low, *Arch.*, LVIII, 3. At Cairnpapple a cairn was set above a henge. *PSAS*, LXXX, 68–123; see also *Antiq.*, XIII, 158.

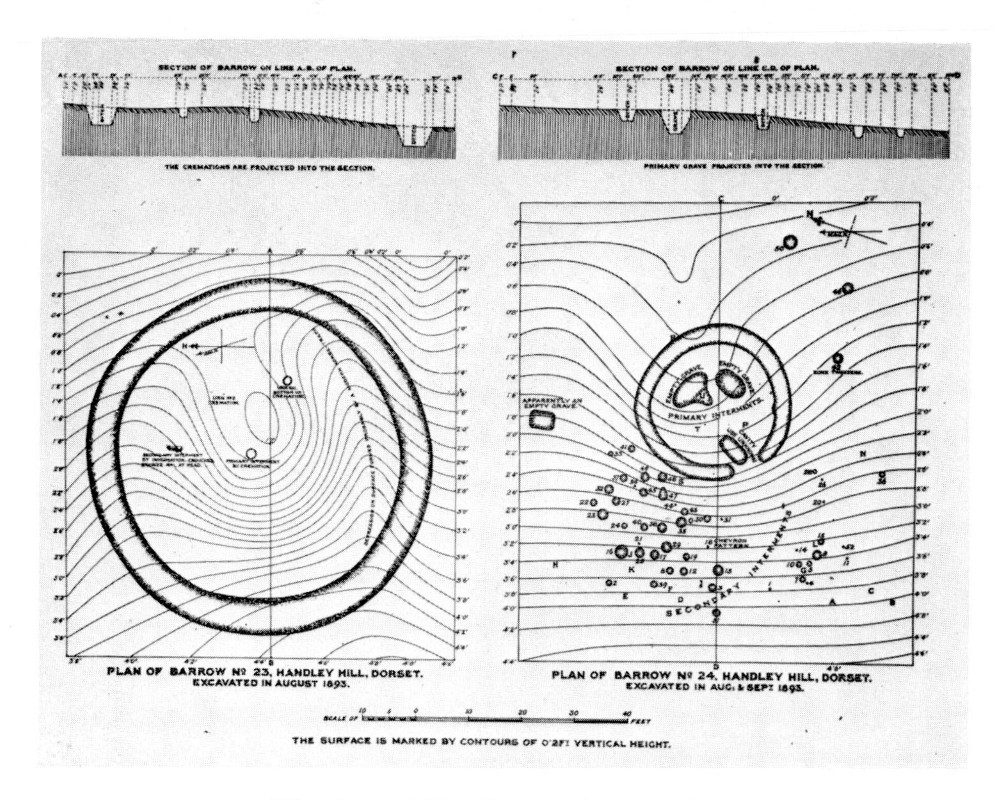

IIIa. General Pitt-Rivers's barrow plans.

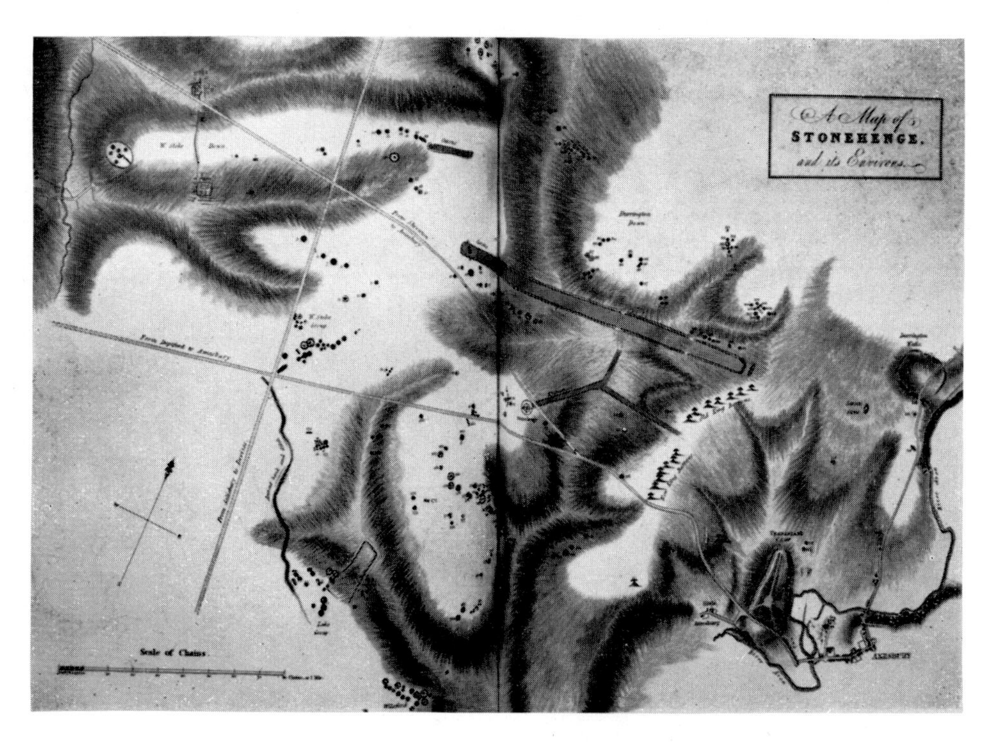

IIIb. Sir Richard Colt Hoare's map of the barrows round Stonehenge.

IVa. A tree-clad barrow at West Hoe, Hampshire.

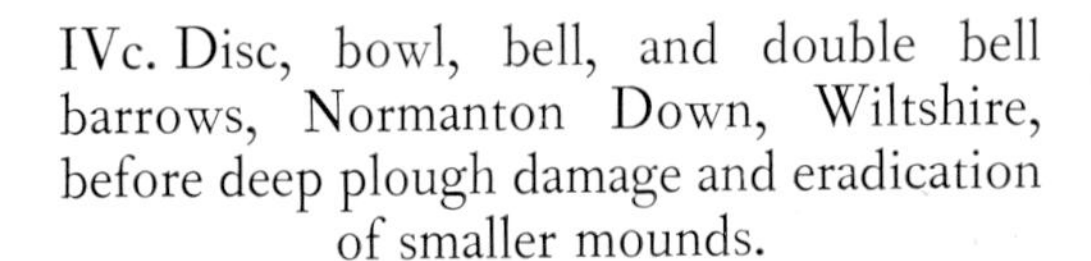

IVb. Barrows on the chalk downs at Overton Hill, near Avebury, Wiltshire.

IVc. Disc, bowl, bell, and double bell barrows, Normanton Down, Wiltshire, before deep plough damage and eradication of smaller mounds.

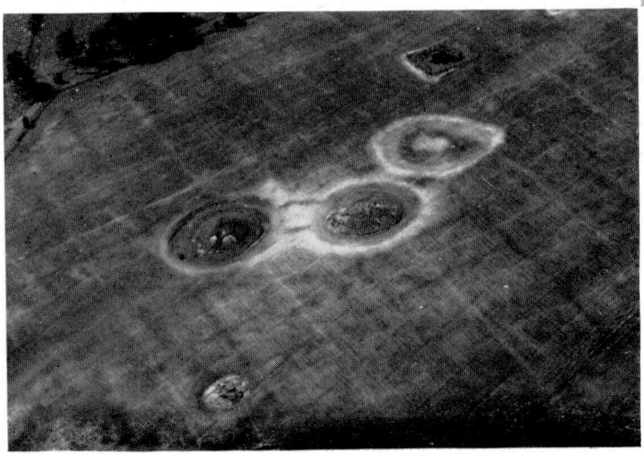

IVd. Two bell barrows linked by a small bowl barrow, a disc barrow, and a bowl barrow, Milton Lilbourne, Wiltshire. All are partially plough damaged.

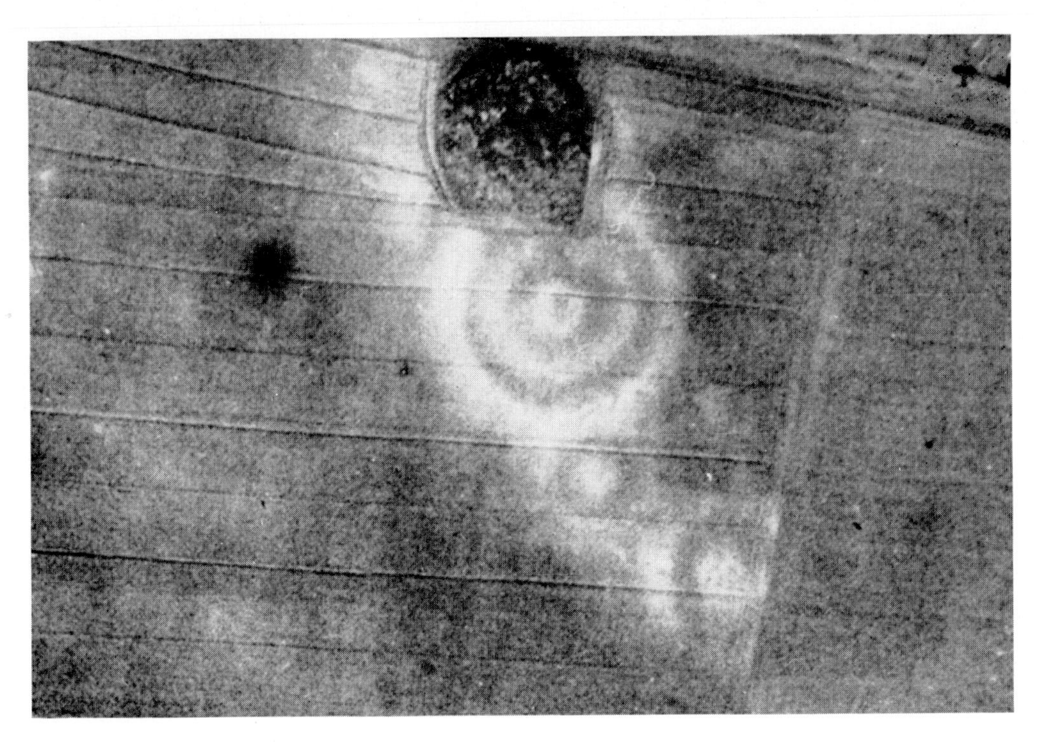

Va. Ploughed-out barrows seen as soil marks: the Grateley Disc Barrow, Hampshire.

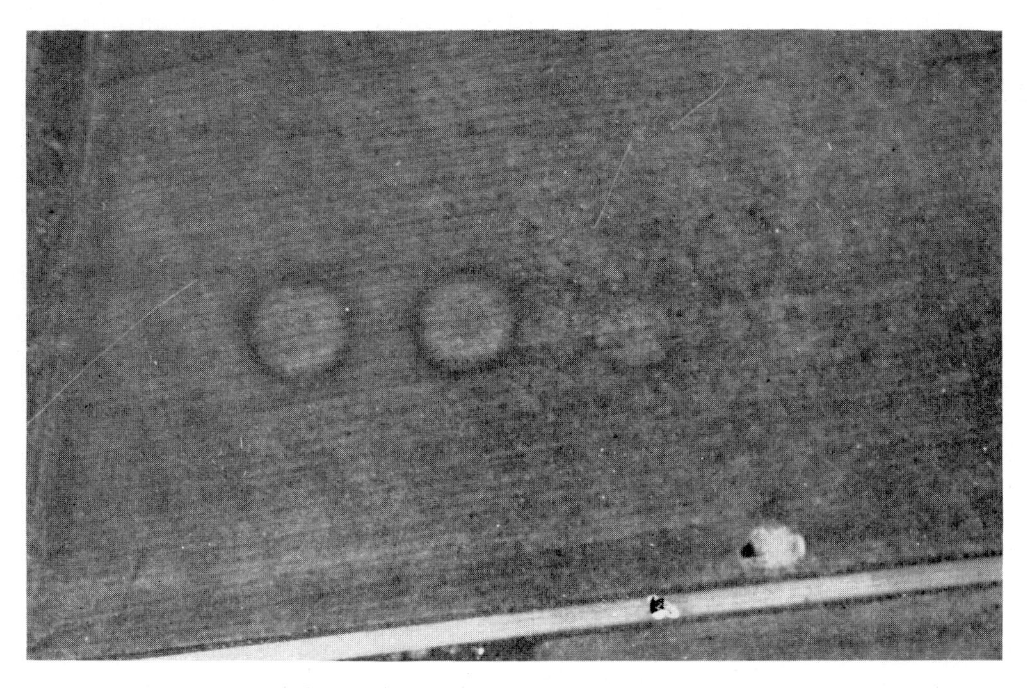

Vb. Ploughed-out barrows seen as crop marks: Everley Barrows, Wiltshire.

VIa. Turf-mound of a podsolized heathland barrow: Dudsbury, Dorset.

VIb. Loam core of a chalkland barrow with a stoneless worm-worked ancient soil beneath; Amesbury (G. 58), Wiltshire.

another case, a marked berm separates the bank and ditch of a North Country henge, calling to mind the principles of the predominantly southern bermed barrow series. These relationships will be discussed in a succeeding chapter.

A few Wessex bermed barrows have been met with in regions distant from their presumed point of origin. To the north-east of Wessex there are bell barrows on Dunstable Downs,[29] near Thetford,[30] and near Bircham and Weasenham,[31] both of which are in Norfolk. There is also some evidence that there were Wessex barrows in the upper Thames Valley.[32] Apart from some peculiar structures in Derbyshire, the Calais Wold bell barrow in Yorkshire,[33] and some barrows in Orkney, there do not appear to have been many of the distinctive Wessex forms north of a line drawn from the Wash to the River Severn. Besides a few bell and bell-disc barrows on and near Mendip,[34] they have been noted in Devon[35] and, still farther to the west, in Cornwall.[36] The round barrows of this last county are relatively unexplored, and, taking into consideration the results of the scrutiny of a single group only,[37] it is possible that more barrows similar to the Wessex forms may be found.

When the great barrow cemeteries in different parts of the country are studied, it can be seen that they generally comprise well-defined groups, a fact early recognized by Stukeley and Colt Hoare. This was realized also, though not pursued, by Thurnam,[38] while it was observed by Greenwell of the Wold barrows.[39] Mortimer,[40] working also on the Wolds, appears, with considerable perspicuity, to have realized that the barrows into which he intended to dig were to be found in groups, often with one or more isolated mounds between them. In his narrative he considers his barrows in terms of groups, numbering them, and indicating by use of numbers the mounds that he dug into. Elgee,[41] when he described the barrows of the Cleveland Moors, also noted groups.

These groups or cemeteries of barrows are most noticeable in the immediate vicinity of Stonehenge[42] (Fig. 6), but are often almost equally impressive elsewhere. That on account of their being grouped together there is a generic relationship between them seems beyond doubt. Furthermore it seems extremely unlikely that they were all constructed simultaneously. A barrow must have been set up on a given site and its companions added over a period of time. One obtains hints of this procedure from certain Stonehenge barrow cemeteries which include distinctive Wessex barrow forms side by side with other types, such as the Winterbourne Crossroads and Normanton groups. Where distinctive forms are lacking this serial construction is, of course, not so obvious from field inspection. Excavation should, ideally, produce a series of burials and relics from such a cemetery which could be arranged in a temporal sequence, thus relatively dating the barrows. Although such cemeteries, e.g. at Amesbury and Snail Down, have now been excavated by modern methods, they have either produced unaccompanied burials, as they have mainly done,[43] or have yielded a series of relics which, in the present state of knowledge, cannot be set in a reliable sequence[44] (Fig. 7).

[29] *PPS*, VII, 101.
[30] *PPS*, VII, 101.
[31] *Arch.*, XLIII, 454, etc.
[32] Stukeley, 1723, 40; Stukeley 1743, 12; *Oxon.*, XIII, 1.
[33] Heathcote, 1947, 10; Mortimer, 1905, 153–6.
[34] *PSANHS*, LXXXV, 151–66.
[35] *Ant. J.*, XXXI, 29.
[36] *PWCFC*, I, 132–5.
[37] *PWCFC*, I, 132–5.
[38] *Arch.*, XLIII, 301.
[39] Greenwell, 1877, 8, 112.
[40] Mortimer, 1905.
[41] Elgee, 1930, 122–3.
[42] 'Stonehenge Reviewed' in Grimes, 1951, 274–292.
[43] *WAM*, LVI, 237–40; 127–48.
[44] Mortimer, 1905: e.g. Garrowby Wold group.

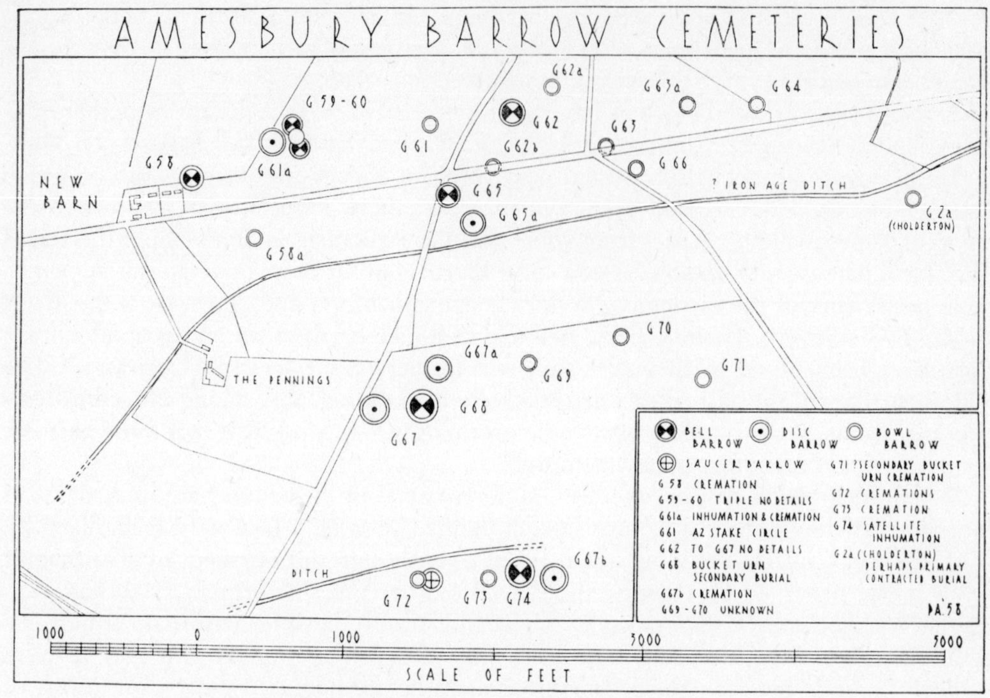

Fig. 7. The Amesbury barrow cemeteries.

The term 'Founder's Barrow' has been suggested for the earliest member of a given barrow group.[45] Some such human term is certainly needed, if only to awaken among certain of our prehistorians cognizance of the fact that these barrow cemeteries are the products of the planning and activities of men and are not mere 'types'.

Three types of barrow cemetery can be seen. I propose to call them *linear*, *nuclear*, and *dispersed*. The linear cemetery form comprises barrows, as in the Normanton and Cursus groups, strung out in a line or lines from or on both sides of the 'founder's', or first, barrow. In a nuclear cemetery such as Lake or Wilsford groups, the barrows comprise a close group around a given barrow or centre. Not enough is known of the grave-goods from such groups to say whether or not centre or nuclear barrows were founder's, or first, barrows, although this seems likely in view of the fact that in one such cemetery on Salisbury Plain a central barrow contained a bell (B) beaker. Dispersed cemeteries include those which appear to have been planned upon neither a predominantly linear nor a markedly nuclear pattern, although they sometimes contain noticeable elements of both principles. They have thus no immediately obvious founder's or first barrow, and are often spread over considerable areas, sometimes of more than two or three square miles.[46]

As examples of well-drilled, regular, linear barrow cemeteries there come most immediately to mind the Normanton, Winterbourne Stoke, and Cursus groups, all near Stonehenge,[47] as well as groups on Bulford, New Barn, and Earl's Farm Downs,

[45] Grinsell, 1953, 256.
[46] *YAJ*, XXXIX, 10, Fig. 1, 3.
[47] Grimes, 1951, 286.

to the east of Amesbury (Fig. 7). However, linear cemeteries are to be met with in other parts of the country. In Yorkshire, Elgee [48] noted barrows set in long lines, while the same principles obtain in Derbyshire,[49] and in many other places where large numbers of barrows exist. It may be remarked in passing that the well-known Lambourn Seven Barrows [50] are basically a group of at least four close-set linear cemeteries.

With regard to nuclear barrow cemeteries it is of interest to note that most of the groups or cemeteries around Avebury are of this type, though the linear one also is present. The well-known group on Oakley Down in Cranborne Chase appears to have been set down on the nuclear principle, and so do many more in that region.

In the North Riding of Yorkshire large bowl barrows are often surrounded by great numbers of quite small circular or elongated barrows or cairns. In some cases the large barrow is clearly the nucleus of the group. Such 'cemeteries' have been dug into but the sepulchral origin of the small cairns has never been proven. During 1953 the present writer excavated a small version of such a nuclear cemetery.[51] The nuclear cairn was clearly for burial, covering as it did a stone setting in a rock-cut grave, but the smaller cairns yielded nothing.

Dispersed cemeteries seem to be mainly a North Country phenomenon, although they do occur in the south-west. Many of the cemeteries planned by Mortimer [52] seem to have been of this type. A group surveyed by the writer at Goldsborough (Fig. 8), on the North Yorkshire coast, had dispersed characteristics.[53] Many of the heath and moorland barrows in the south and south-west come into the dispersed category.

The identification and classification of barrow cemeteries as well as individual mounds is simply an extension of the system of detailed field-work described earlier in the chapter. Much of Britain remains to be surveyed in detail.

In contradistinction to barrow cemeteries there are certain barrows which appear to have stood alone in their surrounding areas.[54] A notable example was the great barrow at Hove,[55] which seems to have been the only one on the Sussex coastal plain.

The topographical consideration of barrows, besides throwing into sharp relief the problems of distribution and settlement, emphasizes among other things the clustering of barrows, in certain areas, upon the enigmatic henge monuments. It will be recalled that these have been classified upon morphological grounds into two forms remarkable at the same time for their uniformity and diversity.[56] These characteristics have been ascribed, respectively, to the relics of the Beaker and 'Neolithic' cultures. Excavation alone can demonstrate the structures, rites, and affinities of the barrows in the vicinities of such henges.

In Ireland, barrows and cairns, which as far as can be seen approximate to those of Britain, as well as low-banked monuments termed 'ring barrows', are distinct from but cluster upon certain passage-grave cemeteries, while they can be seen, in their own right, upon hill-tops [57] in various parts of the country.

In the Boyne valley, where Dowth, New Grange, and Knowth command the countryside around from the ridges that they occupy, are smaller barrows (Coffey's A,

[48] Elgee, 1930, 125–8.
[49] *JDANHS*, IV, X, XIII (Stanton Moor).
[50] *Berks AJ.*, LV, 15–31.
[51] *YAJ*, X, XIX, 179–92.
[52] Mortimer, 1905, 1, Map opp.
[53] *YAJ*, XXXIX, 10, Fig. 1.
[54] *PPS*, XXIII, 137–66.
[55] *BH Arch.*, No. 2, 20–8; *SAC*, LXXXII, 123.
[56] Atkinson, Piggott, and Sandars, 1951, 89–91.
[57] *JRSAI*, LXXXV, 218–25; LXXXVI, 98–101.

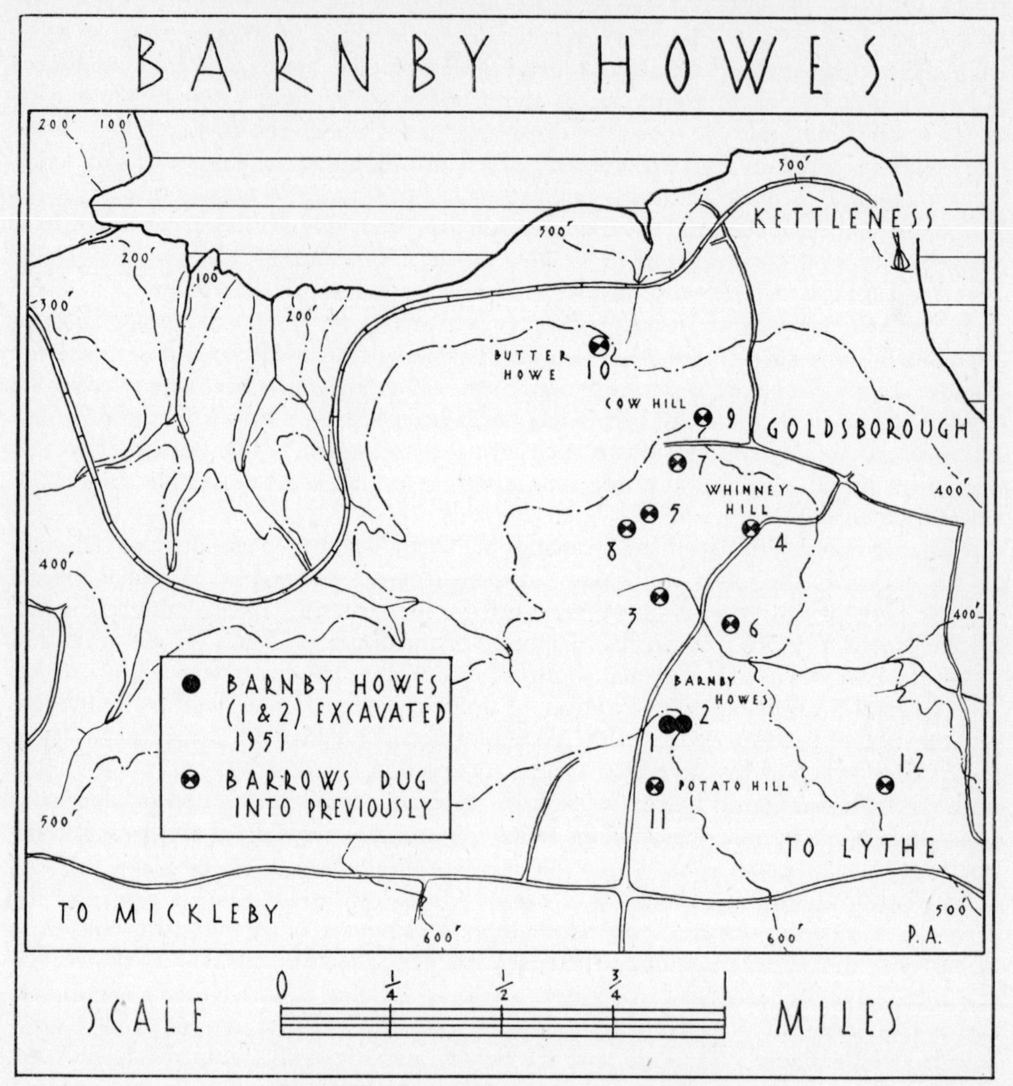

Fig. 8. The Barnby Howes barrow cemetery.

B, E, F, G, H, I, J). Also to be considered together with this complex is the so-called 'fort' at Dowth, possibly 'ritual' in purpose, and a 'henge-like' earthwork, recently noticed from an air-photograph, by the river.

'J' of Coffey's series appears to have covered a closed corbel-roofed chamber with five niches around it. 'A' and 'B' are also of considerable interest. The ditch around 'A', in great part ploughed away, and clothed with a cereal crop when last seen by the present writer, is separated from the mound by a wide berm. Thus the monument is a great disc barrow. 'E' has a berm, at the perimeter of which are orthostats, while no ditch is visible. It appears to be a bell barrow.

The numbers and distributions of barrows and cairns in Ireland, apart from those associated with and actually covering passage-graves, are almost an unknown factor in

Irish prehistory. There has been some record and, indeed, excavation of isolated barrows and groups, but an overall appreciation is lacking.

Bare downs and heaths, the environment in which we mostly see and study barrows today, were not so bare when the first round-barrow builders came to this country. For our contemporary landscape is largely man-made, a fact frequently forgotten in the study of the past. In their natural condition these isles, and indeed much of Europe, would be clad in the deciduous forest of the Temperate Zone,[58] which first assumed this form about seven millennia ago. Only such factors as poverty of soil, climatic extremes, fresh and salt water, and, in the Highland Zone, altitude, inhibited its initial growth. Oak, ash, and elm were the dominant species, even in the northern and western mountain valleys, while the heights would have been clad with hardier pine as are the Alps today.

Rivers, here rushing over rapids and there straggling as slow streams through swamps, and ridgeways were the natural and obvious means of communication. It is only in terms of early environment that the concentrations of barrows, henges, and circles, on chalk downs, limestone hills, rocky moors, and well-drained gravel terraces, can be appreciated. Allowing that at no point in the British Isles is fresh water at any great distance,[59] and in view of the later comparative density of settlement on such soils, it is inescapable that the men of the Bronze Age lived, worked, and moved among the barrows of their forbears.

The general conceptions of forest and climatic history in the British Isles are now firmly established. Palaeobotanical principles and the relevant evidence have been summarized to date by Clark,[60] Movius,[61] and Zeuner.[62] Britain is documented in detail in a series of studies by Godwin[63] and Ireland has been investigated by Jessen[64] and Mitchell.[65] Hencken[66] has endeavoured to reconcile Irish Bronze Age dating with the palaeobotanical record. Climatic change down the ages was inquired into by Brooks as long ago as 1926.[67]

Much remains as yet unknown and unexplored when barrows are considered in relation to their contemporary environment. Evidence of the general exploitation of forest is inherent in coffins, boats, posts, stakes, and mortuary houses, as well as in the charcoal from pyres and fires. Soils and silts, and the pollen preserved in them under favourable conditions, have in recent years told us much, not only regarding local vegetational conditions but also about the climatic variations of the Bronze Age.

The hollowed-out split-tree-trunk coffins were almost invariably of oak, although a plank in a Wessex grave is reported to have been of elm.[68] Similarly oak was almost exclusively used for the monoxylous craft[69] known since Mesolithic times and certainly used in the Bronze Age, found in bogs and the silts and muds of our lakes and rivers. Woodhenge's great trunks[70] were principally of oak, as were the timbers of the

[58] Clark, 1952, 10, Fig. 2.

[59] *Antiq.*, XVIII, 1–15.

[60] Clark, 1936, 1–53.

[61] Movius, 1942, 1–24.

[62] Zeuner, 1950, 92–104.

[63] H. Godwin, *Philosophical Transactions of the Royal Society*, CCXXIX, 323–406, CCXXX, 239–304; *New Phytologist*, Oxford, XL, 108–32, XLIV, 29–69; *The History of the British Flora*, Cambridge University Press, 1956; with A. G. Tansley, *Journal of Ecology*, XXIX, 17–26.

[64] *PRIA*, LII, 85–290.

[65] *PRIA*, L, 1–19, LII, 111–206.

[66] *JRSAI*, LXXXI, 57–61.

[67] Brooks, 1949, 295–302.

[68] *PPS*, VII, 104.

[69] *Ant. J.*, VI, 121–51.

[70] Cunnington, 1929, 73–5.

Sanctuary,[71] although pine, birch, and perhaps hornbeam were also identified at the former. Massive squared and morticed beams have been found on the submerged 'Lyonesse' land surface of the Essex coast,[72] but no report on the species has been published. It is only under natural forest conditions that trunks long and straight enough for canoes and the building uprights postulated at Woodhenge and the Sanctuary can be found. What wood has been found in post- and stake-holes under barrows was of oak[73] or ash[74] although well-preserved oak post-butts and birch-poles were found upon examination of the Bleasdale circle.[75] Both woods would have been eminently suitable for posts and driven stakes. The Beaulieu Heath and East Putford mortuary house's (pp. 53, 54) stakes and timbers did not allow the determination of their species. However, the stakes of the Cassington mortuary house were of oak,[76] as were those of an apparently similar structure unearthed by Mortimer[77] beneath one of the barrows of his Rigg group. Greenwell[78] claims that under a barrow at Kepwick, in the North Riding of Yorkshire, there were birch branches, conceivably the remains of a collapsed structure, some of which had been of a considerable size. It is recorded that the barrow was 'wet at the place in question', the central area of the ancient surface, so waterlogging accounts for the 'bark being as fresh in appearance as if it had been but newly placed there'!

Traces of fires under barrows may remain from initial site clearance, but charcoal mixed with cremations can only be from pyres unless it is part of the burnt remains of bier, coffin, or funerary furniture. Samples from the well-recorded Beaulieu Heath barrows[79] in Hampshire were almost all of oak, although willow was present in one instance. Those from one barrow's ancient surface and grave-pit comprised not only oak but also holly, willow, and purging buckthorn, besides other species not noted. Such a mixture, particularly the thorn, would have burnt well. It is comparable with that from the Sheeplays 293′ barrow,[80] where it was considered that the pyre had been fed with hawthorn and dry grass, and the Chick's Hill barrow,[81] the builders of which had burned pine branches and oak together. In the Lyles Hill cairn,[82] oak and hazel were detected.

Without doubt a detailed analysis of charcoals from barrows would show that specimens of oak are by far the most numerous. Although this might be taken to reflect the predominance of oak in the sub-boreal forests (broadly Zone VII b,[83] to which almost all the material described in this book, except that of the extreme Late Bronze Age, belongs), it must be remembered that oak has the property of being a good heat-producer and will burn long and well.

Pollen analysis of barrow soils[84] shows the impact of man upon the forest. Vegetation change in affected localities has been shown to have been: mixed high forest → hazel scrub → open country. This was a gradual process. The evidence for Dorset and Hampshire has been summarized by Dimbleby,[85] who has pioneered the techniques of

[71] *WAM*, XLV, 484.
[72] *PPS*, II, 184–5.
[73] *PPS*, XVIII, 159.
[74] *PDNHAS*, LXXVI, 50.
[75] *Ant. J.*, XVIII, 156.
[76] *Oxon.*, XI, 12.
[77] Mortimer, 1905, 182.
[78] Greenwell, 1877, 337.
[79] *PPS*, IX, 27–8.
[80] *Ant. J.*, XXI, 107–8.
[81] *PDNHAS*, LXXX, 146–59.
[82] Evans, 1953.
[83] Council for British Archaeology, 1948, 27.
[84] 'Techniques in Archaeology', *BA*, 1954.
[85] *PPS*, XX, 231–6.

pollen analysis of terrestrial soils in this country. It has been possible, with limitations and reservations, to match, upon pollen analysis, other barrows[86] to this sequence. In places as far apart as Cornwall and Yorkshire weeds of cultivation and even cereal remains have been found in barrows, suggesting that either cultivated areas or abandoned plots were at no great distance at the time of construction.

Soils[87] defined[88] as 'products of the decomposition of the land-surface under the influence of weather and vegetation' have much to tell us about barrows and their builders. For when they are thrown up the development of the soil beneath them is abruptly curtailed owing to the suspension of these factors, and a soil begins to grow *upon* their heaped material. By their character (see below, p. 159) these ancient soils under barrows can suggest local environment at the time of their covering, such as forest, grassland, or even cultivation. What is even more valuable is the climatic information obtainable from them. The character of red loams under an Oxfordshire barrow[89] suggested at least seasonal droughts, this being supported by soil evidence for a rather drier Bronze Age climate observed in Dorset.[90] These diagnoses are strengthened by the filling, detected upon analysis as dusty, of one of the 'Y' holes at Stonehenge.[91]

This dry period of the Bronze Age is marked by the drying up of surface peat-bogs and a decrease in the size of lakes. Precipitation is thought to have been about one-half that of the present day. In any future study of this problem cognizance must, however, be taken of the effect of the inroads of man upon the forest. For during this period, as Dimbleby has reminded us,[92] the processes of gradual change from forest to open country were gathering momentum. Soil evidence from under one barrow[93] showed a forest brownearth somewhat altered in the direction of a podsol, either by climatic change, or by deforestation, or by both. The pollen spectra showed that both heath and mixed oak forest were contemporary with this soil. In view of such evidence as this another hypothesis of the whole problem can be entertained. Normally a podsol indicates wet conditions such as obtain in the west, where they are frequent upon moor and mountain. It is possible that during the Bronze Age rainfall remained constant, but that, for the first time in this country, the evaporation rate overtook the rainfall because of the inroads of man upon the forests, already then perhaps a half millennium old. Not only would this account for the progressive drying up of some but not all bogs and lakes, but it would also, with the other factors, inhibit vegetation, allow the formation of localized wind deposits, and promote podsolization. Thus also can the soil phenomenon be equated with the record of the bogs.[94]

Following upon the retreat of the Late Pleistocene ice, the interplay of isostatic land movement and the eustatic rise of sea level has considerably affected the British Isles.[95] The Irish and Scottish coastlines had, by the beginning of the Bronze Age, assumed their present outline, but during this time and, indeed, into historic times, there has been inundation of much of the south coast of England. Submerged sites and monuments of various periods at places distant one from another suggest that the movements

[86] *PDNHAS*, LXXV, 34–5.
[87] I. W. Cornwall, *Soils for the Archaeologist*, Phoenix House, 1958.
[88] *ULIA*, Occasional Papers, No. 9.
[89] *PPS*, XIX, 137.
[90] *PPS*, XIX, 133.
[91] *PPS*, XIX, 138.
[92] *PPS*, XX, 233.
[93] *PPS*, XIX, 133.
[94] H. Godwin, *The History of British Flora*, 1956, denies the hypothesis adhered to by some writers of a warm, dry 'sub-Boreal' period and points to a paucity of evidence from bogs and lakes.
[95] Movius, 1942, 288–93.

were, while intermittent, possibly generally earlier in the east than in the west. On the Essex coast[96] submergence took place shortly after the abandonment of a settlement where Handled beakers and Rinyo-Clacton ware were in use. In the extreme south-west the lowlying land of the Scilly Isles[97] was not overwhelmed until Roman times, for cist graves of broadly that period, set into ancient surfaces, have been found on foreshores. At Yelland[98] in Devon, a stone row on a submerged surface has been planned, and across the Channel in Brittany the half-submerged Er Lannic[99] stone circles have long been known. A Late Bronze Age settlement at Birchington[100] in Kent was abandoned in the face of sea encroachment. Oakley[101] has suggested that these subsidences be equated with the marine transgressions of 'Passage-Grave' and even Iron Age date in the Baltic area. Following upon this Dr Isobel Smith[102] has compared the phenomenon of the Essex coast sites with the flooding of the banks of the Elbe and its tributary the Bille in the Boberg district, and has shown how natural and archaeological evidence exhibit a remarkable degree of correlation.

The foregoing paragraphs seek to emphasize the importance of spatial studies in conjunction with the record of changing environment. We see barrows today together as the final product in space of *x* years of activity, for they were built over a length of time in an environment very different from the artificial circumstances of our own. Our understanding of the original environment of barrows rests largely upon the knowledge which can be recovered by careful selective excavation.

[96] *PPS*, II, 178–210.
[97] *Arch. J.*, CXI, 24.
[98] *PDAES*, III, 109–35.
[99] Le Rouzic, 1930.
[100] *PPS*, IX, 28–47.
[101] *PPS*, IX, 56–9.
[102] *ULIAA Rpt*, XI, 29–42.

CHAPTER IV

BARROW STRUCTURE

WITH NOTABLE exceptions early barrow-diggers recorded no more than particular structural details which had attracted their attention. From the accounts of General Pitt-Rivers [1] one can determine barrow structure, while the notable round-barrow excavations of the past three decades [2] have recorded a wealth of structural detail. Grinsell has paid some attention to structure in his books,[3] and in a paper [4] he has drawn together a mass of structural material from Wessex which is, regrettably, mostly from early accounts and therefore frequently not particularly reliable.

One of the writers of the Council for British Archaeology's *Survey and Policy of Field Research*, published in 1948, remarked that 'Enough material has not yet been published for any general analysis [of barrow structure] to be attempted'.[5] This is still to a great extent true; the numbers of total excavations and partial excavations from which structural evidence can be gleaned are still pathetically small (Appendix III). It can be argued that the information derived from barrow excavations to date plus all that has gone before will permit some expansion of the 1948 view. There are, however, factors which modify this claim, not the least being that of reliability of account. Thus many of the accounts of structural details incidentally noted in earlier and not so early ages have been jettisoned, and only those which have been confirmed by later, methodical work have been retained.

Barrow structure (Fig. 9) was largely conditioned by local geology. Thus the materials to hand, earth or stones, were heaped up. There are, therefore, two basic forms of barrows, namely: *earthen mounds* and *stone cairns*. In many cases, however, barrow structure was *composite*, both earth and stones being used.

Usually a round-barrow mound covered a single interment (Fig. 10), or, in instances, a number of interments (Fig. 10). Normally a single interment was in a grave, or on the ancient surface at the centre of the barrow. This is termed the *primary* burial. When a central primary burial is present other interments made in or on the ancient surface before the barrow was built, or in its body while it was building, are termed *satellite* burials. When no obvious primary in the form of a central burial is present in numbers of barrows which have peripheral burials beneath them, priority is difficult to determine. The same problems of priority obtain with regard to the time relationships of primary and satellite burials. However, a primary burial normally has the prime place

[1] Pitt-Rivers, 1887–98, IV, 136–81.
[2] Fox and Dickens, 1950, 53–73.
[3] Grinsell, 1953, 49–61.
[4] *PPS*, VII, 90–7.
[5] Council for British Archaeology, 1948, 91.

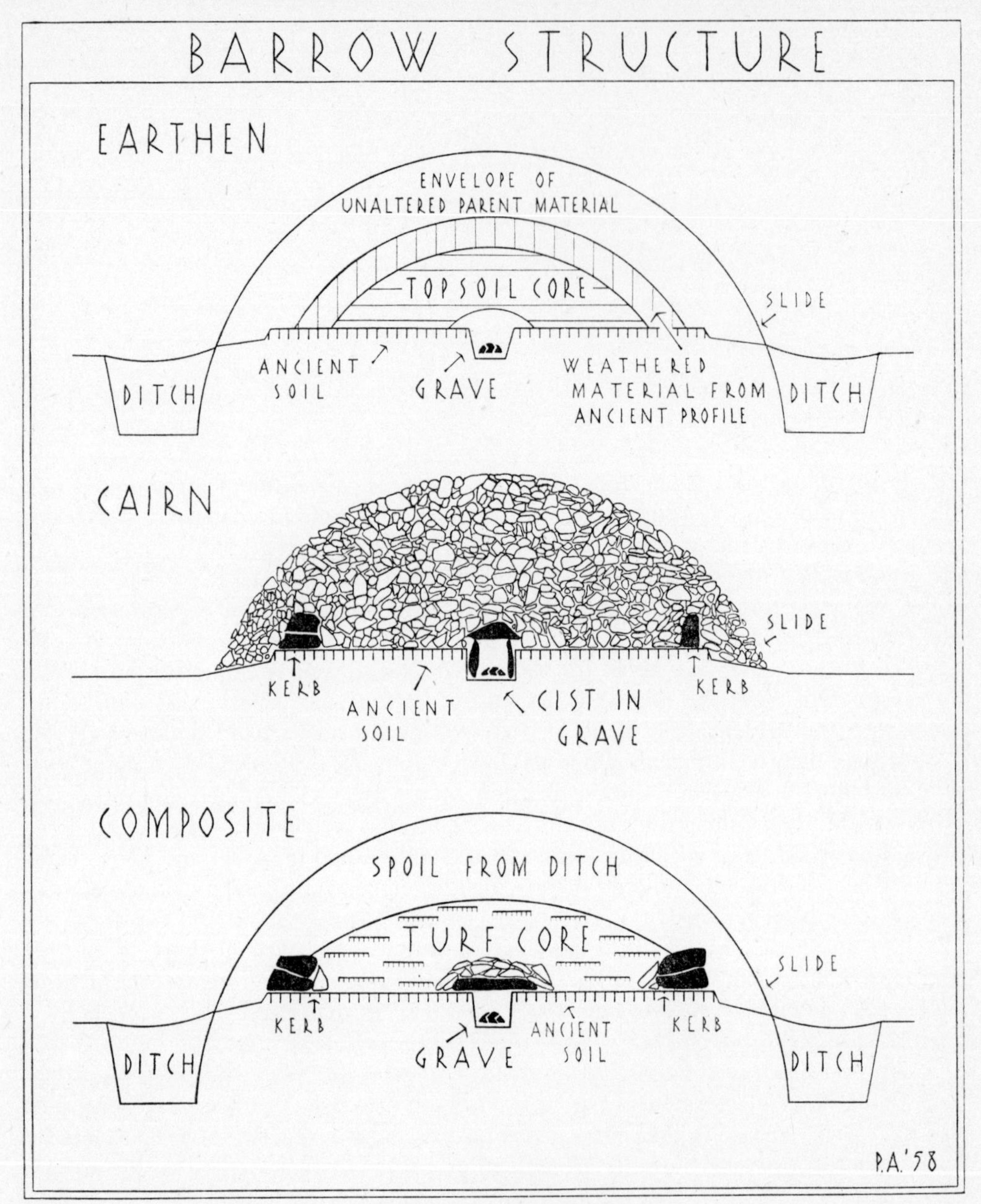

Fig. 9. Barrow structure.

at the barrow centre. Thus in this sense its primacy is reasonably assured, but it must be remembered that the term is but an archaeological assumption.

Interments which have, at some time subsequent to the barrow's completion, been set into its body in dug graves, and which are occasionally of a later age, are *secondary* burials. This term secondary is used in a relative chronological sense when determined by the cold facts of stratigraphy. The term is generally used for all burials later than the

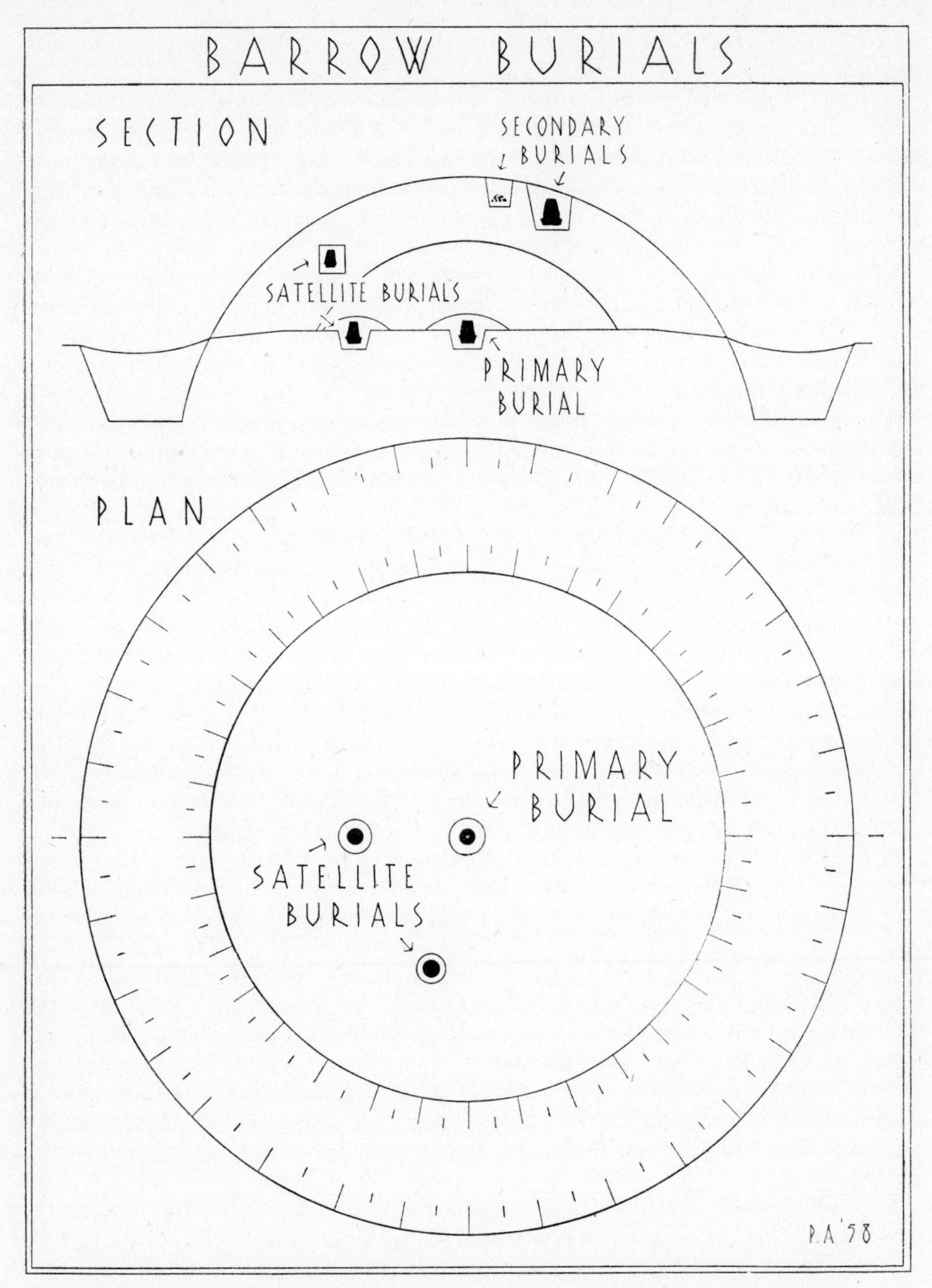

Fig. 10. Barrow burials to illustrate the terms 'primary', 'satellite', and 'secondary'.

barrow's completion, since it is normally impossible to postulate a sequence of such burials.

Beneath all barrows the *ancient* or *pre-barrow* soil is usually met with. It may be remarked in passing that the term 'old turf line' is undesirable, as it connotes a certain type of vegetational cover which may not have existed when the barrow was built.

The foregoing are the structural principles common to all barrows. Before discussing the differing types of barrow structure in detail, two important structural adjuncts must be briefly noted. They will be discussed in more detail in the next chapter.

Circles of stake-holes, and in cases carbonized stake-ends, have been recorded beneath earthen and composite barrows. So far they have not been recognized below cairns. Their discovery depends, largely, upon the factors of total and skilled excavation. Recent work has shown that while they were a feature in certain barrows, they were not used in others.

The recognition of so-called 'ritual' pits, like stake circles, depends upon excavation and mound removal also. Some of these pits are certainly natural, but indubitable carefully dig pits, subsequently infilled, have been recorded beneath both earthen and composite barrows.

Earthen barrows are those built entirely of chalk, gravel, sand, clay, loam, turf, and the like. There were two methods of building—by ditch excavation and the throwing up therefrom, or by collection of materials, from, presumably, a convenient source, and heaping them up, or stacking them, at the required spot. The latter class are sometimes known as *scrape* barrows, a name which suggests a particular mode of building. *Ditchless* barrows is, perhaps, a more precise term.

Excavation has shown that two classes of ditchless barrows are discernible. These are barrows which have been built by heaping up soil or by stacking up turves (Pl. VI a). Excavation alone can conclusively prove the absence or presence of a ditch, as often the denudation of the mound of the barrow completely conceals this feature. Some low ditchless barrows are little more than a heap of soil over an infilled grave.

A number of the barrows excavated on chalk before the last war on Launceston Down, in Dorset,[6] proved to have been built of soil and flints and were ditchless, while Grinsell[7] has listed others, on both chalk and heathland soils, which excavation has shown to have been most probably ditchless. The series of heathland barrows near Beaulieu[8] was excavated during the war years. Certain of these were proved to have been ditchless, one (Stoney Cross I) being of mixed clay and gravelly soils and another (Beaulieu X) of sand. A barrow on Canford Heath, in Dorset,[9] excavated by the present writer, proved also to have been ditchless.

Two barrows excavated in 1946 at Letterston, in Pembrokeshire,[10] illustrate the turf stack method of construction. It would appear that certain of the many barrows excavated in Cornwall before and during the last war, and as yet unpublished,[11] were similarly built.

Ditched barrows of bell and bowl types reflect fairly faithfully their sequence of construction (Fig. 9). The general principle is that a core of soil (Pl. VI b), turf, or even occupation earth, was enveloped by unaltered material dug from the depths of the

[6] *Arch.*, XC, 48–80.
[7] *PPS*, VII, 107.
[8] *PPS*, IX, 1–27.
[9] *PDNHAS*, LXXVI, 39–50.
[10] *Arch. Camb.*, C, 67–87.
[11] *Ant. J.*, XXVIII, 26; *ANL*, II, 110–11.

encircling ditch (Pl. VIII b). Thus, as Stukeley initially observed,[12] barrows in chalk country would, when newly raised, have made a striking spectacle, while on other geological solids they were, probably, also extremely colourful.[13]

Barrow ditches in chalk (Pl. VII a), and other soils, normally annular, tend to be relatively broad-bottomed,[14] although this is not always the case, narrow ones being known.[15] A number of ditches cut into clays and gravels have been found to be more or less V-formed.[16] The sloping sides of a V ditch would retard the processes of silting which must have rapidly filled them.[17]

The constructional principles indicated have been illustrated many times over during the excavation of earthen ditched mounds.[18] Thus in terms of human activity it would appear that, after the initial setting out, the top-soil or turf from the site of the ditch was heaped over the infilled grave, which sometimes appears as a low mound.[19] Finally, as the ditch was completed, the material from its depths was heaped above and around that already dumped, thus completing the barrow.

Sometimes this procedure varied. Material from a certain part of the ditch, or from a distance, was used to delimit the mound and, presumably, to keep it from spreading while building.[20]

The interdigitation of tip-lines, along which moor-pan accumulates in acid soils, suggests that baskets were used for tipping the soil on the mound.[21] This, and possible unfinished ditches, which consist of a series of irregular scoops, have been adduced as pointing to the work of a series of 'gangs', going on simultaneously around the barrow. These should not be confused with finished ditches dug in near-equal segments, with causeways between.[22]

In chalk, 'pick' marks have been noted in graves as in that of Amesbury Barrow G. 58, although not in the well-finished ditches. One could legitimately expect the lower part of the ditch, which must have been soon covered by rapid silting, to preserve such traces. However, antler picks have been found in chalk barrows,[23] for instance, in one upon Earl's Farm Down near Amesbury,[24] apparently discarded. From the turf mound of a Cornish barrow [25] an object claimed to be a shovel was disinterred.

Sometimes, to accommodate more burials an earthen barrow was enlarged by the addition of more material to an existing mound, sometimes from another ditch.[26] Indeed, now and again the original ditch was masked.[27]

The specialized earthen Wessex barrows, disc and pond, were built, as far as can be seen, by material from ditch or central area.[28]

Less is known of *stone cairns* than of earthen barrows because of the considerable amount of labour involved in the examination of an example of even relatively small size.

[12] Stukeley, 1740, 44

[13] *Arch. Camb.*, XCV, 169–91; *PPS*, IV, 169–87, XVIII, 148–59.

[14] *WAM*, XLV, 432–58; *TNDFC*, VIII, 109–15; *PPS*, IX, 22.

[15] *PPS*, IX, 23, Fig. 18; Amesbury G. 61 (excavated 1956).

[16] *Arch. Camb.*, XCV, 169–81; *PPS*, IV, 169–87; XVIII, 148–59.

[17] *Antiq.*, IV, 97–100.

[18] *PPS*, XXIII, 137–66.

[19] *PPS*, XXIII, 137–66.

[20] Chick's Hill, Dorset, *PDNHAS*, LXXX, 146–159; Bishop's Waltham, *PPS*, XXIII, 137–66.

[21] *PPS*, VII, 95, 105.

[22] *Ant. J.*, XX, 39–51.

[23] Greenwell, 1877, s.v. 'antler picks'.

[24] *WAM*, LVI, 237–40 (interim).

[25] *ANL*, II, 110–11.

[26] *PPS*, LX, 11–13.

[27] *PPS*, LX, 11–13.

[28] *Arch. J.*, LVIII, 1–24.

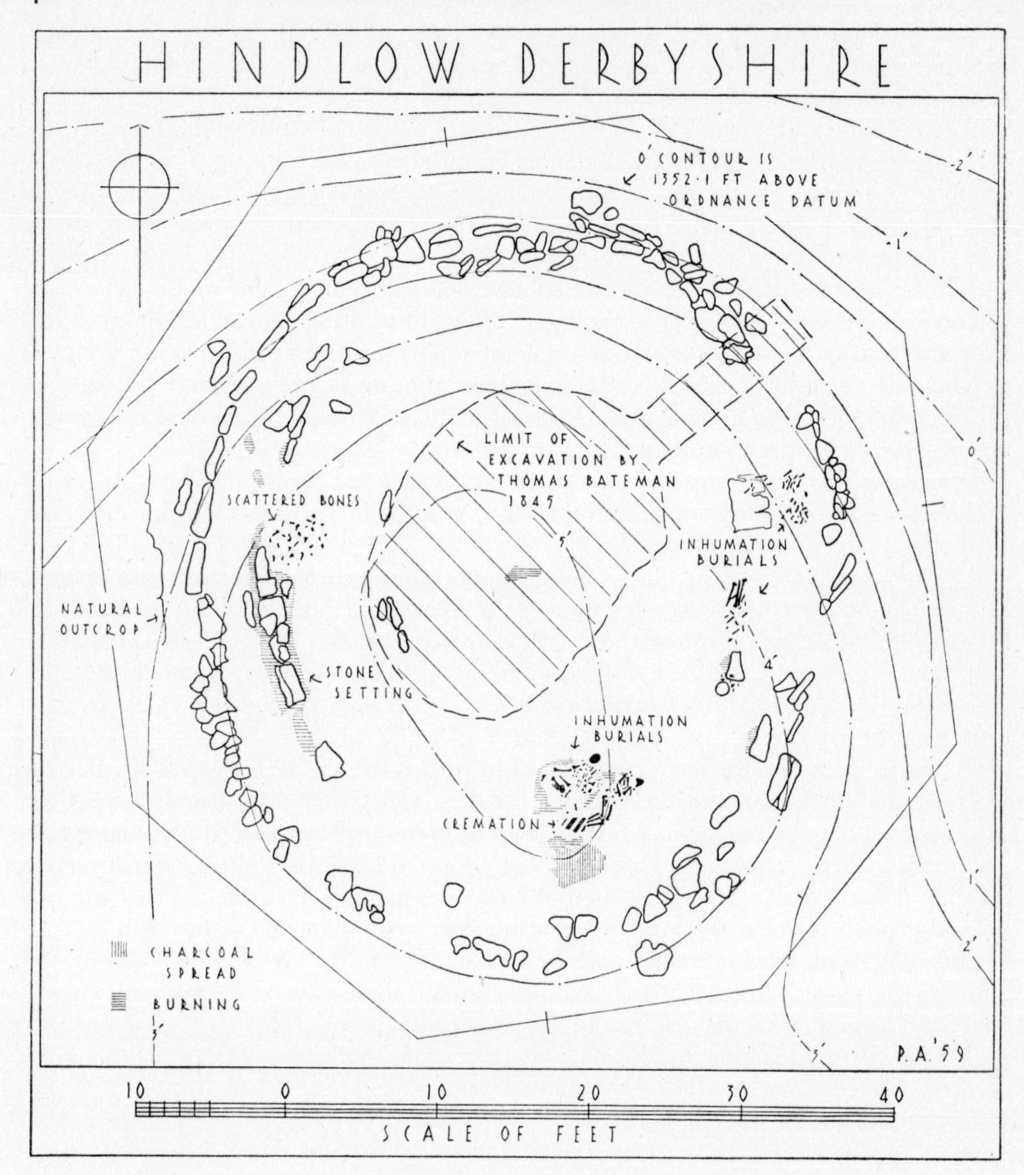

Fig. 11. The Hindlow cairn.

In its simplest form a cairn is a heap of stones, unkerbed, covering a burial often in a covered cist,[29] but sometimes in a grave.[30] Often, however, it is a complex structure.

Cairns often appear upon excavation to have been built of stones and earth. There is little doubt that many cairns recorded as being of such construction were originally constructed entirely of stone. What has frequently happened in such cases is that there

[29] *Arch. Camb.*, LXXXIII, 137–74.

[30] *YAJ*, XL, 179–92.

has been a change of environment, a soil has developed on the cairn, and the interstices between the rocks have been filled with mould by the action of earthworms.

Many cairns are encircled by a kerb of walling or blocks, sometimes near-megalithic, which might well be regarded as a retaining device for the cairn. On the other hand the boulders sometimes seem to be unnecessarily great for the task.

A good example of a retained cairn, completely excavated, is that which was set above the Cairnpapple Henge.[31] A cairn excavated at Simondstown[32] in Wales, sited upon a falling ridge, had a 'thrust block' kerb set to the axis of the barrow. In this case the function of the thrust blocks appears to have been to prevent downhill slip and spread of the cairn material. The present writer examined a similarly sited cairn in Derbyshire (Fig. 11).

Cairns in Kirkcudbrightshire[33] and Ross,[34] in Scotland, covered roughly D-shaped enclosures comparable with those beneath composite barrows in England.[35] In Berwickshire[36] there was a crescentic stone setting beneath a cairn, and a similar crescentic arrangement was noted beneath the great Collessie Cairn.[37] A crescentic setting has been found in Ireland,[38] and the present writer has met with a similar feature beneath a retained cairn in Derbyshire.[39]

A central cist, beneath the Law Cairn, Urquhart, Elgin, Scotland,[40] was encircled by an inner wall of boulders, 2 feet 6 inches in height. Under the great cairn on Kilmartin Glebe,[41] which was more than 100 feet in diameter, Canon Greenwell claimed to have found two concentric rings of uprights. Away to the south, concentric circles beneath cairns appear to have been a regular feature on Dartmoor.[42] In Somerset the 'Wick Barrow',[43] a cairn, covered a well-built annular wall, which must have been built and infilled, and stood drum-like, before being covered by the cairn.

On the Cleveland Moors, in northern Yorkshire,[44] the present writer excavated a ruined cairn (Fig. 12) which covered a rock-cut grave. Sub-megalithic blocks comprised the kerb, while the flat slab that covered the grave was truly megalithic. Minor gaps in this kerb were filled with carefully constructed masonry, as was one large gap on the eastern side, which could have held a stone. A hint of the structural procedure was given by the fact that the cairn stones were more or less uniform in size and were of such a weight that two men might conveniently carry them.

A well-known feature on the north Yorkshire Moors is the large number of small cairns.[45] The only structural feature that the excavation of a number of these small heaps of stones revealed was a tendency for them to have large stones at the core.

Composite barrows, built of both earth and stone, sometimes occur in areas where suitable stone is not a part of the geological solid, and thus must have been collected from a distance.[46] Such barrows usually consist of a mound of soil, or turfs, containing or enclosed by a stone ring, or covering a cairn, or even both. Early writers merely

[31] *PSAS*, LXXXII, 68, 123.
[32] *Arch.*, LXXXVII, 130–41.
[33] *PSAS*, LVII, 65.
[34] Childe, 1935, 109.
[35] *Ant. J.*, XXXI, 1–24.
[36] *PSAS*, LVIII, 318.
[37] *PSAS*, XII, 441.
[38] *JCHAS*, XXXVIII, 81.
[39] *ANL*, V, 134–5.
[40] Childe, 1935, 109.
[41] *PSAS*, VI, 337.
[42] *Antiq*, XII, 450–1; *TDA*, LXIX, 93–101.
[43] *PSANHS*, LIV, 1–77.
[44] *YAJ*, XL, 179–92.
[45] *YAJ*, XL, 179–92.
[46] *PDNHAS*, LXV, 39–52.

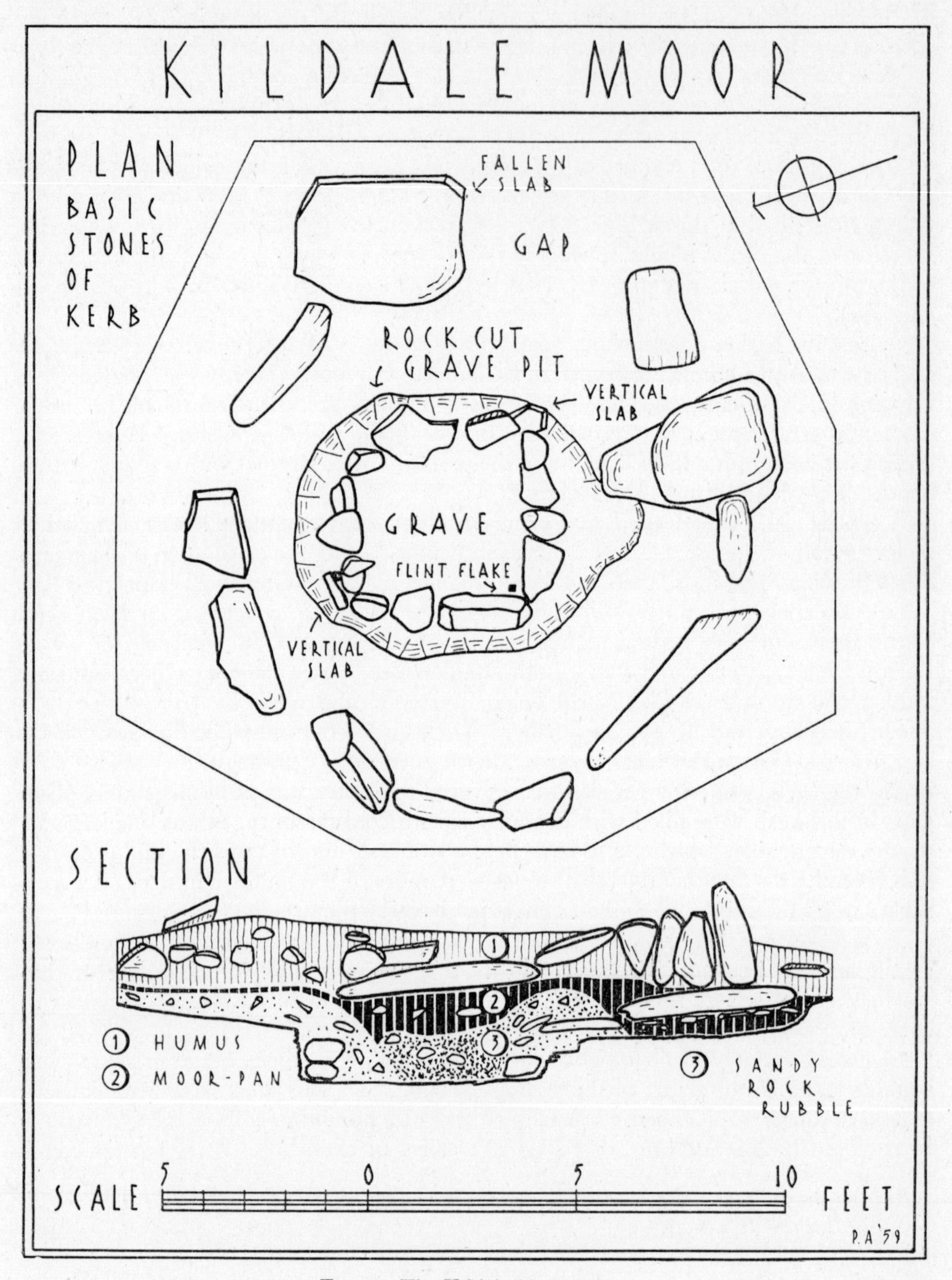

Fig. 12. The Kildale Moor cairn.

VIIa. Intersection of chalk-cut barrow ditches. A double barrow excavated at Earl's Farm Down, Amesbury (G. 72), Wiltshire.

VIIb. Tregulland Burrow: the Cairn ring.

VIIIa. Tip-lines of loam and hearth-sweepings at the core of a chalkland bell barrow; excavated at Milton Lilbourne (G. 4), Wiltshire, in 1958.

VIIIb. Section across a chalkland bell barrow showing loam and core and chalk envelope; excavated at Milton Lilbourne (G. 4), Wiltshire, in 1959.

noted their occasional occurrence;[47] they were given some order by Grimes[48] following upon the excavation of the Breach Farm barrow. He cited a number of examples, demonstrating a wide distribution, and noting that they did not appear to be confined to any particular region. However, it is only in the south and west and in Yorkshire that they have been studied in any detail.

Cairns beneath simple earthen barrows are exemplified by the barrow within the Ysceifiog circle, in Flintshire,[49] where a cairn covered the central grave. Cairns of flints[50] cover central graves under certain chalk barrows, and they may well have their counterpart in the heaps of clay which cover some central burials.[51] Stone cairns covering central burials sometimes occur in association with kerbs and stone rings.[52]

Kerbs of composite barrows, like those of cairns, range from not inconsiderable blocks[53] to quite small stones. They may be neatly laid and be packed behind with smaller stones, as in the case of the Breach Farm barrow[54] and the remaining part of one of the Barnby Howes,[55] or may consist of large blocks interspersed with smaller material as did the kerb around the Crick barrow.[56] A stone-cased turf barrow on Mynydd Epynt[57] had a surrounding kerb of more or less even-sized oblong or cubical boulders without smaller material. A composite barrow in Cornwall[58] was kerbed partly with stones and partly with turfs.

A classificatory scheme, initially used for the kerbs of Dartmoor cairns,[59] was expanded by Payne[60] at the same time as his publication of the Bincombe Barrow.

Some composite barrows reveal upon excavation that they have been modified and enlarged after their initial building. At Sutton, Glamorganshire,[61] and Talbenny, Pembrokeshire,[62] Beaker barrows were enlarged to accommodate each a single Middle Bronze Age cremation burial. At the latter site a new kerb was made by the removal of stones from the earlier mound, and at the former a turf and clay mound, retained by a kerb, extended the earlier structure. A barrow at Tyning's Farm, on Mendip,[63] was extended at a later date in a similar manner.

Stone rings *contained* by mounds fall, broadly, into two categories. First of all there are the well-built, usually annular, rings of stones such as were encountered beneath the turf barrow on Mynydd Epynt[64] or the Charmy Down barrows in Somerset.[65] Certain stone rings, such as that described as being beneath the Bincombe Barrow,[66] were almost certainly around it when placed in position. Subsequent denudation has covered them.

Secondly, there are the rings of cobbles or blocks, generally more or less penannular, such as were found under Quernhowe[67] and Tregulland Burrow (Fig. 13)[68] (Pl. VII b). They have been termed most aptly 'cairn-rings'.[69] While the former cairn-ring

[47] Greenwell, 1877, 6–7.
[48] *PPS*, IV, 119.
[49] *Arch. Camb.*, LXXXI, 48–85.
[50] *Arch.*, XC, 71, Fig. 17.
[51] *Ant. J.*, XXI, 99; *PPS*, IV, 111, Pl. XII.
[52] *TDA*, XXXIV, 107.
[53] *Arch. Camb.*, XCV, 169–91.
[54] *PPS*, IV, 107–21.
[55] *YAJ*, XXXIX, 9–31.
[56] *Arch. Camb.*, XCV, 169–91.
[57] *Arch. Camb.*, XCVIII, 169–94.
[58] *Ant. J.*, XXXVIII, 174–96.
[59] *TDA*, LXIX, 93–101.
[60] *PDNHAS*, LXV, 38–52.
[61] *Arch.*, LXXXIX, 89–125.
[62] *Arch. J.*, XCIX, 1–32.
[63] *PBUSS*, VI, 2, 111–73.
[64] *Arch. Camb.*, XCVIII, 169–94.
[65] *Ant. J.*, XXXI, 1–24.
[66] *PDNHAS*, LXV, 38–52.
[67] *Ant. J.*, XXXI, 1–24.
[68] *Ant. J.*, XXXVIII, 174–96.
[69] *Arch.* LXXXVII, 160.

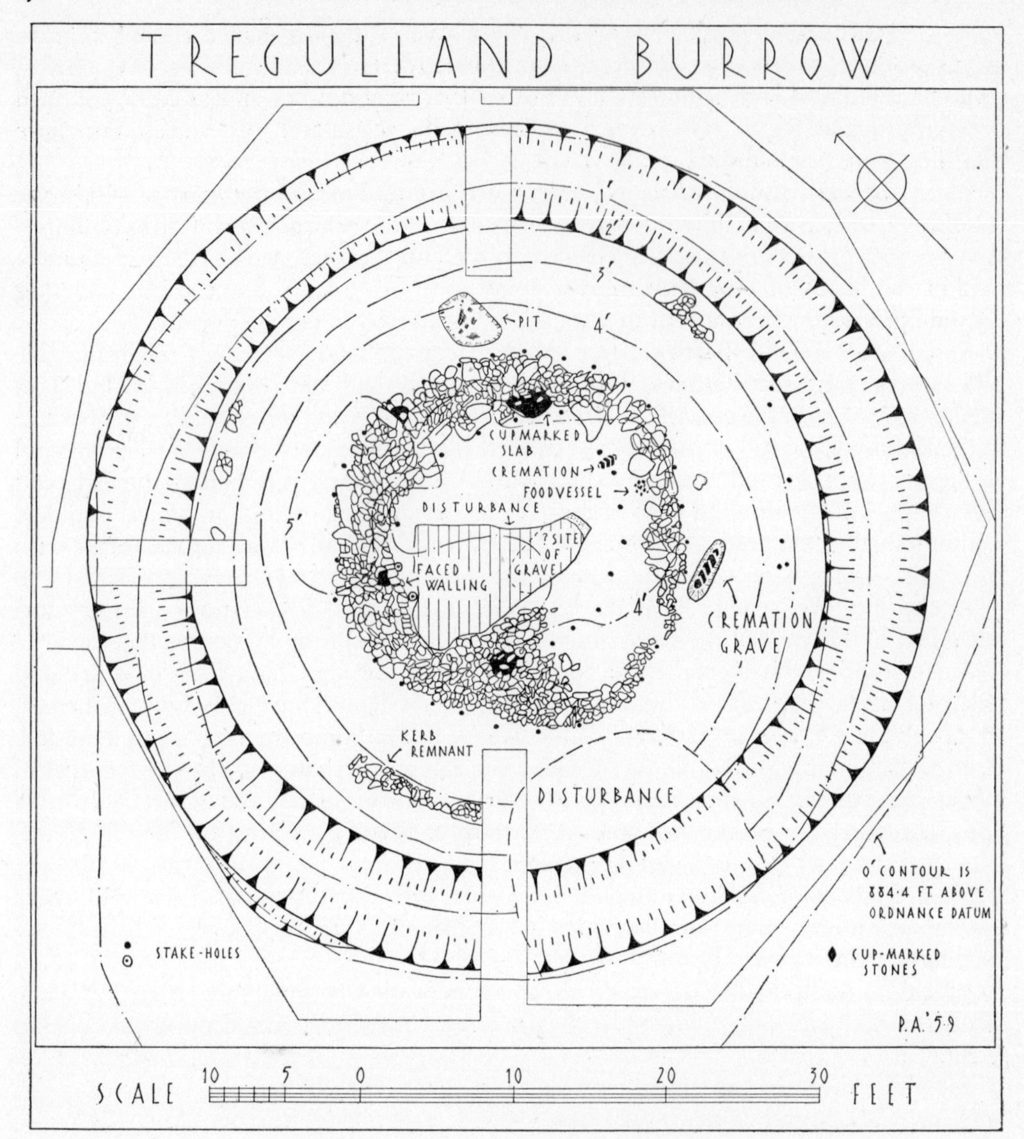

Fig. 13. The Tregulland Burrow cairn-ring.

was a roughly penannular heap of cobbles, the latter had a well-built inner face, and was partly constructed of near-megalithic blocks. It is claimed, with some justification, that such concealed structures are a regular feature of Food-Vessel barrows.[70] Judging from the contemporary account the famous Deverel Barrow covered a large penannular cairn-ring.[71]

Enclosures built of stones similar to these cairn-rings have been noted in regions

[70] Childe, 1947 b, 128

[71] W. A. Miles, *A Description of the Deverel Barrow*, 1826.

where barrows are frequent[72] and adjacent to barrow cemeteries.[73] These enclosures may possibly represent the first stages of the construction of such barrows as Tregulland and Quernhowe, abandoned for some reason before completion.[74] Certain so-called ring barrows in Cornwall may also be an abandoned early stage of barrow building.[75]

'Stake' and 'Post' circles, i.e. settings of stake-holes and post-sockets around and beneath barrows, are being recognized with increased frequency as excavation techniques improve. They are discussed in Chapter V.

Rows of posts and rows of stones have been, and are, related to barrows and cairns in different parts of the country. A line of holes was associated with the entrance to the circle beneath a bell barrow at Poole[76] which had, like its fellow, a penannular ditch, the causeway of which was the entrance to the stake circle. An apparently progressively widening avenue of stakes was found beneath a barrow at Swarkstone,[77] but it seems likely that this was the remains of a structure unconnected with the barrow. Stone rows or avenues are associated with cairns on Dartmoor[78] and in Scotland.[79] They are most numerous on Dartmoor, about sixty known examples occurring of single, double, or multiple rows of stones, usually, and probably originally always, in association with a cairn.

Concealed ditches are a feature which has been met with beneath certain barrows, although from the records at our disposal such ditches do not appear to have been a common feature. A ditch (or trench) was found beneath a composite barrow at Ysceifiog in Flintshire.[80] It was almost exactly 31 feet in diameter, and 3 feet deep, with near vertical sides. Annular in form, it had a sloping passage-way or ramp presumably cut to lead into it. The grave beneath this barrow also had a sloping trench, which gave access into the grave-pit.

Such trenches beneath barrows should not be confused with ditches which appear to be concealed beneath the body of a barrow because of an enlargement after initial construction,[81] or with ditches concealed by the ultimate spread of a barrow.[82] It is possible that trenches beneath barrows recorded by early workers may in certain instances have been for posts.

Greenwell appears to have met with 'trenches' within barrows on the Yorkshire Wolds,[83] while a similar phenomenon has been recorded from Hampshire.[84]

Pits (Fig. 14) which have been dug and then refilled, and which sometimes contain charcoal or traces of organic matter, have been revealed below barrows.[85] Sometimes dug in sand and chalk they have been refilled with turves.[86]

Such a pit, dug in stages in hard sand, the whole having an elongated stepped appearance, was beneath a bell barrow at Bishop's Waltham in Hampshire.[87] It had been refilled with dark loam. A pit under a barrow on Beaulieu Heath had been filled

72 Elgee, 1930, 137, Fig. 44.
73 *PWCFC*, I, 133.
74 Long enclosures were probably the first stage of certain earthen long barrows. Piggott, 1954, 59.
75 *PWCFC*, I, 133.
76 *PPS*, XVIII, 150.
77 *PPS*, XIII, 222.
78 *Antiq.*, XII, 444–6.
79 Childe, 1935, 114.
80 *Arch. Camb.*, LXXXI, 48–85.
81 *PPS*, IX, 1–27 (Beaulieu VI).
82 *Ant. J.*, XXXVIII, 181.
83 Greenwell, 1877, s.v. trench 'within barrows' especially 227, 245.
84 *PBNSS*, XIV, 3 ff.
85 Glasbergen, 1954, II, 150–1.
86 *PPS*, IV, 173.
87 *PPS*, XXIII, 145.

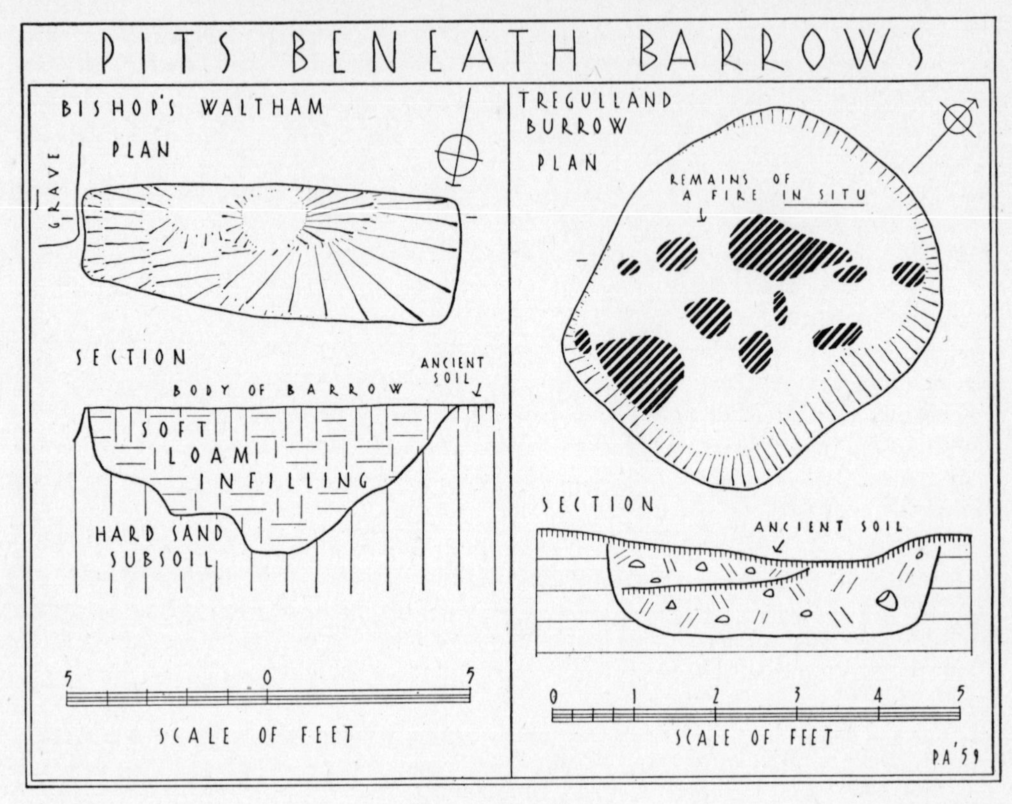

Fig. 14. Ritual pits.

with turves,[88] and a shallow pit beneath Tregulland Burrow in Cornwall,[89] had had fires in it, the bottom of the pit exhibiting reddening and sintering besides containing quantities of burned wood.

In default of more complete barrow excavations, it is impossible accurately to assess the incidence of these so-called 'ritual' pits. Such pits have been found not only beneath round barrows of various forms,[90] but also under earthen long barrows[91] and certain chambered cairns.[92]

'Mortuary houses', which are, strictly speaking, elaborations of the grave, have been disclosed under barrows in southern Britain. They are of three types: square, rectangular, and roughly circular, respectively, in plan.

Mortuary houses of the first type were, during the last war, identified beneath heathland barrows in the New Forest.[93] Under Barrow II here,[94] a square pit contained a setting of stake-holes (Fig. 15). It would appear that they were probably the remains of a small square hut with a gabled roof. It seems that the structure had fallen into decay when the barrow was built over it. The second structure, that under Beaulieu IX,[95] though almost identical in size and purpose with the former, showed a different

[88] *PPS*, IX, 9 (Beaulieu II).
[89] *Ant. J.*, XXXVIII, 178.
[90] *PHFCAS*, XV, 248–62.
[91] *Arch.*, LXXXV, 37.
[92] *Arch. Camb.*, C, 3.
[93] *PPS*, IX, 1–32.
[94] *PPS*, IX, 9.
[95] *PPS*, IX, 17–19.

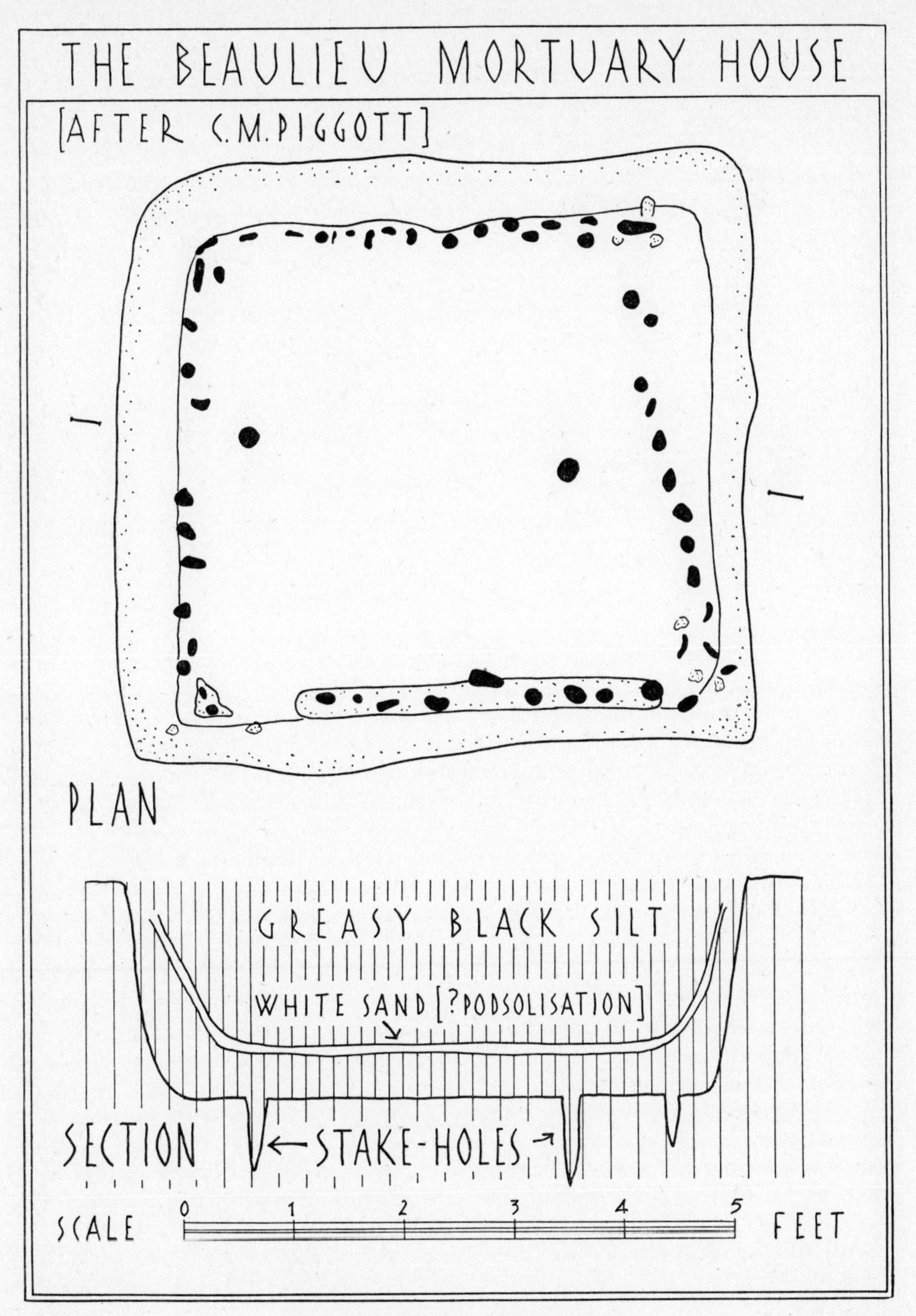

Fig. 15. The Beaulieu mortuary house.

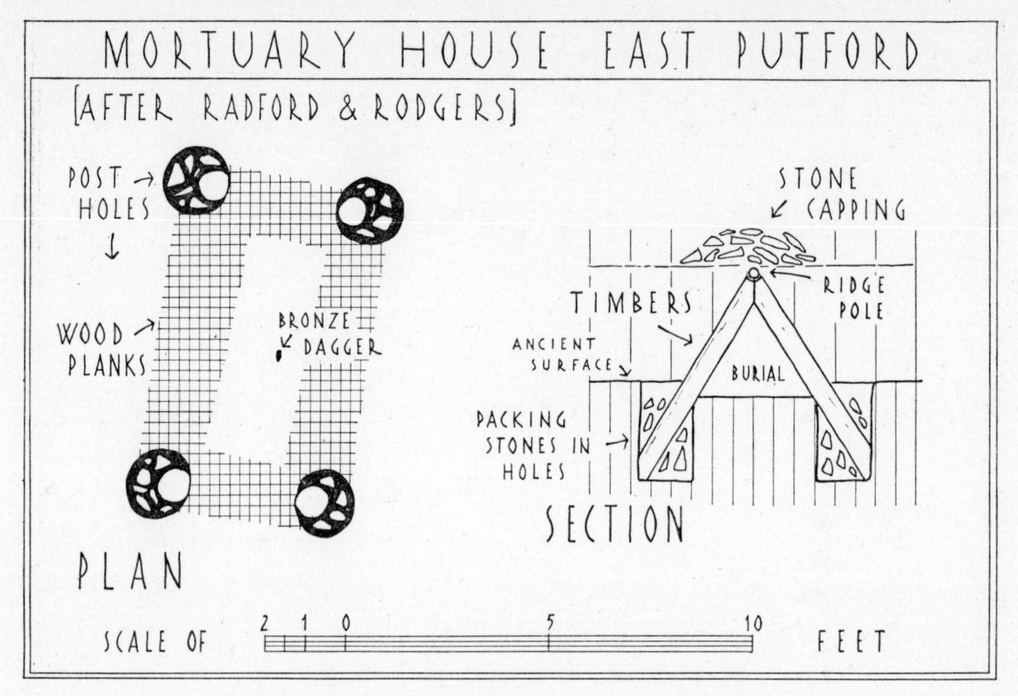

Fig. 16. The Wrangworthy mortuary house.

technique of construction. Its timber sides had been set in a bedding trench afterwards filled in and rammed to support the uprights in position. A central post may have supported the roof or have had bent saplings secured to it.

The remains of mortuary houses of the rectangular class were identified under two barrows at Wrangworthy Cross in Devon.[96] Under the first barrow heavy timbers appear to have formed a gabled structure, some 3 feet in height and 5 feet in length, while above the gable there had been a stone capping (Fig. 16).[97] The mortuary house covered by the second barrow[98] consisted, as far as could be seen, of one wall carried on upright posts, and a pent roof sloping to one side. Stakes had been driven into the filling of a grave beneath a levelled barrow at Cassington in Oxfordshire.[99] It appears that originally they converged inwards and upwards from their base to form the framework for a miniature circular hut or house of mortuary significance. The flattened tops of many, apparently undisturbed, large barrows in Wessex and elsewhere, may be due to the collapse of mortuary structures.

A curious structural method, seemingly allied to mortuary-house building, was detected when a barrow at Drimnagh, County Dublin,[100] was excavated. Logs had been stacked over a mound of turves and covered with turves. When newly erected the structure must have resembled a round house. The whole, some 72 feet in diameter, had after building been set on fire and burned.

Settings of standing stones placed at a distance around barrow and cairn, outside the

[96] *PDAES*, III, 156–63.
[97] *PDAES*, III, 159.
[98] *PDAES*, III, 162.
[99] *Oxon.*, XI, 12.
[100] *JRSAI*, LXIX, 190–225.

ditch, are not unknown. Of note is a barrow on Farway Down in Devon,[101] surrounded by such a circle, and possibly excavation would reveal traces of this practice elsewhere were more generous areas around barrows and cairns excavated. Two stone circles appear to have enclosed a nuclear group of five cairns on Burn Moor in Cumberland.[102]

Another structural feature, difficult to trace on denuded barrows, is a surmounting stone. Sarsens appear to have stood upon certain barrows in Wessex.[103] Whether or not this is an original feature, as in the case of certain Breton passage-graves,[104] is uncertain. In some barrows wooden posts have been recorded as extending from near the primary burial to the surface.[105] Again, whether the impressions of such posts represent the remains of a marker or memorial, or whether they served a practical purpose as planning posts, is not known. However, stake-holes which may have held stakes for planning have, in a number of cases, been recorded from under barrows.[106]

Potsherds (Fig. 17) are often met with in the mounds of barrows that are made of clean soil thrown up from a ditch,[107] a circumstance which suggests deliberate admixture during building. Such a practice appears to have been widespread. Similarly, deposits of dark occupation soil (Pl. VIII a), containing sherds, charcoal, and even pieces of bone, were incorporated in barrows. Such deposits were noted by both Greenwell [108] and Mortimer [109] beneath Wold barrows. Occupation earth was placed around a grave beneath the Cairnpapple cairn.[110] Beaker barrows in Norfolk,[111] and Cambridgeshire [112] seem to have had such deposits in them; as did the remains of a bell barrow on Charlton Down in Berkshire.[113] Sherds and burnt flints were found amongst the flint nodules which comprised a small Beaker cairn on Stockbridge Down in Hampshire,[114] and in two barrows in the Isle of Wight.[115] Such deposits occurred widely, it appears, in the structures of Bronze Age barrows and doubtless lurk within the familiar 'black unctuous earth' of early barrow-digging accounts.

Flint industries (Fig. 18) or, as seems more often the case, sundry implements or knapping debris, were also incorporated into barrow mounds during building. They usually, though not invariably, accompanied sherds and occupation earth. The bell barrows that covered stakes and holes near Poole, in Dorset,[116] contained flints, and an extensive industry was encountered in the mound of the barrow excavated by Sir Cyril Fox at Barton Mills in Cambridgeshire.[117]

In view of the folklore surrounding the use of white quartz pebbles and stones, which were deposited on burial places in Wales even in recent times,[118] it has been claimed that the white stones found in certain barrows were used structurally with ritual intent.[119] This may have been the case in Ireland, where it is claimed, with good reason, that the great New Grange, the largest of the Boyne passage-graves,[120] may have been cased in white quartz stones. However, there is little direct evidence of such

[101] *PDAES*, IV, 1–19.
[102] *PSA*, III, 225; Fergusson, 1872, 159; *TCWAAS*, LVII, 1–8.
[103] *PPS*, VII, 96.
[104] *PPS*, VII, 14.
[105] *Ant. J.*, XIII, 425.
[106] *PPS*, VII, 90.
[107] *PPS*, XXIII, 137–66.
[108] Greenwell, 1877, G. XLII, G. XLVII, G. LXI.
[109] Mortimer, 1905, lxx.
[110] *PSAS*, LXXXII, 68, 123.
[111] *PCAS*, XXXV, 117.
[112] *PCAS*, XXXIX, 33–68.
[113] *TNDFC*, VIII, 110.
[114] *Ant. J.*, XX, 39–51.
[115] *PIOWNHAS*, II, 196, 205.
[116] *PPS*, XVIII, 152.
[117] *PCAS*, XXVI, 19.
[118] Fox, 1952, 41.
[119] Grinsell, 1953, 43–4.
[120] G. Coffey, *New Grange*, 1912.

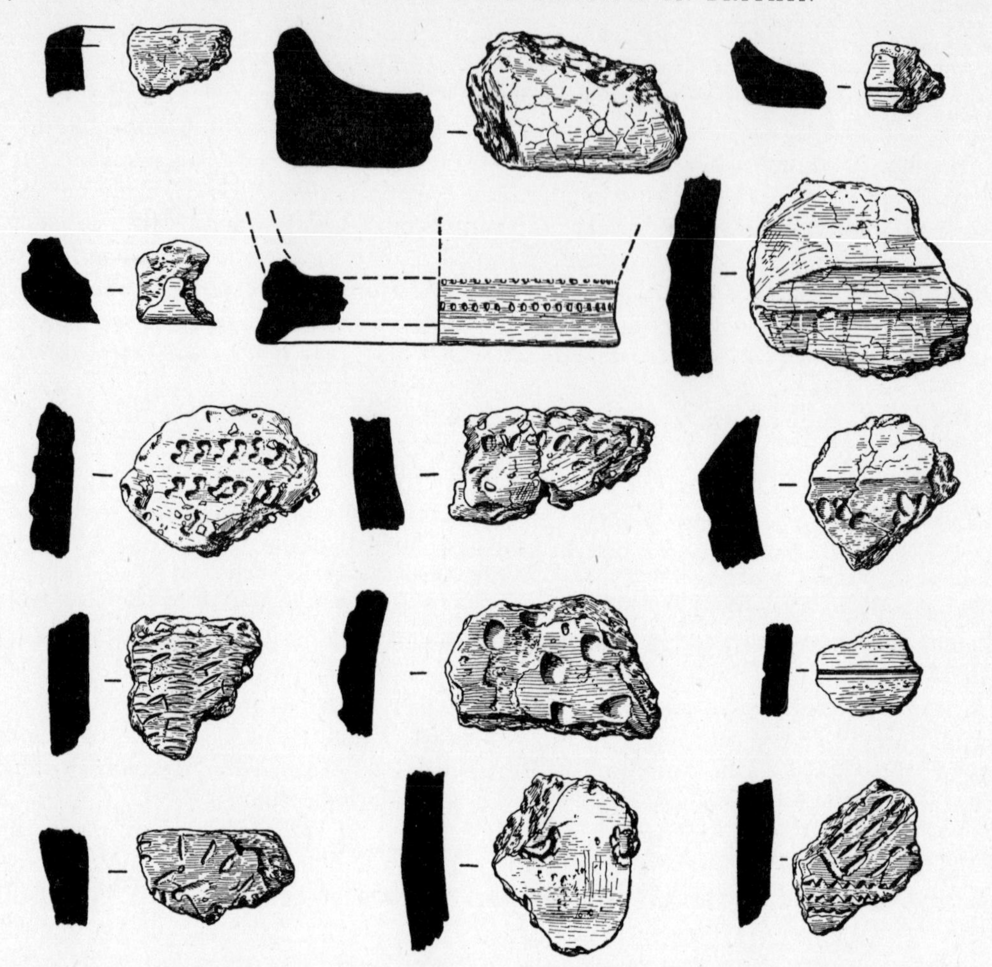

Fig. 17. Sherds from the barrow mound at Bishop's Waltham (1/2).

practices among the barrows and cairns that have been investigated in the areas where quartz appears in nature.[121] It does seem likely, however, that an area of heathland soil, on Canford Heath in Dorset,[122] was stripped of its surface humus before the erection of a barrow, thus exposing the white leached A2 horizon, possibly intentionally.

On the buried surfaces beneath barrows traces of burning, often extensive, are sometimes discovered. Often the ground near what must have been the middle of the conflagration is terra-cotta, while all around is wood-ash and charcoal.[123] An early barrow-digging record mentions an enormous mass of charcoal several feet high,[124] and another claims that 'stakes' had been set into the solid chalk to form a rectangular space, which seems to have contained logs of timber laid lengthways.[125]

It is difficult to distinguish between charcoal and wood carbonized by natural processes, when both have been recovered from barrows. It is possible that some early

[121] *Ant. J.*, XXXVIII, 174–96.
[122] *PDNHAS*, LXXVI, 50.
[123] Amesbury G. 61; *WAM*, LVI, 238 (interim).
[124] *PPS*, IV, 92.
[125] *WAM*, XXXVI, 619.

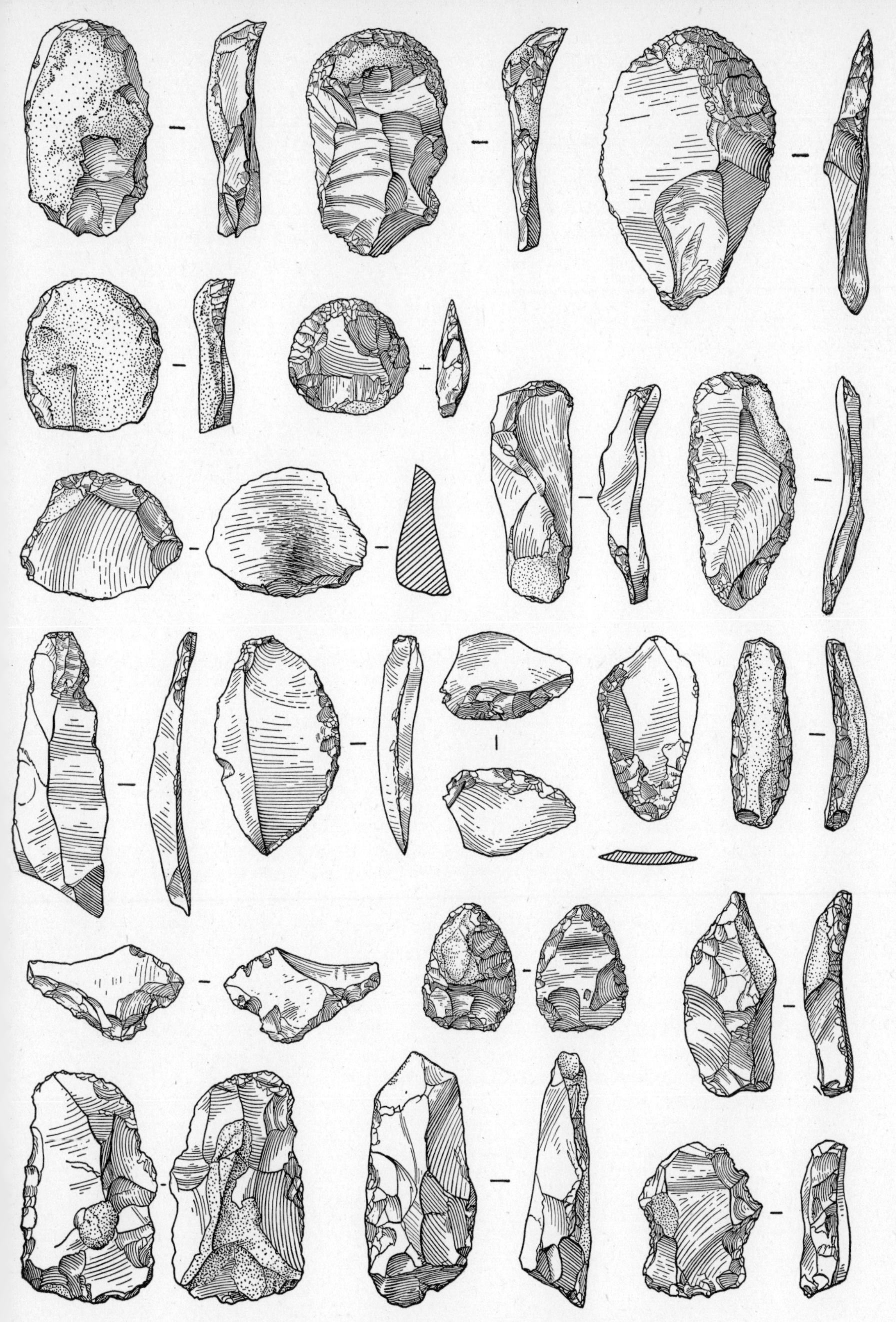

Fig. 18. Flint industry, from the Bishop's Waltham barrow (1/2).

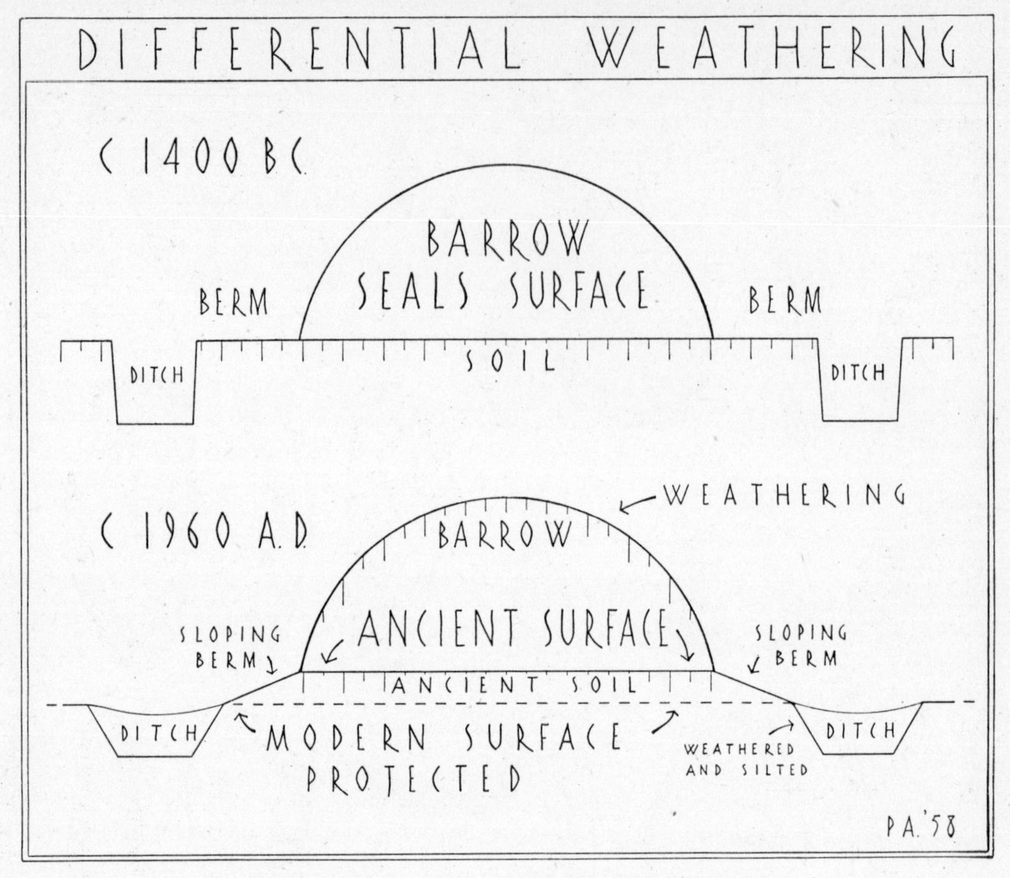

Fig. 19. Sections illustrating differential weathering.

records described the remains of mortuary structures similar to those described above. On the other hand certain settings of stakes claimed as pyre supports [126] may represent the remains of mortuary structures burnt before the barrow was erected.[127]

Apart from these instances, traces of modest fires which have left roughly circular patches of burnt earth and charcoal have been recorded not only beneath barrows in Wessex[128] but also in Yorkshire and Derbyshire.[129] While such traces could possibly be the remains of pyres, it is also likely that they represent the clearing of brushwood and perhaps trees before the building of the barrow (*supra*). It may be noted in passing that it is claimed that in Dorset separate barrows were erected, one to cover the remains of a pyre, and others the urn and the cremation.[130]

Besides bearing evidence of activities connected with the building of the barrow, pre-barrow surfaces sometimes show signs of what might be previous activities of their builders. Alleged traces of tillage in the form of old plough soil, criss-crossed with plough marks, possibly a part of barrow 'ritual', have been recognized beneath barrows

[126] *PHFCAS*, IX, 192.
[127] *Offa*, I, 56–87.
[128] *Arch.*, LII, 60.
[129] *YAJ*, XXXIX, 12.
[130] *PPS*, VII, 92.

at Vesterlund,[131] Sevel,[132] and Aldrupgaarde,[133] in Jutland, Denmark, and near Zwaagdije [134] and Gasteren [135] in Holland. However, the possibility of a natural origin for such phenomenon should not be overlooked.

Soils under barrows in Wiltshire are frequently free (Pl. VI b) from broken pieces of chalk and weathered flints within inches of their surface.[136] This suggests prolonged earthworm activity under undisturbed vegetation. Conversely, buried soils with a high and uniform content of chalk and flint fragments right up to the surface, as has been noted beneath the bank of a disc-barrow at Grafton, may well have been exposed to winter frost weathering. This suggests cultivation right up to the time that the bank was thrown up.[137]

The rounded and in many cases gentle contours of barrows and some cairns are due to the agencies of nature after the building. We have seen how denudation conceals ditches, and it has been remarked that the 'elegant campanile form' of many bell barrows, i.e. the sloping berm, is entirely due to weathering and solution (Fig. 19). Indeed, some slight gauge of the extent of such weathering is given by the fact that buried soils beneath barrows and earthworks of comparable age are sometimes as much as 18 inches above the present-day average soil surface levels.[138] The super-position of a barrow has sealed off the ancient soil, the processes of weathering being transferred to the superimposed mound.

Besides denudation, the processes of nature can change the appearance of the composition of a heaped-up barrow to a marked degree. Thus, depending upon the geological solid, chemical weathering affects a barrow mound in a number of ways.[139] Upon chalk a rendzina soil will form, never more than about 4 inches in depth. Similarly a light soil will cloak cairns, particularly in limestone country, and, where conditions are favourable, worms will fill the interstices between stones.[140]

Barrows built of sands and gravels, consisting of little but quartz and flint, will develop a podsol upon their mounds.[141] This is characterized by the vivid colour contrasts—a dark humus, an often near-white leached layer, below which is a dark brown, sometimes near-black, moor-pan. This last natural feature, entirely the product of chemical weathering, occurs often as a 'burnt layer' or 'marks of fires' in accounts of barrow excavations.

We can do little more, therefore, than speculate intelligently, with all the evidence in mind, about the appearance of a newly built barrow. The craftsman who carved the Frank's Casket,[142] and who belonged to an age when barrow-building was still a living tradition, depicts a steep-sided mound with its top slightly rounded. It may be remarked that this was the form suggested by the present writer for the Bishop's Waltham bell-barrow mound when it was newly built. The suggestion was based upon bulk of sand and rapidity of denudation. On the other hand it seems likely that many barrows, composite and otherwise, which were basically turf-stacks, may well have been flat-topped.

[131] *Acta Arch.*, I, 1.
[132] *Kuml*, II, 9–31.
[133] *Kuml*, IV, 18–29.
[134] *West Friesland's Oud en Niew*, XVII, 121.
[135] *NDV*, 1941, 29, Afb. 31.
[136] 'Techniques in Archaeology', *BA*, 1954, 12.
[137] 'Techniques in Archaeology', *BA*, 1954, 12.
[138] Amesbury G. 58, 18 in; Stonehenge, Bank, 12 in., Atkinson, 1956, 10; *Antiq.*, XXXI, 219–33; *BA*, XV, 165–72.
[139] *PPS*, XIX, 129–47.
[140] Charles Darwin, *Vegetable Mould and Earthworms*, 1904.
[141] *PPS*, XIX, 129–30.
[142] *Anglo-Saxon Guide*, Pl. VIII.

CHAPTER V

STAKE AND POST CIRCLE BARROWS

DURING the past two decades, in war and peace, greater numbers of round barrows than ever before have been excavated, usually as a result of threatened destruction, with method and precision. Under certain barrows (Fig. 20) traces of stake and post circles have been observed and planned. Such are their numbers that it has been possible to order them into types.

The first stake circle ever unearthed in its entirety appears to have come to light from under a bell barrow at Beedon in Berkshire,[1] in the middle of the nineteenth century. A Mr Charles Long, who together with Mr Henry Long directed the digging, wrote in 1850: 'The workmen found seven perpendicular holes, formed almost in a circle, around the centre of the barrow; they were about a foot in depth, and two inches in diameter, and were partly filled with charred wood.'

Seventeen years later, Mortimer,[2] upon reopening Barrow 23, also a bell barrow, of his Calais Wold group in the East Riding of Yorkshire, was to write: 'Within about 14 feet west of the centre, holes made by stakes and posts were noticed in the ground.' With a clear grasp of method, considerably in advance of his time, he adds: 'In each of these a small upright stake was inserted to indicate their arrangement. . . .' Describing the holes, he continues: 'Plaster casts were taken of several of the smaller holes, and although they were partly filled with an earthy deposit left by the percolation of water, it was possible to make out that some of the stakes had been roughly pointed and driven into the ground, whilst the larger—and even some of the smaller ones—had been placed in holes previously made for them, with their thick ends downwards.' These close-set peripheral circles of holes were considered to be the remains of a hut, it being added that the space between the walls 'might have been used for storing grain'! As a corn-chandler Mortimer was a man with a practical mind. With the exception of the initial discovery of the atypical Bleasdale 'circle', not another stake or post circle was to be found beneath a British barrow for more than six decades.

Meanwhile, at the turn of the century, Holwerda,[3] to be followed by Bursch[4] and van Giffen,[5] began work upon the podsolized heathland barrows of Holland. Recently, the Dutch timber circle barrows have been analysed in detail by Glasbergen,[6] and between 1908 and 1953 about 185 were investigated. This represents archaeological endeavour almost unparalleled by any other country.[7]

[1] *Arch J.*, VII, 66.
[2] Mortimer, 1905, 153–6.
[3] *OMROL*, OR I, 7–10.
[4] *OMROL*, NR XIV, 39–123.
[5] Van Giffen, 1930, 44, 45.
[6] Glasbergen, 1954, II, 16.
[7] Glasbergen, 1954, II, 74.

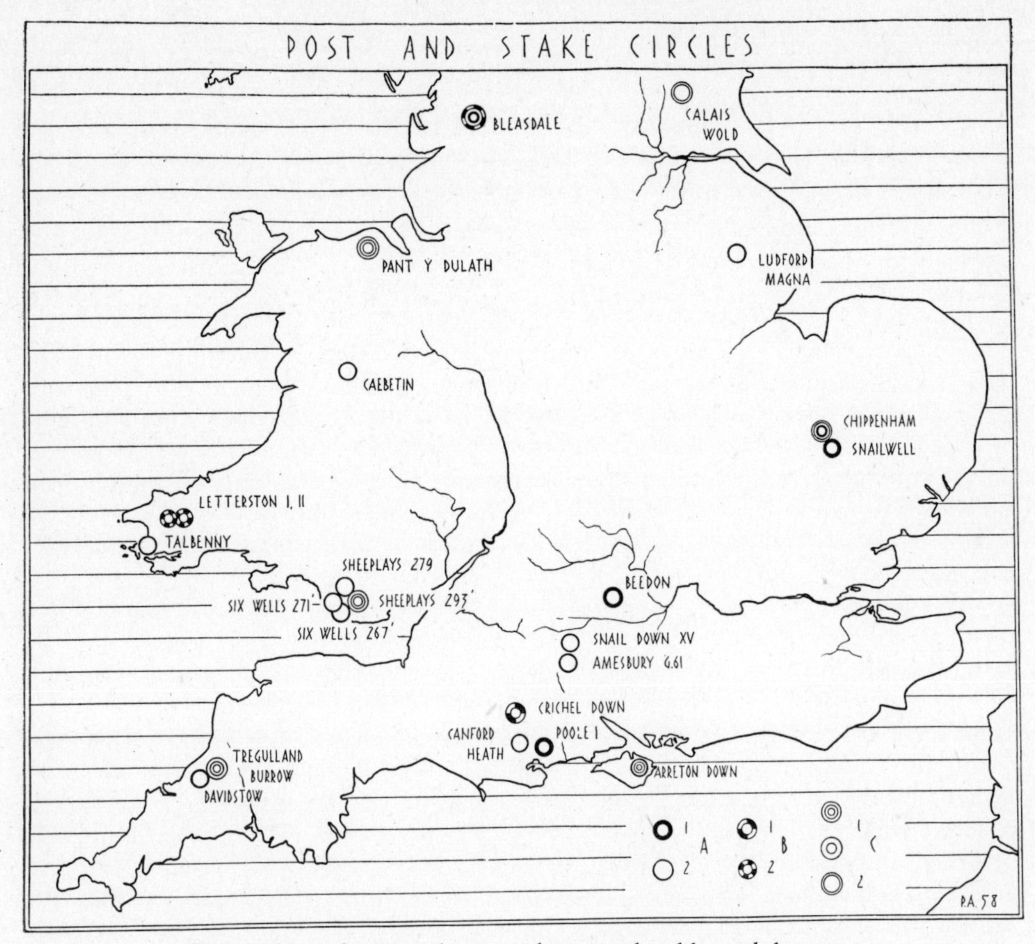

Fig. 20. Map of stake and post circles around and beneath barrows.

Such activity was bound to affect any consideration of similar monuments in neighbouring lands. The excavator of Woodhenge[8] refers briefly to the evidence from Holland, but it was left to Professor Grahame Clark[9] to show clearly, on the one hand, that British henge monuments are essentially different things, and on the other that there are similarities between the Dutch examples and Mortimer's Calais Wold circle, another on Caebetin Hill, Montgomeryshire,[10] and the Bleasdale 'circle' (which was clearly a fenced barrow). After describing this last monument and its apparent affinities to the International Congress of 1932,[11] Varley undertook a re-examination of it.[12] This also focused attention upon the problems of timber circle barrows. All were concerned with the origins of the monuments. Indeed, in 1938, van Giffen[13] put forward an opinion that was the converse of Clark's.[14]

As a result of this work British prehistorians had the problems of timber circles and

[8] Cunnington, 1929, 24–5.
[9] *PPS*, II, 36.
[10] *Mon. Coll.*, 1932, 176–81.
[11] *PFIC*, 1934, 125.
[12] *Ant. J.*, XVIII, 154–71.
[13] *PPS*, IV, 266–71.
[14] *PPS*, IV, 266–71.

barrows much in mind. Operations such as the stripping of part of the berm of a great Sussex bell barrow were an outcome,[15] as was the identification of the circles at Chippenham, Cambridgeshire.[16]

In spite of all this it was apparent that more evidence was needed from British barrows. This was provided by Sir Cyril Fox, who has paid tribute to the influence of the Netherlands school upon British barrow excavation.[17] His work added five examples to the then meagre total, and he was able subsequently to demonstrate differing techniques of construction and setting out.[18] Recently, Case [19] was able to list fifteen stake and post circle barrows, which, together with certain henges, he set into the temporal framework of Childe's period system.[20] In the last few years several more accounts of war-time excavations have added to this total, as have recent excavations.

The physical evidence for stake and post circles, which incidentally, are frequently not true circles, consists mainly of pits of appropriate sizes in the ancient surfaces sealed beneath barrows (Pl. IX a). Mostly they are sealed by the lowermost layers of barrow mounds, although in one barrow they continued up into the body of the mound and were equidistant at a considerable height, suggesting a horizontal tie between the stakes. The stakes and posts used for a small number of circles were housed in *palisade-trenches.*

The evidence [21] points to *driven stakes*, *dug post-sockets*, and *palisade-trenches.* Thus the limits for driven stakes are of the order of 3 inches diameter, more massive timbers being accorded sockets. What are technically post-sockets were, it seems, often dug where obdurate spots were found during the process of stake-driving.

Sir Cyril Fox [22] suggests that driven stakes and socketed posts represent two disparate traditions. The driven stakes of the South Wales circles, he says, demonstrate a hurdle-maker's technique, while the socketed posts and the like are evidence of carpenters' constructions.

There are two basic forms of post or stake circle associated with barrows. They are *peripheral* and *internal.* They range from about 10 feet to about 50 feet in diameter, the internal being the smaller. Peripheral circles appear to have been originally erected around the periphery of the barrow. They may well have performed the function of retention and may subsequently have rotted *in situ.* They are to be found beneath the talus from the mound. An occasional post or stake impression could be preserved, wholly or in part, in this talus, but might not be observed if the excavator were not cognizant of the principles of such circles, their weathering and decay. Internal circles are found beneath the *built* mounds and other structures of barrows. With one exception, noted above, where the barrow appeared to have been built over a standing hurdle structure,[23] all these internal circles, whatever their form and function, were demolished by withdrawal before the barrow was raised. It has been recently put forward that the withdrawal of stakes would distort holes, a phenomenon which is hardly ever seen. Mechanical means of withdrawal may well have been used. This would leave small trace and do little damage to a stake-hole. A composite barrow in Cornwall [24] has shown

[15] *SAC*, LXXXII, 115–21.
[16] *PCAS*, XXXVI, 134–42; XXXIX, 33–68.
[17] Fox and Dickens, 1950, 53.
[18] *Arch. J.*, XCX, 25–9.
[19] *PPS*, XVIII, 153.
[20] Childe, 1947 b, 11.
[21] See Appendix IV for full references.
[22] Fox and Dickens, 1950, 72.
[23] Sheeplays 293′, *Ant. J.*, XXI, 98–114.
[24] *Ant. J.*, XXXVIII, 174–96.

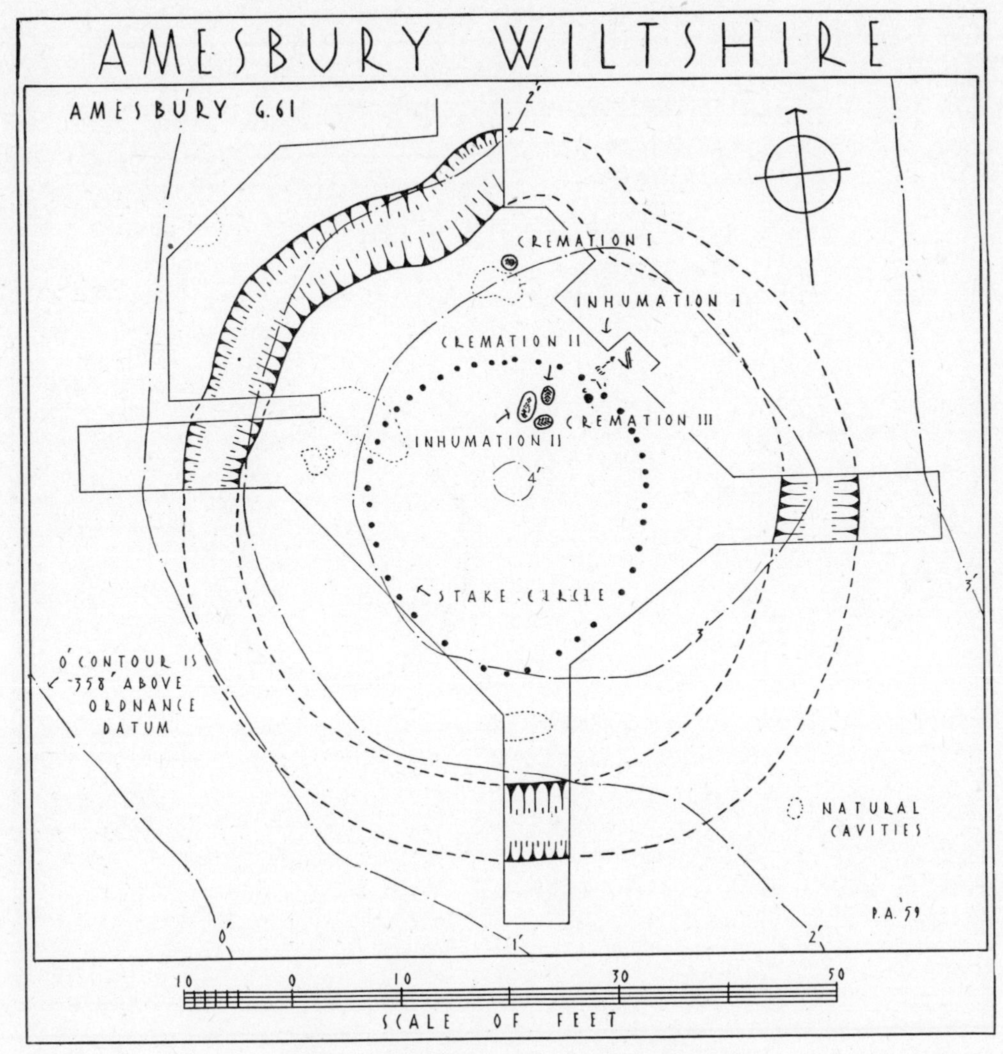

Fig. 21. The Amesbury barrow stake circle.

that here internal stake circles and a closely coincident cairn-ring could not have co-existed as the stake-holes were oversailed and, indeed, covered by set stones.

Post and stake circles are either *simple* or *complex*. Simple circles (Pl. IX b, Fig. 21) are those where only a single circle of posts or stakes has been found. Complex circles consist of from two to four concentric circles. These may be concentric circles of *like* circles, as at Sheeplays 293′ [25] and Tregulland Burrow,[26] or *unlike* circles in which differing constructional techniques have been used, as at Bleasdale [27] and at Chippenham, Barrow 5.[28]

A characteristic of complex circles, of both like and unlike forms, is eccentricity.

[25] *Ant. J.*, XXI, 98–114.
[26] *Ant. J.*, XXXVIII, 174–96.
[27] *Ant. J.*, XVIII, 154–71.
[28] *PCAS*, XXXIX, 33–68.

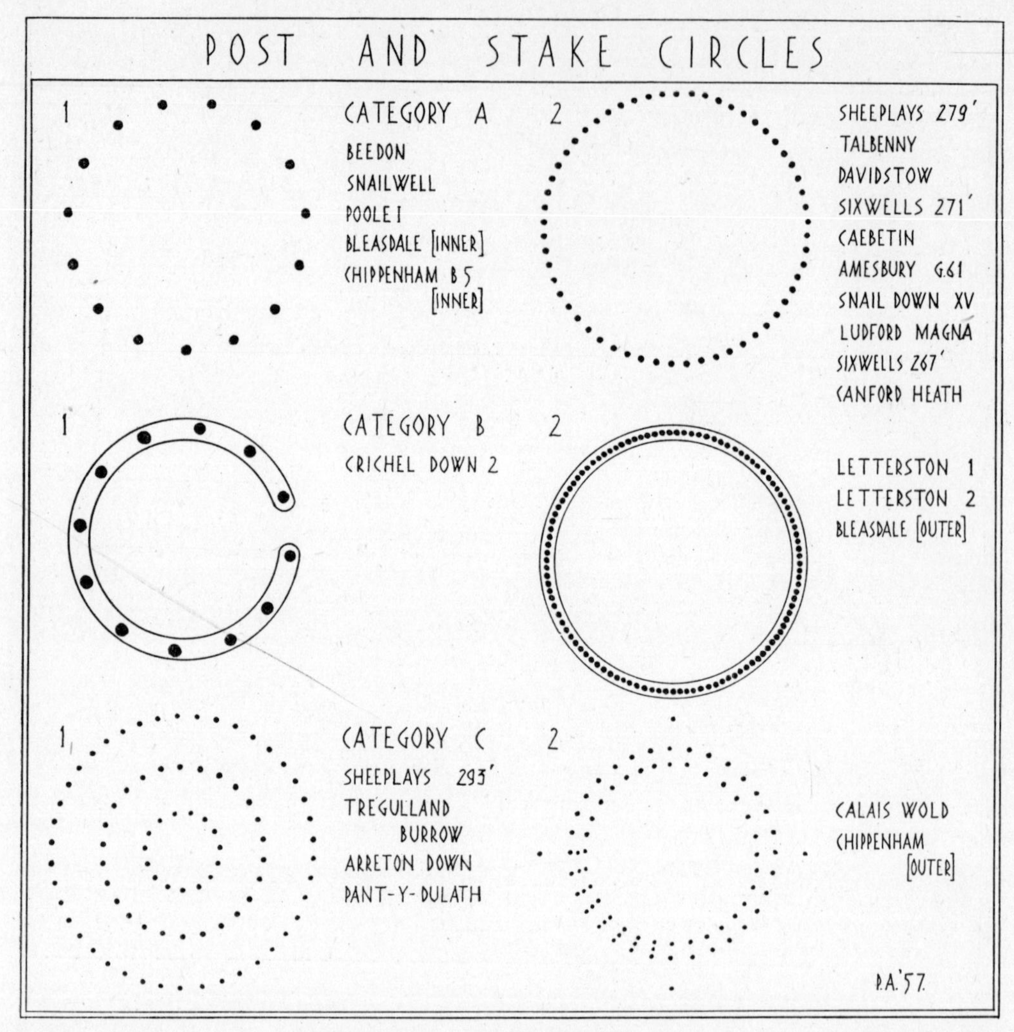

Fig. 22. Types of post and stake circles.

This, initially noted at Calais Wold [29] and Bleasdale,[30] at which latter place the internal post circle almost impinged upon the outer stockade, has been observed at Tregulland Burrow,[31] and, recently and most markedly, beneath a barrow on Arreton Down in the Isle of Wight.[32] At Arreton Down the two inner circles of three like concentric circles merged at one point. This barrow also covered the remains of straight settings of stakes apparently connected with an entrance and with the raising of the barrow.

With all the material now available it is possible to order all post and stake circles into categories (Fig. 22). Under each heading of the scheme set out below are given the names of the barrows under which an example of the particular form has been identified. Circles with a readily identifiable entrance or approach have not been accorded a

[29] Mortimer, 1905, 156.
[30] *Ant. J.*, XVIII, 158.
[31] *Ant. J.*, XXXVIII, 178.
[32] Information from Mr J. Alexander.

IXa. A stake-hole filled with worm-mould in the ancient soil beneath a barrow at Amesbury (G. 61), Wiltshire; excavated in 1956.

IXb. Stake circle (class A2) beneath a barrow at Amesbury (G. 61), Wiltshire; excavated in 1956. Stakes have been set into the ancient holes.

Xa. Cast of a decorated cist slab, from the Pool Farm Barrow, Somerset.

Xb. An enriched slab from Tregulland Burrow, Cornwall.

separate category, as they clearly embody elements of the basic forms. Similarly, in the case of complex monuments, such as Bleasdale and Chippenham, Barrow 5, entries have been made under each heading for the appropriate elements. Full references are given in Appendix IV.

The categories are as follows:

(A) (1) *Single post or stake circles, widely spaced* (Beedon, Snailwell, Poole I, Bleasdale (inner), Chippenham, B. 5 (inner)).

(2) *Single post or stake circles, closely spaced* (Sheeplays 279′, Talbenny, Davidstow, Six Wells 271′, Caebetin, Amesbury B. G. 61, Snail Down XV, Ludford Magna, Six Wells 267′, Canford Heath).

(B) (1) *Widely spaced posts in a palisade-trench* (Crichel Down 2).

(2) *Closely spaced posts in a palisade-trench* (Letterston 1, 2, Bleasdale (outer fence)).

(C) (1) *Widely set concentric circles* (Sheeplays 293′, Tregulland Burrow, Arreton Down, Bleasdale, Pant-y-Dulath, Chippenham, B. 5).

(2) *Closely set concentric circles* (Calais Wold, Chippenham, B. 5 (outer)).

An alleged circle under one of the Chippenham barrows has been omitted as the account of its excavation [33] describes the post-sockets as containing 'charcoal, pot-boilers, broken bones or the like'. There appears to be no positive evidence that these holes were post-sockets, indeed, they could well be considered as a complex of 'ritual' pits in the Dorchester manner,[34] containing deposits. Class A2, closely spaced post or stake circles, is, at the present time, the type most frequently encountered. It would be rash to draw conclusions from this at present, for this numerical relationship may reflect only relative archaeological effort.

It is not possible, with the evidence at present available, to discuss in detail the function of stake circles. Many theories have been put forward, but there is little evidence to prove or disprove them. They seem most likely to have been mortuary huts or houses.[35] Comparisons have been made between them and the post-henges,[36] some of which were surely buildings, which they broadly resemble, while some would see in them posts erected on the occasion of funerary feasts [37] or appropriate religious ceremonies.[38] All that can be said with any certainty is that most of the internal circles were of a temporary nature, the stakes being withdrawn before the erection of the barrow. In the Tregulland Burrow,[39] and Pant-y-Dulath,[40] composite Food-Vessel barrows, it was found that the inner and outer limits of the stone structures coincided almost exactly with the holes which denoted rings of stakes. This circumstance suggests that temporary structures were replaced by the permanent stone cairns, rings, and kerbs. Some of the peripheral circles appear to have been of a more lasting nature, and could well have performed the dual functions of demarcating the limits of the barrow, and its retention and support. No way out of this Hyrcynian wood will be found until competent, critical, and careful excavation gives us a corpus of accurately recorded structural data from our barrows.

[33] *PCAS*, XXXVI, 134–42.
[34] Atkinson, Piggott, and Sandars, 1951, 15.
[35] Mortimer, 1905, 155; *Arch. J.*, XCVI, 218; *Ant. J.*, XXI, 114.
[36] *PPS*, II, 1–51.
[37] J. Röder, *Pfahl und Menhir, Studien zur westeuropäischen Altertumskunde*, 1949, I, 72.
[38] Glasbergen, 1954, II, 152.
[39] *Ant. J.*, XXXVIII, 174–95.
[40] Unpublished information from Mr P. Hayes.

CHAPTER VI

ART

A FEATURE belonging almost exclusively to composite barrows and cairns is the incidence of so-called art, consisting chiefly of cup-marks adorning certain stone structural features. Such art is found generally in one or more of the following circumstances:

(*a*) On cist covers
(*b*) On the stones of kerbs, walls, cairn-rings, etc.
(*c*) On stones built into, or over, graves or cists
(*d*) On stones incorporated into barrow or cairn

The method used for its production was in most cases 'pecking', termed by some 'pocking', although certain cup-marks in the West Country appear to have been produced by techniques akin to drilling, while in places linear motifs have been incised. It is possible that some were once painted, while all could have adorned wood, leather, and other materials. Some have been noted on pottery.

The art motifs can be divided into two groups: Symbols and Real Objects. The symbols include a wide series certain of which, as will be seen below, occur in limited contexts or are near-unique.

Symbols
(*a*) Cup-marks
(*b*) Cup-and-ring marks
(*c*) Rings
(*d*) Concentric rings
(*e*) Spirals and double spirals
(*f*) Ring-enclosed cruciform signs
(*g*) Lines or 'gutters', sometimes attached to, or connecting other signs
(*h*) Triangles
(*i*) Lozenges
(*j*) Eyebrows
(*k*) Rakes
(*l*) Meanders
(*m*) Arcs
(*n*) Horned symbol

Representation of Real Objects
(*a*) Axes
(*b*) Daggers
(*c*) Feet

Simple cup-marks are the most widespread of all these forms, occurring not only apparently in their own right but also side by side with more complex symbols and representations.

Symbols on cist covers are frequent. A cover from a cairn-covered cist at Carnwath in Scotland [1] bore mainly concentric circles and pecked triangles. These triangles, six in number, were the lined-off angles of two larger triangles. Two other small triangles were set apex to apex. There are also indeterminate lines, an arc, perhaps two, and a possible eyebrow motif on this cover. Concentric circle motifs were on slabs, one of them covering an urn, which were above flint cairns in a barrow opened on Camedown, on the Ridgeway, during the nineteenth century.[2] Similar concentric circles, together with four lines making obtuse angles, are to be seen on a cover slab from a cist which contained a food-vessel at Tillicoultry, Clackmannan,[3] which appears to have been a flat grave in a small, embanked stone circle.

A recent scrutiny of the slabs of a cist (Pl. X a) found under a barrow at Pool Farm, north of the Priddy Circles, on the Mendips,[4] dug into by Dom Ethelbert Horne in 1930, revealed that one had pecked into it not only a series of cup-marks but also six representations of human feet, and a horned symbol not previously met with in Britain except upon the problematic Calderstones.[5]

Two daggers, two axes, and five cup-marks adorned a stone in the kerb of a composite barrow at Badbury in Dorset,[6] which when dug into in the nineteenth century yielded a series of food-vessels and urns. The dagger and axe representations, thought at the time to be moulds for bronze casting, were sawn from their parent block, which in its entirety was apparently at least half a ton in weight. Evidently they were unrecognized by the barrow-digger but were noticed by a visitor to the site a few days after the excavators had left. Similar axes, together with a rake symbol, were found on the side stones of a cist, which appears to have been a flat grave, at Ri Cruin, Kilmartin, Scotland.[7] Another site close by, meagrely recorded, seems to have been a cist, on the cover-stone of which were also axes and cup-marks.[8] Cup-marks may well have been on one of the stones of the Ri Cruin cist. Broad-bodied axes, ten in number, and about forty cup-marks were on the underside of the cover-stone of the cist beneath the Nether Largie north cairn,[9] while two further axes, one 16 inches in length, were carved on one of the end slabs. Axes and a possible dagger representation, which could equally well be two superimposed axes, have been found graven on certain of the stones of Stonehenge.[10]

In Cumberland and Westmorland the kerbs of cairns which contained urns, possibly not as primary interments, are claimed to have included stones decorated with pecked ring symbols and spirals.[11] The double spiral on a slab from a cist under a barrow at La Mancha, Peeblesshire [12] appears to be stylized eyes. It is accompanied by concentric rings and arcs.

[1] *PSAS*, X, 62. L. V. Grinsell, *Dorset Barrows*, 1959, 73–5, has, since the time of writing, listed art on stones of henges and in barrows.

[2] *PSAS*, VI (Appendix), 31, Pl. XII.

[3] *PSAS*, XXIX, 193; Childe, 1947 b, 127.

[4] *PSANHS*, LXXVI, 85–90; *PPS*, XXIII, 231–232.

[5] *PPS*, XXIII, 20–39.

[6] *Ant. J.*, XIX, 291.

[7] *PSAS*, LXIV, 131–5.

[8] *PSAS*, LXIV, 131–5.

[9] *PSAS*, LXV, 269–74.

[10] *PPS*, XVIII, 236–7.

[11] *VCH Cumb.*, I, 241; *TCWAAS*, I, 298.

[12] *PPSEA*, VII, 308.

Multi-cup-marked slabs were incorporated into the eastern side of the kerb around the Crick barrow in Wales,[13] and a slate slab bearing three cup-marks was taken from the retaining wall of a barrow at Treligga in Cornwall.[14] Also in the West Country, there is abundant material in the form of cup-marked and part-perforated slabs, as well as the great hog-backed slab bearing cup-marks and an eyebrow motif recovered from the cairn-ring of Tregulland Burrow.[15] A basalt block from the Lyles Hill cairn kerb[16] bore an incised chevron pattern, recalling not only the Carnwath designs but the ornament of Skara Brae and the Irish passage-graves.

Ring-enclosed cruciform symbols, concentric-ring-enclosed cups—some with lines or 'gutters' running from their centres—two rakes, and other rather indeterminate lines, one almost certainly worthy of being claimed as a meander, adorned one of the wall slabs of what seems to have been a Bronze Age cist re-used by Vikings, beneath a small barrow at Aspatria in Cumberland.[17] A cist under the Simondstown Cairn, in South Wales,[18] had a cup-marked slab set in one of the corners. In this general context the Ri Cruin cist, noted above, should be borne in mind.

Slabs of slate, many cup-marked, were recovered from the disturbed central area of the Tregulland Burrow[19] (Pl. X b). It is possible that they were derived from a destroyed cist, or they may have been heaped above the grave, as seems to have been the case under a composite barrow at Brotton, in Yorkshire.[20]

A slab incorporated in a Beaker cairn at Catterline in Kincardineshire[21] bore two pecked simple spirals and a concentric ring symbol. Another slab from the same cairn had a countersunk perforation. Cup-marked stones were met with in the material of the cairn which overlay the henge at Cairnpapple.[22] A highly ornate cup-marked and channelled slab (Pl. X c) was incorporated in the Tregulland Burrow,[23] and it seems that it had been set above a satellite grave. Digging in 1941 in the Nancekuke barrow at Portreath in Cornwall,[24] disclosed a cup-marked and perforated slab which seems to have been incorporated in the mound.

Elsewhere in England, in Derbyshire, Northumberland, and Yorkshire, Bateman[25] and Greenwell[26] disinterred cup-marked slabs from the mound material of some of the many barrows dug into by them during the nineteenth century.

[13] *Arch. Camb.*, XCV, 169–91.
[14] *Ant. J.*, XXVIII, 26.
[15] *Ant J.*, XXXVIII, 174–96.
[16] Evans, 1953, 30.
[17] *Arch.*, X, 105, 111, 113; *PPSEA*, VII, 308–9. See also Elgee, 1930, 92.
[18] *Arch.*, LXXXVII, 129–80.
[19] *Ant. J.*, XXXVIII, 189.
[20] *YAJ*, XXIV, 263.
[21] *PSAS*, LVIII, 30.
[22] *PSAS*, LXXXII, 69–123.
[23] *PSAS*, LXXXII, 68–123.
[24] *Ant. J.*, XXVIII, 26.
[25] Bateman, 1861, 229–30.
[26] Greenwell, 1877, s.v. 'cup-markings'.

CHAPTER VII

BURIALS AND GRAVES

BOTH inhumation and cremation burials are found beneath Bronze Age round barrows.

Inhumation burials are found in *contracted*, *flexed*, and *extended* postures. They should be considered as contracted when the knees are drawn up to the chin, the resultant angle in relation to the spinal column being 90° or less, as flexed when this angle is more than a right angle, and as extended when spinal column and legs are in a line.[1] In this last case the skeleton is usually supine. Although the distinction between contracted (Pl. XI a, b) and flexed inhumation burials, on the one hand, and extended inhumation burials, on the other, is often reasonably clear, the difference between contracted and flexed burials is often obscured in description. Indeed, ambiguities exist even in relatively modern accounts.

The primary burial beneath round barrows, whether inhumation or cremation, has usually been found to be a single burial. Indeed, the term 'single-grave' burials [2] has been proposed for the earliest round-barrow burials in contradistinction to the impersonal collective burial rites of the earlier long barrows.

While single burials are those most frequently found, the rite of collective burial was practised also. Thus, round barrows are known to have covered groups of inhumation burials, inhumation and cremated burials, and groups of cremated burials. Such collective burials were the primary interments—that is they were laid down before the barrow was raised. They should in no circumstances be confused with secondary or satellite burials. In instances where such collective burials have been encountered it has been seen that pride of place at the centre of the barrow may sometimes suggest a primary interment.

Inhumation and cremation burials beneath round barrows were, at times, accompanied by what is termed grave-furniture or grave-goods. Grave-furniture or goods comprise the remains of nourishment, weapons, tools, vessels, ornaments, and objects both personal and ritual, symbols of authority, fire-producing equipment, and the like—all, presumably, for use by the deceased in the echoing vaults of eternity. All this material is dealt with in Chapter VIII. By means of classification and typology, the objects can be brought into chorological and chronological order, a process which gives both breadth and depth to our concepts of the Bronze Age. The remains of clothing and cerements have been considered apart from grave-furniture.

Graves were dug into the ground, and after burials were put into them they were infilled and the barrow raised above them. They range from extremely large pits, usually elongated, and of which the burial sometimes occupied but part, to small, often

[1] Childe, 1947 a, 346.

[2] *ANL*, VI, 15.

circular, cavities in which an urned or unurned cremation was placed. Inhumation burials were often in graves, but sometimes, when the barrow covered a number of burials, bodies appear to have been laid on the ground surface with no grave being dug.

Certain burials have been found within timber coffins. Such were *composite* or *monoxylous*, that is, they were either constructed of wicker, or planks of wood, or else hewn from a suitable trunk. Sometimes certain monoxylous coffins had the form of boats, though it is doubtful if such 'boats' were ever used as such.

In areas where cairns and composite barrows are relatively common, cists built of selected slabs of stone, occasionally of great size and perhaps even dressed, housed the burials. In some cases such cists appear to have been designed as the precise counterparts of certain timber composite coffins. Some graves were hewn, surely with great labour, into rock. Other stone-built graves are difficult to describe as cists, being mere settings or edgings of stones.

A few interments were set beneath structures which are clearly mortuary houses. These have been described in Chapter IV in conjunction with aspects of barrow structure.

Possibly some of the earliest readily identifiable single-grave inhumation burials are a group in Wessex housed in roughly rectangular graves. They are not uniformly well documented, but the earlier accounts accord reasonably well with the results of more recent critical excavations so general observations are possible.

On Stockbridge Down in Hampshire,[3] a low barrow (Fig. 23 a), comprised mainly of flint nodules, had round it a ditch with five causeways. Such segmented ditches frequently surrounded sequential burials. Because of the cinerary urn from the ditch, it is uncertain whether or not the ditch is a primary feature. Beneath this barrow in a chalk-cut 'boat-shaped', grave, some 3 feet in depth and 5 feet in length, the skeleton of a young woman lay flexed and on its right side. The fragments of a larger B1 beaker lay at the foot of the grave. A copper awl was also in the interment and two cremations were in the grave-filling. These cremations had been put into the filling, presumably as the grave was infilled, but there are instances of the re-use of barrow-graves. An A beaker burial was inserted into the grave-pit of a B beaker interment at Cassington, Oxfordshire,[4] while a Food-Vessel burial was similarly inserted into an inhumation grave-pit on Rockbourne Down, Hampshire.[5] In a Scottish cist[6] it was found that the bones of a previous burial and a food-vessel had been heaped into one corner to make room for a subsequent occupant.

Equally well recorded was a low barrow covering a B1 beaker accompanied burial, on Crichel Down, Dorset[7] (Fig. 23 b). Here, in a roughly D-shaped grave-pit 6 feet by about 5 feet and about 2 feet 6 inches deep, a skeleton lay on its left side, contracted and with the beaker by its legs. This burial is of considerable interest, as the skull, like a few others of comparable age, had been trepanned before death. The roundel of bone detached by this operation had been placed back into position at the time of burial. A circular pit, into which a cremation had been put, partially cut into this grave.

Also reliably excavated was a 'ring-ditch' in Barrow Hill Fields, Radley, Berkshire.[8] An ovoid ditch enclosed two low bermed barrows, which appeared to have resembled

[3] *Ant. J.*, XX, 39–51.
[4] *Oxon.*, XI–XII, 164.
[5] *PHFCAS*, XVI, 156.
[6] *PSAS*, LXXXII, 299–301.
[7] *Arch.*, XC, 75–6.
[8] *Oxon.*, XIII, 1.

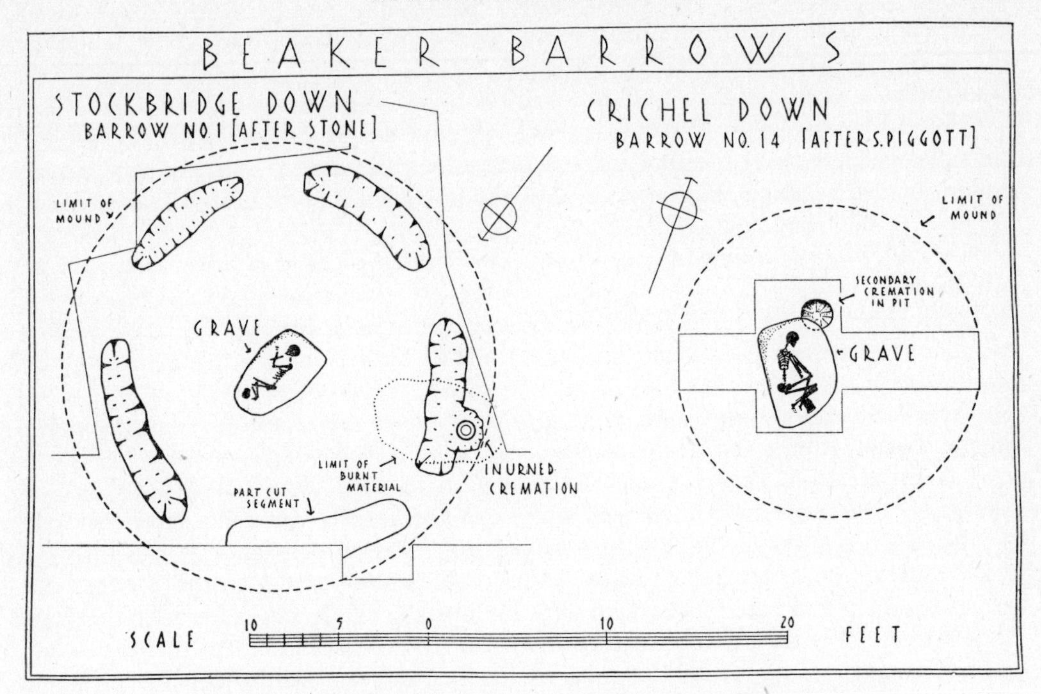

Fig. 23. The Stockbridge Down and Crichel Down Beaker barrows.

certain Wessex double forms. The smaller of the two barrows covered a roughly rectangular grave-pit about 7 feet long, 4 feet wide, and 3 feet deep, which was encircled by a V-sectioned ring-ditch. In this grave was a contracted male skeleton, supine and with head and legs turned to the left. It appears that this youth was wearing gold 'basket' ear-rings when buried, and a B1 beaker had been placed on its side near the sole of the left foot. In the grave infill were three barbed and tanged arrow-heads, and a fourth was in the body of the mound. On the bottom of the trench encircling the grave-pit was the horn-core and the metatarsus of an ox. Similar 'offerings' with Beaker burials have been noted at Crichel Down [9] and Linch Hill Corner.[10] Also on top of this encircling trench was a child burial which may have been encoffined in wood. The larger mound of this remarkable monument, in the construction of which turf may have been used, covered a cremation tipped into a little conical heap just to the west of its central point. In the middle of this was a small flat dagger blade, its condition suggesting that it had been placed in position after the cremated bones had cooled.

Less reliably recorded, but coinciding in detail with those described above, are the contracted burials from graves beneath low barrows at Roundway and Mere in Wiltshire.

That from Roundway [11] was opened by William Cunnington in 1855. The grave appears to have been of oval form and 5 feet long and about 2 feet 6 inches in width, and of the astonishing depth of 5 feet 6 inches. The skeleton in the grave was contracted and is depicted as on its left side. The B1 beaker was, as in the graves noted above, at its

[9] *Arch.*, XC, 74.
[10] *Oxon.*, VIII–IX, 34.
[11] *WAM*, III, 185; *Arch.*, XLIII, 289, Fig. 7; Forssander, 1936, 64.

feet, while by the head was a flint barbed and tanged arrow-head. Near the left hand was a long, tanged West European bronze dagger, while an archer's wrist-guard and a flat-headed pin or, perhaps, razor were between the bones of the left forearm.

A low barrow on Mere Down [12] covered a grave 6 feet in length and about 3 feet in depth, in which were, it is claimed, the skeletons of a man and a 'younger person' . . . 'embracing each other'. In this grave, although in what relationship to the skeletons is not clear, was a tanged dagger similar to that from Roundway, a B1 beaker, an archer's wrist-guard, a bone implement, and two small discs of gold bearing a cruciform ornament.

To the 'low barrow' series should be added yet another at Roundway,[13] said to have had a 'drinking cup', Colt Hoare's usual term for a beaker, in the grave. Although in each case it was claimed that a low barrow covered the graves, the evidence at Crichel Down at least suggests the mere infilling of a fair-sized grave, not necessarily supplemented by soil from elsewhere.

Other types of B beaker graves beneath barrows have been noted. In Wales at Llandow,[14] a U-shaped cairn, encased with earth and kerbed, covered a great rock-cut grave-pit. In this was a roughly boat-shaped stone setting or edging in which was a flexed skeleton on its left side. The skeleton occupied only half the length between the stones, but had been compressed with difficulty into the width. Packed around the skull were pieces of a beaker, comprising a whole pot. Arrow-heads, perhaps the remains of the broken arrows of a funeral salvo, lay by the feet, and one of them adhered to one of the beaker fragments. Like other Beaker barrows this was subsequently enlarged for more burials to be put down.

B beakers appear sometimes to have accompanied burials beneath barrows which were not in graves. An early account of the excavation of the 'Gospel Hillock', Buxton, Derbyshire,[15] describes skeletons laid on a pavement of stones, protected by a walling of stones and accompanied by a beaker.

Low barrows also covered A beakers on Crichel Down.[16] A large sub-rectangular grave-pit 7 feet by 6 feet and 3 feet deep contained a flexed skeleton on its right side. At the feet was a bronze awl and by the left elbow an A beaker, which had apparently been placed upright but had collapsed. A vessel of food-vessel affinities had been inserted into the filling.

Several other Beaker graves in Wiltshire,[17] as elsewhere,[18] may well have been covered by low barrows all traces of which have vanished. Indeed, in this connection, such Beaker flat grave cemeteries as Cassington [19] and Eynsham [20] should be considered. In the north in Yorkshire [21] relatively large barrows cover numbers of Beaker burials, which include vessels of several types, some of which are in graves, while others were placed on the ground surface. In the south-west the Wick Barrow [22] showed upon excavation that, although the central area had been robbed, eccentric cists contained contracted disarticulated skeletons accompanied by beakers of B and A types.

A recent analysis of the nineteenth-century work of Bateman,[23] in the Peak District

[12] Hoare, 1812–19, II, 44.
[13] Hoare, 1812–19, II, 98.
[14] *Arch.*, LXXXIX, 89–126.
[15] Bateman, 1861, 70.
[16] *Arch.*, XC, 76.
[17] *WAM*, XXXVIII, 44.
[18] *PSA*, X, 29.
[19] *Ant. J.*, XIV, 272.
[20] *Oxon.*, III, 10–20.
[21] Mortimer, 1905, 54.
[22] *PSANHS*, LIV, 1–77.
[23] *JDANHS*, LXXV, 66–172.

of Derbyshire, is of considerable interest when compared with the foregoing evidence regarding Beaker graves and burials. The writer demonstrates that by far the greater number of Beaker burials in the area come from pit-graves of varying though often considerable depth, and that these graves contained contracted inhumations and were originally beneath low barrows. It has been further shown that out of the eighteen complete beakers found by Bateman, fifteen come from pit-graves, one apparently from an extended burial not in a pit, and one uncertain. One more seems to be from a slab cist on the pre-barrow surface.

In the south food-vessels sometimes accompany inhumations, and are in instances [24] closely associated with beakers. However, it appears that they occur more frequently with cremations. In the north, especially in Scotland, beakers and food-vessels are mostly found in cists, set into the ground with little or no trace of a covering barrow or cairn.

In Scotland, C beaker graves have been listed,[25] and it is possible to analyse the mass of accumulated material. The following figures are for good C beakers, fragments being excluded. Cairnless cists numbered 106, and there were only 17 cists under cairns although 5 more, poorly recorded, appear to have been in or under cairns. Where some attempt has been made to sex skeletons, 21 are claimed as male and only 5 as female. However, 53 are merely described as 'skeletons'. As far as can be ascertained the skeletons were contracted or flexed.

From this Scottish material apparent variations of the essential 'single' burial rite emerge. Thus at Broomend, Inverurie,[26] two male skeletons were found in one cist with two beakers, while at Keir Bellhelvie [27] there were three beakers with the skeleton of what is claimed as a young female. Three skeletons and one beaker were in a cist under a cairn at Ballymeanoch.[28]

Food-vessels are also well documented in Scotland.[29] Thus, while 127 flat graves are known there are only 15 which were below cairns. Of all these, 52 were identified as inhumation burials and only 42 were cremations. Two of these have been claimed as male burials and 4 as females. There were also 2 infants.

A C beaker burial in a cist under a large barrow at Kellythorpe in Yorkshire,[30] is of considerable interest as it appears to have been of a person of some social standing. The barrow contained satellite burials, one of which appears to have been associated with a food-vessel. The central cist, which was about 4 feet long, 3 feet wide, and about 2 feet 6 inches deep, was built of obviously selected slabs of stone, paved and covered by a cap-stone. All the stone was, as far as can be seen, brought to the barrow from a considerable distance. A block and tackle had to be used to remove the cap-stone from the cist. This cap-stone was level with the ancient surface, the cist having been built in a grave. In the cist was a contracted skeleton on its left side. There was an archer's wrist-guard with gold rivets on the right arm, a small dagger near the pelvic girdle, and a C beaker by the feet. At the neck were three V-perforated conical amber buttons, suggesting some kind of ornamented collar rather than functional clothes fastenings. An object described as the 'head of a hawk', possibly an intrusive rabbit's skull, was also recorded from the cist.

[24] *Ant. J.*, XXX, 41; *PDAES*, IV, Pt. I, 1–19.
[25] *PSAS*, LXVIII.
[26] *PSAS*, LXVIII, 174.
[27] *PSAS*, LXVIII, 176.
[28] *PSAS*, LXV, 270.
[29] Childe, 1946, 106–18.
[30] Mortimer, 1905, 271–83; Elgee, 1933, 54.

Certain contracted or flexed burials were accompanied by 'axe-hammers' of the type normally associated with A beakers. Possibly the most reliably recorded grave of this type was that enclosed by two concentric ditches, the barrow having apparently been destroyed, near Woodhenge.[31] Here a large grave, 7 feet long and 5 feet wide, had been dug to a depth of about 3 feet 6 inches into the chalk. It contained the contracted skeleton of a man with hands folded across his chest, lying on his left side and facing the east. An A beaker was by the head, and the axe-hammer was found actually touching the forehead, resting upright on its 'axe' end, the perforation parallel with the skeleton. It was suggested by the excavators that the shaft had been held between the folded arms at the time of burial.

Side by side with the Beaker burials a series of inhumation burials, mainly collective, of Neolithic affinities should be considered. A round barrow at Ditton in Wiltshire,[32] thrown up from a ring of pits, covered seven or eight disarticulated skeletons, lying presumably on the pre-barrow surface. A barrow on Therfield Heath, near Royston,[33] covered skeletons also disarticulated. Associated with these was a bone pin.

Further burials beneath round barrows are included within the cultures termed 'Secondary Neolithic'. Under Barrow 26 on Handley Hill, Dorset,[34] was a fragmentary central inhumation, while another, about 8 feet distant, had a jet so-called 'belt-slider' at the hip. Around this 40-foot diameter barrow was a penannular ditch. Sherds of Peterborough pottery were in the mound and ditch-filling.

More burials from round barrows in southern and northern England have been included by Piggott[35] as a group within his 'Dorchester Culture'. Thus Colt Hoare's Upton Lovell Barrow 4[36] covered a grave 3 feet deep, in which were two inhumations. At the foot of the larger skeleton were, in Colt Hoare's words 'more than three dozen' perforated bone points, three flint axes, and stones, including an 'arrow straightener'. Boar's-tusk blades and natural hollow flints were by the legs, and near the chest were more bone points (? a necklace of perforated teeth) and a perforated stone battle-axe. A jet ring, jet and bone beads, a bronze awl, stones and pebbles, and also a broken battle-axe all appear to have been in loose association. Burials associated with antlers must be included in this group; they surely point to ultimate Mesolithic origins!

The most remarkable barrow of this group was Duggleby Howe, or Howe Hill, Duggleby, in the East Riding of Yorkshire, explored by Mortimer.[37] This great bowl barrow, some 120 feet in diameter and still 20 feet high, had at some time been decapitated for a mill-stance. Centrally beneath this mound, Mortimer found a grave-pit 9 feet in depth which had at the bottom a skeleton which is claimed to be that of an adult male. With this skeleton was a bowl of Neolithic A (Windmill Hill) ware, now lost. In the grave-pit filling were a number of skeletons of adults and children. Close by this pit was a smaller grave, in and on the edge of which were two adult skeletons. One had by it a 'skewer' pin, five *petit tranchet* derivative arrow-heads, boar's-tusk blades, beaver's teeth, and flint flakes, the other a polished rectangular flint knife. Near by, and over the central grave-pit, was an adult male skeleton with an antler mace-head, a flint axe, and a lozenge arrow-head. All these burials were beneath a core of earthy chalk

[31] Cunnington, 1929, 148–51.
[32] Hoare, 1812–19, 54.
[33] Fox, 1923, 32.
[34] Pitt-Rivers, 1887–98, IV, 58–61; 140–1.
[35] Piggott, 1954, 351–63.
[36] Hoare, 1812–19, 75.
[37] Mortimer, 1905, 23.

rubble, some 50 feet in diameter, which contained at least five unaccompanied skeletons of adults and children. In this core, and in a chalk-rubble layer above, were some fifty cremations, with bone pins and more *petit tranchet* derivative arrow-heads. All were sealed by what is described as a 'clay layer' overlaid by a sterile chalk envelope.

Another burial of this series was that beneath the cairn called 'Liff's Low' at Biggin in Derbyshire,[38] explored by Bateman during the nineteenth century. Bateman said that there was beneath it a male skeleton which was contracted and on its left side, with the head to the north. By the knees there was an antler mace-head, elsewhere in the 'octagonal' cist was a small-necked pottery flask, two polished flint axes, two flint knives with polished edges, 'lance-' and arrow-heads, boar's tusks, and pieces of red ochre.

Contracted inhumation burials in the Beaker manner are a feature of the Wessex culture, the peculiar barrow forms of which have been discussed in Chapter IV.

The rite of contracted inhumation burial was noted from a number of graves furnished with battle-axes, normally considered as part of the Wessex culture. Of the Hove-Snowshill battle-axe graves, five were flexed or contracted inhumations, namely Snowshill, Hove, Upton Lovell, Ashton Valley, and Chippenham. The Stourton-Loose Howe hammer-ended battle-axes were all associated, as far as could be seen, with cremations, but two of the Wilsford-Crichie series were with inhumations.

Not all the Wessex graves are particularly well documented, but reasonable accounts are available of two which contained both daggers and battle-axes.

A cist at Snowshill, Gloucestershire,[39] was dug out by Canon Greenwell. He wrote: 'At the centre [of the barrow] and partly sunk below the level of the natural surface was a cist formed of four slabs of stone set on edge, with a single stone for a cover. It was 4 feet long, 3 feet wide, and 2 feet deep. It contained the much decayed skeleton of, presumably a man, with whom were associated two bronze daggers [an ogival dagger and a tanged and socketed spearhead, both patently the work of the same craftsman], a bronze pin [crutch-headed], a perforated axe-hammer of stone.'

A similarly furnished burial was found beneath a denuded bowl barrow about 60 feet in diameter, at Chippenham in Cambridgeshire.[40] The body had been laid on the ground surface beneath the barrow, and the skeleton, which was at approximately the centre, was described as being on its back with its knees up, presumably contracted. It was noted at the time of excavation that there was no sign of a cist or grave. The dagger and battle-axe were on the left side of the skeleton at approximately chest level. A scrap of beaker pottery, perhaps included in the grave-filling, was noted in the vicinity of the skull.

Besides the warrior graves with daggers and battle-axes, one at least of three of the richer Wessex female graves[41] was a contracted inhumation burial. Precise details of the rite in the other two is lacking.

Reasonable details exist regarding the excavation of the rich, surely female, grave beneath a ploughed bowl barrow, about 66 feet in diameter, and 3 feet 6 inches high, at Manton, Preshute, in Wiltshire.[42] The primary burial was a contracted skeleton on its left side on the pre-barrow surface. No trace of a grave was recorded. It appears that

[38] Bateman, 1848, 286; *Arch. J.*, LXXXVIII, 132.
[39] *Arch.*, LII, 70–2.
[40] *PCAS*, XXXI, 134; *Ant. J.*, XV, 61.
[41] *ULIAA Rpt*, X, 53.
[42] *WAM*, XXXV, 1.

before burial the corpse had been wrapped in cloth, the impression of which remained in the soil. Beside the skeleton was a small bronze knife which had an amber pommel, a halberd pendant, a gold-capped and banded lignite bead, some 150 small, flat, circular beads of jet or shale, three bronze awls, a gold-bound amber disc, a labial plug of 'earthenware', a fluted oblate bead of lignite or shale, a 'grape' cup, and a small straight-sided pot. Some nine feet from the skeleton was a small cinerary urn which had apparently been used as a food-vessel. A bifacially trimmed arrow-head was found on the pre-barrow surface.

A number of unusually large barrows covered well- and in some instances exotically furnished graves which contained extended inhumation burials. Besides burials in Wessex [43] a number have been found in northern England,[44] and in Scotland.[45] Some of these were housed in cists and others in timber coffins; the latter will be discussed below.

What must have been a royal burial was beneath the 'Bush Barrow'—a huge bowl barrow in the Normanton group of barrows to the south of Stonehenge.[46] Colt Hoare, who dug into it in September 1808, does not say that it was an extended inhumation burial, but his remarks regarding the deposition of the grave-furniture suggest that it was (Fig. 24). Colt Hoare [47] wrote:

'The first attempts made by Mr Cunnington on this barrow proved unsuccessful, as also those of some farmers, who tried their skill in digging into it. Our researches were renewed in September 1808. . . . On reaching the floor of the barrow we discovered the skeleton of a tall and stout man, lying from south to north; the extreme length of his thigh bone was 20 inches. About 18 inches south of the head we found several brass rivets intermixed with wood, and some thin bits of brass nearly decomposed. These articles covered a space of 12 inches or more; and it is probable, therefore, that they were the mouldered remains of a shield. Near the shoulders lay the fine celt, the lower end of which owes its preservation to having been originally furnished with a handle of wood. Near the right arm was a large dagger of brass, and a spearhead of the same metal, full 13 inches long, and the largest we ever found. . . . These were accompanied by a curious article of gold which I conceive had originally decorated the case of the dagger. The handle of wood belonging to this instrument exceeds anything we have yet seen, both in design and execution, and could not be surpassed (if indeed equalled) by the most able workman of modern times . . . you will immediately recognize the British zig-zag or the modern Vandyke pattern which was formed with a labour and exactness almost unaccountable, by thousands of gold rivets, smaller than the smallest pin. The head of the handle, though exhibiting no variety of pattern, was also formed by the same kind of studding. So very minute indeed were these pins that our labourers had thrown out thousands of them with their shovels, and scattered them in every direction, before, by the necessary aid of a magnifying glass, we could discover what they were, but fortunately enough remained attached to the wood to develop the pattern. Beneath the fingers of the right hand lay a lance head of brass, but so much corroded that it broke to pieces on moving. Immediately over the breast of the skeleton was a large plate of gold in the form of a lozenge, measuring 7 inches by 6 inches. It was

[43] *PPS*, VII, 98.
[44] Greenwell, 1877, s.v.; Mortimer, 1905, s.v.
[45] Childe, 1946, 119.
[46] Hoare, 1812–19, 203.
[47] Hoare, 1812–19, 203. See *PPS*, IV, 63, for description of grave-furniture.

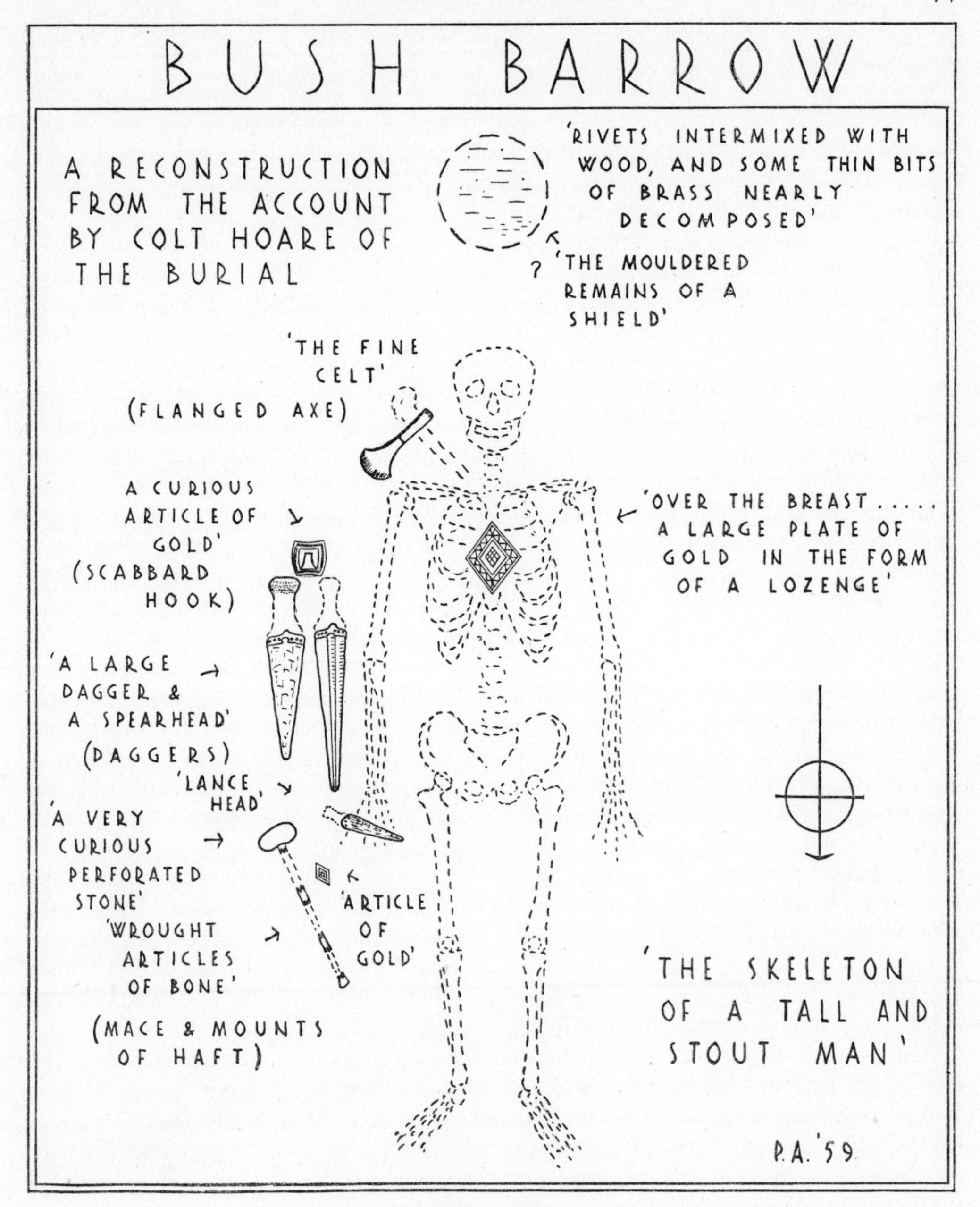

Fig. 24. The Bush Barrow burial.

fixed to a thin piece of wood, over the edges of which the gold was lapped. It is perforated at the top and bottom for the purpose probably of fastening it to the dress as a breastplate. . . . We next discovered, on the right side of the skeleton, a very curious perforated stone, some wrought articles of bone, many small rings of the same material, and another article of gold. The stone . . . had a wooden handle which was fixed into the perforation at the centre, and encircled by a neat ornament of brass, part of which still adheres to the stone.'

Elsewhere in Wiltshire, at Figheldean,[48] beneath a small bowl barrow, a grave cut into the chalk to the depth of 4 feet was 8 feet long and 3 feet 9 inches wide. In this was an extended skeleton with a small bronze knife behind the skull and a small pot at the feet. The extended inhumation rite appears also to have been met with in a barrow on Ballard Down in Dorset[49] where it is claimed that the skeleton of a boy was 'laid out straight with the heels touching each other'.

A large barrow at Towthorpe in Yorkshire[50] covered, besides what appear to have been 'ritual' pits and a satellite infant cremation, a grave about 3 feet 6 inches deep and probably about 7 feet long and 3 feet 6 inches wide, containing an extended supine skeleton. The skeleton was claimed to be male, and it had carbonized matter beneath it and large pieces of chalk lay below its sides and all around it. A dagger of Bush Barrow type lay by the left humerus, which, judging by the account, may have been encased in a leather sheath, and, as in other instances, wrapped in fabric. On the left side of the skull was a stone mace-head, and on the right, a plano-convex flint knife.

Greenwell appears to have found an extended inhumation, accompanied by a cremation, the grave-furniture being a food-vessel and a 'flint knife' under a barrow at Rudstone.[51] He disinterred two extended skeletons in the same grave under a barrow at Goodmanham,[52] another which appears to have been in a timber coffin, also at Goodmanham,[53] and another which was within a stone setting under a barrow at Hartburn in Northumberland.[54]

A number of burials mostly from cists, beneath cairns of some size, in Scotland,[55] have been said to have been extended burials. While the dimensions of graves and cists suggest this, no skeletal remains have been found, as they appear to have vanished in the lime-hungry soils of that region. Rich grave-furniture and the remains of great cists that could well have housed extended inhumation burials are known from Cornwall.[56] The bones have vanished, as acid soils are present in that region also.

Skulls from inhumation burials in Dorset[57] and Oxfordshire[58] have been trepanned at some time before deposition in the grave. A cranial disc from the parietal bone of the skull was amongst the *cremated* bones of a burial within a stake circle beneath a low, ditchless, bowl barrow recently excavated on Snail Down, in Wiltshire.[59] The Dorset burial has been discussed above (p. 70), and it is sufficient to note that that from Oxfordshire was from a so-called flat grave in a cemetery.

The practice of trepanning,[60] or the removal of a piece of bone from the skull and consequent exposure of the cerebral *dura-mater*, was widespread in prehistoric Europe. At Crichel Down, where a B1 beaker was resting against the right tibia of the skeleton, the associations were most satisfactory. It would appear that the operation had been performed by grooving with a sharp point, presumably of flint, and indeed scratches on the skull and the roundel indicate strokes made before the instrument had incised a

[48] *WAM*, XXXVI, 621.
[49] *Arch.*, XLIII, 317–18.
[50] Mortimer, 1905, 3.
[51] Greenwell, 1877, 269.
[52] Greenwell, 1877, 299.
[53] Greenwell, 1877, 303.
[54] Greenwell, 1877, 434.
[55] Childe, 1946, 121.
[56] Hencken, 1932, 73–6.
[57] *PPS*, VI, 112.
[58] *Oxon.*, III, 31–40.
[59] *WAM*, LVI, 145.
[60] *PPS*, VI, 113; *Man*, LIX, 93–6.

workable channel in the outer table of the skull. The inner table had been partly cracked by the levering out of the roundel, in final removal, to avoid cutting and damage to the subject's *dura-mater*. It would seem that this subject did not survive the operation as there was no evidence of healing on the edge of the cavity. The roundel must have been replaced and secured in position before burial.

The skeletal remains found beneath certain round barrows suggest mutilation, ritual or otherwise, before burial. Thus a skeleton, found on the ancient surface under a bowl barrow at Amesbury, had the right arm missing, while the other was disarticulated and the hand had been severed by a cut through the forearm. The ribs of this skeleton were crushed, and the skull and mandible were some distance from the trunk.[61] The inhumation burial recovered from a grave within the enclosure of a disc barrow not far distant also showed signs of such treatment.[62] Grinsell[63] records a burial where the head had apparently been severed from the body before burial. It seems probable that many other examples of similar treatment would have been disclosed by precise excavation: it is to be expected that more will be discovered in the future.

Such inhumation burials as those noted in the previous paragraph should not be confused with those where it seems that bones rather than bodies had been buried. According to the latter rite the bodies had apparently been exposed, the remains later collected and interred, either laid out or heaped, individually or communally. The absence of feet and hands and the occurrence of bones in patently unnatural positions all suggest some such rite.[64]

The arrangement of the bones as found in certain inhumation burials suggests that the corpse had been trussed into a contracted position before burial. Although this may well have been the case in some instances[65] no evidence of the materials used for such a purpose has been forthcoming.

Much has been written regarding skeletal material from barrow graves but it has been mostly inconclusive and tells us little except in a general way. Outstanding amongst the earlier works are the relevant descriptions in the great *Crania Brittanica* of Davis and Thurnam, Rolleston's study of crania appended to Greenwell's *British Barrows*, General Pitt-Rivers's precise descriptions, and the note by Mortimer upon the physical characteristics of the individuals buried beneath the Wold barrows. Since Abercromby's ethnographical account[66] it has been generally accepted that the sturdy bones and brachycephalic skulls, which contrast markedly with the gracile skeletons and consistently dolichocephalic skull forms of the Neolithic population, represent immigrants and are most probably to be identified with the Beaker folk. None the less, scrutiny of bone assemblages of the period reveals mixed populations. Coon,[67] noting how the British Beaker population as a whole diverges from the more uniform continental counterpart, would see an admixture of tall dolichocephalic 'Battle-axe' folk. Such a contention accords well with archaeological evidence. It is likely that examination

[61] Amesbury, 1956; *WAM*, LVI, 237–40 (interim).

[62] Amesbury, 1956; *WAM*, LVI, 237–40 (interim).

[63] *PPS*, VII, 97.

[64] *Oxon.*, III, 22, Pl. II, c.

[65] Grinsell, 1953, 39.

[66] Abercromby, 1912, I, 66. G. M. Morant in *Biometrika*, XVIII, 56–98, noted a dual division of skull form.

[67] C. S. Coon, *The Races of Europe*, New York, 1939, 159; the most recent account is J. C. Trevor, 'The Racial History of Britain, the Bronze Age', Munro Lectures, University of Edinburgh, February 1956 (not yet published).

and comparison of regional groups by an anatomist might show coincidence with regional cultures.

Grinsell in his first paper on bell barrows[68] tabulated the primary interments and showed that inhumation burials became progressively few in relation to cremation burials. ApSimon's analysis of the dagger graves[69] at last positively demonstrated that the rite of cremation appears to have supplanted and finally superseded inhumation in Wessex. In the earlier Bush Barrow phase, inhumations were more numerous than cremations (8 : 4), and in the later 'Camerton-Snowshill' phase cremations were more numerous (28 : 13). Beneath certain barrows such as Amesbury G. 60 and G. 85[70] the rites of inhumation and cremation occurred side by side. It is of interest to note in this connection also that only little more than a quarter of the burials accompanied by 'flat-riveted knife-daggers', listed by Fox and Grimes,[71] were cremations.

In cremated burials the pieces of burned bone, which may sometimes be mixed with the charcoal from the pyre, were interred either unurned or urned. In the former case they often appear to have been merely tipped or heaped into the grave, sometimes while still hot from the pyre. In some cases it has been found that they were covered by bast or some such substance, while in others it is possible that they were enclosed in a bag or a basket. Urned cremations were contained within an urn which was inverted or standing upright in its appropriate grave or cist.

An apparently early cremation was the primary burial in a round barrow at Kingston Deveril in Wiltshire, explored by Colt Hoare.[72] The burnt bones would appear to have been in and around the vessel, a two-handled bowl of Windmill Hill ware (Piggott's Form J), found, it is said, on a *knob of chalk*, perhaps the proud ancient surface, in the centre of the barrow.

Multiple cremation burials in elongated trenches, in the local 'Windmill Hill' Neolithic earthen long-barrow style, and associated with appropriate material, are alleged beneath round barrows in Yorkshire.[73] Other round barrows covering such crematorium trenches are known, but they appear to have had Beaker and Food-Vessel associations. At Ford in Northumberland, Greenwell[74] claims to have found a number of cremations with sherds, a leaf-shaped arrow-head, flint flakes, and charcoal, beneath a round barrow recorded as being 'almost identical in size with the last' (G. CLXXXVII), which was apparently 16 feet in diameter and 3 feet in height and built of earth and stones.

The rite of cremation occurs in the Secondary Neolithic in Britain,[75] and has even been found in an isolated Mesolithic context in Denmark.[76] The chronological relationships of these cultures to certain Bronze Age groups is at present nebulous and undefined. There are grounds for the belief that the rite of cremation is allied with the spread into Britain of 'Corded Ware' and specific types of battle-axes, namely those typified by the Ashton Valley-Winwick forms, found in this country, as far as can be seen, almost exclusively with cremations.

The researches of Grinsell[77] have shown that in Wessex cremations are frequently

[68] *PPSEA*, VII, 203–30.
[69] *ULIAA Rpt*, X, 53.
[70] *WAM*, XLV, 432–58.
[71] *Arch. Camb.*, LXXXIII, 137–74.
[72] Hoare, 1812–19, 45; *Arch. J.*, LXXXVIII, 141.
[73] Piggott, 1954, 112.
[74] Greenwell, 1877, 410.
[75] Atkinson, Piggott, and Sandars, 1951.
[76] *ANL*, III, 12.
[77] *PPSEA*, VII, 207–8.

(a)

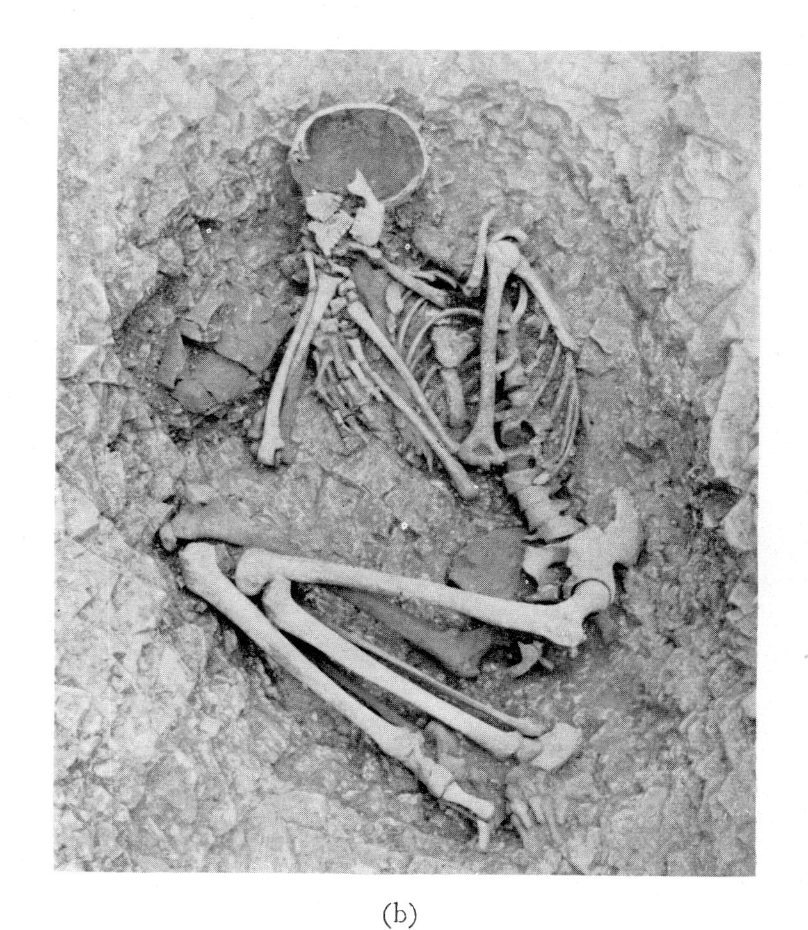

(b)

XI. Necked (A) Beaker burial (a), and Bell (B) Beaker burial (b). Satellite and secondary burials in Barrow Amesbury G. 59; excavated in 1960.

XIIa. Cremation and grave-furniture in a chalk-cut disc-barrow grave; Amesbury (G. 61a), excavated in 1956.

XIIb. Timber coffin containing a cremation beneath a bell barrow at Milton Lilbourne (G. 4), Wiltshire; excavated in 1958.

XIIc. An inverted cinerary urn in a circular grave-pit, Milton Lilbourne (G. 5), Wiltshire; partially excavated.

XIIIa. A selected granite slab cist beneath a cairn on Samson, Isles of Scilly.

XIIIb. The cist on Samson: detail of joint.

XIIIc. A stone-setting in a rock-cut grave: Kildale Moor, Yorkshire.

XIVa. (LEFT). The Roundway tanged 'West European' dagger; length 10 inches. b (CENTRE). The longer Bishop's Waltham hilted dagger; length 8 inches. c (RIGHT). The Brigmerston round-heeled dagger (hilt restored); length 8·25 inches.

found beneath specific types of bell barrows, generally wide-bermed. ApSimon's work on daggers[78] has shown also that cremation is the preponderant rite of the dagger-graves of his Wessex II. All this evidence, when considered together with the fact that cremations were sometimes put into graves large enough to have contained inhumations, might suggest that the rite may have been intrusive in the area. Much more careful excavation of barrows is needed before its affinities can be defined with any precision.

Modern excavation has revealed many examples of unurned cremations deposited in barrows in varying circumstances.

An unurned cremation placed in a shallow scoop was found to be the primary burial under a low, penannular-ditched barrow on Crichel Down,[79] and another barrow close by covered a penannular enclosure defined by a palisade-trench. This enclosure had in it an unurned cremation in a shallow scoop, and another was by the entrance.[80] The barrow, like its fellow, had been thrown up from a penannular ditch. A penannular-ditched barrow at Wallis Down in Dorset[81] also yielded an unurned cremation, although the full burial record from this barrow is not known owing to disturbance.

Unurned cremations were frequently in other than a primary context. Fifty cremations, four with bone pins, were in the chalk envelope of Duggleby Howe.[82] Recently the excavation of the Mound of the Hostages, at Tara in Ireland,[83] has revealed a similarly placed cremation cemetery in the clay envelope and indeed even in the ground around the base of the mound. With regard to this it should be remembered that cremations set in cavities in the ground have been found *between* barrows in Dutch barrow cemeteries.[84] These are areas that it is not usually possible to explore in this country. In this context the cemetery-cairn at Knockast,[85] in Ireland, which yielded thirty cremations, in and beneath the cairn, should also be considered.

Cremations associated with beakers are rare and are thus of note. In Yorkshire a number have been recovered from beneath barrows on Broxa Moor.[86] As yet no precise details are available. Greenwell found cremations and inhumations under his Barrow LXII at Rudstone.[87] In Scotland certain beakers may have accompanied cremations, and a beaker was in the mound of the 'Fairy Knowe' at Bridge of Allan,[88] the primary burial of which appears to have been a cremation contained in a cist.

In Wessex the excavation of a bowl barrow at Amesbury[89] disclosed cremations placed in shallow scoops in the ancient surface side by side with inhumations, a rite frequently noted. Bell-beaker sherds were recovered from the remnant of chalk envelope left after ploughing, and from the ditch.

At least forty-two food-vessels in Scotland accompanied cremations,[90] but they were almost all from cist or flat graves. In the East Riding of Yorkshire cremation was the rite in 20 per cent of the Food-Vessel graves explored by Mortimer.[91]

The publication of Quernhowe,[92] this well-excavated complex composite barrow,

[78] *ULIAA Rpt*, X, 37–62.
[79] *Arch.*, XC, 72.
[80] *Arch.*, XC, 66.
[81] *PPS*, XVIII, 148.
[82] Mortimer, 1905, 23.
[83] *PPS*, XXI, 164; XXIII, 220–1.
[84] Glasbergen, 1954, II, 142.
[85] *PRIA*, XLI, 232–84.
[86] *ANL*, III, 37.
[87] Greenwell, 1877, 234.
[88] *PSAS*, LXVIII, 187.
[89] *WAM*, LVI, 237–40 (interim).
[90] Childe, 1946, 106–18.
[91] Mortimer, 1905, xxxiv.
[92] *Ant. J.*, XXXI, 1–24.

has thrown much light on Food-Vessel cremations in the Yorkshire region. It appears that the bones were cleansed before disposal, and in two cases at least were interred while still hot from the pyre. The structural history suggests the deposition of primary and satellite cremations, and the erection of the mound, followed by modifications to house secondary cremations. A series of food-vessels was associated with the burials.

In Wales, where food-vessels are few, cremation was the normal practice.[93] It appears also to have been used in Cornwall.[94] The Tregulland Burrow[95] yielded cremations, one of which was accompanied by a Type III food-vessel.

A pond barrow at Winterbourne Steepleton[96] in Dorset, produced, besides specific Sheep Down urns, Type III food-vessels. In this barrow, the only example of its kind excavated by modern methods, only four out of twenty pots appear to have accompanied burials. The burials were mainly cremations, but dismembered inhumations were also present. It was argued that the primary purpose of this pond barrow was not sepulchral, as only eleven of the thirty-four pits contained substantial quantities of human remains, and while one was at the centre the other ten were peripheral and thus perhaps satellite. The remaining twenty-three pits consisted of three classes, namely: empty pits, pits with cremations, and pits with pottery.

Cremations have been noted elsewhere with food-vessels in the Wessex area. A cremation was a secondary burial in a large barrow at Long Ash Lane, Frampton, in Dorset,[97] and was accompanied by a Type III food-vessel and faience beads. Recent work at Amesbury[98] has produced a similar food-vessel from a disc barrow, the primary burial from which was a cremation.

Piggott listed ninety-nine Wessex graves.[99] These included many of the dagger-graves. Of these some sixty-three appear to have been cremations.

The association of cremations with bell barrows has been shown by Grinsell. His lists were in great part compiled from accounts of early explorations, as relatively few bell barrows have been excavated under modern conditions. Indeed, in 1954 the present writer was able to find only about a dozen, a number since augmented by the Amesbury and Snail Down barrow excavations. Certain Wessex burials, both unburnt and burnt, were enclosed in timber coffins or allegedly laid on planks.

A cremation which was the primary burial of a bell barrow at Amesbury, recently excavated, was heaped in an elongated grave. This grave had been dug to a depth of almost 2 feet below the ancient soil, and with vertical sides. Vertical striations had been left in the graveside, presumably by the 'picks' used to dig it. Ash from the pyre and fine pieces of burnt bone had first of all been tipped into the bottom of the grave, and then larger pieces, and finally the largest heaped up in the centre. Upon the cremation was a small knife-dagger, sheathed, with the hilt intact but the pommel lacking, wrapped in cloth and a substance which was probably moss, and also a piece of iron pyrites. It appears that the cremation was cold when put in the grave, as the grave-goods were unmarked by heat. The grave had been infilled with the spoil dug from it and the residue heaped over it.

Disc barrows, as was noted by Thurnam[100] almost all contained cremations. These

[93] *Arch. Camb.*, LXXV, 329.
[94] *Arch. J.*, CI, Table V.
[95] *Ant. J.*, XXXVIII, 174–96.
[96] *Arch. J.*, CVIII, 1–24.
[97] *Ant. J.*, XXXI, 30.
[98] *WAM*, LVI, 237–40 (interim).
[99] *PPS*, IV, 102–6.
[100] *Arch.*, XLIII, 294.

were hardly ever urned, only four examples being recorded. In most instances the cremations appear to have been placed in small graves dug into the chalk. Two recent excavations of disc barrows have thrown much light on the types of burials in them.

A disc barrow on Earl's Farm Down was explored during 1956,[101] and in the central area, besides a small, near-rectangular grave containing the cremation, there was a small pit into which charcoal, presumably from the pyre, had been placed. It is of interest that the practice of interring a portion of charcoal in a small pit near the primary burial has been noted under a barrow, the primary interment of which was a Deverel-Rimbury globular urn covering a cremation, at Chick's Hill in Dorset, and elsewhere under similar barrows.[102]

Another disc barrow, an oval example on New Barn Down,[103] not far distant, enclosed two burials. One was a disarticulated skeleton placed in a large pit, possibly a partly natural one, the other a cremation accompanied by grave-furniture. This cremation burial was in a rectangular grave (Pl. XII a) about 15 inches in depth, 2 feet long, and about 1 foot 8 inches broad. The cremation was heaped in the bottom of the grave. At one end of the elongated heap was a globular miniature vessel. Against this was a beaver-tooth pendant, a fragment of bronze, and a bronze awl. Beneath it were beads of amber, faience, steatite, and cowrie shell.

A cremation burial, accompanied by grave-furniture with Wessex affinities, was recovered from beneath the composite barrow explored on Breach Farm, Llanbleddian, in Glamorganshire.[104] The burial-pit was a roundish oval in plan, 2 feet 4 inches across, and of about the same depth below the ancient soil surface. The cremated bones were in the bottom of the pit and the associated objects had been placed on top. The miniature vessel was on its side with its base against the west side of the pit, while the stone and bronze artefacts were on the other.

A well-recorded cremation in an overhanging-rim urn, set upright in the grave, was that from beneath the composite Pond Cairn in Glamorgan.[105] Although the urn was found in a crushed condition, it was possible to see that it had been set upon the ancient surface, with a flat stone slab covering the mouth. Blocks of sandstone had been piled around and above it to form a small cairn.

Not far distant, also in Glamorgan, the barrow Sheeplays 293′ [106] also had a cinerary urn as a primary burial. This urn had been placed upright in a neat round hole 13·5 inches in diameter, its rim being 5 inches below the ancient surface. The space between the side of this pit and the urn was just wide enough for the excavator to insert his fingers and lift it out, and thus, presumably, just wide enough for the funeral party to insert the urn. In this space, besides black material from the pyre, were small stones inserted to secure the urn in the pit. In the urn were the clean cremated bones of a youth, a calcined flint flake, and a bronze awl. The condition of the awl suggested that the bones were inurned when cold. In Wessex cinerary urns were buried in this manner, often beneath low bowl barrows (Pl. XII c).

Inverted urns were found in profusion beneath one of the two palisade barrows, the structure of which has been described on page 44, at Letterston in Pembrokeshire.[107]

[101] *WAM*, LVI, 237–40 (interim).
[102] *Ant. J.*, XIII, 432.
[103] *WAM*, LVI, 237–40 (interim).
[104] *PPS*, IV, 107–121.
[105] *Arch.*, LXXXVII, 142.
[106] *Ant. J.*, XXI, 98.
[107] *Arch. Camb.*, C, 67.

The primary urn burial was in a circular pit, slab covered and clay and slab lined. It had been inverted over a cremation which had with it a plano-convex flint knife. It is thought that this barrow was on the site of the actual cremation, after which the bones were swept into the pit and the urn inverted above them. Three secondary burials were cremations contained in inverted urns, one with a miniature vessel, each being within a poorly constructed slab-cist.

Besides being single burials under barrows, satellite burials as at Latch Farm in Dorset,[108] or secondary burials, overhanging-rim urns have been found in 'cemeteries' set in structures which sometimes may well be uncompleted barrows. At Loanhead of Daviot [109] in Scotland, thirty cremations, only fourteen of which were unurned, had been deposited in pits in a circular area 35 feet in diameter, which was surrounded by a narrow trench, said to be broken at two points, and which abutted upon a recumbent stone circle. In Lancashire, at Todmorton,[110] an earth bank, reported to be about 3 feet in width, enclosed a circular area described as 90 feet across. In the centre was a cremation in a cinerary urn, while four other urned cremations, four miniature vessels, and a number of unurned cremations were around it.

On Easton Down in Wiltshire,[111] cinerary urns and unurned cremations were set out in a row or arc, though these may also have represented preliminary burials made before the erection of a barrow. Yet another form of collective urn-burial has been noted beneath small barrows in Derbyshire,[112] each of which cover three to twelve interments.

Deverel-Rimbury cremations,[113] urned and unurned, were collected in flat-cremation cemeteries or were single or multiple burials under barrows, or were, frequently, inserted as secondary burials into barrows (Fig. 25). In flat cemeteries, such cremations were often in circles, while in the Deverel Barrow [114] they are said to have been placed, together with overhanging-rim urns, at the foot of a penannular cairn-ring of massive stones. When such Deverel-Rimbury cremation burials are found in the mounds of barrows they tend to be restricted to a quadrant or arc towards the south or south-east.

Early antiquaries often made useful observations about graves and the burials within them. These accounts of the barrows which they opened, compiled for the great part in an age when collection was a prime archaeological aim, though they are suspect in many ways, can sometimes be consulted side by side with more modern work.

Thurnam,[115] a pioneer in all respects, took Colt Hoare's observations and combined them with his own. He notes how in Wessex inhumations were frequently placed on the ancient surface, or at the most in a shallow grave. However, the occurrence of deep pits, and even 'shaft' graves for the reception of inhumations is not unknown. These latter have been listed by Grinsell,[116] while one such grave was met with recently during the immediate pre-war excavation of barrows on Crichel Down.[117] Regarding cremations, Thurnam remarks that they were deposited in appropriately sized graves 'generally of irregular form and rudely circular or oblong'.[118]

[108] *PPS*, IV, 169–87.
[109] *PSAS*, LXX, 279.
[110] *Reliquary*, IX, 278.
[111] *WAM*, XLVI, 218.
[112] *JDANHS*, LI, 1–44; LVII, 21–35; LX, 105–115.
[113] *Ant. J.*, XIII, 414–54.
[114] W. A. Miles, *A Description of the Deverel Barrow*, 1826.
[115] *Arch.*, XLIII, 285.
[116] *PPS*, VII, 102.
[117] *Arch.*, XC, 73.
[118] *Arch.*, XLIII, 325.

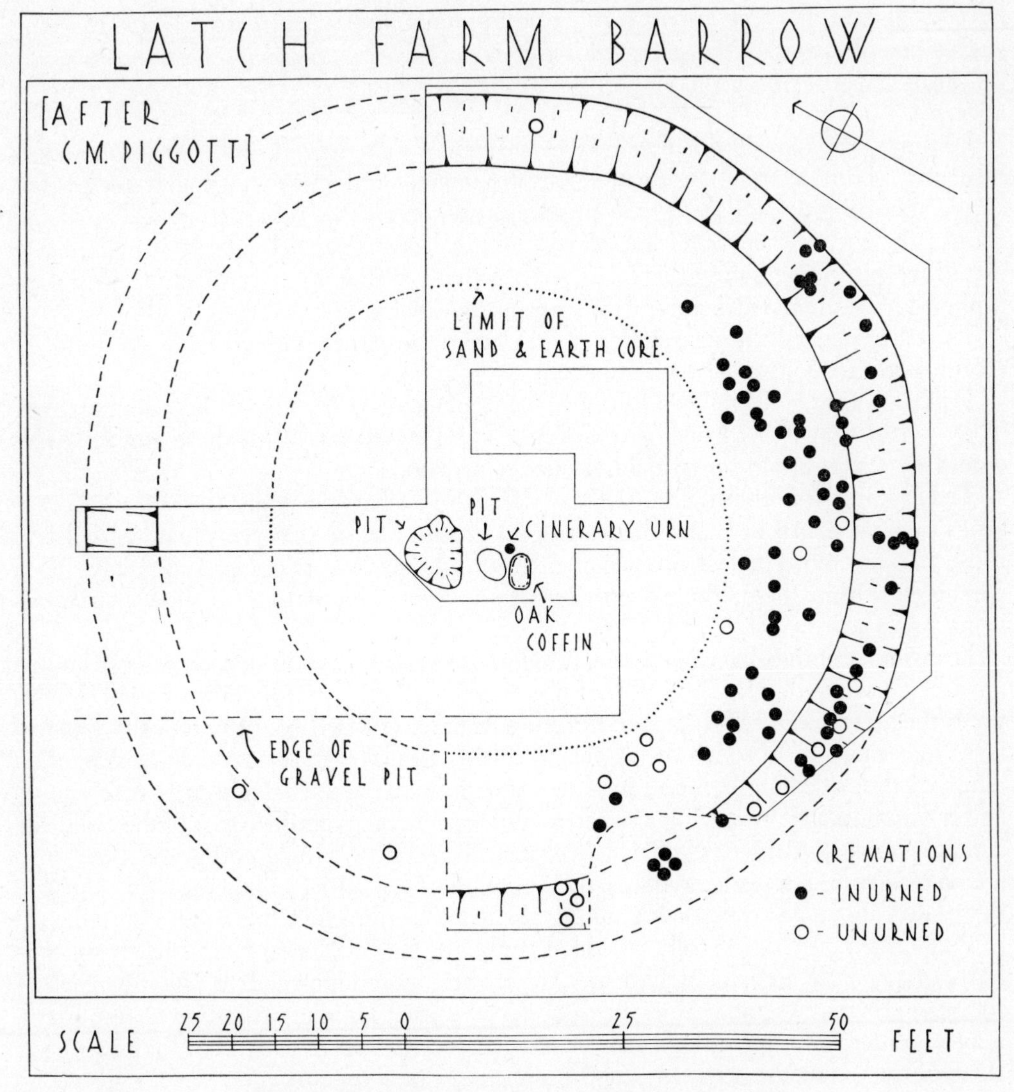

Fig. 25. The Latch Farm Deverel-Rimbury burials.

Greenwell [119] wrote, after 'opening' innumerable barrows: 'The central, which in case of no after disturbance is the primary burial, was usually made in a grave sunk to a greater or less depth in the chalk rock. The grave is either oval or circular, and its shape or size were no doubt in some measure regulated by the way in which the makers were able to work out the chalk rock at that particular point.' He also observed regarding 'secondary' burials (which must include certain satellite burials), to the effect that they were 'much more frequently on the south and east than on the north and west, indeed', he continues, 'they are but rarely found on the last mentioned sides'.

Mortimer [120] to some extent reiterates Greenwell's contentions regarding graves and

[119] Greenwell, 1877, 12.

[120] Mortimer, 1905, xxv.

burials. He said that 'the graves containing inhumed bodies are mainly oval, whilst the graves or holes containing cremated bones are almost invariably circular and more or less dish-shaped'. Greenwell's belief regarding the digging of graves into chalk rock he rejects.

Recent work has shown that graves dug into clay, gravel, and sometimes even relatively obdurate rock preserve the approximately ubiquitous forms. It seems that large oval or slightly squared grave-pits are entirely typical of Beaker graves,[121] to which culture the rite of contracted and flexed inhumation burial belongs. It would follow that grave-pits perpetuating this form, such as that which housed the Bishop's Waltham timber coffin, discussed below, demonstrate the continuance of these traditions.

The early generalizations regarding graves and burials hold good today, and indeed recent work has confirmed their validity.

Timber coffins [122] have been found in many places in graves or set beneath barrows. They are of two types, namely: *monoxylous* and *composite*. With these some writers would associate certain burials laid on planks of wood.

The examples of monoxylous coffins (Fig. 26) that have been disinterred, and sometimes preserved, can be marshalled into two groups: those that are square-ended and those that are more or less boat-shaped. Both inhumations and cremations have been contained within them, the proportion of fourteen inhumations to nine cremations being known.

Few timber coffins have been unearthed under modern conditions, so early accounts must be considered. The condition of preservation of all types of coffins varied. Sometimes they were only soft scraps of fibrous substance (Pl. XII b), or practically replacement material, soft to touch or trowel. In other cases they were sound and substantial. The Gristhorpe coffin,[123] found in water, was removed to a local museum. A few years ago it was mutilated by sawing apart to facilitate removal to another part of the building, and was subsequently patched with cement. The Loose Howe coffin and boat, also recovered from a waterlogged barrow, were removed, dried, and were for a period suspended above a showcase containing the grave-furniture in the British Museum.

Perhaps the first objectively recorded timber coffin in a barrow was that from Stoborough, near Wareham in Dorset. An account communicated to the *Gentleman's Magazine* [124] in the same year as the discovery by John Hutchins, the Dorset antiquary, is of considerable interest, and has therefore been quoted in full: 'On digging down King-barrow, January 21, 1767, at the south end of Stowborough . . . in the road to Grange, to make the turnpike-road, the following discovery was made. The barrow was 100 feet in diameter, its perpendicular height 12. In the centre, at the bottom, even with the surface of the ground, in the natural soil of sand, was found a very large hollow trunk of an oak, rudely excavated, but probably by hand, 10 feet long; the diameter from out to out was 4 feet; that of the cavity, 3 feet: it lay horizontally, S.E. to N.W.: the upper parts of the ends were much rotted. The barrow was composed of strata on layers of turf, in some of which the heath was not perished. In the cavity were found as many human bones as might be contained in a quarter of a peck, about 12 in number, viz., an arm-bone, two thigh bones, two blade bones, the head of the humerus,

[121] *Arch.*, XC, 52.

[122] *WAM*, XLIV, 101–5; *TAASDN*, VIII, Pt I (1937); *PPS*, XV, 101–6; *Man.*, LIII, 129.

[123] W. C. Williamson, *Tumulus opened at Gristhorpe, Scarborough*, 1872.

[124] *Gents. Mag.*, Archaeology, Pt I, 94–5.

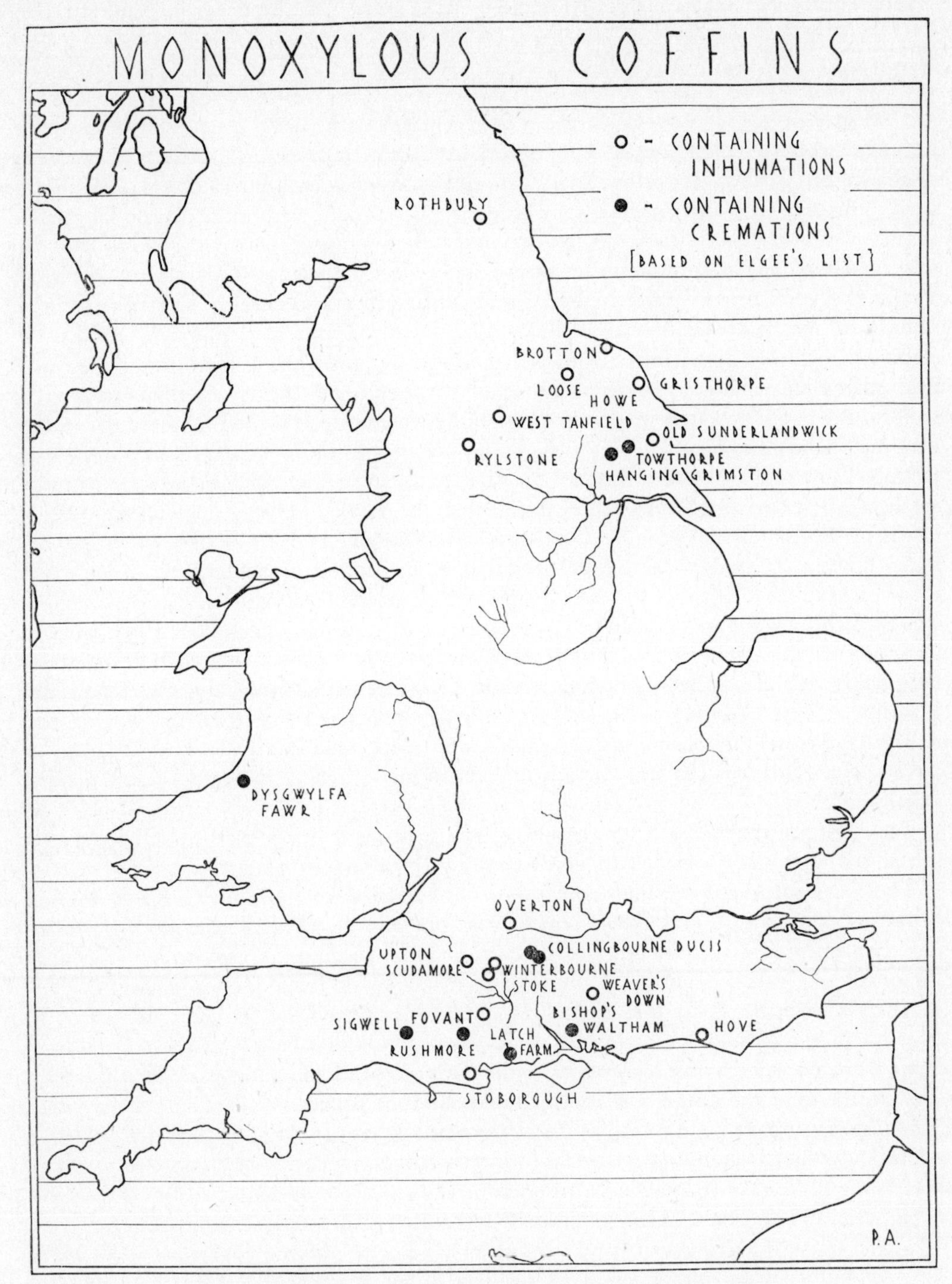

Fig. 26. Distribution map showing monoxylous timber coffins.

part of the pelvis, and several rib bones. They were unburnt, soft and black; the ribs would lap round one's finger. There were no remains of the skull; many were scattered and lost, more were entirely consumed. These bones were wrapped up in a large covering, composed of several skins, some as thin as parchment; others, especially where the hair remained (which showed they were deer-skins), were much thicker; they were generally black, and not rotten; they were neatly sown together, and there were many small slips whose seams or stitches were scarce two inches asunder. As the labourers expected to find money, they were pulled out with much eagerness and torn, so that the shape of the whole could not be discovered. This covering seemed to have been wrapped several times round the body, and in some parts adhered to the trunk: in the middle of which covering most of the bones were compressed flat in a lump, and cemented together by a glutinous matter, perhaps the moisture of the body, which was not inflammable. The covering did not reach to the N.W. end, and perhaps not much beyond the body, towards which the thigh bone was found; this and the situation of the urn, may determine the position of the body. On unfolding it, a disagreeable smell was perceived, such as is usual at the first opening of a vault; near the S.E. end was found a small vessel of oak, the colour black; it was much broken, but enough preserved to show it was in the shape of an urn. . . . On the outside were hatched (no doubt with a graver) many lines, some horizontal and others oblique: its longest diameter at the mouth was three inches; the short one two; its depth two; its thickness, two-tenths of an inch. It was probably placed at the head of the corpse. There was no appearance of any ashes in it, or any part of the covering. There was a piece of gold-lace, as imagined, four inches long and two and a half broad, stuck on the covering inside, black and much decayed. Bits of wire appeared in it, and here were no fragments of brass or iron from whence one might have concluded any arms or armour were deposited here. . . . The largeness of the barrow evidences that the person interred under it was a person of note and distinction. . . .'

This description of the King Barrow opening paints a lively picture of a log-coffin burial, with probably a shale cup, similar to that from Hove or Gristhorpe.

The Gristhorpe coffin came from the central barrow of three on Gristhorpe Cliff, between Scarborough and Filey, which was 'opened' in 1834. The coffin, preserved together with some of the contents in Scarborough Museum, appears to have been, as far as can be gleaned from the accounts of its discovery, 7 feet 6 inches in length, 3 feet 3 inches wide at the head, and 2 feet 10 inches wide at the foot. At this end it was just over 1 foot in depth. The lid which covered the coffin, and which appears to have been made from the same trunk, was 1 foot in depth at the head and 9 inches deep at the foot, The head end of the coffin was rounded and the foot square.

It appears to have been found at the bottom of a grave-pit which was about 10 feet in depth and which, when dug into, was found to contain water. It can safely be assumed that in the bottom of its pit, dug into boulder clay, it was waterlogged for a great part of the year and deprived of oxygen for the remainder, and so preserved.

The coffin as it lay in the grave-pit is said to have been covered with what is described as 'a quantity of oak-branches laid together'. The same early account describes the coffin when the 'branches' have been removed as an 'immense log of wood'.

Within the coffin lay the skeleton of a powerfully built man about 6 feet tall. It would seem that the body had originally been wrapped in an animal skin with soft, fine hair, which had been fastened at the breast by a bone pin. By the side lay a flat-bottomed, circular dish, made of pieces of bark stitched together with what is presumably sinew, and which presumably contained a food-offering. Other grave-goods comprised a bronze dagger with a pommel, claimed to be of whale-bone, a small spatula of wood, part of a horn ring, and three fragments of flint, possibly *petit tranchet* derivative arrow-heads as found in other barrows in the area.

All this material is preserved in Scarborough Museum, but it is little known. The composite vessel, if still extant, is unique, and the whole would amply repay study and definitive publication.

Perhaps the best known of all the timber coffin burials is that found at Hove in Sussex,[125] when a great barrow was destroyed during building operations in 1857. While digging away the barrow, the workmen came upon 'a rude oak coffin, hollowed out of a single tree-trunk, and shaped with an axe. It was 6 or 7 feet long, and had been placed roughly east and west. In this coffin, which crumbled to pieces, were found many fragments of decayed bones, but it could not be determined with certainty whether the body had been cremated or not. In the centre of the coffin, as if they had rested on the breast of the body, were found four objects, viz., a cup of red amber, a polished stone axe-head, an object shaped like a small whetstone, and a bronze dagger'.

The state of preservation of the oak coffin found beneath a bell barrow excavated at Latch Farm, Christchurch, Hampshire,[126] was such that only skilled excavation and observation detected its presence. Under the barrow three pits were found, the coffin being in the smallest one of these. To quote the excavator's account:

'Pit 3. Dimensions: 2 feet by 3 feet. Depth below the old turf line: 1·5 feet. This oval pit was cut closely beside Pit 2. The upper part of the filling was indistinguishable from the natural loam, but as soon as the solid level was reached, an oval area of loam surrounded by a band of heavily carbonised material, see photograph, pl. xxxiv [of paper], showed the presence of a pit, and the section was then obtained.

'The whole pit was lined with this carbonized material, which proved on examination by Mr Maby to have been an oak coffin, and into this a cremated burial, presumably wrapped in some form of bag, had been placed, and packed round with loam and gravel. No signs of cloth were recovered, but the fact that the bones were clean and in a compact mass, unmixed with the surrounding soil, suggests that they were contained in some perishable substance.

'A bronze awl was found with the bones, and may have served as a pin to fasten this material together. It was placed definitely outside the mass of bones, and not embedded amongst them.'

Similar conditions of preservation obtained in the square-ended oak coffin excavated by the present writer from a bell barrow at Bishop's Waltham (Fig. 27), also in Hampshire,[127] during the winter of 1953–4.

Beneath the barrow centre was an approximately rectangular grave, about 8 feet in length, 5 feet in breadth, and 1 foot 6 inches in depth. In this grave were the readily recognizable remains of a rectangular tree-trunk coffin 5 feet in length and just under 3 feet in width, and remaining to a depth of about 1 foot. Carbonized and in places of almost sand-like consistency, it had obviously been hewn from a tree-trunk.

[125] *BH Arch.*, No. 2, 20–8; *SAC*, LXXXII, 123.
[126] *PPS*, IV, 169–87.
[127] *PPS*, XXIII, 137–66.

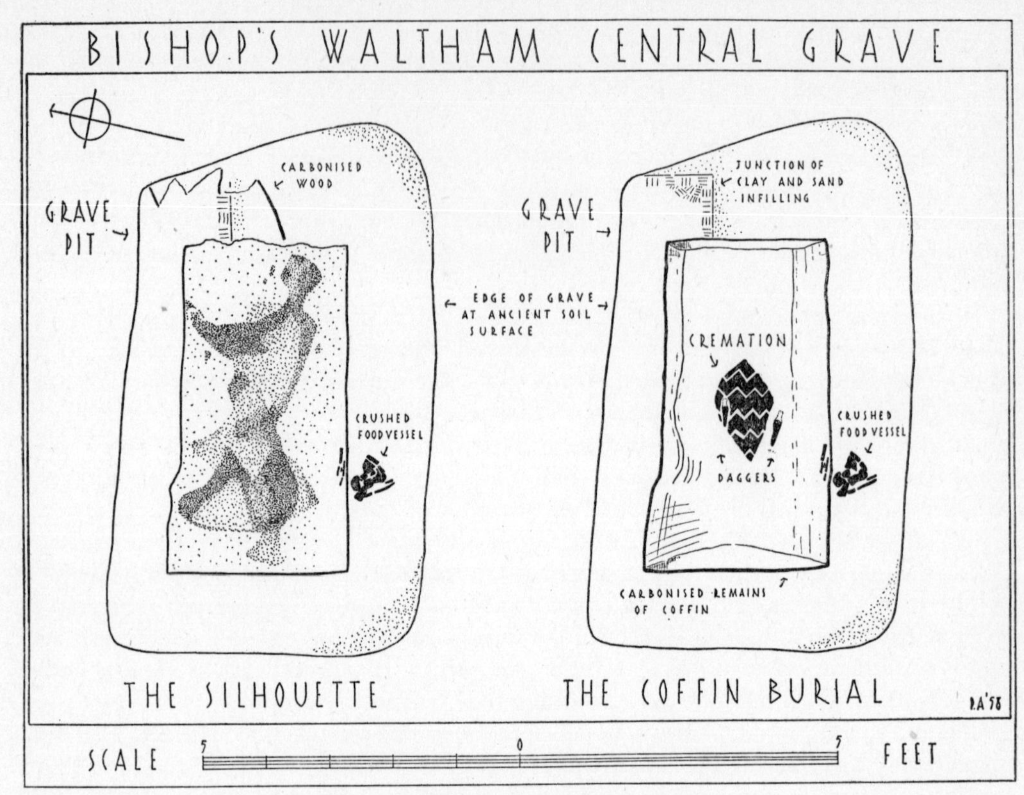

Fig. 27. The Bishop's Waltham burials.

In the centre was found a cremation which had been laid upon straw placed in the bottom of the coffin. It had been piled into a neat ovate heap and covered by a sheet of bast, which had also covered the daggers placed upon either side of it. At the side of the coffin was a food-vessel which had been crushed by soil settlement when the lid collapsed, as shown by broken pieces inside the coffin and pieces of carbonized wood also inside it. Above the cremation and inside the coffin was an anthropomorphic silhouette,[128] there having most probably been a double burial in the coffin.

Certain monoxylous timber coffins have been found to be boat-shaped, and indeed it is suggested by some that they were symbolic boats.[129] Others maintain it as likely that concepts analogous to those held in the ancient Orient regarding the Boat of the Dead [130] obtained in north-west European Bronze Age funerary ritual.

A boat-like coffin, its cover, and an actual canoe were unearthed when Loose Howe,[131] high on the eastern moorlands of Yorkshire, was explored in 1937. As the excavators struck the massive end of the coffin gallons of water poured out of it. When the lid was raised a black greasy substance was seen in which, apparently, the lineaments of the interment were invisible, although, curiously, it was claimed that 'there was evidence to show that the coffin had enclosed an inhumation at full length'.

[128] *Antiq.*, VII, 468.
[129] Elgee, 1930, 75.
[130] *Antiq.*, XV, 367, XVI, 160–74.
[131] *PPS*, XV, 87.

Examination of the coffin contents disclosed a fragment of foot-wrapping and a shoe, and the remains of a small bronze dagger were by the left hip. In the coffin were also three pieces of flint and hazel branches and the husks of nuts. The body, perhaps wrapped in a linen shroud, or in linen clothing, had been laid on what were considered to have been rushes, reeds, or straw. It will be remembered that traces of straw were found beneath the cremation in the Bishop's Waltham timber coffin, and may well have existed in many others.

In Loose Howe an inurned richly equipped warrior cremation burial was also found.[132]

Other coffins are considered to be boat-shaped. One containing a cremation at Scrubbity Coppice [133] in Cranborne Chase was square at one end, rounded at the other, and flat-bottomed. A full-size replica of this coffin was constructed at the behest of General Pitt-Rivers, who had excavated the barrow, and is to be seen in the Farnham Museum. Colt Hoare [134] described a coffin which he came upon in a barrow at Winterbourne Stoke as being a 'shallow wooden case of boat-like form'.

Because of the unsatisfactory nature of many early accounts, a precise description of composite timber coffins, made from planks of wood fitted together, is nearly impossible. These records continually refer to 'wooden boxes'.[135] However, although much decayed, the coffin found under a carefully excavated bell barrow at Pewit Farm in Berkshire [136] appears to have been made of separate planks. Similarly, the ephemeral remains of such a coffin have been revealed by skilled excavation in a site on the gravels near Oxford.[137] It is possible that such coffins were a much more regular feature of earlier barrow graves than has been generally thought, and that many have been overlooked because of uncritical excavation.

Indirect evidence of composite timber coffins lies in the grooving of stone cists. The side slabs of one such cist beneath a barrow on Samson (Pl. XIII a), in the Isles of Scilly,[138] had been grooved to receive the end slabs.[139] Similar cists, nine in number, have long been known near Ri Cruin in Argyllshire.[140] These grooved cists suggest the perpetuation in stone of features more normal to wood, as, for instance, the mortise and tenon joints at Stonehenge,[141] and the internal fittings of the well-known huts at Skara Brae in Orkney.[142]

Burials, both inhumations and cremations, have sometimes been placed in the grave on a simple plank of wood. Colt Hoare [143] records one from Amesbury G. 15, which has been described as the finest bell barrow near Stonehenge. Here the skeleton appears to have been lying on 'a plank of elm wood'. A similar plank has been noted from under the barrow Collingbourne Ducis, G. 12.[144] Here beneath the inhumation on the plank was a cremation. Greenwell met with a number of such burials in Yorkshire,[145] and the present writer examined a damaged example in a grave-pit under one of the Barnby Howes, also in Yorkshire.[146]

[132] *PPS*, XV, 95.
[133] Pitt-Rivers, 1887–98, II, 40.
[134] Hoare, 1812–19, I, 124.
[135] *PPS*, VII, 91.
[136] *TNDFC*, VIII, 110.
[137] *Oxon.*, VIII–IX, 34.
[138] *Antiq.*, II, 420.
[139] *Antiq.*, XV, 81–3.
[140] *PSAS*, LXIII, 161, LXIV, 146.
[141] Atkinson, 1956, 25, 176.
[142] Childe, 1931, 39.
[143] Hoare, 1812–19, I, 205–6.
[144] *WAM*, X, 91.
[145] Greenwell, 1877, 13–14.
[146] *YAJ*, XXXIX, 24.

The principle of placing burials on a plank appears to be allied to that of placing them, in the grave, on a bed of organic substances, such as moss, straw, rushes, hide, etc., rather than as a form of coffin burial.

A burial, with grave-furniture in the form of a beaker, tanged knife, riveted knife, and bracer, which had been covered by a low mound, at Dorchester, near Oxford,[147] had been buried in what is claimed as a wicker coffin.

Stone cists are, in essence, stone composite coffins. In its simplest form a cist consists of four slabs of stone set at right angles to one another, and covered by a fifth. Sometimes the sides may consist of more than one slab, as may the cover, while dry-walling is not unknown as a method of constructing the sides. Such cists may be set in a grave or upon the ancient surface beneath mound or cairn. In the north, as has been noted above, numbers of cists appear to have been flat graves, no definite trace of mounds or cairns being found above them.

Whether or not stone cists were a substitute for timber coffins in regions where suitable stone was plentiful is not clear. Stone cists have been found in places far removed from suitable stone, which has been transported. On the other hand, the skeuomorphic 'grooved' cists (Pl. XIII a, b) suggest that substitution may well have occurred in certain places.

A good example of a Highland Zone cist is that found beneath a cairn, 50 feet in diameter and 5 feet high, at Corston Beacon in Wales.[148] The cist was 6 feet long, 2 feet 6 inches wide, and of the same depth, and it was covered with large stones. The side stones of this cist overlapped one another. In it there had been an extended inhumation burial, accompanied by a dagger, of which little trace remained.

Cists beneath barrows, and others, were discussed by O. G. S. Crawford early in the life of *Antiquity*, and those in the Wessex area have been listed by Grinsell.[149] Professor Childe in his lists of Beaker and Food-Vessel burials in Scotland incidentally recorded cists, and listed certain cists, as did Sir Lindsay Scott in his work on the nature of prehistoric trade.[150] In Yorkshire, where numbers have been met with beneath barrows and as flat graves, Elgee [151] saw two forms, a larger and a smaller. This is a division which is in a general sense ubiquitous where cists occur. He noted that numbers of Yorkshire cists were beneath barrows, and that they had been inserted into the fabric of local long barrows.

On Kildale Moor in Yorkshire,[152] a square rock-cut grave had stones set round the bottom (Pl. XIII c), and a standing stone at each of two opposing corners. The grave had been infilled and a great stone slab had been laid above it, on the ancient surface. Around and above, the cairn had been built.

Stone settings such as these—and others, as for instance that which enclosed the burial in the barrow Sutton 268′[153]—should in no circumstances be confused with cists.

In graves, cists, and coffins, burials, both by inhumation and cremation, have been found to lie on what appear to have been prepared layers of materials, such as moss,

[147] *ANL*, IV, 58.
[148] *Arch. Camb.*, LXXXIII, 137–74.
[149] *Antiq.*, II, 419; *PPS*, VII, 103.
[150] Childe, 1946, 106–18; *PPS*, XVII, 71, XXIII, 74–90 (Wales).
[151] Elgee, 1933, 63.
[152] *YAJ*, XL, 179–92.
[153] *Arch.*, LXXXIX, 94.

reeds, rushes, straw, or cloth, or a plank of wood. Probably this practice was widespread, but has only been recognized where optimum conditions of preservation have obtained. Thus reeds and rushes were found in the Loose Howe coffin, straw in that from Bishop's Waltham,[154] moss under a burial in the barrow Amesbury G. 85,[155] and fern leaves at Shuttlestone, near Parwick in Derbyshire.[156]

Evidence of textiles[157] has been found in inhumation and cremation burials. As with other organic materials, our knowledge of them is scanty, but their use was probably more frequent than is normally supposed.

In the Kellythorpe cist,[158] cloth was said to have been under the entire length of the skeleton. While a shroud or clothing is not out of the question the practice noted above cannot be excluded. At Manton,[159] in the primary burial, the cloth is reported to have extended above the head. Here a shroud may be likely, but some kind of face covering, even perhaps a mask, such as was suggested by the carbonized wood at Cairnpapple,[160] is possible. At Rylston in Yorkshire[161] a trunk coffin held an inhumation which was 'enveloped in a woollen fabric reaching from head to foot'.

There is also some evidence that when inhumation burial was practised the dead went to the grave in articles of clothing. As well as the remains of textiles of both wool and substances of varied origins[162] there is the constant occurrence of buttons,[163] and in some cases pins.[164] Greenwell[165] and Mortimer[166] list the evidence for dress found in the large numbers of barrows that they explored. It would appear that the peoples represented there by beakers and food-vessels, probably one and the same, had clothing that buttoned in front. A male burial in Yorkshire[167] had a pair of buttons 6 inches apart at the outer side of each lower leg and ankle, suggesting some form of gaiter or spat.

Female and perhaps male hairdressing and securing is suggested by the bone pins in certain graves.[168] Under the skull of a female burial accompanied by a food-vessel, at Garton Slack in Yorkshire,[169] were 'fragments of string or fine rope, a little thicker than coarse worsted, made of two strands', and small pieces of woven fabric were also found suggesting some form of headdress.

Ear-rings have been found in certain graves[170] while small plugs were probably for insertion in the lips.[171] Both these articles sometimes appear to have been worn at the time of interment rather than to have been deposited as grave-furniture.

Cloth remains have also been recovered from cremation burial. The urn from Colt Hoare's Woodyates, Dorset, Barrow 17,[172] had eleven holes around the rim, presumably to enable a cover to be secured, and the actual remains of cloth were present. Another urn had a piece of cloth perhaps to block the mouth.[173] Indeed, the overhanging rim or 'crown' of a cinerary urn would facilitate the use of such a cover of cloth, leather, or the like, and this, incidentally, would be admirably suited for drumming! It must be

[154] *PPS*, XXIII, 162.
[155] *WAM*, XLV, 432–58.
[156] Bateman, 1861, 34–5
[157] *PPS*, XVI, 130–62.
[158] *Arch.*, XXXIV, 255.
[159] *WAM*, XXXV, 12.
[160] *PSAS*, LXXXII, 68.
[161] Greenwell, 1877, 376.
[162] *PPS*, XVI, 151–6.
[163] Childe, 1935, 172; Childe, 1947 b, s.v.
[164] Mortimer, 1905, xli.
[165] Greenwell, 1877, 31.
[166] Mortimer, 1905, xl.
[167] Mortimer, 1905, 85.
[168] Mortimer, 1905, xli.
[169] Mortimer, 1905, 328.
[170] *Oxon.*, XIII, 1.
[171] Elgee, 1930, 111 (Toggles).
[172] *Stourhead Cat.*, 253.
[173] *WAM*, XLVIII, 177.

admitted that little evidence for such practices exists. In many cases cinerary urns, if not inverted, were covered by flat stones[174] or, as in a barrow at Battlegore in Somerset,[175] by a shaped and rimmed lid of wood, or by a wooden slab, as at Crichel Down.[176]

In three instances cloth has been found mixed with cremations in a charred state. This may represent the remains of clothing burnt on a pyre, although judging from the condition of an average cremation one would expect it to be entirely consumed. There is some evidence for the deposition of cremations in bags[177] of woven grasses as well as of more normal materials, and indeed in baskets. Mortimer mentions what appears to have been a cylindrical basket, 1 foot 5 inches in diameter and 1 foot 4 inches high, as having contained a cinerary urn, in Barrow 241 of his Blanch group.[178]

All this evidence leads to the general conclusion that the differences in grave and burial rites of the Bronze Age are criteria which should be taken into as much account as pottery and other grave-furniture. Such variations reflect social change perhaps more clearly than grave-furniture. Early Bronze Age *single* or *individual* inhumation burial, contracted, flexed, or even supine, in coffin, cist, or grave, accompanied sometimes by satellite or secondary burials, under or in the same barrow, was the form of burial which, early in the second millennium B.C., superseded the *impersonal collective* rites of the Neolithic communities. In exceptional circumstances the rite of extended inhumation was used also. Later, in what is termed by some the Middle Bronze Age, inhumation gave way to similar single, primary, satellite, or secondary depositions of cremated bones. This seems to be due in part to the development and expansion of those groups termed *Secondary Neolithic*.

[174] *Arch J.*, XCIX, 15.
[175] *PSANHS*, LXXVII, 7–36.
[176] *Arch.*, XC, 61–2.
[177] *PDNHAS*, XXVI, 29.
[178] Mortimer, 1905, 328.

CHAPTER VIII

GRAVE-FURNITURE

THE GRAVES beneath barrows were often furnished. This means that when the burial took place, whether by inhumation or after cremation, objects, presumably significators or for use in a nether world, were placed in the grave.

As distinct from objects and materials which are clearly the remains of dress or cerements, the considerable and heterogeneous grave-furniture can be ordered into four approximate categories. These are: *tools and weapons*, *ornaments of the person*, *equipment of ritual and parade*, and *ceramics*. This last comprises a wide and disparate range of vessels. Often such vessels appear to have contained food and drink offerings. Others, chiefly 'urns', contained, or were inverted over, cremation burials. Upon a functional basis these urns should be classed with coffins, but they have for long been bracketed with such pots as are more clearly grave-*furniture*, and there is no purpose in altering customary usage. In graves, the prehistorian sometimes meets with natural objects, animal bones and the like, these being frequently, for want of a better term, called *ritual deposits*.

The artefacts which furnished barrow graves are regularly used to illustrate the divisions of the Bronze Age. By means of classification and the subsequent formulation of typological sequences, they are brought into chorological and chronological order. Upon such bases rest, in great measure, our concepts of the Bronze Age.

While it is generally assumed that objects deposited with the remains of a person were used during his lifetime, both obviously new and unused artefacts and also very worn and abraded articles have been found. Refinements of typology suggest that the latter may have been heirlooms. If several objects are found to have been placed in the grave at the time of burial, they are considered to have been in current use together and thus to be contemporary. This is an example of *association*.

Not all burials were accompanied by grave-furniture, and not all barrows covered furnished burials. As complete and reliable barrow excavations are the exception rather than the rule, it is difficult to assess the precise proportion of barrows which covered furnished burials in relation to those which covered unfurnished burials. However, some early archaeologists recorded the relative numbers of furnished and unfurnished *burials*. Of the 379 burials examined by Greenwell[1] only 94 were accompanied by objects. Mortimer's tables[2] show that in the 288 Yorkshire barrows dug into by him, most of which covered more than one burial, 300 burials were furnished while 258 were not. Mortimer also commented upon the relative rarity of bronze implements in the

[1] Greenwell, 1877, 51.

[2] Mortimer, 1905, 398–442.

Wold barrows, only 25 being found, the majority of which were awls. In Wiltshire, as has recently been shown,[3] 147 cremations had an object buried with them and 140 had not.

In inhumation graves it seems likely that grave-furnishings were put to hand, or, in the case of certain categories, attached to the body as in life. Thus the position in the grave of battle-axe or sceptre might suggest that the shaft was placed in the dead man's hands; [4] while his dagger was almost certainly at his waist.[5] Insignia have been found on a man's chest [6] and ear-rings at a youth's ears.[7]

In cremation graves furnishings were comparably placed. Thus a dagger has been found wrapped and laid on a cremation,[8] while two had been put in a coffin prior to a cremation, this being heaped above them.[9] In female graves such objects as a miniature vessel, an awl, and beads were placed by cremations.[10] Such cremation graves must, initially, have been infilled with considerable care as grave-furniture often appears to be undisplaced.

Objects found with burials had sometimes been broken, presumably intentionally, before interment. Thus pommels have been snapped from dagger-hilts,[11] a beaker smashed and the pieces placed around a person's head,[12] flint implements fractured,[13] and in the mound of one barrow three broken bronze flanged axes were found.[14] Whether in this last instance the axes were associated with a secondary or a satellite burial is not clear.

Objects found with cremations are often fire-twisted, having been burned, or exposed to not inconsiderable heat, presumably on the funeral pyre. It seems likely that some of these relatively frail objects were in the fire for only a short time, as prolonged exposure to heat would have fused them out of all recognition. Some of the small bronze scraps sometimes found with cremations [15] may be all that is left of knives, daggers, etc., and the possibility should not be overlooked that apparently unaccompanied cremated bones are all that is left of bodies initially accompanied by objects consumed in the pyre.

Grave-furniture is normally considered in terms of relatively durable artefacts such as bronze daggers, stone battle-axes, and pottery vessels. The evidence from regions where there are better conditions of preservation [16] shows that in Britain we see mostly the bare bones of prehistory. Not only did the dead go to the grave clothed, but we can also sometimes see traces of head cushions and even mattresses in the layers of organic material occasionally detected beneath skeletons.[17] Much grave-furniture, or vital parts thereof, would be made of materials which would normally leave little trace, but which can at times be detected by skilled excavation. Thus daggers and knives were hafted,[18] sheathed,[19] or sometimes carefully wrapped before committal to the grave, battle-axes and sceptres were shafted,[20] as were most probably certain spears,[21] and there was a

[3] *VCH Wilts*, I (Part I), 231–40.
[4] Cunnington, 1929, 42.
[5] Hoare, 1812–19, 203.
[6] Hoare, 1812–19, 203.
[7] *Oxon.*, XLIII, 1.
[8] *WAM*, LVI, 237–40.
[9] *PPS*, XXIII, 149.
[10] Amesbury G. 61 a (disc barrow), *WAM*, LVI, 237–40.
[11] Amesbury G. 58, *WAM*, LVI, 237–40; *Arch. Camb.*, LXXXIII, 137–74.
[12] *Arch.*, LXXXIX, 94.
[13] Mortimer, 1905, 59, 162.
[14] Curwen, 1954, 151, Pl. xiv.
[15] Mortimer, 1905, 109.
[16] *PPS*, XXI, 104.
[17] *PPS*, XV, 90, XXIII, 148–9.
[18] *PPS*, XXIII, 164–5.
[19] Hoare, 1812–19, I, 207; Greenwell, 1877, 359.
[20] Cunnington, 1929, 42; *PPS*, IV, 87.
[21] Grinsell, *The Archaeology of Wessex*, Methuen, 1958, 129.

XVa and b. The Bush Barrow daggers (proportionate sizes). Lengths: (a) 13 inches; (b) 10·6 inches.

XVc. The Snowshill ogival dagger; length 8·4 inches.

XVd. The Snowshill spear-head. Length 9·4 inches.

XVIa. The Ridgeway (Dorset) gold pommel (2/1).

XVIb. The Hammeldon pommel and its cruciform *pointillé* ornamentation (2/1 approx.), from above.

XVIc. The Hammeldon pommel: side view showing repair of edge and underside (2/1 approx.).

XVIIa. Necked Beaker axe-hammer (Type I); length 5·7 inches.

XVIIb. Hove-Snowshill battle-axe, Snowshill; length 6·1 inches.

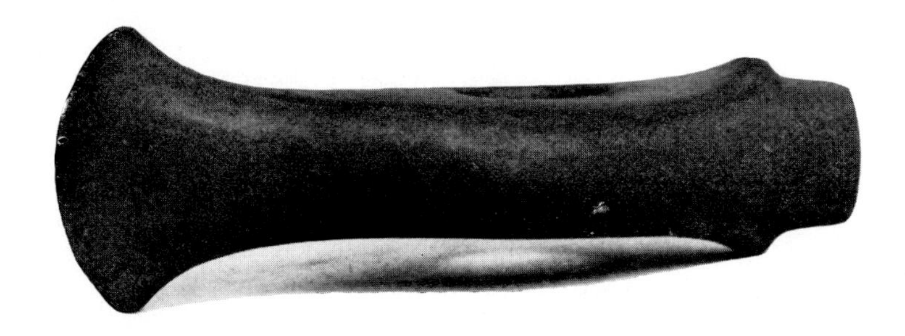

XVIIc. Stourton-Loose Howe battle-axe; length 6·3 inches.

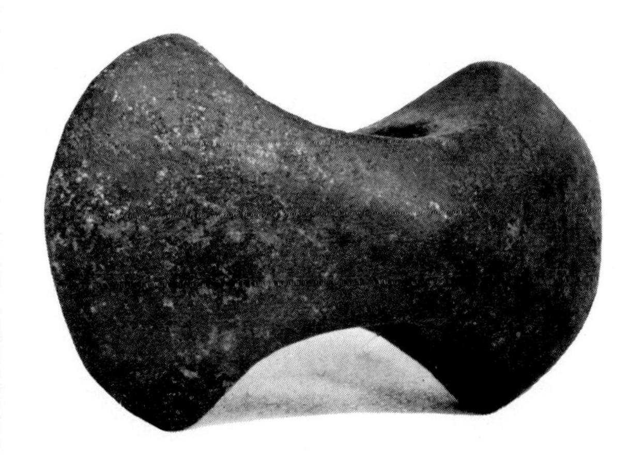

XVIId. Wilsford-Crichie battle-axe; length 4 inches.

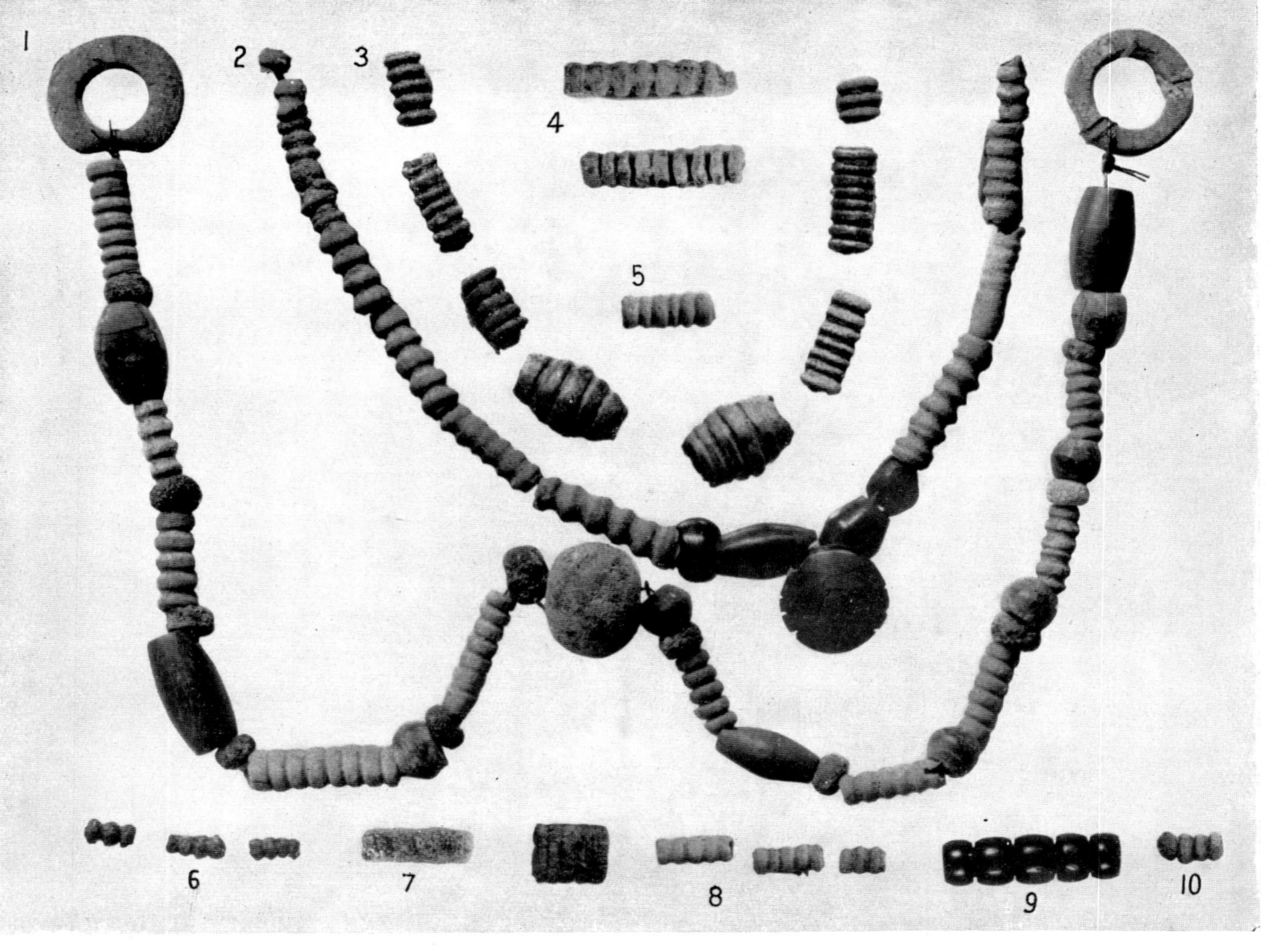

XVIII. British segmented faience beads (1/1). 1. Upton Lovell, Wiltshire (Devizes Museum). 2. Figheldean, Wiltshire (British Museum). 3. Boscregan, St Just in Penwith, Cornwall (British Museum). 4. Wilsford G. 54, Wiltshire (British Museum). 5. Easton Down, Winterslow, Wiltshire (Salisbury Museum). 6. Amesbury G. 54, Wiltshire (Devizes Museum). 7. Doll Tor, Stanton Moor, Derbyshire. 8. Crinoid and associated beads; Aldbourne G. 5, Wiltshire (Devizes Museum). 9. Jet bead; Lockton Pastures, Yorkshire (Yorkshire Museum, York). 10. Segmented

wooden club in one Yorkshire grave.[22] The remains of a composite shield, wooden with bronze fitments, are recorded from a Wessex barrow.[23] An oak boat-bowl, embellished with gold ornament, from a Welsh bog [24] suggests composite wooden vessels, which have not as yet been detected in entirety. Certain food-vessels are clearly derived from wooden prototypes [25] and turned amber and shale cups [26] can only be luxury versions of their more normal wooden or pottery fellows. Beads, where their relative positions are recorded,[27] imply strings, while such things as archers' wrist-guards were mounted on leather, or some such substance, for attachment to the wrist.[28]

That barrows covered burials, sometimes furnished, has long been known, and they have suffered accordingly. Medieval treasure-seeking commissions digging into barrows may have met with the success that their recurrence suggests.[29] It may be that research in appropriate quarters would reveal the report of such a commission, although it is doubtful if a barrow's contents would be detailed. Stukeley was one of the first to excavate and record in detail a barrow's contents [30] although, almost two centuries before, one of Leland's correspondents [31] had noted 'yerthen pottes with the mouthes turnid douneward' when cairns in Anglesey were destroyed. A barrow near Stonehenge [32] was the scene of Stukeley's investigation. He pronounced its occupant 'a heroin, for we found the head of her javelin in brass'. Colt Hoare, aided by Cunnington, filled his cabinets with the often exotic relics of the Wessex culture, and his folios with descriptions and drawings of them. Although many of these early accounts of grave-furniture are reasonably objective when considered against the state of knowledge of their time, little progress could be made until the methodology of the Dane, Thomsen, was applied.[33]

Thurnam's monograph 'On Ancient British Barrows ... (Part II. Round Barrows)', published in 1871,[34] is the basis of all subsequent study of barrow grave-furniture. Not only did he set in sensible order the external forms of round barrows (Chapter II), but here for the first time is a scientific functional and typological description and classification of their contents. After nearly a century this work is still essential to serious study.

The following year (1872) saw the initial publication of Sir John Evans's *Ancient Stone Implements*, which included numbers of artefacts from barrow graves. The methods of classification, borrowed from geology and palaeontology, were to bear even finer fruit nine years later, in 1881, when the same writer brought out *Ancient Bronze Implements*, relying again upon barrow graves for certain of his categories.

Archaeology owes more, perhaps, to these works of Thurnam and Evans than is generally realized. By their methods it ceased to be a cultured diversion of the squirearchy and became a science in its own right. They were honoured, and their names are writ large in the Victorian Valhalla of the Natural Sciences beneath the Puginesque Gothic roof of the Blackmore Room in Wiltshire's Salisbury Museum.

Here the matter rested until Abercromby,[35] extending Thurnam's work, sought out

[22] Greenwell, 1877, 278.
[23] Hoare, 1812–19, 202.
[24] Grimes, 1939, 83, 171.
[25] Childe, 1935, 92; *PPS*, I, 83; Clark, 1952, 206.
[26] *WAM*, XLIV, 111–17.
[27] *PSAS*, LXIII, 164 ff.
[28] Mortimer, 1905, 274.
[29] Grinsell, 1953, 110.
[30] Stukeley, 1740, 45, Tab. XXXII.
[31] Clark, 1947, 19.
[32] Stukeley, 1740, 45, Tab. XXXII.
[33] C. J. Thomsen, *Ledetraad til Nordisk Oldkyndighed*, Copenhagen, 1836.
[34] *Arch.*, XLIII, 285–552.
[35] Abercromby, 1912.

and classified Bronze Age pottery, first in monographs [36] and then, definitively, in the two volumes of his *Bronze Age Pottery*. To Abercromby we owe the innovation of the near Teutonic term 'beaker' [37] in place of the 'drinking-cup' usage of Colt Hoare and Thurnam.

Besides ceramics, other artefacts have been studied with considerable precision during the past four decades. Notable are Newall's list of amber and shale cups,[38] Fox and Grimes's account and list of flat daggers and knives,[39] Newall's list and appreciation of ogival daggers,[40] Smith's work on battle-axes [41] and arrow-heads,[42] Beck and Stone's definitive publication of faience beads,[43] Ó Ríordáin's comprehensive consideration of British and European halberds,[44] Piggott's definition of the Wessex culture,[45] and ApSimon's ordering of the Wessex daggers.[46] Besides all these there are excavation reports and works on specific localities [47] which enumerate and describe, often in considerable detail, artefacts from barrows. The British Association's Card Index of Bronze Implements includes those from barrows,[48] while recently a Register of Bronze Age Pottery has been embarked upon.[49]

Apart from implements clearly representative of an industrial process, such as woodworking saws, it is difficult to distinguish certain tools from weapons. Stone battle-axes or bronze halberds can be used only in the chase or for martial purposes, but a bronze axe has potentialities as a woodworker's tool. A dagger can be either a hunter's weapon or a flayer's knife.

The tools and weapons can, however, be approximately differentiated, according to their apparent manner of use.

(*a*) Stabbing and cutting implements, namely daggers, spear-heads, knives, razors, etc., and their ancillaries.
(*b*) Missile points and archers' equipment.
(*c*) Striking appliances, namely axes, adzes, battle-axes, maces, halberds, etc.
(*d*) Industrial equipment.

Recently [50] the term 'dagger' has been restricted to implements with a blade length of between 5 and 13 inches. Smaller blades have been termed 'knives' or 'knife-daggers', following Thurnam. This distinction is often difficult to maintain as sometimes quite small blades have the precise lineaments of larger daggers. However, Occam's razor has been applied and normal methods of classification have been followed. It should be noted that no reliable accounts exist recording the discovery of rapiers or swords [51] in barrow graves. One would expect that had they ever been placed in graves one would have been disinterred under reasonably reliable conditions.

Four principal types of bronze daggers and knives have been recovered from barrow graves. Refinements of classification show sub-types within certain of the groups, and allied to them are a series of hybrids, derivatives, and copies in flint. First of all there are

[36] *JRAI*, XXXII, 391 ff.; *PSAS*, XXXVIII, 323–410.
[37] Abercromby, 1912, I, 17.
[38] *WAM*, XLIV, 111–17.
[39] *Arch. Camb.*, LXXXIII, 137–74.
[40] *WAM*, XLV, 432.
[41] *Arch.*, LXXV, 77–108.
[42] *Arch.*, LXXVI, 82–106.
[43] *Arch.*, LXXXV, 203.
[44] *Arch.*, LXXXVI, 195.
[45] *PPS*, IV, 52–106.
[46] *ULIAA Rpt*, X, 37–62.
[47] *VCH*; County Archaeology Series (Methuen), etc.
[48] *PFIC*, 145–7.
[49] *ANL*, VI, 11.
[50] *Antiq.*, XXVII, 67–78.
[51] *PPS*, XVII, 195–213.

the tanged daggers termed *West European*,[52] then the class of *Riveted Knife-Daggers* defined by Fox and Grimes,[53] thirdly the almost exclusively Wessex group termed the *Bush Barrow Type*,[54] and lastly the distinctive ogival daggers recently named *Camerton-Snowshill Type*.[55]

Tanged, or West European, daggers (Fig. 28) which are normally associated with 'B', or Bell, beakers, have been found, together with archers' equipment, in inhumation

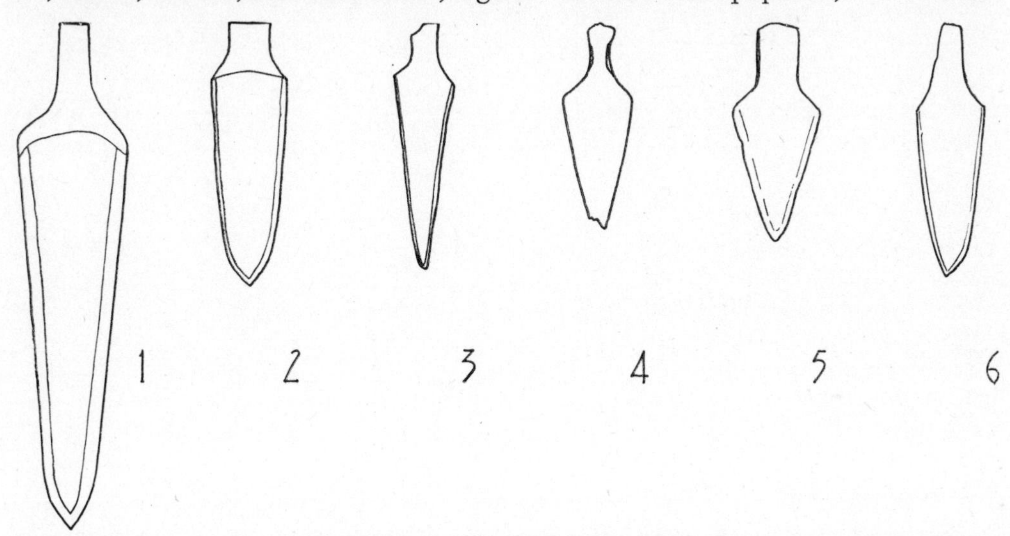

Fig. 28. West European tanged daggers (1/4). 1, Roundway; 2, 3, Winterslow; 4, Dorchester (Oxon.); 5, North-east Scotland; 6, Mere.

graves under low mounds in Wiltshire[56] and Oxfordshire.[57] Although they have been called 'flat', a recent re-examination has demonstrated their complex workmanship and hollow-ground edges.[58] The renowned example from Roundway[59] (Pl. XIV a) is 10 inches in length, this being exceptional as their length is normally about 4 or 5 inches. Beaten-up tang flanges on a dagger from Dorchester, Site XII,[60] suggests hilt- or tang-plates, while one from Sittingbourne[61] had not only a flanged tang but also a single rivet through it, presumably to secure plates. Most of the daggers appear to retain their original form and are unwhetted. Although found mainly in southern England, an example is known from Scotland.[62] Scrutiny of the unpublished material in museums would probably reveal many more.

Flat riveted knife-daggers (Fig. 29) range from the large northern series, one or two being almost 8 inches in length, to small blades about 2 inches long, thin, and sometimes whetted down. Research would possibly detect local variants. It was pointed out in 1938 that Fox and Grimes's list included daggers not strictly flat,[63] and the examination of such daggers shows that while reasonably flat ones such as the distinctive and classic

[52] Childe, 1930, 78.
[53] *Arch. Camb.*, LXXXIII, 137 74.
[54] A. M. ApSimon, *ULIAA Rpt*, X, 37–62.
[55] A. M. ApSimon, *ULIAA Rpt*, X, 42.
[56] Hoare, 1812–19, I, 44; *WAM*, III, 186; *Arch.*, *XLIII*, 449.
[57] *ANL*, IV, 58.
[58] *WAM*, LV, 135–8.
[59] *WAM*, III, 185–6.
[60] *ANL*, IV, 58.
[61] *PSA*, X, 29.
[62] Childe, 1935, Fig. 23, 2.
[63] *PPS*, IV, 59.

examples from Homington[64] and East Kennet,[65] in Wiltshire, are to be found, many, including even small knives, are medially thickened. A few of these daggers or knives have been found with their hilts or remnants thereof.[66] Such hilts usually consisted of two separate wooden (Pl. XIV b) or antler plates riveted to the blade and perhaps stuck, or secured together with numerous smaller decorative rivets and fitted with a trough pommel. A fine hilted dagger from Brigmerston[67] (Pl. XIV c) in Wiltshire has long

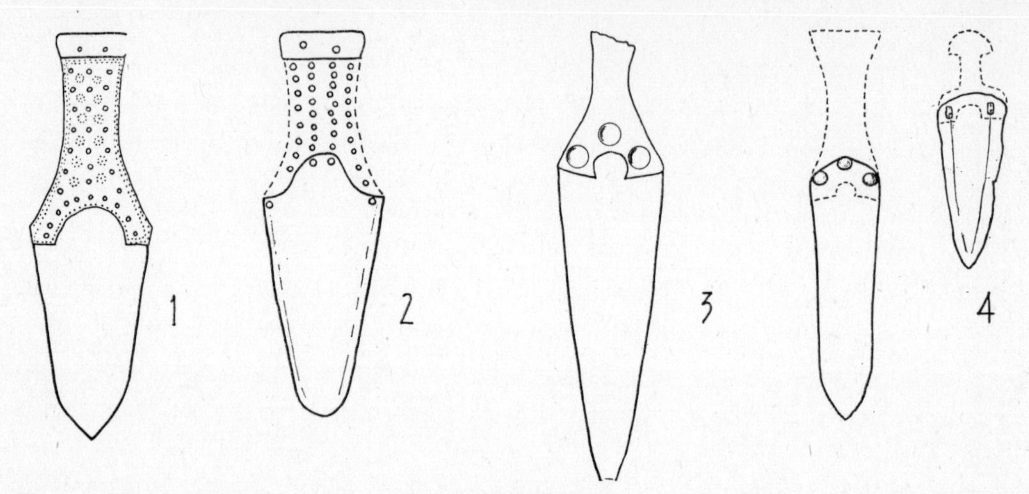

Fig. 29. Flat riveted knife-daggers (1/4). 1, Brigmerston; 2, Garton Slack; 3, Corston Beacon; 4, Bishop's Waltham.

been known, and there is another closely resembling it from Garton Slack[68] in Yorkshire. These riveted hilts, which are the exception rather than the rule, appear to be simplified versions of the complex *pointillé* hilts of the Bush Barrow and Breton type of dagger. The plates of composite unriveted hilts found at Corston Beacon[69] and Amesbury[70] lacked pommels. The pommel had clearly been snapped from the latter hilt before burial.

Obviously copying certain of the broad, flat, riveted bronze knife-daggers is a series of flint daggers. Initially noted by Evans[71] they were discussed by R. A. Smith[72] and given final precision by Grimes.[73] Besides apparently simple leaf-shaped blades (perhaps spear-heads), there were two forms, one suitable for direct use, the other for hafting. Notches and marked tangs facilitated the fitting of a haft, perhaps of leather. A flint dagger, hafted and in its sheath, recovered from a German bog,[74] resembles our series and shows how they were hafted and sheathed.

Bush Barrow type daggers (Fig. 30_1) have a triangular blade, flat or with a well-defined mid-rib (Pl. XV a, b). Sometimes a small tang is present, though this never carries rivets. These, six in number, are set in almost a straight line across a broad

[64] *PSA*, IV, 329.
[65] *Arch. J.*, XXIV, 29.
[66] *PPS*, XXIII, 164–5.
[67] Hoare, 1812–19, I, 195.
[68] Mortimer, 1905, 230–2.
[69] *Arch. Camb.*, LXXXIII, 137–74.
[70] *WAM*, LVI, 237–40.
[71] Evans, 1897, 349–54.
[72] *PSA*, XXXII, 6–22.
[73] *PPSEA*, VI, 340–55.
[74] *PPS*, III, 178–9.

shallow heel. Certain of these daggers were formidable weapons when hafted. A hiltless blade from Cranborne, in Dorchester Museum, is 12·75 inches in length, and the larger of the Bush Barrow blades is 13 inches in length.[75] A blade from Idmiston[76] is only 5·5 inches long. Whether the hafts of these daggers were composite or one-piece is not clear. The wooden shaft fragment from the Bush Barrow bore a zigzag pattern executed in minute gold pins driven flush with the surface. A drawing made at the time

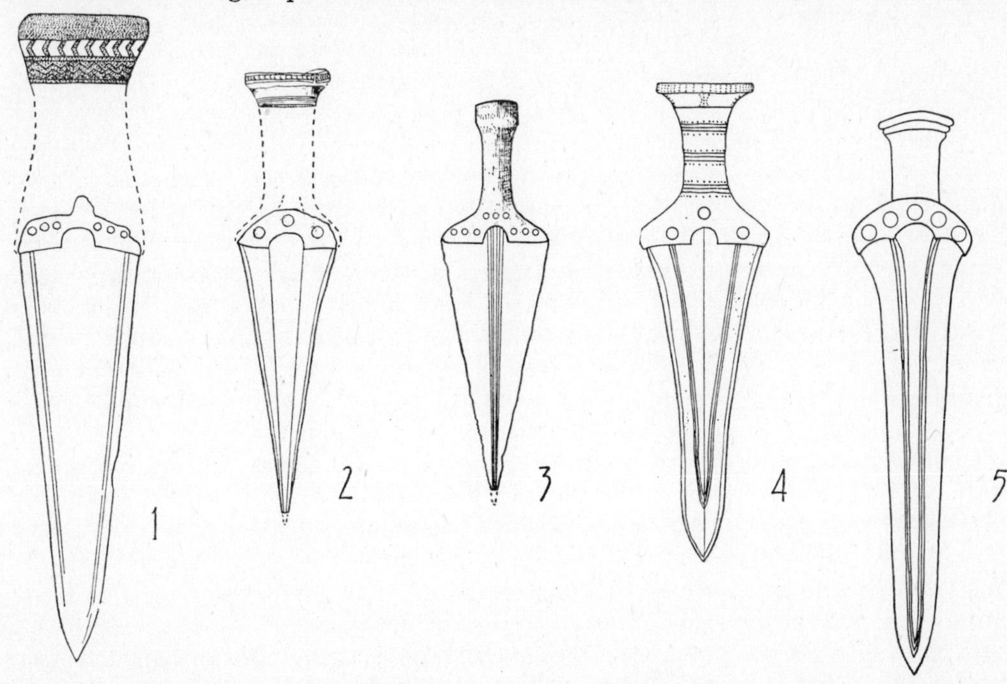

Fig. 30. Bush Barrow and ogival daggers (1/4 approx.). 1, Bush Barrow; 2, Ridgeway Barrow 7; 3, Angus, Wester Mains of Auchterhouse; 4, Camerton-Snowshill blade with a conjectural hilt restoration; 5, Roke Down.

of its discovery shows that it resembled such hilts as that from Brigmerston. *Pointillé* decoration was not restricted to hilts, but was often executed by punch-marks on blade mid-ribs, not only on Bush Barrow daggers but also on some of the ogival class. Several barrow graves in Dorset and Wiltshire have yielded these exceptional weapons, while one has been found in Norfolk, and four in Yorkshire.[77]

A number of daggers from sites distant from Wessex appear to have been allied to or influenced by the Bush Barrow daggers. Three from Scottish cairns had ribbed golden pommel-mounts. The best preserved example, from Collessie,[78] shows that these daggers must have had trough pommels not dissimilar from those of Wessex. A triple-reeded, mid-ribbed dagger from a grave in Angus[79] (Fig. 30_3) has an antler hilt resembling closely the metal hilts of the European mainland.

Daggers of the ogival Camerton-Snowshill type (Fig. 30_4, $_5$), initially listed by

[75] Hoare, 1812–19, I, 77.
[76] Evans, 1881, Fig. 296.
[77] ApSimon, *ULIAA Rpt*, X, 54–5.
[78] Anderson, 1886, 5–10.
[79] *PSAS*, XXXII, 205–20.

Newall,[80] are homogeneous in form, and relatively numerous. Although near-triangular blades are known, they are usually of curved outline (thus ogival) and incised or cast grooves are found on either face. A stout, relatively broad, mid-rib (Fig. 30_2) reinforces these blades, which were secured to their hilts by three stout rivets. The third, central, rivet is lacking from some specimens and it is difficult to tell whether or not it was originally present. No fewer than nine blades of this series bear upon their mid-ribs *pointillé* decorations.[81] A blade from Great Torrington[82] in Devon is 9·25 inches long, and one ploughed from a barrow at Winterbourne St Martin, now in Dorchester Museum, 9 inches. Though few are smaller than 6 inches in length, a miniature blade from Wilsford[83] only 3·4 inches in length is of note.

Although most of these daggers were recovered from graves, some, as at Chippenham Barrow I,[84] within recent years, few pommels have been found. Such is their rarity that it can be suspected that they may have been broken from daggers before consignment to the grave. An oval cross-sectioned pommel of sheet gold (Pl. XVI a) (Fig. 30_2) was found in association with three daggers, allied to the ogival class, in Ridgeway, Barrow 7,[85] in Dorset. Similar to this is the large amber pommel from Hammeldon Down[86] in Devon (Pl. XVI b, c), also found with fragments of a near-ogival dagger. Instead of a socket for the hilt-plates, like the trough pommels, there is a tenon for securing it to the haft. Wrought from a single block of amber, it bears on its end a cruciform design, and on its edges and underside lines executed in gold pins. This is an adaptation of the Bush Barrow *pointillé* technique to a different and more obdurate medium. Such was the value of this pommel that it had been repaired with gold pins, perhaps even by the craftsman who made it. Oval pommels have been found made of bone,[87] and small knives from the Manton[88] and the Winterbourne Stoke[89] barrows had small oval amber pommels. A dirk from Roke Down[90] in Dorset, with a blade allied to the ogival form, had a hilt of antler or some such material. It was destroyed in a fire, but a likeness was preserved which is sufficiently accurate to show that it is an example of a European series[91] of normally metal-hilted dirks. There can be little doubt that all these oval pommels of amber, gold, and antler are copies of the metal-hilted daggers of the European mainland as collected by Uenze.[92]

The principal concentration of ogival daggers is in Wessex, but examples are known from Cornwall and Yorkshire. Outstanding and well-known specimens are from Arreton Down, now in Carisbrooke Museum, and Camerton,[93] and from Snowshill[94] (Pl. XV c). At this last place the dagger blade was associated in the grave with a battle-axe and a tanged and ferruled spear-head (Pl. XV d). Dagger and spear-head were both clearly the work of the same craftsman.

Sometimes daggers were consigned to the grave in their sheaths or wrapped in various materials, and sometimes the scabbard hooks, by means of which sheathed

[80] *WAM*, XLV, 448–58.
[81] ApSimon, *ULIAA Rpt*, X, 57–9.
[82] *TDA*, VII, 102.
[83] *Arch.*, XLIII (ii), Pl. XXXIV, 4.
[84] *Ant. J.*, XV, 61; *PCAS*, XXXI, 134.
[85] *PDNHAS*, LVIII, 20–1.
[86] *Ant. J.*, XVIII, 313.
[87] *PDNHAS*, LVIII, Pl. VI, 9; Evans, 1881, 228, Fig. 283.
[88] *WAM*, XXXV, 1.
[89] Hoare, 1812–19, I, 124.
[90] Evans, 1881, 233.
[91] *Germania*, XXVI, 4.
[92] Uenze, 1938.
[93] *Arch.*, XLIII, 169.
[94] *Arch.*, LII, 70–2.

daggers were allegedly suspended from belt, girdle, or sling, have come to light. Whetstones fairly frequently accompany daggers, although examination of large numbers of the larger daggers suggests sparing use of these, only small knives apparently being regularly whetted.[95]

A long flat dagger from Fovant[96] is recorded as having been found in a wooden scabbard, and the remains of one of the same material were detected with the piece of a small riveted knife-dagger in a barrow grave at Roundway.[97] Mortimer noticed that a dagger which was with a contracted burial on Acklam Wold[98] bore traces of a scabbard. The larger of the Bush Barrow daggers was found in a wooden sheath, presumably suspended, for parade purposes because of its flimsy nature, from the magnificent scabbard hook from the same grave.[99] A similar dagger was in a Yorkshire barrow[100] enclosed in a bronze sheath seen as a green powder, while a wooden Scottish sheath from Collessie[101] in Fife appeared to have been hide-covered. At least three other ogival daggers were recorded as being sheathed when found, but the details of the materials are only assumptions.

Daggers were wrapped presumably to assure their safe-keeping. Mortimer saw traces of such wrapping around the Towthorpe[102] dagger. He described it as 'dark matter, resembling decayed and compressed leaves'. A knife-dagger from a bell barrow at Amesbury,[103] recently excavated by the present writer, had a fur sheath, its texture being preserved by the processes of oxidization, and it had been wrapped in moss and then in finely woven cloth.

Besides the unique golden scabbard hook from the Bush Barrow, more modest hooks, often described as of bone, but, as far as can be seen, of antler, have been found in a few graves. All are carefully made. Colt Hoare took one from one of the Normanton barrows,[104] another from Wath, in the East Riding of Yorkshire, is illustrated by Thurnam,[105] and recently one has come to light from a small barrow on Broxa Moor,[106] also in Yorkshire.

Whetstones were with a number of Wessex daggers of both types. Some were perforated and some unperforated, the former having often countersunk holes and careful finish. That from Camerton[107] was square in section, while one from Brigmerston[108] was broad and flat. One from Normanton[109] had carefully finished convex surfaces, the perforation being in the end lug. Two Wessex whetstones, one from Amesbury, the other a more dubious specimen from Upton Lovell, have, in recent years, been examined petrologically.[110] The former was considered likely to be a siliceous hornstone, the latter slate.

The dagger-wielding warrior class may have worn leather caps[111] of which the bell-helmets[112] are a rendering in metal. At least four such bronze bell-helmets appear to have been found early in the nineteenth century by men digging for

[95] *Arch.*, LII, 67 (Fig.); *Arch. Camb.*, LXIV, 211–220, LXXXI, 356.
[96] *DMC*, II, 25.
[97] *WAM*, III, 185; *Arch.*, XLIII, 289, Fig. 7; Forssander, 1936, 64.
[98] Mortimer, 1905, 87–8.
[99] Hoare, 1812–19, I, 207.
[100] Mortimer, 1905, 5.
[101] Anderson, 1886.
[102] Mortimer, 195, 5.
[103] *WAM*, LVI, 237–40 (interim).
[104] Hoare, 1812–19, I, 200, Pl. XXIV.
[105] *Arch.*, XLIII, 441, Fig. 144.
[106] *ANL*, III, 37.
[107] *Arch.*, XLIII, 169.
[108] Hoare, 1812–19, I, 194.
[109] Hoare, 1812–19, 199.
[110] *PPS*, XVII, 146.
[111] *Germania*, XXVI, 115–16.
[112] *PPS*, XVIII, 36–46.

limestone on Ogmore Down [113] in Glamorganshire, apparently during the destruction of a barrow.

Spear-heads were an extension of the dagger principle. Numbers have been found in Britain, mostly in hoards or singly, and numerous types have been identified.[114] Tanged spear-heads, to which is closely allied the tanged and ferruled spear-head from Snowshill,[115] which appears to be the only authenticated spear-head from a barrow grave, closely resemble the triangular (Bush Barrow) and ogival (Camerton-Snowshill) daggers. Many bear *pointillé* decoration on their mid-ribs, as do certain daggers. A small heat-twisted, socketed, and basal-looped spear-head was reported by Thurnam [116] as being from a cremation burial under one of the Wilsford barrows. Subsequent work has shown this identification to be incorrect.[117]

The name razors has been given to implements thought to be for shaving and therefore indicative of a male grave, numbers of which have been recovered, mostly from cremations. One from Priddy was described by Skinner [118] as 'sharp enough to mend a pen'. Classified and assigned to the Later Bronze Age by C. M. Piggott,[119] they have recently been shown as having been current earlier.[120] Indeed, the so-called pin from Roundway may well be an early example, and should be compared with such narrow-tanged blades as those from Kirkcaldy,[121] Fifeshire, and Well Glass Spring Cairn, Co. Londonderry.[122] The Priddy razor, now lost, was in a wooden sheath when found, as was an example from Laughton's Knowe, Holm Parish, Orkney Mainland.[123] The Kirkcaldy blade apparently had a haft of hazelwood.

Certain razors have thin oval blades and flat perforated tangs, and are decorated with patterns of triangles and lozenges.[124] Similar blades, tangless, with rivet holes at the base, and undecorated, have been found in Beaker contexts.[125] A localized type is met with in Northern Ireland.[126] In view of the early affinities of these razors or knives it is possible that this bronze form was a metal perpetuation of the distinctive flint plano-convex knives.[127] These knives, found mainly with food-vessels, although a variant with Secondary Neolithic affinities has recently been recognized,[128] are broad, more or less oval, or roughly triangular, flint-flakes, smooth on the bulbar face, but skilfully pressure-flaked on the upper surface.

Neolithic and Bronze Age flint arrow-heads were described, and their associations listed, by R. A. Smith [129] following Evans.[130] The flint arrow-heads found in barrow graves are almost exclusively barbed and tanged. They were made with either short or long barbs. Smith urged that a definite Beaker type of barbed and tanged arrow-head be recognized, this being comparatively small in size and having the barbs and tang terminating at the same level. Apart from this there were, he claimed, two tendencies, to exaggerate the length and breadth of the tang at the expense of the barbs, or to diminish the tang and prolong the barbs into swallow-tail curves. Arrow-heads with the latter tendency are rather rare.

[113] *Arch.*, XLIII, 553–5, Pl. XXXVI.
[114] *Arch.*, LXI, 439–72, LXXXIII, 187–202.
[115] *Arch.*, LII, 70–2.
[116] *Arch.*, XLIII, 447, Fig. 153.
[117] *PPS*, VII, 130.
[118] *Arch. J.*, XVI, 151.
[119] *PPS*, XII, 121–41.
[120] Butler and Smith, *ULIAA Rpt*, XII, 20–52.
[121] *PSAS*, LXXVIII, 109.
[122] *UJA*, I, Pl. XX.
[123] *PSAS*, LXXXI, 173, Pl. XX, 2.
[124] *PSAS*, X, 431.
[125] Butler and Smith, *ULIAA Rpt*, XII, 28.
[126] Childe, 1947 b, 154–5.
[127] *Ant. J.*, XII, 158–62.
[128] Atkinson, Piggott, and Sandars, 1951, 71–2.
[129] *Arch.*, LXXVI, 81–106.
[130] Evans, 1897, 360–411.

In contrast with the normally neatly, but irregularly, finished arrow-heads, found mostly in Beaker graves, is the group of what are sometimes called 'Breton' arrow-heads, mainly from the graves of Wessex.[131] These are for the most part square-barbed, and are usually of superb workmanship. They are, nevertheless, not all precisely similar to the Breton forms, as Grimes[132] observed when describing those from the Breach Farm Barrow (Fig. 31) in South Wales. Furthermore, in other parts of the country,[133] and even in Scotland,[134] arrow-heads closely comparable to the Wessex series have been found. Recently a Cornish grave[135] has yielded a hollow-based variant of this type, few others having been found in Britain.

In a Cornish barrow[136] explored in the nineteenth century great numbers of arrow-heads are reputed to have been found. Whether or not assemblages of arrow-heads represent the remains of funeral salvoes rather than grave-furniture in the normal assumed sense is impossible to determine. It should be noted that broken arrows have come to light in Ireland,[137] though from bogs not barrows.

Beside barbed and tanged arrow-heads, derivative forms of the *Petit tranchet* or transverse arrow-head, of Mesolithic ancestry, have been found in, mostly, the mounds of barrows. Clark[138] demonstrated their derivation and associations. It is likely that they were secured to their shafts by birch pitch, or some such substance, the facets of the retouch affording the adhesive a purchase.

Archer's wrist-guards are also found in Beaker graves, and are considered part of that complex.[139] These wrist-guards, or 'bracers' as they are sometimes called, consist of flat, rectangular, or convex and waisted plaques, perforated once at either end[140] or at the four corners,[141] or even three times at each end.[142] It is thought that they protected the wrist of the archer against the recoil of the bowstring. The plaques, frequently well finished, were apparently mounted on leather or some such substance. Rivets were sometimes used, and the plaque from the Kellythorpe[143] cist had been fastened by gold-headed rivets.

Implements thought to have been used for straightening and smoothing arrow-shafts have also been found in a number of graves.[144] Bun-shaped and suitably abrasive stones had a groove, or sometimes more than one, set across them. Such arrow-straighteners, as they are termed, could have been used singly or in pairs.

Apparent bow-tips have come to light in a Wiltshire grave,[145] and implements tentatively termed 'netting needles', from both Wiltshire and Derbyshire[146] barrows, could well be the remains of composite bows.

A few typologically early bronze axes have been found in barrow graves or apparently deposited in barrows at the time of their raising. An axe from the Bush Barrow[147] may well be early in the series. It has a pointed butt, and, scrutinized longitudinally, the edge and butt can be seen to taper each way from a medial thickening. It

[131] *PPS*, IV, 69
[132] *PPS*, IV, 119.
[133] Greenwell, 1877, lxiii, 249, Fig. 29.
[134] Smith, 1931, I, Pl. X, 14.
[135] *Ant J.*, XXXVIII, 174–96.
[136] Hencken, 1932, 301.
[137] Raftery, 1951, 134, Fig. 121, 8.
[138] *Arch. J.*, XCI, 32–58.
[139] *Antiq.*, V, 415–26.
[140] Hoare, 1812–19, I, 44, Pl. II.
[141] *WAM*, III, 185–6.
[142] *Arch.*, XLIII, 428; *WAM*, XLVIII, 174; *Bronze Age Guide*, 68; *ANL*, IV, 58.
[143] Mortimer, 1905, 274.
[144] Evans, 1897, 267; Childe, 1947 b, s.v.
[145] *DMC II*, 59, Pl. XVI, 13.
[146] *Arch.*, XLIII, 436–7; Howarth, 1899, 55.
[147] Hoare, 1812–19, 202.

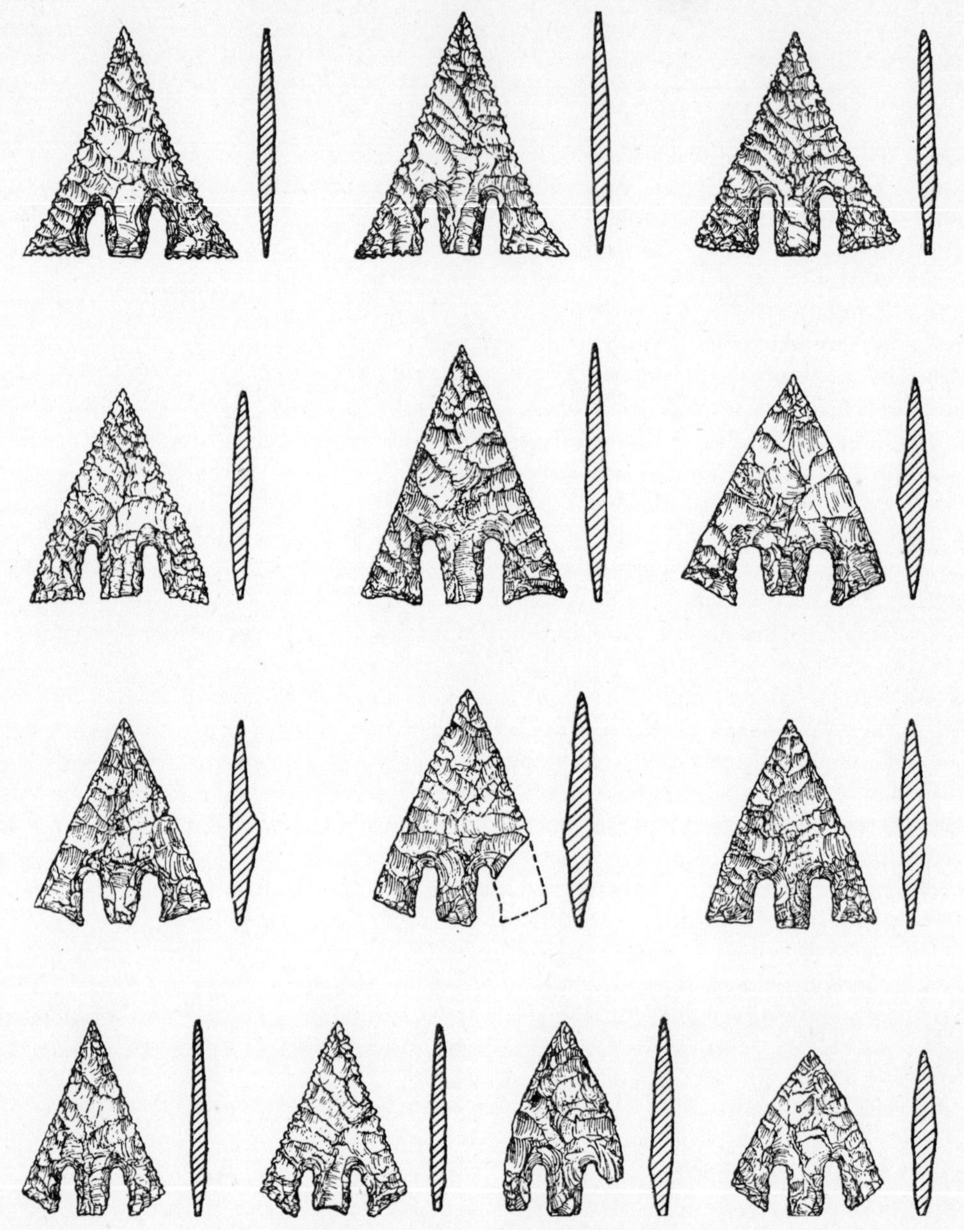

Fig. 31. The Breach Farm Barrow arrowheads (1/1).

may well have gone to the grave wrapped, as traces of cloth, described [148] as a plain weave, are visible on it. An axe of similar form, although of slightly differing type,[149] was found, together with two daggers, accompanying an inhumation burial in a cist of tufa slabs at Aylesford [150] in Kent. Whether or not the cist was below a barrow is not

[148] *PPS*, XVI, 158.
[149] *Arch. Cant.*, LXV, 183.
[150] *PSA*, XVII, 373.

known. A small axe is recorded by Colt Hoare as having been found in a grave with flat dagger and crutch-headed pin, on Overton Hill [151] near Avebury. Three or four flanged axes found in a barrow on Coombe Hill, Jevington,[152] in Sussex, had been broken, presumably ritually (a process requiring considerable effort). Greenwell [153] found four axes, three of which were decorated, in a barrow on Wold Farm, Willerby, in Yorkshire. There seems to be no real reason to doubt his assertion that the axes were deposited during the building of the barrow. An axe with a markedly expanded cutting edge, central thickening, and incipient cast side flanges was the only bronze implement remaining of four which had been placed in a grave-pit, together with a miniature vessel, arrow-heads, scrapers, knives, and an arrow-shaft smoother, to accompany the cremated bones of three individuals [154] in the Breach Farm, Glamorganshire, composite barrow.

Numbers of maces found in barrows belong more properly to the recently isolated Secondary Neolithic Cultures.[155] Plain antler mace-heads, made from a proximal brow-end, have been recovered mostly from Yorkshire barrows.[156] However, one is known from Lambourn [157] in Berkshire, where it had been accompanied by a tanged dagger, an incense cup, and a stone battle-axe of the Hove-Snowshill class described below. A similar, though faceted, antler mace-head was dug from Liff's Lowe.[158] Stray mace-heads of this type have been recovered from the Thames,[159] but few have as yet been found in any south country barrows. Faceted stone maces are also known,[160] mostly from the north, although one has been found in Wales.[161]

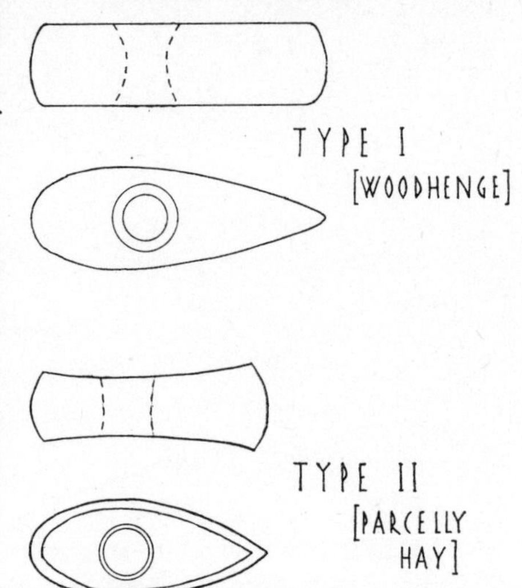

Fig. 21. Types I and II axe hammers (1/4).

Three more distinctive forms of Secondary Neolithic mace-head, all in stone, have been found in barrows. They are the pestle, cushion, and edged-cushion forms. A pestle mace-head, together with a Bush Barrow dagger and a plano-convex flint knife, were found in a grave at Towthorpe.[162] A typical cushion mace-head was with a cremation in a cist at Cleughead [163] in Kincardineshire, an edged-cushion mace-head was found in Dorchester II.[164] A cushion mace-head has been found at Stonehenge.[165]

Distinctive axe-hammers [166] have been recovered from a number of graves, usually with inhumations. Sometimes they accompanied daggers.[167] Two types (Fig. 32) comprise the series. Type I (Pl. XVII a) has parallel upper and lower faces, and the

[151] Hoare, 1812–19, II, 90.
[152] Curwen, 1954, 151, Pl. XIV.
[153] *Arch.*, LII, 1–72; *PPS*, IV, 283–4, Fig. 10.
[154] *PPS*, IV, 113.
[155] Piggott, 1954, s.v.
[156] Mortimer, 1905, Pl. VIII, 63, Pl. XVIII, 152, Pl. CV, 906; Greenwell, 1877, 217, Fig. 33, 390, Fig. 154.
[157] *Arch.*, LII, 60.
[158] *Arch. J.*, LXXXVIII, 132.
[159] *Arch.*, LXIX, 7, Figs. 5, 6, 7.
[160] Childe, 1935, 100.
[161] Grimes, 1939, 156.
[162] Mortimer, 1905, 7, Pl. I, Figs. 8, 9, 10.
[163] Anderson, 1886, 320, Fig. 302; *PSAS*, LXXVIII, 16–24.
[164] Atkinson, Piggott, and Sandars, 1951, 114.
[165] Piggott, 1954, 358, Fig. 63, 5.
[166] *Ant. J.*, XXX, 147.
[167] *Arch.*, LXXV, 85, 86; *Arch. J.*, XXIV, 28.

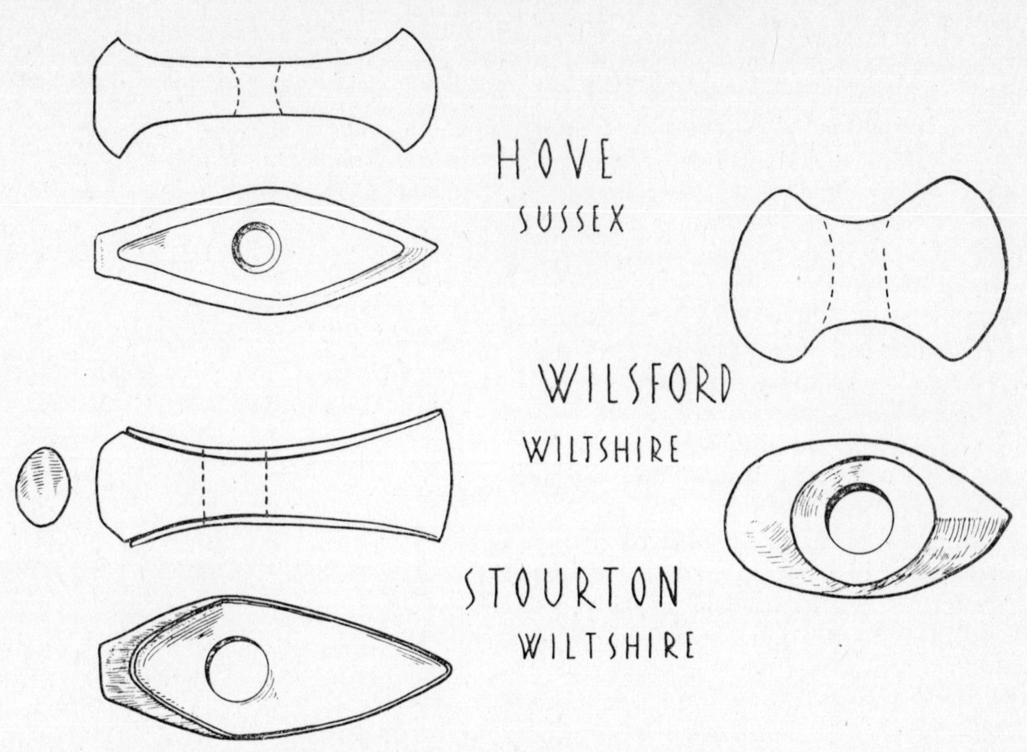

Fig. 33. The three types of battle-axe (1/4).

shaft-hole is set relatively close to the hammer or blunt end. Type II has edge and hammer ends, while the shaft-hole is set more medially. The shaft-holes of both forms are usually straight. Type I is best represented by examples from the Woodhenge,[168] East Kennet,[169] Garton Slack,[170] and Rudston [171] graves. In the first instance, the shaft of the axe-hammer was, at the time of internment, most probably between the hands of the deceased. A bone wedge secured the shaft of the axe-hammer from Bulford Down.[172] Type II axe-hammers were with flat daggers in two Derbyshire graves,[173] and others have been found in Cornwall [174] and Yorkshire.[175]

Both these forms of axe-hammer occur in a series made of preselite, recently isolated by Stone,[176] and related by him to Secondary Neolithic sources. Side-fluting on a specimen from Wollaton Park [177] suggests, as do the splayed ends of the Type II, that one or two of this fine-grained rock series may have been inspired by massive metal originals [178] as this ornamentation is not natural to stone.

Three types of implement (Fig. 33) warranting the graphic term battle-axe and intimately associated with the Wessex culture can be recognized (Pl. XVII b, c, d). They can be given appropriate names. *Hove-Snowshill* battle-axes are boat-shaped with

[168] Cunnington, 1929, 148–51.
[169] *Arch.*, XLIII, 410, Fig. 96.
[170] Mortimer, 1905, 209.
[171] Greenwell, 1877, 126.
[172] *WAM*, XXXVI, 617, 622, Fig. 5.
[173] *Arch.*, LXXV, 85–6.
[174] Borlase, 1872, 87.
[175] Mortimer, 1905, 154.
[176] *Ant. J.*, XXX, 147.
[177] Evans, 1897, 203, Fig. 132.
[178] Forssander, 1936, Taf. L.

convex, tending to angular, upper and lower surfaces. The axe-edges are splayed, and the blunted hammer-ends, which are ovate or rounded, are nearly equally expanded. Several approximate to double-axe form, and all have medially set shaft-holes. Several, such as that from the Snowshill barrow,[179] are proportionately slender. All are of exceptional workmanship, surely by specialists, the uniformity of the group being remarkable. At Chippenham,[180] Hove,[181] (Fig. 33), and Snowshill [182] they were accompanied by equally uniform ogival daggers. At the second place an amber cup was a feature of the assemblage. Battle-axes of what I have termed the *Stourton-Loose Howe* type [183] (Stourton, Fig. 33) are distinguished by their broad oval or circular, pronounced and elongated, hammer-end. Their axe-edges are less splayed and thus their upper and lower surfaces are less convex and far flatter than those of the first group. These, like others, sometimes bear beading [184] or grooving [185] at the interfaces. Shaft-holes, sometimes of hour-glass character, are mostly medial, although there is a tendency for them to be closer to the hammer-end. The *Wilsford-Crichie* [186] (Wilsford, Fig. 33) battle-axes are short and broad, with a deep, almost hemispherical concavity, in the middle of which is the shaft-hole, on both upper and lower surfaces. The angle of the axe-edge is oblique, in one instance blunted, while the other is usually wide and rounded. One example [187] bears triple incised lines on its sides defining the interfaces. Evans [188] and Smith [189] emphasized the close resemblance of these battle-axes to those from the Bann in Ireland. The Wilsford battle-axe was found in a bell barrow where it was associated with a flanged axe. A shale bead from one of the Normanton barrows [190] reproduces clearly the lineaments of this class, and thus demonstrated their affinities.

No stone battle-axe is a true double-axe, although they were perhaps influenced by the design of the latter. Recently there has been defined a small group of metal double-axes with ovate shaft-holes and apparently of alien origin.[191] All were chance discoveries, none being from barrows, but their affinities lie with such exotic objects as the Pelynt dagger.[192]

There seems to be no record of a halberd [193] having been found in a barrow, although they have come to light in Irish and Scottish cist graves.[194] However, one possibility must be noted. According to Stukeley [195] 'a very large brass weapon of twenty pounds weight, like a pole-ax' was found in a barrow near Amesbury. Grinsell [196] has suggested that this might have been a metal-shafted halberd, similar to the East German range.[197] This fascinating possibility is enhanced by the fact that three Wessex graves [198] have yielded halberd pendants, two of which reproduce in some detail the lineaments of these distinctive weapons.

[179] *Arch.*, LII, 72.
[180] *Ant. J.*, XV, 61.
[181] *BH Arch.*, No. 2, 20–8.
[182] *Arch.*, LII, 72.
[183] Stourton: Hoare, 1812–19, I, 39; Loose Howe: *PPS*, XV, 98.
[184] *PSAS*, IX, 386; Munro, 1899, 149.
[185] *Arch.*, LXXV, 91.
[186] Wilsford: Hoare, 1812–19, I, 209; Crichie: *PSAS*, LIV, 164.
[187] Crichie, *PSAS*, LIV, 164.
[188] Evans, 1897.
[189] *Arch.*, LXXV, 102.
[190] H156, Hoare, 1812–19, I, 202; *PPS*, IV, 70, Fig. 8, 7.
[191] *PPS*, XIX, 224–6.
[192] *PPS*, XVII, 95, Pl. II.
[193] *PRIA*, XXVII, 94–114; *Arch.*, LXXXVI, 195–321.
[194] *PPS*, XVII, 72; *JRSAI*, LIX, 113.
[195] Stukeley, 1740, 46.
[196] *VCH Wilts.*, I, Pt I, 150.
[197] *Mannus*, IX, 157.
[198] *PPS*, IV, 84–5.

Scrapers, struck flakes, and even cores are sometimes found in graves.[199] So are flint and pyrites, presumably for fire-making. Antler, a source of raw material for many purposes, has often been met with,[200] as have pebbles and pieces of fine-grained rocks. There is no direct evidence of specialist craftsmen's graves as in the later Iron Age.[201]

Awls are found in graves in all parts of the country. They have recently been classified into types (Devizes Museum). Their function, whether for leather working or for tattooing, two suggestions, remains obscure. These awls are sometimes hafted in a manner similar to a modern bradawl.

Tweezers have been found in a number of graves. Like awls, their purpose is not clear. The toilet is a suggestion, although industrial uses are possible.

As distinct from buttons and pins which, together with other remains, testify to clothed bodies going to grave or pyre, numbers of objects fulfil the definition of ornaments of the person. Such things as ear-rings, studs, beads, pendants, certain pins, clasps, armlets, torques, and the like adorned (or were at least possessed by) a minority in life and accompanied them in death. These ornaments were, on account of their relative rarity, clearly the labels of social strata.

Two types of ear-rings have been found, associated in two instances with beakers, and all apparently from inhumation graves. They are (*a*) basket and (*b*) strip types. Basket ear-rings consist of a more or less oblong sheet of gold or bronze with rounded ends and a side hook for attachment to the ear-lobe. The sheet has been partially bent around a cylinder, giving an elongated basket effect, hence the name. Sometimes they bear traced or punched ornamentation. Only one example of a pair of strip ear-rings has been found, at Goodmanham.[202] It is a longitudinally corrugated strip of bronze, provided at one end with a point for the ear-lobe, the strip being bent to form a loop.

Bateman[203] and Greenwell[204] both record, in a dramatic manner, the discovery of bronze ear-rings. The former notes of a skeleton, in a barrow on Stakor Hill, near Buxton: 'Both mastoid bones were dyed green from contact with two small plates of thin bronze, bent in the middle.' The latter writes that in a barrow at Cowlam 'touching the temporal bones, which were stained green by the contact, were two ear-rings of bronze'.

A single gold ear-ring came to light in a Northumbrian[205] Beaker barrow; its edges were decorated with punched bosses, recalling *pointillé* work. A gold pair, now in the Ashmolean Museum (Pl. XXVIII c), had been worn at the time of burial by a youth, at the feet of whose skeleton was a beaker, buried in the smaller mound of the Radley double barrow. Neck-rings with spatulate terminals, not unlike the ear-rings in principle of workmanship, are known from Scotland.[206]

Studs of amber,[207] jet,[208] shale,[209] and pottery,[210] flat on one or both surfaces, and sometimes convex or conical on both, or on the other, have been found, sometimes in

[199] e.g. Mortimer, 1905, flint, s.v.

[200] e.g. Hoare, 1812–19, 183.

[201] Joseph Dechelette, *Manuel d'Archaeologie Prehistorique, Celtique, et Gallo-Romaine*, II, Pt 3, Paris, 1914, 1051; *PPS*, XXI, 231.

[202] Greenwell, 1877, 324.

[203] Bateman, 1861, 80.

[204] Greenwell, 1877, 223.

[205] *Arch. Ael.* (4th ser.), XIII, 207.

[206] Evans, 1881, 379, Fig. 470; D. Wilson, *Prehistoric Annals of Scotland*, 2nd ed., 1863, 473–4, Fig. 98.

[207] Stukeley, 1740, tab. XXXII.

[208] Elgee, 1930, 111, Fig. 37; Mortimer, 1905, 47, Figs. 74–5.

[209] *PCAS*, XXXIX, 44.

[210] *WAM*, XXXV, 1.

pairs. Their form, and the fact that they have been found near the heads of inhumation burials, suggest that they have been inserted in the lips or the ear-lobes, a purpose for which they would be admirable, rather than have served as 'dress fastenings'.

Amber, faience, jet, shale, and metal are the principal materials from which beads were made.

By far the greatest concentration of amber beads is in Wessex [211] and its immediate environs, although occasionally they have come to light in rich burials in northern and eastern England,[212] in Wales,[213] and in Scotland.[214] Those from Wessex are spherical, oblate, tabular (spacers with complex borings), or pestle and mace forms. The exotic Lake [215] lunula-necklace is a compound of the first three elements. Another such necklace seems to have been in the Upton Lovell 'Golden' Barrow,[216] and about a thousand oblate beads were allegedly recovered from it. Pestle beads, found also in East Anglia,[217] have their counterparts in other mediums in the Irish passage-graves.[218] A smooth-wrought functional 'pestle' of dark fine-grained rock—perhaps a metallurgist's tool—reproducing this precise form, was found in a barrow at Collingbourne Ducis.[219] The amber beads from the Knowes of Trotty [220] in Orkney, some of which were lost, included triangular and lunate beads, and would appear to be all that is left of a complex compound, possibly lunate, necklace, similar to that from Lake.

It was early realized that blue faience segmented beads (Pl. XVIII) from southern England resembled in colour and material numbers of beads from Egypt. Their many problems, distribution (Fig. 34), and affinities were decisively defined by Beck and Stone [221] in 1936, and have, in the light of the last quarter of a century, been reassessed by Stone.[222] As Stone emphasized, the total number of such beads from Britain (Fig. 34) is only about 250, less than the load of a packman. A single Sicilian hoard contained more segmented beads than have been found in the whole of Britain! Four classes have been defined: (1) segmented, (2) star (3) quoit, (4) sundry types, which includes (*a*) oblate and spherical, (*b*) cylindrical, (*c*) spiral, and (*d*) spacing beads. Segmented beads, the most numerous, are found chiefly in Wessex; the remainder, including a number from Ireland, being, with one exception, from coastal sites.

Jet for beads, derived mostly, so far as is known, from the coal measures of Yorkshire and Scotland, is a northern phenomenon. The basic bead types are enumerated by Evans,[223] and they include, as do the amber series, fusiform and quoit beads, as well as tabular spacer beads with complex borings. Callander [224] collected the facts relating to the Scottish material, while Elgee examined those obviously from Yorkshire sources.[225] Craw [226] has studied the problems of jet beads and necklaces and has shown that they formed, like the amber from Lake, compound lunates (Fig. 35), incorporating smaller beads and spacer-plates. He showed how Irish gold lunulae [227] copy jet necklaces, often

[211] *PPS*, IV, 80–3.
[212] *PPS*, IV, 100.
[213] Grimes, 1939, s.v.; *PPS*, XIX, 166.
[214] *PPS*, XVII, 78–9.
[215] Hoare, 1812–19, I, 212.
[216] Hoare, 1812–19, I, 98. Apparently without tabular spacer beads: see *JRAI*, XC, 122–7.
[217] *Arch.*, XLIII, 454; *PPS*, IV, 93.
[218] *PRIA*, XXIX, Pl. XXIV. For amber in the Irish Bronze Age see *JCHAS*, XLIX, 122–7, and *JRSAI*, XC, 61–6.
[219] *WAM*, X, 96; *DMC II*, 37.
[220] *PSAS*, III, 195.
[221] *Arch.*, LXXXV, 203, 52.
[222] *IPEK*, XVII, 43–6; *Ant. J.*, XXXI, 27–31; *PPS*, XXII, 37–84.
[223] Evans, 1897, 452–64.
[224] *PSAS*, L, 238.
[225] Elgee, 1930, 108–19.
[226] *PSAS*, LXIII, 164.
[227] Armstrong, 1933, 10.

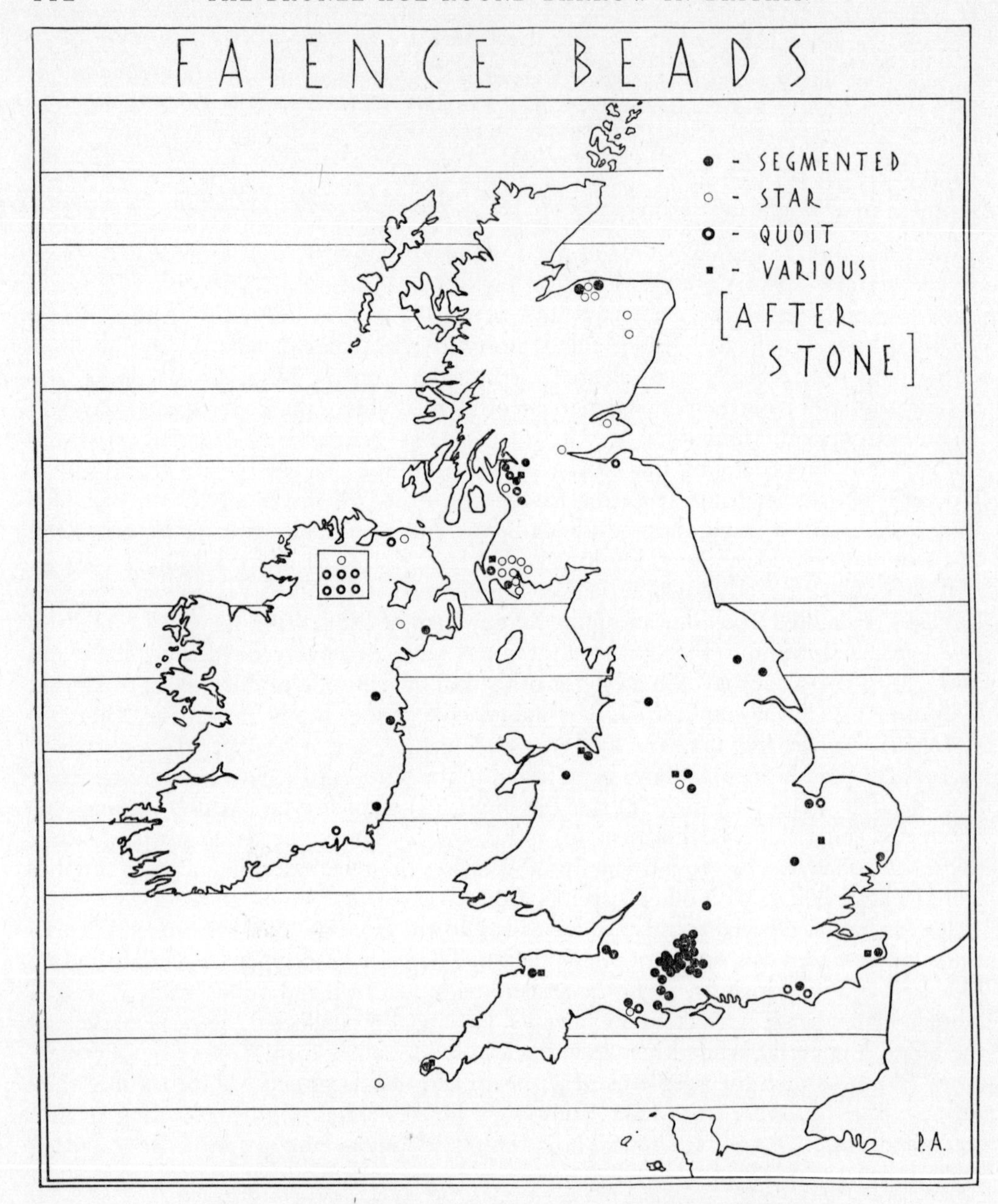

Fig. 34. Distribution map of faience beads from Great Britain.

in some detail, and are but a rendering in gold of the same form. This manner of simulating beadwork in gold was similar, in principle, to that which produced the inlaid and engraved collar, which copies beadwork, adorning the portrait mask of the Egyptian Tutankhamun.[228]

[228] P. Fox, *Tutankhamun's Treasure*, Oxford University Press, 1951, Pl. 28.

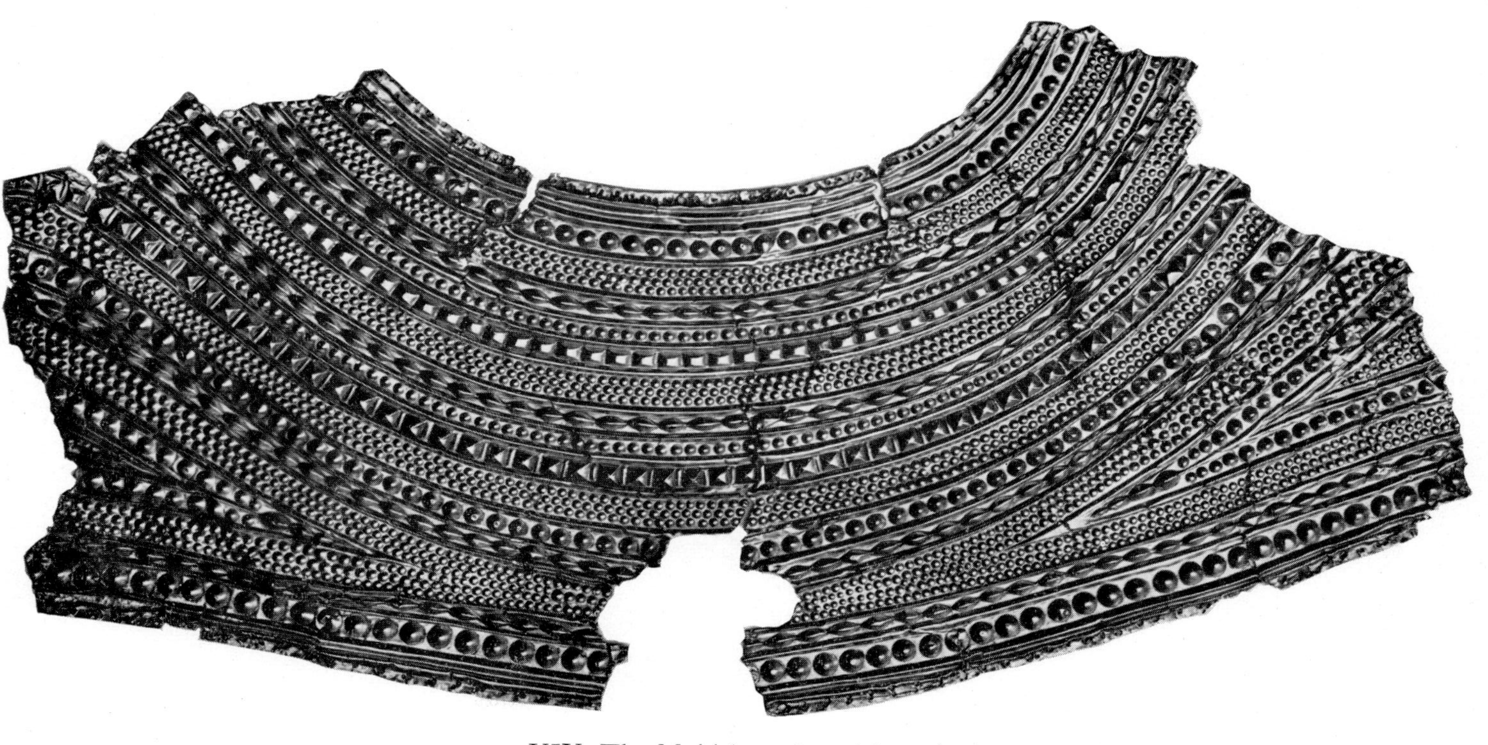

XIX. The Mold 'cape', or 'tippet'.

XX. The Mold 'cape' as worn.

XXI. The Folkton drums. Carved chalk idols from a barrow in Yorkshire. LEFT, 'faces'; RIGHT, tops of the idols. Diameters 4·1, 4·8, 5·6 inches.

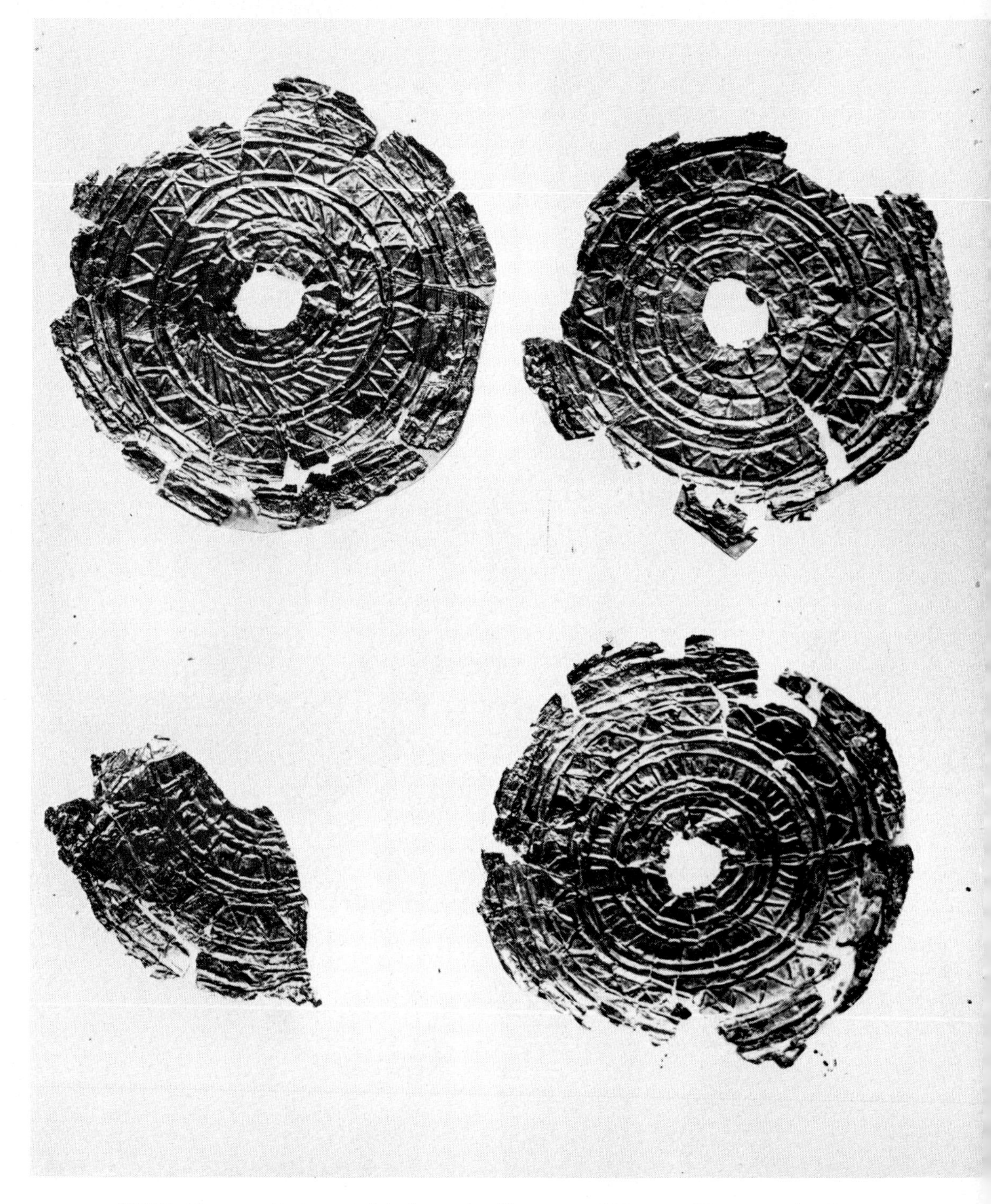

XXII. Sheet-gold discs (1/1) from the Knowes of Trotty, Huntiscarth, Orkney.

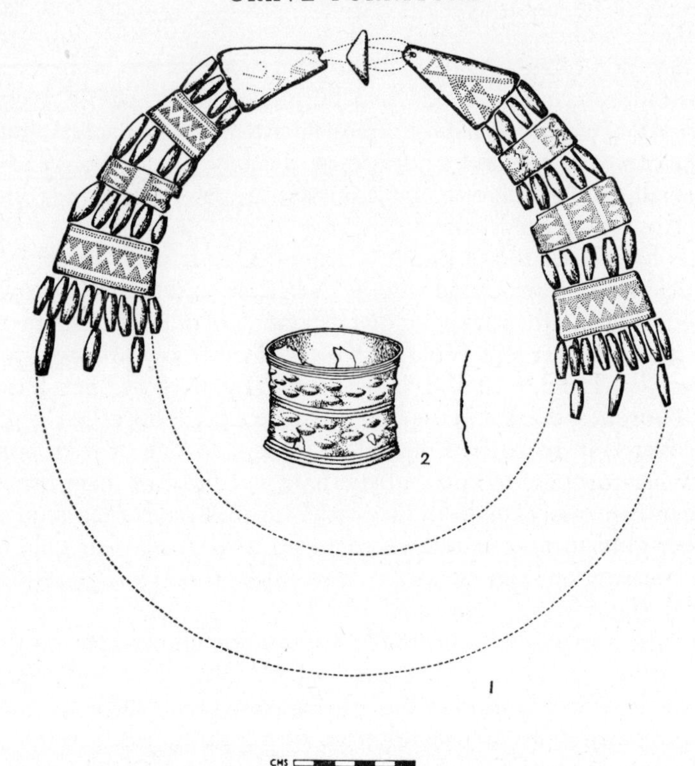

Fig. 35. The Melfont jet beads and armlet.

Beads described as being of shale or lignite have been found in different parts of Britain, but no comparative study has been made of them. There is some evidence that the shale deposits at Kimmeridge [229] in Dorset, exploited in Roman times, were a source of material in the Bronze Age.

A tin segmented bead was recorded by Colt Hoare,[230] and cylindrical bronze-leaf beads are known from Dorset [231] and Sussex.[232] Segmented gold beads have been found in Ireland,[233] but from a bog not a barrow. Cylindrical side-perforated drums of thin gold from the Upton Lovell 'Golden' Barrow [234] may well have been used as beads. Also of note are the sheet-gold globular and fusiform beads from Bircham [235] in Norfolk, and Normanton.[236]

Made from the same materials as beads, apart from metal, are a series of objects designated pendants. Of especial note are 'pulley-rings',[237] ring-pendants,[238] perhaps girdle-fasteners, and axe-pendants.[239]

[229] *Ant. J.*, XX, 44–6; for Kimmeridge shale, see *Arch. J.*, XCIII, 200–19. Such beads have their forbears in Early Post-glacial times: see *Arch. Camb.*, LXXXI, 94 and Pl. V; and J. D. G. Clark, *Excavations at Star Carr*, Cambridge University Press, 1954, 165–6.

[230] Hoare, 1812–19, 103, Pl. XII.

[231] Abercromby, 1912, II, 39.

[232] *JRAI*, XXXII, 381.

[233] Armstrong, 1933, Pl. XIV, 244.

[234] Hoare, 1812–19, I, 98.

[235] *Arch.*, XLIII, 525.

[236] Hoare, 1812–19, I, 202.

[237] Hoare, 1812–19, I, 172; Mortimer, 1905, 90–2.

[238] *PSA*, X, 29; *Oxon.*, VIII–IX, 34.

[239] *WAM*, VI, 324.

Apart from Late Neolithic antler or ivory pins [240] which were possibly used to secure the hair, pins are not often found in British barrows. There is a series, single and complex ring-headed, crutch-headed, and bulb-headed respectively, current in the Wessex Bronze Age,[241] derived from those of Germany, if not actual imports, while a number of bone copies of certain Continental forms have been identified.[242] Hawkes [243] has defined a small group of exotic pins from south-eastern England, one example of which may be from a wrecked barrow.

Sheet armlets have been found in a few graves. One from Normanton,[244] a similar example from Knipton,[245] associated with an A beaker, and the well-known Melfort [246] (Fig. 35) armlet, probably the surviving one of a pair, are of note. Mortimer found strip-armlets with a hilted dagger in a Wold barrow.[247] Two heavy bronze torques found in a barrow on Penninis Head,[248] St Mary's, Isles of Scilly, may well be a localized version of massive ingot torques, current in the Early Bronze Age.[249] So-called 'Sussex loops' [250] have been discovered in barrows. Other than these, and one or two more ill-attested early finds, few bar-torques are known from barrows, most of them being chance discoveries, frequently unassociated. Gold 'Tara' torques have been studied by Crawford [251] and other gold torques by Hawkes.[252] An Irish twisted bar gold torque found with a late Unětice pot at Regensberg,[253] in south Germany, suggests that they were current during the later Wessex Bronze Age.

Richly furnished burials, often in timber coffins, sometimes beneath great barrows, have been alluded to in Chapter VII. From such burials, which comprise only a small part of the funerary record, objects have been recovered which by their character, material, or workmanship leave little doubt as to the prominent position in society of the individual they accompanied. The character of the material permits approximate classification thus:

(*a*) Regalia, e.g. the Mold 'cape'.
(*b*) Cult objects such as idols and sun-discs.
(*c*) Cups of gold, amber, and shale.
(*d*) Aggrandized equipment such as gold buttons, scabbard hook, wrist-guards, embellished daggers, etc.

The greater number of barrows which have produced material of this last category, objects spectacular in their implication of wealth, are concentrated on Salisbury Plain, some at no great distance from Stonehenge and hardly unconnected with the floruit of the monument. Collected by Colt Hoare, these relics have attracted the attention of many writers who would see there the premier province of Early Bronze Age Britain. The analysis and listing of the graves, together with others which contained elements, sometimes exotic, more or less peculiar to the region, was undertaken by Piggott [254] and the whole collocation was termed by him the Wessex Culture.

[240] Atkinson, Piggott, and Sandars, 1951, 142–4.
[241] *PPS*, IV, 85–7.
[242] *DMC II*, Pl. XVI, 3; *PPS*, XV, 100, Fig. 12; Childe, 1957, 332, fn. 1.
[243] *PPS*, VIII, 26–47, XV, 109–12.
[244] Hoare, 1812–19, I, 160; *Arch.* XLIII, 469; Evans, 1881, Fig. 480; *PPS*, XV, 120 (ribbed examples).
[245] *Ant. J.*, XV, 60.
[246] *PSAS*, XIX, 134; *PPS*, XIX, 169.
[247] Mortimer, 1905, 232.
[248] *Arch. J.*, IX, 96; *PSA* (2nd ser.), V, 406, 422; Hencken, 1932, 308.
[249] Forssander, 1936, Taf. XXXVII, 1.
[250] *PPS*, XV, 107.
[251] *PSA*, XXIV, 41, Fig. 2.
[252] *Man*, XXXII, 222.
[253] *Germania*, XXII, 7–11.
[254] *PPS*, IV, 52–106.

It seems likely that a number of wealthy barrows were at one time a feature of the West Country, particularly Cornwall,[255] but few now remain, the barrows having been methodically robbed in medieval times. Others occur in apparent isolation. The Knowes of Trotty,[256] Orkney, in which gold and amber were found, is at no great distance from the great Maeshowe passage-grave from which Vikings removed, so they record, a wealth of gold.[257]

The premier and unique object in the first category, that of regalia, is the Mold 'cape' or 'tippet' (Pl. XIX). Recently and definitively published by Powell,[258] this great sheet of bossed and ribbed gold, bronze-backed and leather-mounted, at one time thought to be an ornament for a pony, was found in a composite barrow destroyed in the early nineteenth century. With it were numbers of amber beads, only one, oblate, specimen surviving, and it apparently enclosed unburnt bones. From the extant remains it has been shown that it was most likely a rigid ceremonial cape (Pl. XX), made, three-dimensionally, by a master craftsman, by beating from a single gold ingot. Presumably it was worn by the person whose bones it enclosed. No similar objects exist, although the techniques of its workmanship have been equally skilfully applied to other contemporary pieces. A burial found near Castle Martyr,[259] Co. Cork, reported to have been covered with gold plates (Pl. XXIII a), was cited as similar in principle, as were Wessex gold lozenges.[260]

Although the difference between the Mold cape and the lunulae of sheet gold and the lunate necklaces of amber and jet, discussed earlier in the chapter, has been emphasized, it seems likely that they also come into the category of regalia, and were worn only upon specific occasions. An oak case [261] enclosing a lunula, found in an Irish bog, hints at how carefully they were conserved when not worn. Indeed, this is an argument that can be used for much of Britain's gold. Gold collars or gorgets, recently discussed by Raftery,[262] which are renderings in gold of cord, bead, or braided necklaces gathered beneath discs, seem also similar in principle to lunulae, and can likewise be considered as regalia. Their similarities of workmanship to the Mold cape have been emphasized.

As cult objects the three Folkton 'drums', like the Mold cape, are unique. They were associated with the skeleton of a child in a satellite grave under a composite barrow, which, perhaps, covered the palisade-trenches of post circles and central adult burials, on Folkton Wold,[263] in the East Riding of Yorkshire. These solid, squat, cylindrical chalk-cut idols (Pl. XXI), seemingly wood-inspired, bear 'pick-axe' faces, eye-symbols, and owl-faces as well as elaborate lozenge, concentric circle, and false relief ornamentation. Similarities of detail with miniature vessels,[264] as well as Rinyo-Clacton pottery and mural art,[265] food-vessels,[266] and the art of the Boyne passage-graves,[267] can be detected. The lineaments of a miniature vessel with a cremation at Goodmanham,[268] in Yorkshire, appear related to these idols.

A series of ornamented golden discs, hailed as evidence of sun worship [269] must be

[255] *PWCFC*, I, 132–5.
[256] *PSAS*, III, 195.
[257] Piggott, 1954, 253–4.
[258] *PPS*, XIX, 161–79.
[259] *JCHAS*, L, 23; Armstrong, 1933, Pl. X, 57.
[260] *PPS*, IV, Pl. X.
[261] Armstrong, 1933, 11, Fig. 4; *JCHAS*, XXXIX, 1–14.
[262] *ANL*, IV, 177.
[263] *Arch.*, LII, 14.
[264] Curwen, 1954, Pl. XII, 4.
[265] Piggott, 1954, Pl. XII, 1–4; Childe, 1931, 150–154, Pl. LIII, 3.
[266] Childe, 1947 b, 121 (false relief).
[267] Piggott, 1954, 208–18.
[268] *LPA*, Figs. 5, 9.
[269] *PPS*, III, 371.

included in the category of cult objects. From a barrow on Lansdown Hill,[270] near Bath, and in the same grave as pieces of cinerary urns, came a fragmentary golden foil disc, set on bronze and about 6·75 inches in diameter. As tentatively and perhaps unjustifiably reconstructed, its centre appears to have been a boss surrounded by smaller bosses, chevrons, concentric line-infilled circles, more bosses, and more infilled concentric circles. It is comparable in size to certain of the Irish sun-discs,[271] but its affinities lie not only with the designs on the terminal ends of gorgets but, as R. A. Smith [272] pointed out, with the disc on the Trundholm cult vehicle.[273] This is a small two-wheeled frame carrying the sun-disc to which the figure of a horse, borne on four wheels, is attached. It is thought to represent the sun drawn across the heavens by his steed.

Two other types of golden 'sun disc' have been met with in graves. First of all there are the small, double perforate, cruciform ornamental discs. Two were found with a B beaker in a grave on Mere Down [274] in Wiltshire, and recently two more have come to light at Monkton Farleigh.[275] Secondly, there are chevron-ornamented discs. Two pairs of discs, one chevron-ornamented and one plain, were in the rich Lake barrow, and two discs resembling them, though by no means precisely, were found with amber in the bell-barrow-like Knowes of Trotty [276] (Pl. XXII) in Orkney. Devotees of both usages also used pottery discs [277] incised with these designs, and reproduced them on the bases of certain pottery vessels.[278]

In this context of cult objects, certain discoveries from bogs and marshes, not barrows, though probably of approximately the same period, must be mentioned. Foremost are the coracle-like boat-vessels. The Caergwrle [279] boat—for long termed a bowl—of oak, carved and decorated with thin sheet gold, was found in a bog. Its edge or 'gunwale' is lined with 'sun-discs', or perhaps circular shields, beneath them 'oars'. It has eyes, a ribbed keel, and a schematic representation of waves on each side of it. A boat-model (Pl. XXIII b) of the shape, of beaten sheet-gold, was found at Broighter,[280] Co. Londonderry, in a field during ploughing. It was equipped with seats, separate oars, and a mast, or boat-hook. Although apparently found at the same time as the famous Broighter torques of Iron Age date there is no evidence that they were directly associated. The character and form of the Broighter model suggests that it may be in the same tradition as the Caergwrle boat. Both may even be ancestors of the golden and silver-gilt nefs, the symbols of wealth and power which have stood proudly upon English dining tables for time immemorial.

Anthropomorphic representations are rare in the early Bronze Age. Reminiscent of northern rock carvings, the mutilated white-quartz-eyed schematized wooden warriors, dowelled by their thin legs to an equally schematized boat, found in Roos Carr [281] in Yorkshire, probably held circular shields and battle-axes. Five figures were found, three attached to one boat and two to another, now lost, deep in the blue clay of the carr. It seems likely that they are sinister cult figures, perhaps cast into a mere, that stimulated

[270] *PSA* (2nd ser.), XX, 6–13.
[271] Armstrong, 1933, Fig. 17.
[272] *PSA* (2nd ser.), XX, 12.
[273] Ebert, 1924, XIII, Taf. 76.
[274] Hoare, 1812–19, I, 44, Pl. II.
[275] *WAM*, LII, 270.
[276] *PSAS*, III, 195.
[277] *Arch.*, XLIII, 383, Fig. 78.
[278] Mortimer, 1905, Pl. XIII, Fig. 102; *Arch.*, XLIII, 370, Figs. 58–60; Greenwell, 1877, 101 Fig. 90.
[279] Grimes, 1939, 83, 171.
[280] Armstrong, 1933, frontis., 450–73.
[281] *Transactions of the East Riding Archaeological Society*, IX, 62–74; Elgee, 1933, Pl. X; *Acta Arch.*, XIII, 235–42.

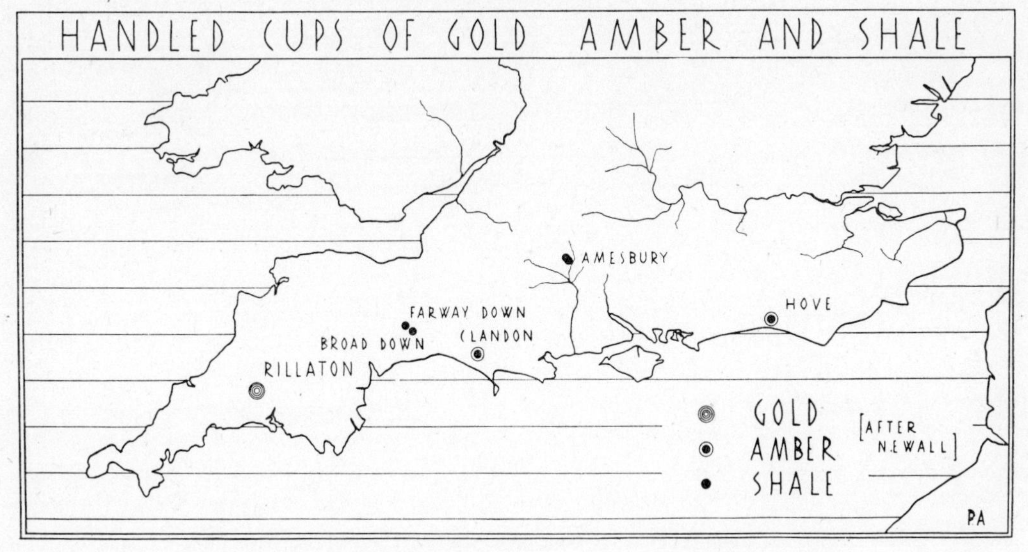

Fig. 36. Map showing distribution of gold, shale, and amber cups.

the builders of barrows, and were possibly even the remains of an act of sympathetic magic calculated to ensure the success of a war-party. Such acts might have been quickened by the piping of bone flutes such as those found in barrows at Normanton and Avebury.[281a]

Other such figures are known to have been found singly. Two, one from Shercock, Co. Cavan,[282] and another from Dagenham in Essex,[283] were male representations. All, including the Roos Carr warriors, are thus distinguished by the penis sockets now empty. Another from Ballachulish in Scotland,[284] accounted female by reason of its pronounced pubal regions, was found covered with wickerwork and with several pole-like sticks near it, perhaps the remains of a baldachin. A fourth figure found at Kingsteignton in Devon [285] was of indeterminate sex, although the head and elongated neck, also the flexed knees, recall the Roos Carr figures.

Cups of gold, amber, and shale (Fig. 36) accompanied certain inhumations, with either daggers or both daggers and battle-axes. The cups, and the methods of manufacture of the amber and shale specimens, were studied comprehensively by Newall.[286] In the small muster there are three distinct forms. They are:

(*a*) B1 beaker-form (Rillaton: beaten gold).
(*b*) Hemispherical (Hove: amber) (Fig. 37_6).
(*c*) Pointed base, with carinated body, two from a barrow near Amesbury (Fig. $37_{1,2}$): shale. Broad Down, Honiton (Fig. 37_3): shale. Farway Down, Honiton (Fig. 37_4): shale. Clandon Barrow, Dorset (Fig. 37_5): amber.

[281a] *Antiq.*, XXXIV, 6–13.
[282] *Antiq.*, IV, 487.
[283] *Transactions of the Essex Archaeological Society*, XVI, 288.
[284] *PSAS*, XV, 158.
[285] *TDA*, VII, 200.
[286] *WAM*, XLIV, 111–17.

Fig. 37. Shale and amber cups (1/4). 1, 2, Near Amesbury; 3, Honiton, Broad Down; 4, Honiton, Farway Down; 5, Clandon; 6, Hove.

The gold cup (Pl. XXIV a, b) was beaten from a single ingot, and its handle was attached by rivets passing through lozenge-shaped washers. A gold cup recently found in the Rhineland (Pl. XXIV c) [287] has a similar handle attached and similar washers used for the same purpose, and its form approximates to that of British shale cups (Pl. XXIV d). The other cups have been turned from blocks of amber or shale, presumably by means of a pole-lathe with which provision could be made for their handles. Decoration is predominantly bands of horizontal grooves, while all types of cup, gold, amber, and shale alike, have vertical channelling on the handle. The only vessel, apart from the Wessex handled bowls, comparable to the series is a pottery cup from a Cornish barrow.[288] Hencken [289] refers to the beaker shape of the Rillaton Cup, which is most marked. Indeed if the corrugations, derived ultimately perhaps even from leather working,[290] be compared with the predominantly zonal ornament of B1 beakers, the likeness is enhanced. One of the two shale cups from Amesbury has a flat base, and its form, like that of the others except for their pointed bases, recalls angular B1 beakers.[291]

Aggrandized equipment in line and line *pointillé* ornamented [292] sheet gold, accompanied by weapons and a wealth of amber, and in two instances sceptres, can only be from the graves of princelings. They are few in number and not one such grave has been excavated in modern times. The Bush Barrow is perhaps the best recorded.

Certain graves, containing daggers frequently embellished with gold, are clearly male burials, while others have been claimed as female assemblages because of small knives, quantities of beads, awls, and trinkets. Most of the barrows that covered these

[287] *The Times*, London, 23 April 1955.

[288] *Arch. J.*, CVII, 47.

[289] Hencken, 1932, 70.

[290] *PRIA*, XXVII, 259. So close was the connection that Minoan copper ingots had the form of oxhides! *ABSA*, XXX, 74–85. The techniques of sewing sheet-metal with wire, and rivets, are probably adaptations from the same source. *PRIA*, XLIV, 181–228.

[291] *Arch.*, LXXXIX, 100.

[292] *PRIA*, XLIV, 187.

richly furnished burials were bowl barrows, often of considerable size. Only two were bell barrows.

It is impossible in the present context to describe the Wessex gold in detail; this has been done to some extent by several writers. The most recent, concise, and authoritative account is that of Piggott[293] in his classic paper.

The sceptres of the princelings from Bush Barrow[294] and the Clandon Barrow[295] (Fig. 38) are basically cushion mace-heads, resembling closely certain of the Secondary Neolithic group described earlier in this chapter. That from the former barrow is of simple finish. Found with it were bone mounts which ornamented the shaft. They comprise two ferrules and two intermediates all cut to a dentated pattern, the intermediates forming continuous zigzags. Only the shale head with four inset gold bosses remained of the latter sceptre, the shaft, presumably of wood, having vanished. Similar gold studs or bosses were recovered from a barrow on Hengistbury Head.[296]

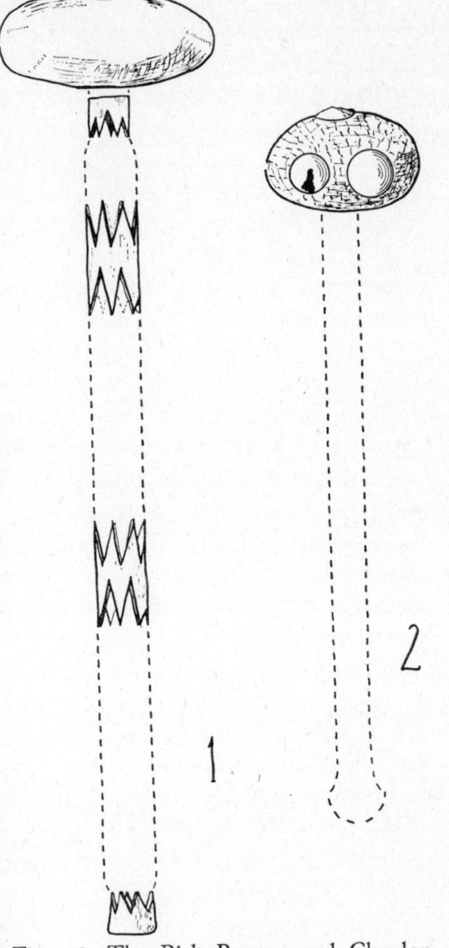

Fig. 38. The Bish Barrow and Clandon maces (1/4 approx.).

Prominent amongst the gold equipment are the lozenge plates which, judging from the report to the effect that one lay on the skeleton's chest,[297] were attached to garments. One, accompanied by a similar smaller plate, was from the Bush Barrow (Pl. XXV), the other from the Clandon Barrow. Such garments were enriched and secured by shale cones, encased in thin gold and V-bored at the base. These appear to be enlarged and embellished V-bored buttons of Beaker affinity. Golden buttons, apparently used singly, were found in the Upton Lovell 'Golden' barrow[298] (Pl. XXVII a), at Normanton (H. 155),[299] probably at Piddletown[300] in Dorset, and recently in a grave, possibly that of a destroyed disc barrow on Portsdown,[301] near Portsmouth. Shale beads gold-mounted or encased were a feature of many of these burials.

In the Bush Barrow was the renowned and unique scabbard hook (Pl. XXV), a regal rendering of the modest bone hooks. Two small golden boxes, with Irish counterparts[302] were in the Upton Lovell assemblage, as well as a rectangular plaque (Pl. XXVI a) mounted on what was described as wood, and perforated at the four corners.

[293] *PPS*, IV, 52–106.
[294] Hoare, 1812–19, I, 202.
[295] *PDNHAS*, LVIII, 18.
[296] Bushe-Fox, 1915, 16, Pl. III, 2.
[297] Hoare, 1812–19, I, 202.
[298] Hoare, 1812–19, I, 98.
[299] Hoare, 1812–19, I, 201.
[300] *Arch.*, XLIII, 530.
[301] *Portsmouth Reader*, II, No. 3, 38.
[302] Armstrong, 1933, frontis., 485–8.

A similar gold plaque (Pl. XXVI b) was in the Cressingham [303] dagger grave. In the absence of precise evidence as to their usage it could be that, like the buttons and the hook, they were royal versions of archers' wrist-guards.

Amber discs mounted in gold (Pl. XXVII b) were found in a number of graves.[304] Such a disc may have been exported to the contemporary eastern Mediterranean world, where one was found in the Tomb of the Double Axes.[305] Faience pendants modelled upon these encased discs have been found at Claydon Hill [306] and Oxteddle Bottom [307] in Sussex. Bone-mounted stone discs were in the shaft graves; [308] stone discs have been found in both long and round barrows in Britain.[309] A bone disc, encased in gold [310] ornamented with diagonal cross-hatching, from Normanton, may have been from a cranium.

Glimpses of the far-flung connections of this virile royal house, whose members took with them beneath their barrows so much wealth, are provided by the gold ingot-torque pendant (Pl. XXVIII a) [311] and the halberd pendants,[312] both representations of objects which do not occur in Britain.

Thurnam [313] initially brought order and precision into the realm of Bronze Age pottery with a system of classification and terminology much of which is with us today. A half-century later, Abercromby,[314] following upon earlier papers,[315] published his great study *Bronze Age Pottery*, which has conditioned British archaeological thought to this day. His avowed intent was chronology, thus, with appropriate acknowledgments, he adapted Thurnam's system to his ends, examining not only pottery but the variegated grave-furniture associated with it.

Abercromby devoted Volume I to beakers and food-vessels, Volume II to cinerary vessels. Basically his beaker types were A, B, and C, replacing the α, β, and γ of Thurnam. He distinguished six types of food-vessel, while cinerary vessels, subdivided into two classes, viz., Urns and Pygmy Vessels, comprised seven more groups.

His work had the effect of directing all conception of the Bronze Age into ceramic channels, and many subsequent studies of pottery from barrows and cognate sites have tended to equate the material with the *systema* of Abercromby, rather than examine it upon its own merits. Hence the term B1 had long obscured the Cord-zone class of beaker. However, he set the precedent for the *corpus*, so essential to archaeology, happily perpetuated in many papers on pottery, and reaching its zenith in the recently begun Register of Bronze Age Pottery,[316] which will supplement the British Association's Card Index of Bronzes.

A neglected aspect of ceramic studies, that of construction and firing, has recently been pursued by R. B. K. Stevenson.[317] The ring-building principles governing the construction of Bronze Age pottery have had considerable light thrown upon them.

Abercromby's A-B-C classification of beakers was based upon distinction between the globose body and relatively long or short neck of the ideal 'A' or 'C' beaker and

[303] *Arch.*, XLIII, 454.
[304] *PPS*, IV, 80, Pl. IX.
[305] *Ant. J.*, V, 68–70.
[306] *Arch.*, LXXXV, Pl. LXIV, Figs. 2, 5.
[307] Curwen, 1954, Fig. 42.
[308] Karo, 1930, Taf. I, 154, Abb. 73, 892.
[309] *PPS*, V, 132.
[310] Hoare, 1812–19, I, 201.
[311] Hoare, 1812–19, I, 201.
[312] *PPS*, IV, 102–6, Nos. 23 a, 68, 71.
[313] *Arch.*, XLIII, 331–400.
[314] Abercromby, 1912.
[315] *JRAI*, XXXII, 391; *PSAS*, XXXVIII, 323–410.
[316] *ANL*, VI, 11.
[317] *Man*, LIII, 97.

the ovoid profile of his ideal 'B' beaker. To this tripartite division he added the subtype B2, and the hybrids AC, AB, and BC.

Subsequent beaker studies have been the distributional, coupled with a continuation of the *corpus*, undertaken by Sir Cyril Fox,[318] investigation of specific aspects and features, such as handled beakers,[319] and the regional researches. Outstanding amongst these last are Crichton-Mitchel's [320] analysis of Scottish beakers supplemented by

Fig. 39. British beaker forms.

Professor V. G. Childe's subsequent lists,[321] and the *corpus* and studies of Welsh beakers by Savory and Griffiths.[322] Other studies concerned with cultural movement and ethnic origins are discussed in Chapter X.

As in part a counteraction to the effects of Abercromby's *systema*, Professor Stuart Piggott [323] has put forward a descriptive cognominal terminology for the different types of beakers (Fig. 39). Thus B1 beakers rightly become Bell-beakers, as they are but the insular counterpart of the ubiquitous European form. B2 beakers are to be called Barrel-beakers, C beakers become Short-necked beakers, and A beakers become Long-necked beakers.

Thus precisely descriptive terms can be used to define specific basic classes. Other groups masked by alphabetical terminology can be given similar descriptive names. Thus Sir Cyril Fox's [324] B1β group of B beakers could well be termed Rim-cordon beakers. Professor Childe's [325] B3 beakers should be known as Cord-zone beakers, and his B3a type would become a Cord-spiral beaker. A small group defined by Willmot [326] could well be called Collared beakers as the decoration is confined to the upper part of the pot.

Beaker pottery is fine and hard, and, by the use of slip and in firing, it has been brought to a pleasant reddish colour. This may sometimes vary from a dark red to a light ochreous hue. There is some evidence that decoration was occasionally infilled with white material (Pl. XXIX a). The zones of bell-beakers are executed by incision

[318] *Arch. Camb.*, LXXX, 1–31.

[319] *Antiq.*, IX, 348; cf. *Ant. J.*, XV, 280; *PPS*, IV, 98 (bowls).

[320] *PSAS*, LXVIII, 132–89.

[321] Childe, 1946, 99.

[322] *BBCS*, XVI, 215–41; *PPS*, XXIII, 57–90.

[323] To the Prehistoric Society, 29 February 1956.

[324] *Arch.*, LXXXIX, 100.

[325] *Actas*, XXI, 196–201.

[326] in litt. (1951).

or by the use of a square-toothed comb which produced an almost continuous hyphenated line. Barrel-beakers are inferior in finish to bell-beakers, but the same techniques of decoration were used, although cord impressions were not infrequent. Cord-zone beakers were simply ornamented with cord impressions arranged in zones, and a cord was evidently wrapped around in a spiral to produce much the same effect for cord-spiral beakers. Rim-cordon beakers, besides being more angular, are sometimes of poor

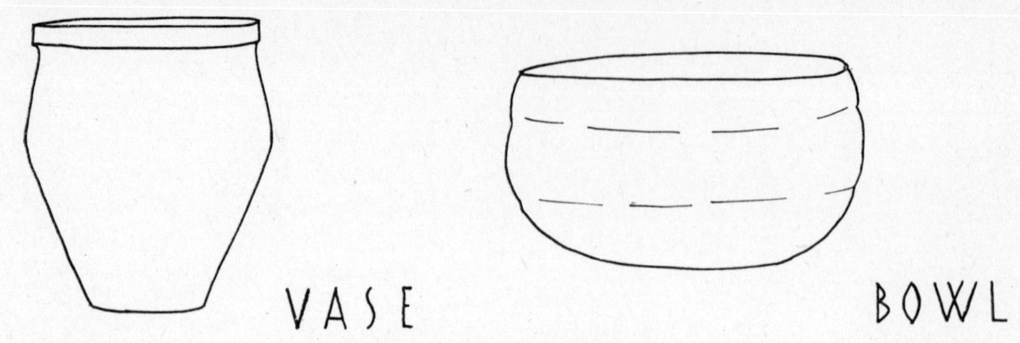

Fig. 40. Food-vessel forms.

workmanship, and have ornament bands of hyphenated diagonals separated by horizontal lines. Short-necked and long-necked beakers never bear cord impressions. Hyphenated lines, finger-nail impressions, hollow-bone end impressions, and similar devices are arranged not only horizontally but often vertically, in triangles sometimes panelled, lozenges, saltires, etc. Ridges are sometimes a feature of the former. With the exception of the collared-beakers, decoration covers the whole pot.

Beakers, termed *drinking-cups* by Colt Hoare and Thurnam, so called by Abercromby for the sake of convenience and international usage, are normally found empty with the burial. It has long been thought that they were vessels suitable for drinking from, hence their name, but, unfortunately, little evidence has been forthcoming as to the nature of the beverage allegedly consumed from them. Suggestions include both alcoholic and non-alcoholic potions. An age-bent antler ladle found in a beaker at Inverurie [327] in Scotland, hints only at a liquid perhaps carefully measured!

Food-vessels were, from the beginning, containers which, like beakers, did not have burnt bones in them. They were distinguished from them by their coarse texture, shape, and general unsuitability for drinking from. It was suggested, as sediments were noted in them by many early antiquaries, that they were eminently suitable to contain pottage or porridge.

Food-vessels (Pl. XXIX b) are concentrated mainly in northern Britain and Ireland.[328] Two principal forms (Fig. 40) can be recognized. These are the vases sometimes termed *Yorkshire*, seen in their simplest and southern form in the Type 3 of Abercromby, and the bowls often known as *Irish*.

Vases are of two parts: the body, an inverted truncated cone, and the neck, a shallow concavity. The rim is generally broad,[329] and it is usually bevelled internally. The juncture of the two members can be a sharp shoulder (Type 3) (Fig. 41), or there can be

[327] *Arch.*, XLIII, 395, Fig. 87.
[328] Fox, 1952, Pl. IV, s.v.
[329] *PPS*, XXIII, 128.

a groove (Type 2), spanned by stop-ridges (Type 1). Further types (2*a* and 1*b*) have the groove duplicated, with or without stop-ridges. Decoration is sparse, but, when present, is concentrated on rim and neck, consisting of for the most part simple motifs executed with cord (Pl. XXIX c), point, bone, or comb, while sometimes a shell-edge is to be suspected.

Irish bowls, Abercromby's type A, are lotus-shaped vessels; sometimes their smooth

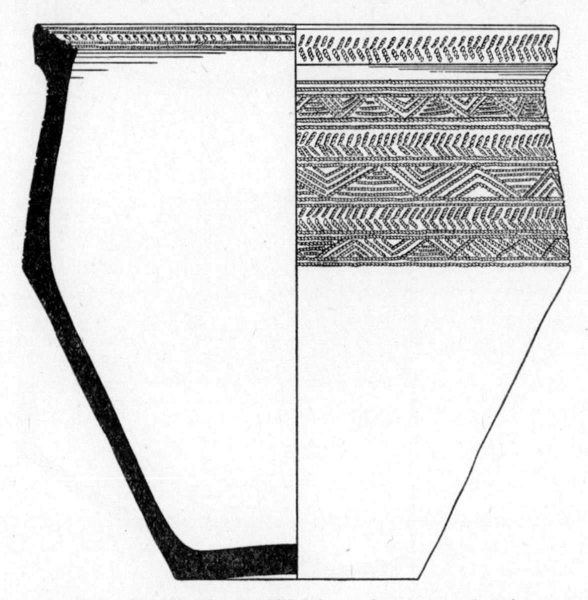

Fig. 41. The Bishop's Waltham food-vessel (1/3).

profile is interrupted by a constriction. Type B has the same form and is banded by two broad ridges. Type C is a bowl rather like A but with deep grooves—or raised mouldings around the body. Type D has a globular body and an everted rim. Type E has an inverted truncated conical body, and above a pronounced shoulder it has an everted neck. Types B–E have prominent bases. False relief is a feature of some bowls, while comb, cord, and point have been frequently and skilfully used to cover the entire bowl.

It seems likely that some food-vessels, like the A beaker 'mugs', are pottery renderings of wooden vessels. This likeness is enhanced by surface texture and base ornamentation that recalls, always distantly, the annular rings and medullary rays of wood. Certain food-vessels with feet [330] owe much to wood also, and indeed a wooden polypod bowl has recently come to light in a German grave.[331]

Cinerary urns are containers for cremated bones, and pygmy vessels, better termed *miniature vessels*, are the small, presumably ritual, vessels which sometimes accompanied them. These latter are sometimes called 'incense cups' after Colt Hoare, who thought that the slotted cups were suited to that purpose. In a few graves cinerary urn forms were used as food-vessels.[332] They are coarsely made and built up in rings, as are food-vessels. As with these, stamping and cord ornament is the method of decoration

[330] Greenwell, 1877, 193; Mortimer, 1905, 330.
[331] Schultz, 1939, 43, Abb. 45.
[332] *Arch.*, XLIII, 379, Fig. 68.

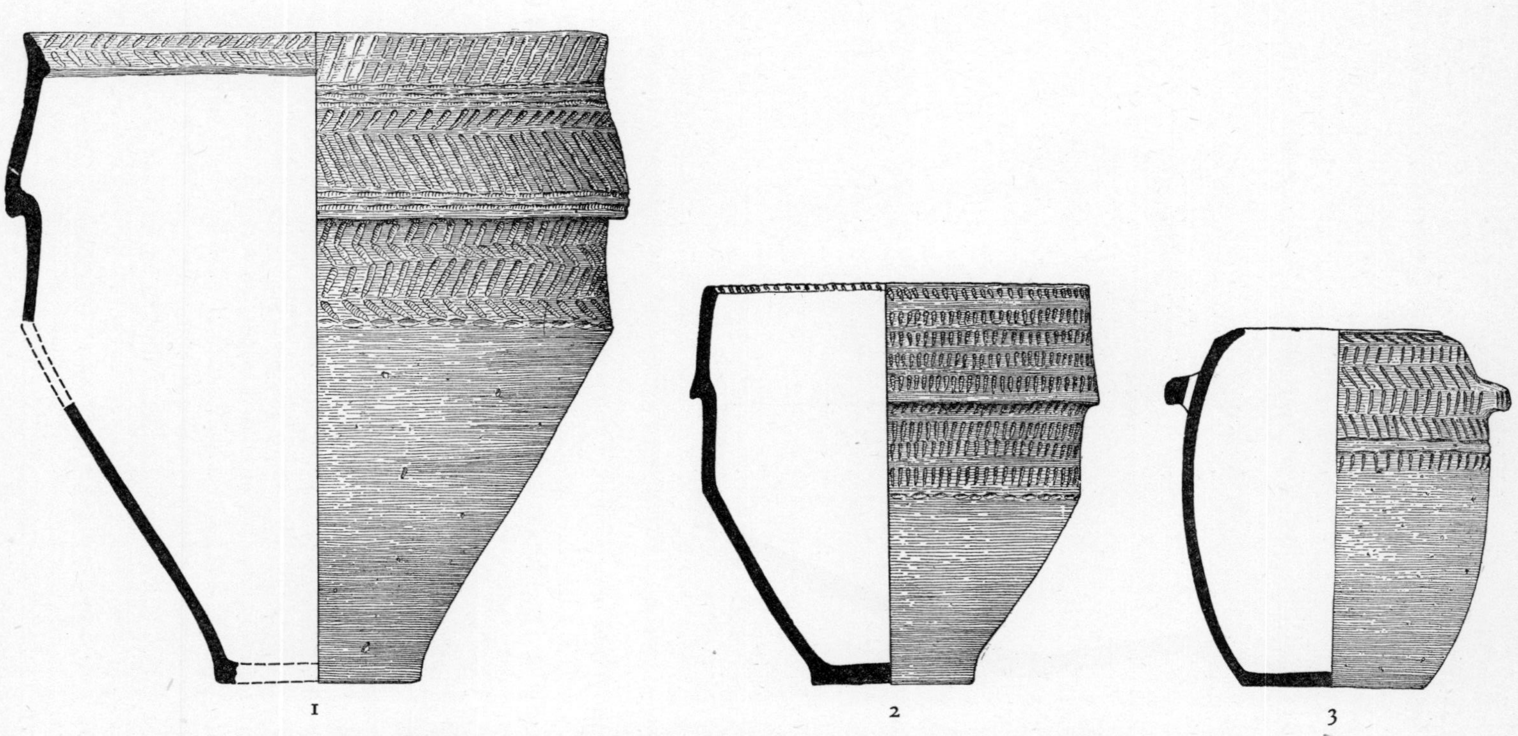

Fig. 42. The Kirk Ireton urns. 1. Height 15·75 inches; 2. Height 9·8 inches; 3. Height 8·75 inches.

of overhanging-rim urns (Fig. 42). It is confined to the rim, or as it is called by some, the *crown*, and occasionally the upper part of the pot. Cordoned urns, as their name suggests, are decorated with applied cordons, and on a small series, horseshoes (Fig. 43), often finger-printed and either deep or shallow. Enlarged food-vessels are large versions of the Yorkshire type and are decorated with similar motifs. The decorative

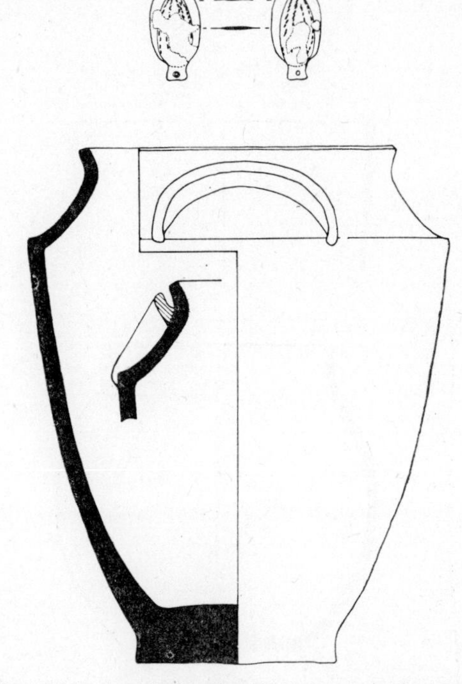

Fig. 43. The Amesbury handled urn (height 15·25 inches) and razors (1/5).

technique used for encrusted urns was most complex; applied mouldings and blobs, smeared with a thick slip, were enriched with jabbed and incised patterns.

Excluding Deverel-Rimbury urns found normally in cremation cemeteries, though sometimes in barrows, four basic types, named in the preceding paragraph, can be identified. While no detailed over-all study of cinerary urns, apart from that of Abercromby, has been made, the basic forms have been studied separately. Thus, in 1927 Fox [333] demonstrated the northern British and Irish distribution of encrusted urns, and, recently,[334] cordoned urns. Varley [335] has isolated the Pennine urns, Patchett [336] has listed Cornish urns, and Brailsford [337] has provided possible progenitors for overhanging-rim urns. To these must be added Powell's study of the little known pottery of the East Midlands.[338]

Besides distributional studies the cinerary urns have, on account of the not inconsiderable period of time they allegedly occupy, typological value although uncertain.

[333] *Ant. J.*, VII, 115.
[334] Fox, 1952, Pl. VIII.
[335] *Ant. J.*, XVIII, 169–71.
[336] *Arch. J.*, CI, 17–49, CVII, 48–64.
[337] *Arch J.*, CVIII, 20.
[338] *PPS*, XVI, 65–80.

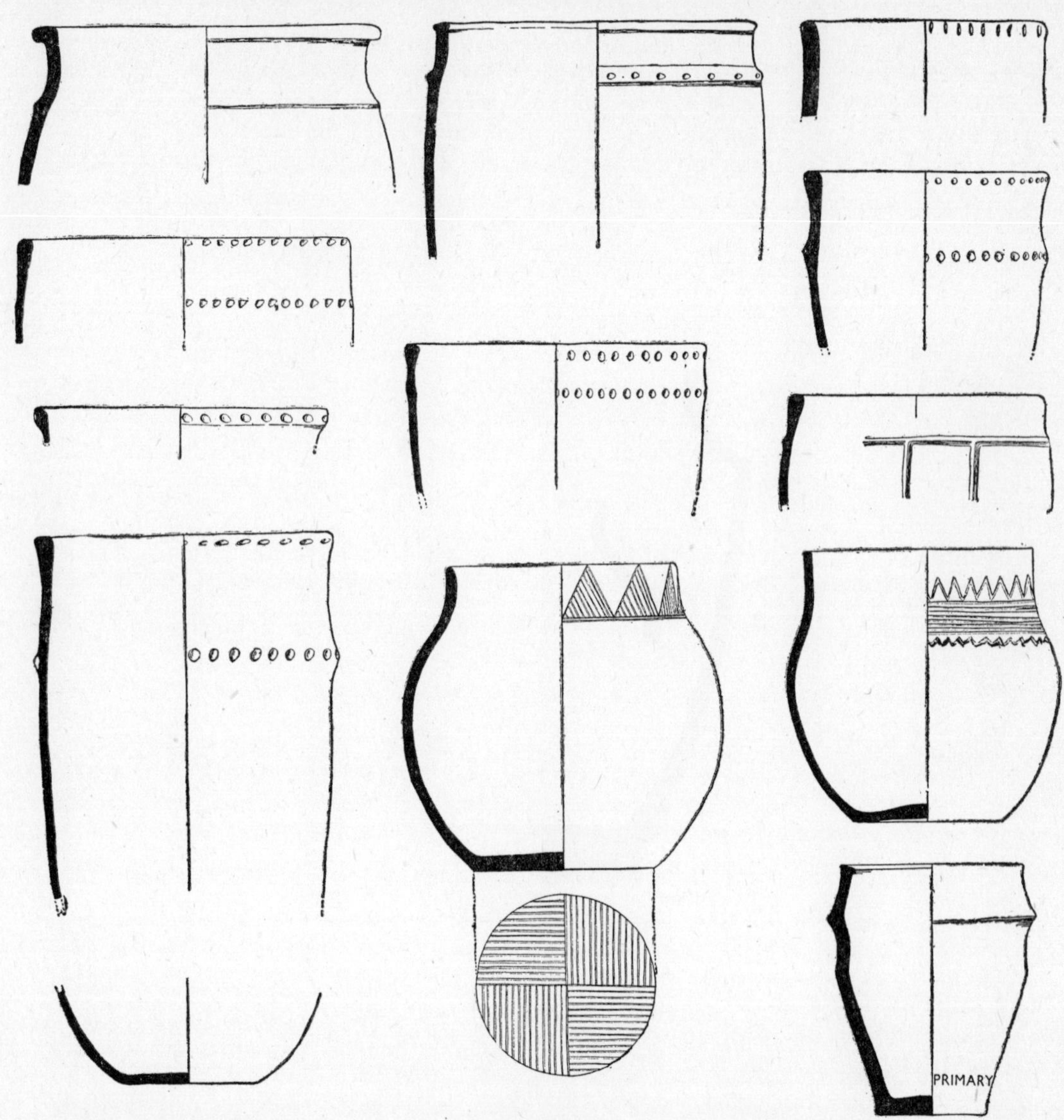

Fig. 44. Deverel-Rimbury urns and the overhanging-rim urn from the Latch Farm Barrow (1/6).

Abercromby [339] put forward a devolution which has been extended, in respect of Wales, by Grimes.[340] Thus the northern cordoned urns, like the Cornish 'Late Bronze Age' class, are a product of the overhanging-rim urns, the ultimate ancestors of which are the Ebbsfleet and Mortlake bowls, followed by Dr Isobel Smith's Fengate Pottery [341] and Brailsford's narrow-rimmed Sheep Down urns.[342] Following Fox [343] encrusted urns are envisaged as the end-product of food-vessels, though the possibility of a Secondary Neolithic ancestry [344] cannot be overlooked.

[339] Abercromby, 1912, II, 10–16.
[340] Grimes, 1939, 92.
[341] Childe, 1957, 332.
[342] *Arch. J.*, CVIII, 20.
[343] *Ant. J.*, VII, 115–34.
[344] Childe, 1947 b, 150.

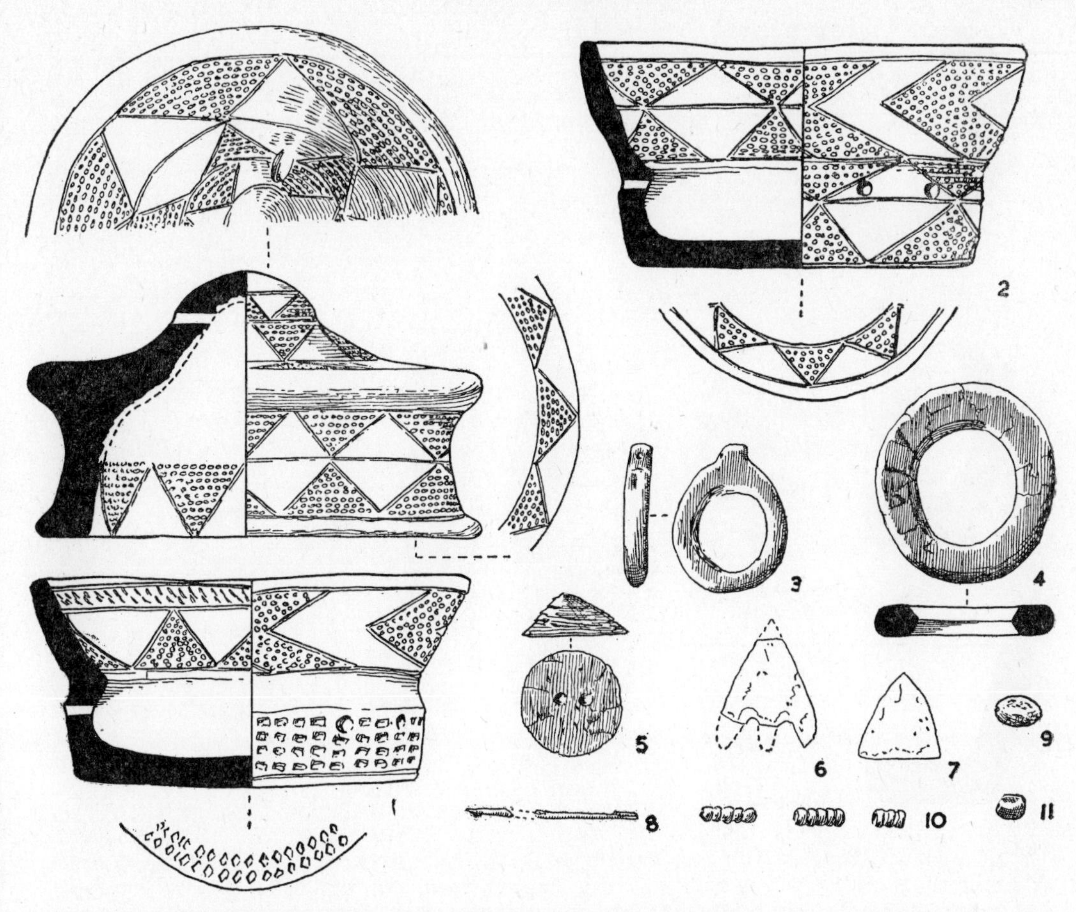

Fig. 45. Aldbourne cups (one with cover) and associated shale (3–5, 11), amber (9), bronze (8), flint (6, 7), and faience objects (1/2 approx.).

There are three varieties of Deverel-Rimbury urn.[345] (Fig. 44). Globular urns are hard-faced and smooth, have a barely recognizable neck decorated with shallow fluting or tooling, with vestigial handles at the base. Barrel and bucket urns are of coarse ware and often flat-rimmed, and as decoration bear cordons which are frequently finger-printed. The globular urns are rare beyond Dorset, and all three types occur only in southern and eastern England. Cordons, ribbing, and base reinforcement all suggest an ancestry in Secondary Neolithic wares.[346]

Miniature vessels, many of which have twin perforations, were set into six categories by Abercromby.[347] Of these the first two, the Aldbourne (Fig. 45) and Grape cups (Fig. 46), are intimately associated with the Wessex culture,[348] as is the third, the 'cup with perforated walls', and a small globular type, recently found for the first time in a Wessex context.[349] Categories 4, 5, and 6, respectively, 'biconical with everted lip',

[345] *Ant. J.*, XIII, 414–54.
[346] *ULIAA Rpt*, XII, 43.
[347] Abercromby, 1912, II, 24–37; *BBCS*, XVIII, 89–118 is the most recent study.
[348] *PPS*, IV, 52–106.
[349] *WAM*, LVI, 237–40 (interim).

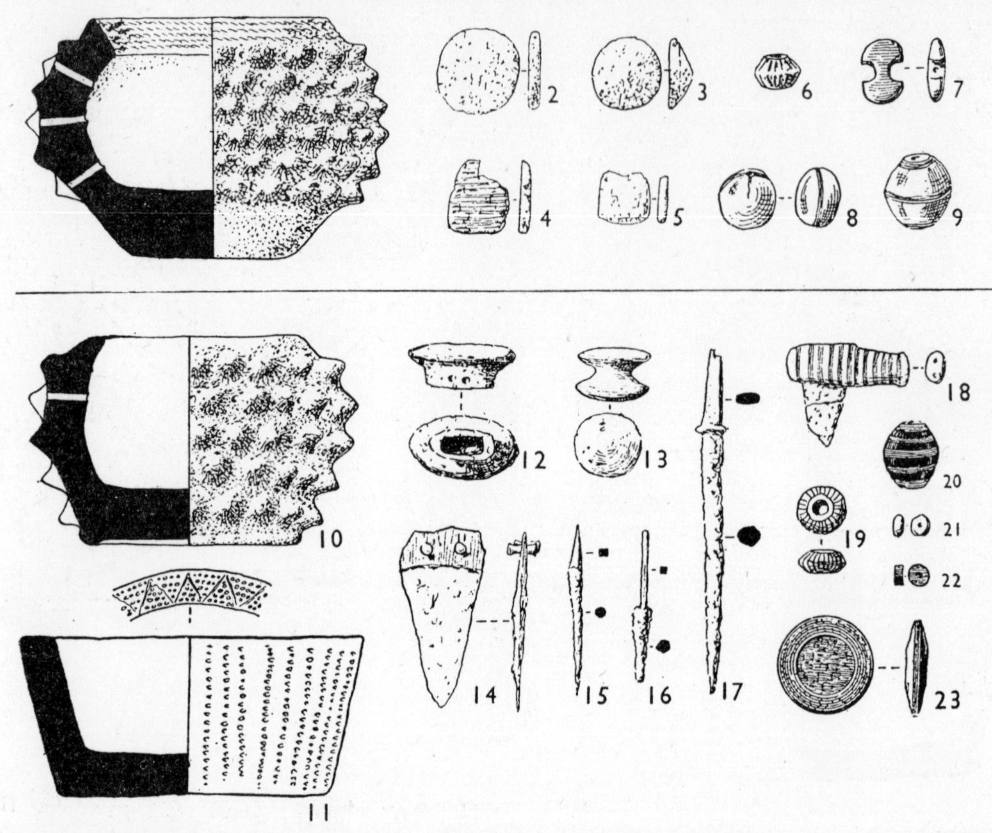

Fig. 46. ABOVE. Grape cup with associated amber (2–5), shale (6–7), and gold (8, 9) objects from Normanton. BELOW. Grape cup with associated cup and bronze (14–17), amber (12, 21), and shale (19, 20, 22) objects: halberd pendant (18) and gold-mounted amber disc from Manton (1/2 approx.).

'straight-sided, etc.', and 'biconical' are clear-cut categories. The seventh variety, 'miscellaneous', covers several forms largely undefined. Side by side with these distinctive small vessels are numbers inspired by different varieties of funerary and other, even perhaps metal,[350] vessels—some are unmistakably miniature food-vessels or urns. The bases of many miniature vessels bear ornamentation. Designs were used similar to those on food-vessels, reminiscent of wood, or circles and cruciform designs, the last recalling sun-discs. Pairs of perforations in the sides of certain vessels are thought to derive from the ritual *oculi*, such as were graven upon the Folkton idols.[351]

When barrow grave-furniture, particularly the bronze daggers, knives, pins, etc., is set against the typological sequences of Bronze Age metal artefacts, it emerges that it represents the earlier periods only. Later artefacts such as palstaves, rapiers, swords, and socketed celts are *not* found in graves. Inhumations and some cremations are furnished, only comparatively few inhumations and a great number of cremations are unfurnished. There is then an increasing impoverishment of grave-furniture, first really apparent in the Middle Bronze Age.

[350] *Arch. J.*, XLII, 29.

[351] PPS, XVI, 76.

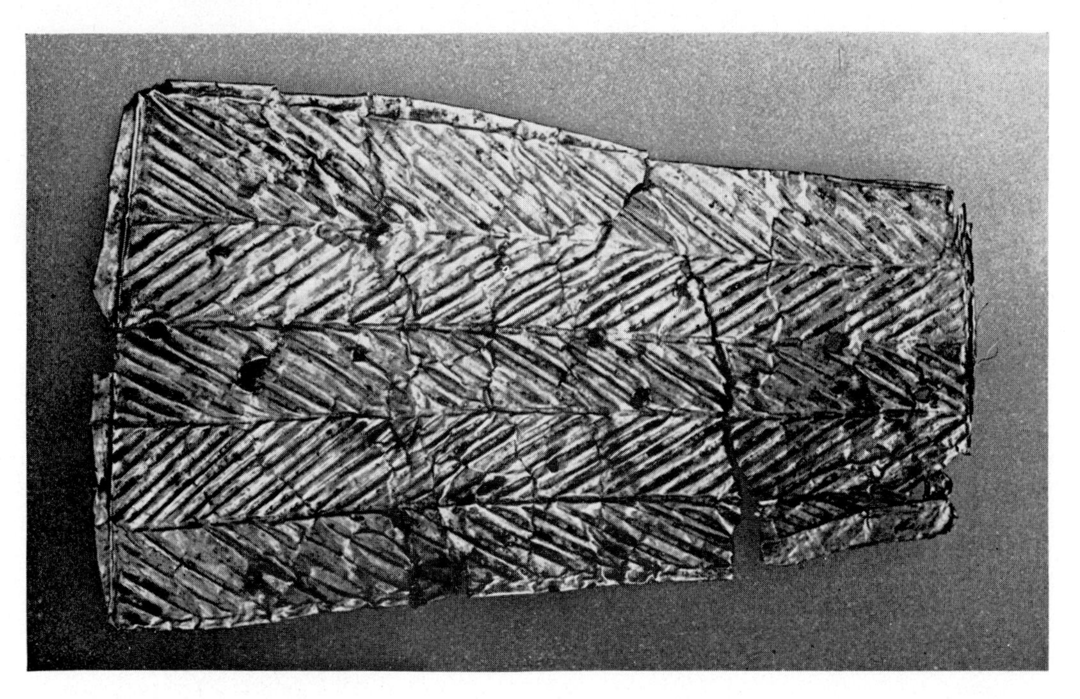

XXIIIa. Sheet-gold plate (2/1 approx.) from a burial at Castle Martyr, Co. Cork.

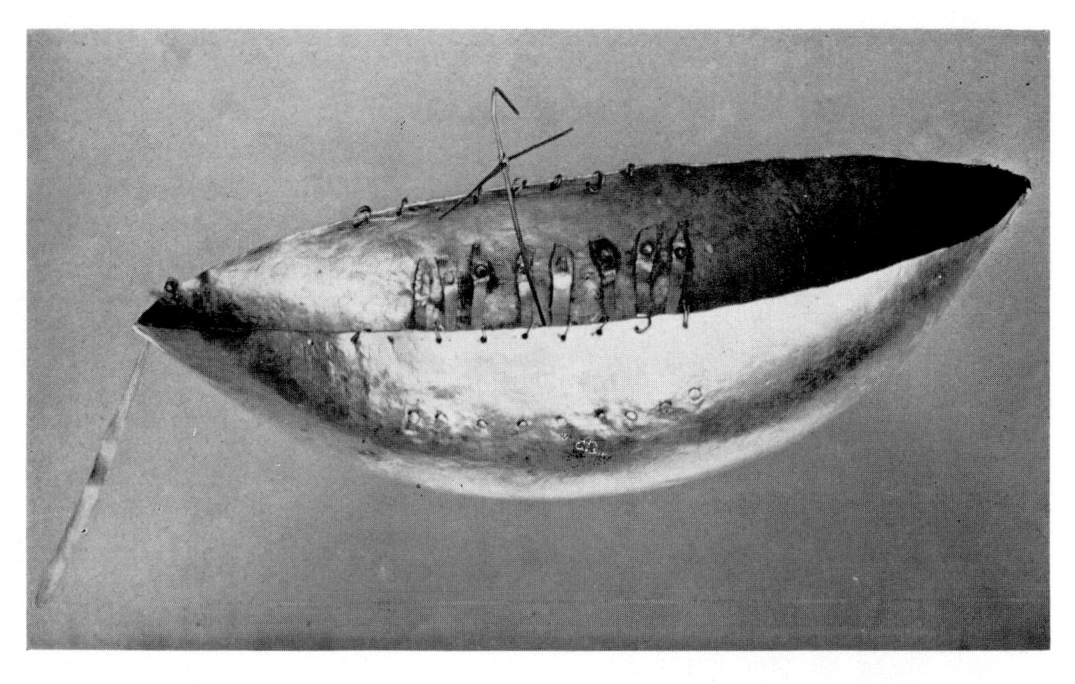

XXIIIb. Votive miniature boat of sheet gold (2/3 approx.); Broighter, Co. Londonderry.

XXIVa. The Rillaton gold cup, showing handle decoration; height 3·5 inches.

XXIVb. The Rillaton gold cup, showing attachment of handle.

XXIVc. The Fritzdorf gold cup; height 4·75 inches.

XXIVd. The Farway Down shale cup; height 3·6 inches.

XXV. Lozenge-shaped sheet-gold plaques and scabbard-hook (1/1); Bush Barrow, Wiltshire.

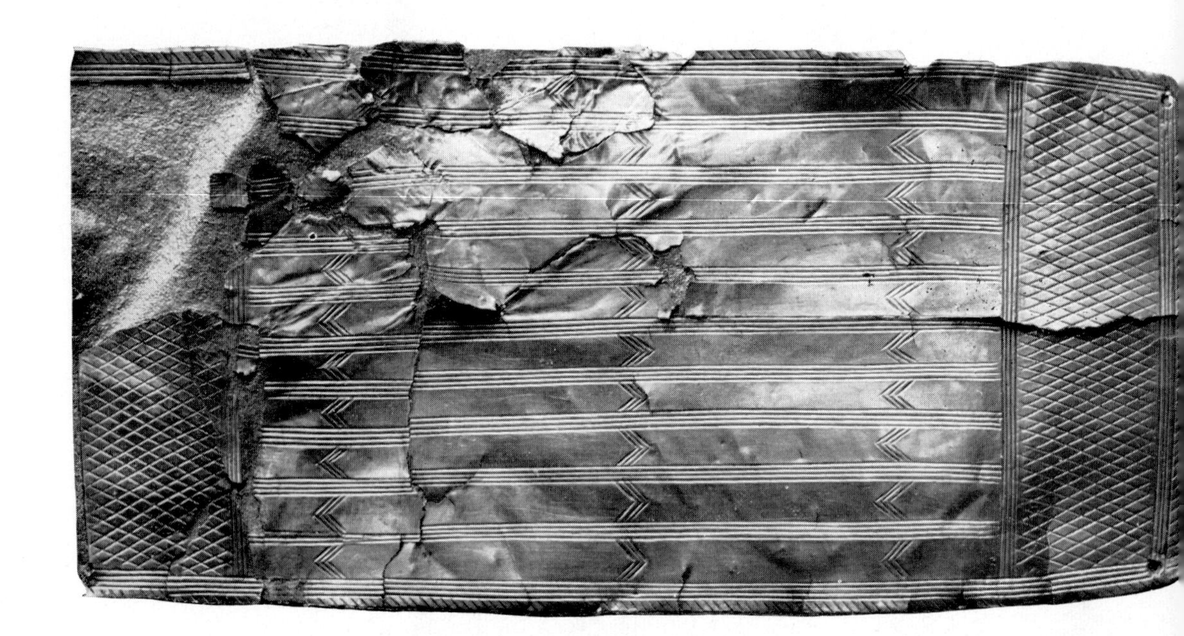

XXVIa. Sheet-gold wrist-guard (1/1); Upton Lovell.

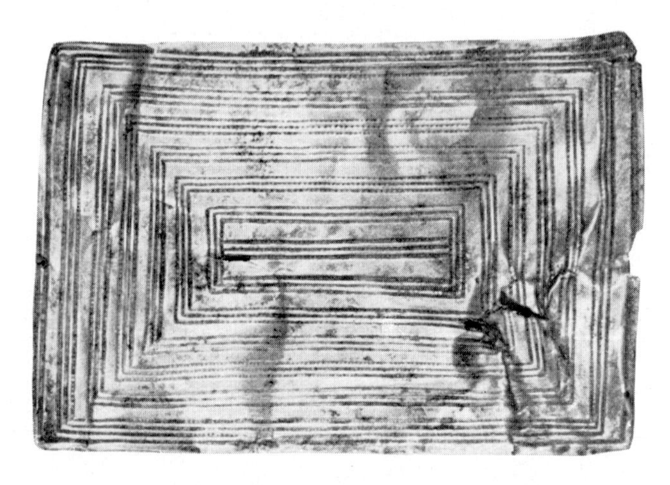

XXVIb. Sheet-gold wrist-guard (1/1); Cressingham.

CHAPTER IX

HENGES, STONE CIRCLES, AND BARROWS

THE TERM 'henge' was first used by Kendrick,[1] who initially listed a number of such sites. The subject was treated in detail by Clark [2] as an appendage to his report on the Arminghall timber circle. As a result of the Dorchester, Oxfordshire, excavations it has been treated afresh by Atkinson.[3] There has been no exhaustive treatment of stone circles, although those of certain localities [4] or of specific types [5] have received recognition and publication.

'Henge' should, strictly, be applied only to monuments which possess a 'hanging' structure, namely lintels. Lintels are peculiar to Stonehenge, which has a structural competence and architectural sophistication unique in the West. Although it cannot be denied that other monuments, where timber was used instead of stone, may have had lintels, this is impossible to prove. Yet the term *henge* for a peculiar type of monument has passed into English usage.

Atkinson [6] defines henges as having the common feature of an approximately circular earthwork in the form of a ditch *within* a bank, broken by either a single entrance, or two opposing ones. Certain of such earthworks are known to enclose, or to have enclosed, stones, posts, pits, and burials.

Circles of posts and stones which do not have a surrounding bank and ditch have been excluded from the henge class although they are allied. Atkinson also excluded a few henge-like monuments which, from field inspection, appear to have been surrounded by or embedded in apparently continuous and unbroken earthworks. Recent excavation [7] has shown that such monuments must have had entrances.

Certain henges, sometimes relatively small and unsubstantial, must certainly have had their internal features open to the sky and could even have surrounded the 'groves' noted by classical writers. Some were funerary monuments conceived and executed for a specific series of rites. The great enclosures such as Marden and Durrington served more generalized purposes. Others, particularly those sometimes called 'timber circles', may well originally have been roofed buildings. The excavator of the Arminghall henge [8] was inclined to the side of 'the pillars, as it were, of an open-air temple', yet a roofed building may have existed here. Even were Arminghall a horseshoe of uprights, it is unlikely that they would have been bare trunks; they may well have been

[1] Kendrick and Hawkes, 1932, Chap. VII.
[2] *PPS*, II, 23 ff.
[3] Atkinson, Piggott, and Sandars, 1951, 81–107.
[4] *PPS*, II, 106; *Antiq.*, XIII, 140; Childe, 1935, 111–15.
[5] Childe, 1947 b, 110; *PRIA*, LIV, 37–74.
[6] Atkinson, Piggott, and Sandars, 1951, 81–107.
[7] *PBUSS*, VIII, 1.
[8] *PPS*, II, 23 ff.

carved and embellished, like those seen by White[9] in the seventeenth century in the forests of temperate North America, in a manner recalling distantly the wooden figures from our bogs and marshes.

The detection of these timber circles was one of the major triumphs of aerial photography during the third and fourth decades of this century. First there was the discovery of Woodhenge[10] by Wing-Commander Insall, followed by that of Arminghall.[11] Air photography was enlisted in an endeavour to locate the Sanctuary,[12] a stone circle appended to Avebury's Avenue, lost to sight since the days of Stukeley, but without success. It was located, finally, by a topographical clue,[13] and, upon excavation, proved to have been a composite stone and timber circle.

Henges and stone circles are near-exclusive in distribution.[14] This could mean that in western England, where there are no henges, stone circles fulfilled their function. On the other hand, a few henges have recently been recognized in the south-west,[15] so it is possible that more may come to light in the apparent stone circle areas.

Stone circles vary in size. Most are modest, but, as with henges, there are large and impressive sites. The Stanton Drew, Somerset, circles are about 368 feet, 145 feet, and 97 feet, respectively, in diameter, while the overall diameter of the great circle at Grange Townland, Lough Gur,[16] Co. Limerick, is about 215 feet. Excluding those contained within henge earthworks, they are of two types, free-standing and embanked. The former are sometimes associated with avenues. There is a tendency for them to be grouped together in certain areas, while certain circles are in complexes as at Stanton Drew[17] or Lough Gur. Sometimes entrances are denoted, in the former class by large or small stones, in the latter by an entrance through the embankment.

Round barrows of the Bronze Age tend to cluster upon henges. The marked concentrations of barrows in the vicinities of these monuments can hardly be accidental and unconnected with them. Indeed, sometimes barrows have even been built within them, or upon their banks.

Stukeley[18] was the first to emphasize the great number of barrows in the immediate vicinity of Stonehenge, when he wrote: 'We may very readily count fifty at a time, in sight, from the place; easily distinguishable: but especially in the evening, when the sloping rays of the sun shine on the ground beyond them.' He made a similar observation[19] regarding his much loved Avebury, writing in his chapter heading: 'Of the barrows or sepulchral tumuli about Abury, very numerous here, as having for ages been a metropolitical temple.' Stukeley's remarks were amplified by Thurnam,[20] who deplored the lack of a map of the barrows around Avebury in Colt Hoare's 'Ancient Wiltshire'. Thurnam gave details of his own record, and remarked that at Avebury there was only about a third of the number of barrows that were around Stonehenge.

Allcroft and Sumner[21] have noted barrows in the vicinity of the Knowlton Circles. The latter was careful to point out that the greatest concentration of barrows in the region was a short distance to the west, at Oakley Down. However, air photography

[9] *Arch. J.*, XCVI, 215, Pl. I.
[10] *Antiq.*, I, 92; Cunnington, 1929.
[11] *Antiq.*, III, 257, Pl. I.
[12] *WAM*, XLV, 300–35.
[13] Stukeley, 1743, 36.
[14] Atkinson, Piggott, and Sandars, 1951, 92, Fig. 29.
[15] *Ant. J.*, XXXII, 67; *PWCFC*, I, 35.
[16] *PRIA*, LIV, 37–74.
[17] Dobson, 1931, 60.
[18] Stukeley, 1740, 43.
[19] Stukeley, 1743, 40.
[20] *Arch.*, XLIII, 306.
[21] Allcroft, 1908, 564; Sumner, 1931, 28.

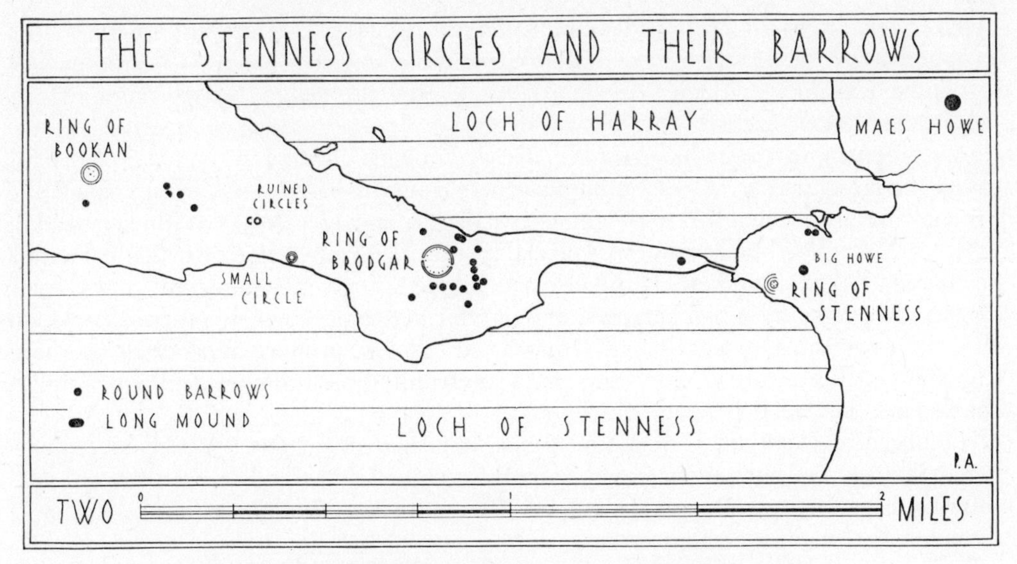

Fig. 47. Concentration of barrows around the Orkney circles.

shows great numbers, part destroyed, in the immediate vicinity. Many Mendip barrows are at no great distance from Gorsey Bigbury [22] or the Priddy Circles.[23] Recently, the fact of the proximity of barrows to the Thornborough and Hutton Moor Circles [24] has been restated. These last circles have a broad berm separating bank and ditch, a feature which has been compared with the bermed barrows of Wessex.

In much the same way as there is a relationship between henges and barrows, a relationship between stone circles and barrows is apparent. A factor is the occasional circles of stones, free-standing and set at a distance from the periphery of the barrow, and surrounding it. Notable examples are one of the Farway Down [25] barrows in Devon, and an apparently unchambered bell barrow in the Boyne passage-grave cemetery [26] in Ireland. Silbury Hill,[27] part of the Avebury complex of monuments, is also reputed to have been surrounded by a circle of stones.

Barrows do not always cluster upon stone circles. The circles at Stanton Drew in Somerset, which have a 'cove', a setting of three stones, similar to that in the centre of the northern circle at Avebury, and so called by Stukeley,[28] are remarkable for the absence of barrows in their immediate locality. On Dartmoor cairns appear to be associated with stone rows rather than with circles. However, a barrow is close by the Rollright Circle [29] and a cairn and circle were similarly closely associated on Mynydd Epynt.[30] Numbers of barrows are in the vicinity of certain stone circles. Clark [31] has shown how barrows cluster upon the Stenness Circles (Fig. 47), one of which is a henge.

At Arbor Low [32] a barrow has been set into the bank of the monument, a feature

[22] *PBUSS*, V, 3.
[23] *PBUSS*, VIII, 1.
[24] *YAJ*, XXXVIII, 425–45.
[25] *PDAES*, IV, 1–19.
[26] Ó Ríordáin, 1953, Pl. 57.
[27] *WAM*, XLII, 215.
[28] Stukeley, 1743, Tab., XIV.
[29] Crawford, 1925, 176.
[30] *Arch. Camb.*, XCVII, 169–94.
[31] *PPS*, II, 28, Fig. 13.
[32] *Arch.*, LVIII, 461.

noted in relation to the Mount Pleasant [33] henge in Dorset. The Eggardon Circle [34] has a round barrow sited in the centre of it, while another abuts the bank. At Cairnpapple [35] in Scotland a cairn succeeded and partially covered the henge. A large mound was within the Marden circle.[36]

A relationship between henges and barrows has been claimed in the form of the so-called 'henge-barrows'. A discontinuous ditch around a barrow at Chippenham,[37] the primary burial of which had with it an ogival dagger and a battle-axe, both discussed in Chapter X, enclosed what was most probably a series of pits, some of which contained occupation debris. Symmetrical ditches with single entrances, reminiscent of a Class I henge, surrounded two bell barrows, one of which covered a widely set post circle, on Wallis Down [38] in Dorset. Grinsell [39] has listed at least ten more barrows in southern England which had one or more causeways interrupting their ditches, and which might equally well be hailed as henge barrows.

The bermed barrows are also considered as related to henges.[40] It will be remembered that certain bermed barrows, namely some bell and the disc barrows, are surrounded by a ditch with an external bank. This feature is thought to be the fusion of the two elements henge and barrow.

It seems that the interment of bodies or cremated bones might be undertaken within or beneath henges, stone circles, or barrows. Indeed in Scotland the recumbent stone circles [41] are exclusively funerary. Many henges, circles, and barrows must be roughly contemporary, as will be seen below, but there is as yet no evidence as to what determined the particular place of interment.

Henges occur throughout Britain, and a few have been found in Ireland [42] also. Most are between about 175 feet and 400 feet in diameter. Avebury (about 1,400 feet diameter) and Durrington Walls (about 1,600 feet diameter) are the largest.

Avebury in North Wiltshire and Stonehenge on Salisbury Plain, geographically at the nodal points of southern England and two of the outstanding prehistoric monuments of the Old World, might each be cast in the role of cathedrals, to which all other henges would be as parish churches. Although Aubrey used a similar simile when describing Avebury, viz. 'that it did as much excell Stoneheng as a Cathedrall does a Parish Church', a case can be made for seeing Stonehenge as significant of a shift of power from the former to the latter. Sarsens of a size satisfactory for Stonehenge can be found only around Avebury, and there is no evidence of a supply elsewhere. It has thus been plausibly argued [43] that Avebury was the starting point for the sarsen phase of Stonehenge.

Side by side with Avebury and Stonehenge it would be well to consider Tara,[44] set commandingly at the key point of the Plain of Meath and among its many features possessing monuments resembling henges as well as a proven barrow of commensurate date. This last may be some indication of the origins of the site.

Recent study has shown that Stonehenge, in its final form, was most probably the product of the Wessex chieftains whose barrows throng its vicinity. If it be accepted that

[33] *Antiq.*, XIII, 159.
[34] *Antiq.*, XIII, 152.
[35] *PSAS*, LXXXII, 68–123.
[36] *VCH*, *Wilts.*, I, Pt. I, 37.
[37] *PCAS*, XXXVI, 134–42.
[38] *PPS*, XVIII, 150.
[39] *PPS*, VII, 106–7.
[40] Atkinson, 1956, 160.
[41] Childe, 1935, 173–6.
[42] *JRSAI*, LXXXIV, 93, Pl. IV.
[43] Atkinson, 1956, 110–17.
[44] Macalister, 1931; Ó Ríordáin, 1954.

the monument, in its various phases, was in use for three-quarters of the second millennium B.C., at the most conservative estimate, then its coexistence with not only the barrows but like monuments in its immediate vicinity is assured. It is thus hardly likely that they are unconnected, and they should be considered as a group or complex, rather than as a number of isolated monuments, as they have been up to now. Such grouping has been commented upon, but it must be emphasized that they are invariably thought of in isolation.

Thus Stonehenge and its Avenue, the Cursûs, Woodhenge, and Durrington Walls should be considered together as a single entity, as should Avebury, the Avenue and Sanctuary, plus Silbury Hill. The Knowlton Circles, the Thornborough Circles, the Stenness Circles form groups of like monuments. The apparently disparate monuments on the Hill of Tara have long been seen as a complex of associated monuments. Here in Ireland historical records and tradition can provide hints regarding their function, and excavation has shown that certain features of the site, namely the faience beads and the burials from the Mound of the Hostages, are coeval with the heyday of Avebury and Stonehenge.

Pradenne,[45] in 1938, compared Stonehenge (Pl. XXX a) with the framework of the 'earth-lodges' of the Omaha Indians of North America, whose material culture and environment was at one time not dissimilar from that of Early Bronze Age Britain. He suggested that were it roofed it would closely resemble such earth-lodges. It will be recalled that in a note on the Sanctuary, Cunnington[46] had envisaged a building utilizing all the post-sockets there, although in his mind Woodhenge remained the timber prototype of Stonehenge.

Pradenne's earth-lodge, Cunnington's pioneer building work, and the Germanic *Siedlungsgeschichte* (settlement-archaeology) practised by Bersu[47] to recover the circular-house plans at Little Woodbury, led Piggott[48] to study timber circles afresh. He was able to show the inherent possibility that Woodhenge may well have been a great circular building (Pl. XXX b), resembling in principle an Elizabethan theatre, and that the Sanctuary was a three-phase structure, composite and housing a stone circle in its final phase.

In view of this interpretation of the maze of post-sockets that are these monuments, it should be considered whether or not Stonehenge and other henges and stone circles were indeed circular roofed buildings along the lines suggested by Pradenne. It has recently[49] been possible to see long barrows as the counterparts of long houses; the alliance of round barrow with round house would be equally logical. Pradenne also stressed, although he apparently had in mind chambered barrows, how Stonehenge and Woodhenge, turf-roofed, would be, in their external appearance, almost identical with barrows!

Stake and post circles beneath and around barrows have long been compared with Woodhenge and the Sanctuary,[50] a process still current.[51] Piggott[52] has pursued the problems of this possible relationship between barrows, henges, and circles and suggested that a Dutch barrow incorporated a collapsed earth house. Now that a number

[45] *Antiq.*, XI, 87–92.

[46] *WAM*, XLV, 486–8.

[47] *PPS*, VI, 30–111; see also *Journal of the Manx Museum*, V, 177, and *UJA*, X, 30, in this general context.

[48] *Arch. J.*, XCVI, 193 ff.

[49] *Antiq.*, XXXII, 106–11.

[50] Van Giffen, 1930, 115–22.

[51] *PPS*, XVIII, 153.

[52] *Arch. J.*, XCVI, 193 ff.

of different types of post and stake circles are known from barrows it would be tempting to take the analogies further. Many of the stake circles, especially those under composite barrows, appear to have been temporary in character, while others performed at the most the function of peripheral retention. One can suggest enclosures or temporary mortuary houses. The latter function seems more possible if it is thought that the 'passage' arrangements of stakes at the entrances to certain circles were porches.[53] There is no evidence to warrant the contention that certain round barrows covered functional houses.[54] A further link between house and barrow lies in the deposits of occupation earth, together with struck flints, artefacts, and sherds, often abraded, which were presumably brought from houses and incorporated in barrows. The excavator of the great stone circle in Grange Townland, Lough Gur[55] found, as have the excavators of similar sites in Northern Ireland[56] and Morbihan,[57] traces of what can only be the 'ritual' breaking of pottery. This is thus a rite common to barrows and circles.

Although certain henges have yielded relics attributed to the Secondary Neolithic cultures,[58] it must be remembered that much material recovered from barrows in the form of sherds is closely comparable.[59] While it is possible to demonstrate evolutionary relationships between Secondary Neolithic wares and funerary pottery such as food-vessels, overhanging-rim and ribbed urns, etc. (see Chapter VIII), it is equally possible that the general relationship was, instead, parallel. Thus much of the pottery that we recover from barrows, often as more or less perfect vessels, may well have been the purely funerary vessels, separate and distinct from those for domestic usage.

Attested Bronze Age domestic sites, with undoubted household pottery and the remains of unmistakable dwellings, have scarcely ever been discovered. There are the remains, from lowland areas, of what can hardly have been more than squattings,[60] with Beaker, Secondary Neolithic, and sometimes Food-Vessel pottery mixed together. In the highland zone there are the remains of a distinctive series of often cellular and sometimes courtyarded stone houses,[61] and there are raths in Ireland.[62] On the other hand, in the vicinity of Woodhenge[63] there is evidence of domestic usage, in the form of occupation debris, though perhaps of specific feasts, interred, in pits. Elsewhere, unfortunately, the excavation of henges has been restricted to the internal features and areas. Here, except under the exceptional circumstance of soil increment, the detection of a floor with occupation debris is so unlikely as to be almost impossible, as soil weathering would have long since removed all traces.

Henges and related structures have long been claimed as temples, but it is a strange society that constructs imposing groups of temples and no houses. Some henges and circles, as has been shown above, could have been roofed and been dwelling houses, although for a ruling minority. With all this evidence in mind it seems likely that the builders of barrows continued to dwell amongst the barrows of their ancestors, that house and temple, such as the dwellings of priest-kings at Avebury, Stonehenge, and Tara, and their subject princelings at Knowlton and other centres, were one and the same.

[53] *Ant. J.*, XXI, 118–22; *PPS*, XVIII, 150; *PDNHAS*, LXXVI, 39–50.
[54] *PPS*, XXIII, 222.
[55] *PRIA*, LIV, 37–74.
[56] Evans, 1953, 12.
[57] Le Rouzic, 1930, 32.
[58] Atkinson, Piggott, and Sandars, 1951, 90–1.
[59] e.g. *PPS*, XXIII, 154, Fig. 10.
[60] Childe, 1947 b, 98 (Beaker); *PCAS*, XXXV, 126 (Beaker); *Ant. J.*, XIII, 266.
[61] *TDA*, LXXXIX, 18–77.
[62] *PRIA*, XLV, 83–181.
[63] *WAM*, LII, 287; *PPS*, XV, 122–7.

CHAPTER X

CULTURES, ORIGINS, AND AFFINITIES

DISTINCTIVE types of barrows and forms of barrow structures, timber circles around and beneath barrows, forms of burial, graves, and the pots, daggers, battle-axes, and objects termed grave-furniture recurring together constitute cultures. Just as today houses, cars, and cutlery embody the social traditions of nations or continents, the Bronze Age barrows, and the relics therefrom, are considered to do likewise. The differing types of barrows circumscribed in their specific regions, the differing types of vessels, daggers, and axes, embody the differing social heritages of their makers. Thus, when the prehistorian considers cultures compounded of certain elements he seeks details of the preliterate societies of which they are the material expression.

The entrenched epochal entities, based upon impressive typological sequences, of Montelius and Müller, were undermined by Schliemann's 'Mycenaen'. They were finally superseded by Gordon Childe's first *Dawn of European Civilization* (1925) and by the lucid argument and exposition of the cultural methods [1] of prehistory contained within his *The Danube in Prehistory* (1929). Today contemporary and overlapping cultures are an integral part of our conceptions of the Bronze Age.

It is frequently claimed that certain traits in the British Bronze Age originated on the mainland of Europe. Initially they most probably did. However, subsequently, traffic and intercourse can only have been reciprocal—that is, many things must have originated in the British Isles and have spread to the Continent. Thus there was an intricate pattern of exchange which ebbed and flowed down into historic and even modern times.

With two exceptions British Bronze Age cultures bear names derived from funerary vessels found in barrows. At the present time [2] it is customary to refer to the *Beaker folk*, the *Food-Vessel people*, the *Wessex culture*, the *Urn folk*, and the *Deverel-Rimbury culture*. Certain burials discussed in Chapter VII, although beneath round barrows, are normally considered with the *Secondary Neolithic cultures* and have thus not been accorded a label here. Though they overlapped considerably in time this is their apparent sequence of origin. While the characteristic content of the first three groups is fairly comprehensive, the last two *cultures* are defined by little more than sepulchral vessels. As grave-furniture was not deposited in any quantity in what appear to be later barrow graves, the question of the precise types of bronzes used by the later cultures is problematical.

The Beaker folk comprised a number of groups expressed, almost entirely, by the

[1] Childe 1956, cultures, s.v.

[2] Childe, 1947 b.

complexes 'A' and 'B' formulated by Clark,[3] which are the necked- and bell-beakers of Piggott.[4]

Bell-beakers are a ubiquitous European form, found from Bohemia to Britain.[5] Their ubiquity means that they are the earliest type, while localized forms can only be later. Everywhere they are accompanied by characteristic tanged West European daggers, archers' wrist-guards, and, in Britain and western Europe only, barbed and tanged arrow-heads. Elsewhere the hollow-based variety was used. Gold discs, pendants, ear-rings, and what may have been razors do not seem to have been a primary feature of this widespread European culture.

Certain West European daggers with flanged tangs, namely those from Dorchester and Sittingbourne[6] in southern England, very closely resemble their continental counterparts.[7] Analysis of the metal of one of these daggers has shown that the metal may reasonably be compared to metals from the Saale region, while the metal of the other also most probably has affinities with that quarter. The enlarged tanged dagger from the Roundway[8] Beaker grave recalls the not dissimilar, massive tanged dagger in the Neuenheligen hoard,[9] and its metal may also be from that region.[10] However, the tanged dagger from the Winterslow[11] grave appears to have been the product of Irish metallurgists.

Ring-pendants, found in at least two southern English bell-beaker graves,[12] have been found in varying contexts in northern and central Europe,[13] and in the eastern Mediterranean.[14] The Radley sheet-gold basket ear-rings in the Ashmolean Museum have their counterparts in Belgium[15] and Spain.[16] Although one has been found in Poland,[17] they are apparently a western form, presumably inspired, originally and distantly, by the wire basket ear-rings of Egypt[18] and Anatolia.[19] Strip ear-rings, comparable to those from Goodmanham,[20] have been found in Silesia[21] and Poland;[22] these are apparently a mid-European form. The Scottish spatulate-ended neck-rings are comparable with a north European series now defined by Glasbergen.[23]

The distribution of bell-beakers in England suggests two points of penetration and two areas of primary settlement. Piggott[24] has suggested a south-coast landing and settlement, while colonization south of the Thames valley was initially conceived by Abercromby.[25]

B2, or barrel-beakers, can at present only be regarded as a pottery type. Their shape is reminiscent of certain of Becker's coarse beakers with 'short-wave' moulding.[26] Such 'wave' decoration, incised or scored, is a feature of one B2 beaker,[27] and a cordon or

[3] *Antiq.*, V, 415–26.

[4] To Prehistoric Society, 15 March 1952.

[5] Childe, 1957, beakers s.v.

[6] Dorchester, *ANL*, IV, 58; Sittingbourne, *PSA*, X, 29.

[7] *MAGW*, LVII, 88; Castillo, 1928, Pl. LXXX.

[8] *WAM*, III, 185–6.

[9] Childe, 1929, Fig. 143.

[10] *PPS*, XXIII, 99 (Case and Coghlan).

[11] *PPS*, XXIII, 100.

[12] *Oxon.*, VIII–IX, 34; Sittingbourne, *PSA*, X, 29.

[13] Sprockhoff, 1938, Taf. 63; Forssander, 1936, Taf. XXIV; Childe, 1957, 98.

[14] Schliemann, 1880, 430, Fig. 557.

[15] *Matériaux*, 1885, 318, Fig. 89.

[16] *Ethnos*, II, 458 ff; Childe, 1950, 79.

[17] *Fontes*, VII, Ryc. 111, c.

[18] Aberg, 1930–5, IV, 11.

[19] Childe, 1950, Fig. 22, 1.

[20] Greenwell, 1877, 324.

[21] *Altschles.*, I, Abb. 44; Ebert, 1924, II, Taf. 81, 382.

[22] *Man*, XLVIII, 24; *Fontes*, VII, 85–6, Ryc. 110–11.

[23] *Palaeohist.*, V, 53–71.

[24] *PPS*, IV, 57.

[25] Abercromby, 1912, I, 80.

[26] *PPS*, XXI, 65–71.

[27] *Antiq.*, V, 415 (opp.), 1.

moulding has been found below the rim, enhancing this likeness, on another.[28] This wave-decorated B2 beaker is markedly similar to a beaker from a Dutch *Hünenbett*.[29] The rolled bronze-leaf beads found with a B2 beaker in Sussex [30] have their fellows, not only with Dorset urns, Oxfordshire A beakers, and in the Scottish Migdale hoard,[31] but in northern Europe and the south German Straubing culture.[32] An indigenous origin for the type seems not impossible. Most marked is the absence of any armament, although a wrist-guard was with a B2 beaker at Brandon [33] in Suffolk. Cord-ornamented bell-beakers [34] may also be another insular innovation, for the British series are distinct from the zoned corded bell-beakers of the Middle Rhine and south-western France recently defined by Gersbach.[35] None the less the use of British-inspired beakers spread to Holland and the Rhineland beyond.

The AC beaker group, which is Clark's complex 'A', namely the necked-beakers, was, when other grave-furniture was present, accompanied by battle-axes, 'flat' knife-daggers with rivets in five or six instances, flint daggers which like some of the battle-axes copied metal,[36] conical V-perforated buttons, pulley-rings, and barbed and tanged flint arrow-heads. Some of this equipment, which appears to denote male warrior graves, has a bell-beaker ancestry, as have the archers' wrist-guards. Here lies the British version of the widespread Battle-axe cultures [37] and the basis of our insular bronze working.

C beakers, the short-necked variety, are predominant in Scotland and the North. Abercromby believed that they resulted from the degeneration of A beakers, noticing that, after A beakers, they became more numerous the further one went from the Thames estuary landing places of the bell-beaker immigrants. It seems unlikely that necked-beakers, 'C' or 'A', owe anything directly to bell-beakers, although there must have been parallel development. However, there are coincidences between certain of the former [38] and Dutch beakers of the Veluwe type.[39] While these vessels may represent incidental intercourse, the possibility of actual immigration into Scotland, from across the North Sea, cannot be overlooked. Thus ancestors for the short-necked beaker group as a whole could be found. However, in view of the popularity of panelled ornament on Veluwe beakers, and the predominance of zoned decoration on the Scottish series, this derivation is rather unconvincing.

As for B2 beakers, an indigenous origin seems likely for A beakers, the long-necked variety, since convincing continental ancestors are entirely absent. Indeed it has been suggested that Abercromby's sequence be reversed and that it be considered that they evolved from the C series. These, however, are, as has been emphasized, predominantly zoned, and never have the great vertical panels of the A beakers, which resemble the panelling frequently found in Holland on the alleged ancestors of the C beakers. Thus for the time being their precise origins must remain obscure. The long neck and sometimes rather globose body give the vessels almost more than a superficial

[28] *PPS*, II, 189, Fig. III, 1.
[29] *Antiq.*, V, 415 (opp.), 2.
[30] *JRAI*, XXXII, 381.
[31] *PSAS*, XXXV, 266, LVII, 127.
[32] Broholm, 1943–9, I, 83, G. 728; Ebert, 1924, VIII, 247, Taf. 75 b, 7; *MBV*, 11, Katalog Straubing, Taf. 8, 9: 11, 8: 12, 4: 15, 12.
[33] *Bronze Age Guide*, 68.
[34] *Actas*, XXI, 196–201.
[35] *JSG*, XLVI, 1–12.
[36] Forssander, 1936, Taf. L.
[37] Childe, 1950, 148–74.
[38] Abercromby, 1912, I, 217, 230, 236, 245, 255, 266, 268, 269.
[39] Bursch, 1933, Taf. II.

resemblance to certain Saxo-Thuringian corded beakers,[40] although the zoned, corded, neck decoration of the latter has never been found on A beakers.

The bronze armlet found under an A beaker at Knipton,[41] and others from Normanton [42] and Melfort,[43] and certain corrugated armlets [44] may well be inspired by the manchette armlets of the central European Unětice culture.[45] However, analysis of a knife-dagger from an A beaker grave at Eynsham [46] in Oxfordshire has shown the probable western origin of the metal.

That food-vessels represent a distinct society, apart from the Necked-Beaker folk, seems unlikely as the two types are frequently found together in dwelling sites and from time to time in barrows.[47] Thus they have, in Britain, an almost identical distribution, and the relics found with them, and their burials, perpetuate Beaker traits. Plano-convex flint knives, and, in the north, lunate jet necklaces, are the only consistently accompanying relics. Flat knife-daggers and a dagger related to the Bush Barrow type have been found with food-vessels. The only halberds found in graves have been assigned to them, as has a flat axe. V-perforated buttons identical with those from Beaker-graves are found with them. Art, described in Chapter VI, is a trait associated more closely with food-vessels than with any other type.

Food-vessels have been found in the same grave as a necked beaker in Wiltshire,[48] and in the same barrow in Devon.[49] In Scotland [50] there are beakers that closely resemble food-vessels in fabric and workmanship. These factors, the common burial rites and relics, together with the lack of armament in all but a handful of graves, hint that these vessels might have been buried with a certain class of Necked-Beaker society—perhaps the women?

Some would see the origins of food-vessels outside the British Isles, in the Iberian Peninsula [51] and southern France, and the polypod bowls with their lug-interrupted shoulder groove, from the gallery-grave of La Halliade [52] also closely resemble food-vessels. It will be remembered that an Iberian ribbed cylinder pin-head has been found in a grave in Galway [53] and that lunulae close to Irish forms are known from Galicia and Portugal.[54] In Germany bowls comparable to the small number of British footed food-vessels have been found.[55] A 'twin' vase, two food-vessels joined at the shoulder, has been considered as the British representative of a popular Mediterranean ritual vessel.[56] On the other hand, Stone [57] has pointed out that certain Yorkshire vases owe much to Secondary Neolithic sources for their decoration. It seems inescapable that they owe much to Neolithic forms such as bowls of Form G.

It is possible that art of MacWhite's [58] Irish 'Galician' group, usually found in burial cairns, on natural rock surfaces and boulders, and sometimes on standing stones, has the

[40] e.g. Hoernes and Menghin, 1925, 321, 3.
[41] *Ant. J.*, XV, 60.
[42] Hoare, 1812–19, 160.
[43] *PSAS*, XIX, 134; *PPS*, XIX, 169; cf. *Inv. Arch.*, A 1.
[44] *PPS*, XV, 120–1.
[45] Childe, 1929, 231, Fig. 134.
[46] *PPS*, XXIII, 99.
[47] *PPS*, XXIII, 40–56. Further propositions regarding the affinities and development of food-vessels have been made by ApSimon in *ULIAA Bulletin*, I, 24–36.
[48] *WAM*, XLVIII, 360.
[49] *PDAES*, IV, 1–19.
[50] Childe, 1935, 84.
[51] *PPS*, XVII, 45.
[52] *Matériaux*, XVI, 1881, Pl. XVI.
[53] Childe, 1957, 338.
[54] MacWhite, 1951, 48–64.
[55] Schultz, 1939, 43, Fig. 45.
[56] *Ant. J.*, LX, 137.
[57] *PPS*, XV, 125.
[58] *JRSAI*, LXXVI, 59–80.

connection with food-vessels that his maps imply. This art in Scotland is also found on cist covers or stones. MacWhite sees its origin in north-western Spain and Portugal, in Obermaier's latest group of rock carvings,[59] with Mediterranean connections beyond. Such a derivation strengthens the case for a Western origin for food-vessels. On the other hand it should not be forgotten that such art in a simple form is not unknown in northern Europe.[60]

However, food-vessel connections with the Mediterranean and Iberia went deeper than pottery styles. It is with food-vessels that the famous Folkton 'drums', the cylindrical chalk-cut idols, are normally considered. Although, as has been shown, the affinities of this ornamentation lie with British and Irish cultures, their 'pick-axe' faces are inspired, ultimately, from more distant sources. Such faces have been traced to Anatolia[61] and appear to manifest an ideology[62] discernible throughout the Mediterranean littoral, which spread, ultimately, throughout western Europe, where it assumed localized and distinctive forms. Doubtlessly the Folkton idols are one such localized manifestation.

Irish bowls, like other elements in the Irish Bronze Age, have been shown as having affinities with northern Germany. The gold vessel from Gonnebek,[63] in Holstein, apparently closely copies a north British or an Irish bowl-type food-vessel,[64] and two more bowls from Langendorf, near Stralsrund, may show Irish influence. It is of considerable interest, in this present context, to remember that in 1692 a gold so-called 'hat', comparable with that from Schifferstadt[65] and the one recently found at Etzelsdorf-Buch,[66] was found in a bog in Tipperary.[67] These so-called 'hats' were most probably ritual vessels, used, perhaps even as were the Minoan rhytons, for pouring libations. Also comparable with Irish sheet-gold work, notably the Broighter boat, and its composite fellow from Caergwrle, are the one hundred sheet-gold concentric-circle ornamented miniature boats from Nors in Denmark.[68] They were found one inside another, so it is alleged, in a pot covered with a flat stone apparently deposited in a gravel bank. Irish craftsmen in metal must have taken to themselves concentric-circle ornament from northern European sources, and continuation of this connection is attested by the sunflower pins, Hersprung shields, trumpets, trumpet-ended bracelets, perhaps amber,[69] and the bracelets in the Gorteenreagh,[70] Co. Clare, hoard.

A precise origin for Irish bowls, the panelled decoration of which recalls long-necked beakers, could be sought in the movement from the region of the Netherlands of peoples who used beakers of the Veluwe type, although descent from the local Neolithic seems more likely. Indeed, there are sherds in the assemblages from such sites as Knockadoon[71] which could be considered as pieces of proto-food-vessels.

One Irish Type E food-vessel was found, together with a Bush Barrow derivative dagger in an inhumation grave, under a considerable cairn on Topped Mountain,[72]

[59] *IPEK*, I, 59.
[60] Ebert, 1924, III, 212.
[61] Blegan, 1950, I, Pt. II, 190, 257.
[62] Crawford, 1957.
[63] Kersten, 1936, Taf. XXI.
[64] *Altschles.*, V, 179 ff, Taf. XXXII; *PPS*, III, 327.
[65] Ebert, 1924, XI, Taf. 69.
[66] *Germania*, XXXII, 1.
[67] J. C. Walker, *Irish Dress*, Dublin, 1788, Pl. III, Fig. 5.
[68] *Aarbøger*, 1886, 236.
[69] *PPS*, III, 394; *Germania*, XX, 10; *JRSAI*, LXXXI, 57–61.
[70] *ANL*, IV, 177.
[71] *PRIA*, LVI, 297–459.
[72] *PRIA* (3rd ser.), IV, 651–8.

Fermanagh, while more recently another was found associated with a segmented faience bead. In spite of the excavation and research of the past two decades, there have been relatively few beakers found in Ireland, while those brought to light resemble British forms so closely[73] that they must represent settlement from that land. Can it be that these angular Type E vessels, which resemble short-necked beakers, are the local equivalent of the beakers? On the other hand it could be argued that male relics have also been found with bowls, as was the case at Croghan[74] in Westmeath, while Gogan[75] and others have compared these vessels with Marnian pots of the Early Iron Age! These excesses have been curbed by Childe,[76] who cites the Fermanagh dagger. The predominantly zoned, and sometimes panelled, decoration of these food-vessels clearly resembles that of long-necked beakers.

A social relationship existed between the Irish Food-Vessel people and the builders of the Boyne passage-graves. Not only were food-vessels often, it is claimed, the final burials in the chambers, but the distinctive pecked art symbols of the Boyne culture were on the underside of the capstones of cists, containing a food-vessel, and a cremation, at Ballinvally,[77] Co. Meath, and a heat-twisted halberd and a cremation at Moylough,[78] Co. Sligo. Boyne art motifs are sometimes found on the bases of food-vessels, and they are also found on certain British miniature vessels.

The ornamental stones set in the kerbs and cairn-rings of cairns and composite barrows recall distinctly the enriched stones in the kerbs of the great Boyne passage-graves. It is becoming increasingly evident that much of this barrow 'art', and some of the related passage-grave 'art' hitherto thought of as almost exclusively Western is present in Central Germany.[79] It is possible that its origins lie here like so much in our Round Barrow cultures.

The Wessex culture (App. V) must inevitably loom large in any account of Bronze Age Britain. The culture comprises the frequently richly furnished graves, often with exotic content, set within the circumscribed area termed Wessex and beneath the sometimes distinctive barrows[80] clustered mainly upon Avebury and Stonehenge (Fig. 6). It is an amalgam of which the ingredients can be detected and examined. If these warriors and amazons were not mere aggrandized A-Beaker-Battle-axe-Food-Vessel-Secondary Neolithic folk, enriched by the proceeds of their control of the metal trade, the dominant class at least may originally have come from the Saale valley.

Thus from Beaker sources came the V-perforated buttons, sometimes of amber, sometimes enlarged and cased in sheet-gold, the sheet-gold wrist-guards, the finely finished barbed and tanged arrow-heads. The hilts of the Bush Barrow daggers are aggrandized and developed versions of the Brigmerston type. It is possible that the battle-axes (Fig. 48), which, like daggers, denote warrior graves, were also of A-beaker ancestry, although much modified to incorporate likenesses to exotic double-axes! However, hammer-ends, on the Stourton-Loose Howe battle-axes, are clearly a battle-axe feature. From this same source must come the technique of tubular perforation which is so markedly different to the laborious 'hour-glass' method which is likely to

[73] *Ant. J.*, XXVIII, 151.
[74] *PRIA*, LV, 388; *JRSAI*, LXX, 61.
[75] *JCHAS*, XXXIV, 65–70.
[76] Childe, 1947 b, 133.
[77] Raftery, 1951, 148, Fig. 154.
[78] *JRSAI*, LIX, 113.
[79] Schrickel, 1957; Kramer, 1958, 93–106.
[80] L. V. Grinsell, *The Archaeology of Wessex*, Methuen, 1958, 102–3.

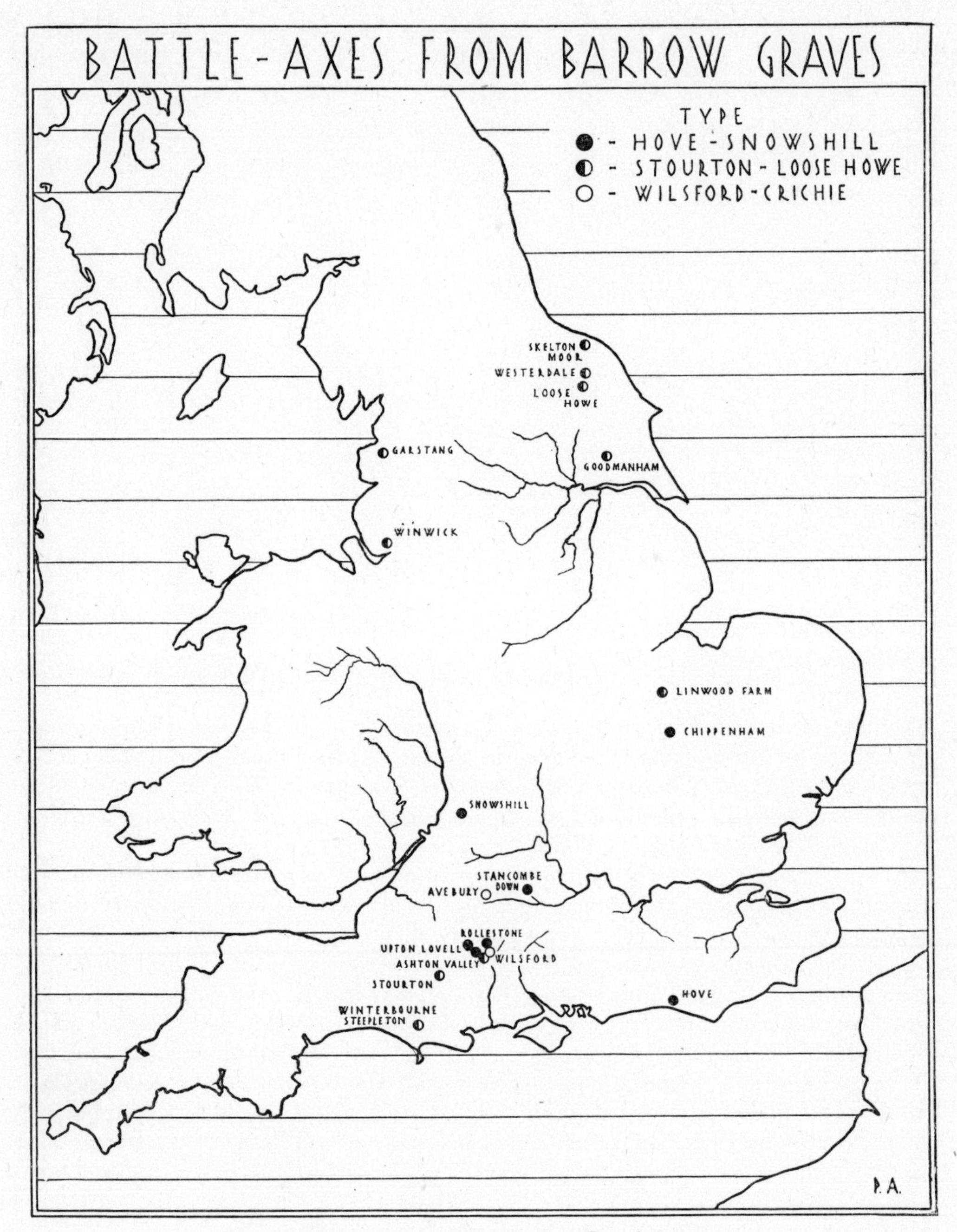

Fig. 48. Map showing battle-axes from British barrows.

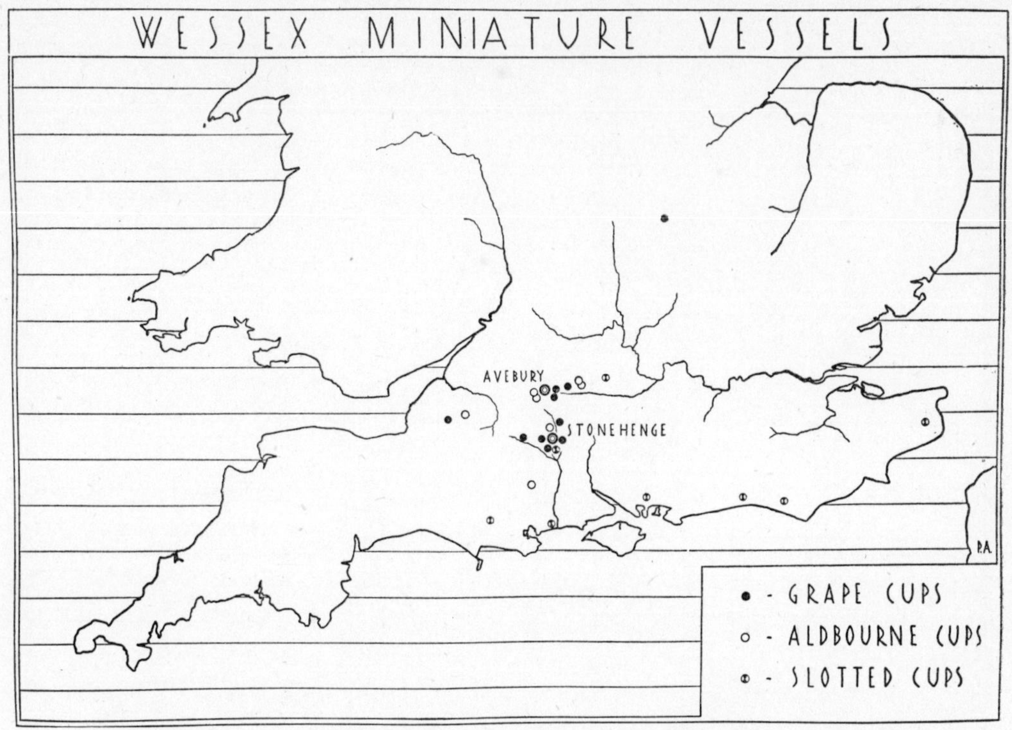

Fig. 49. Map showing the distribution of Aldbourne, Grape, and Stonehenge cups.

have been of ultimate Mesolithic origin. Food-vessels make their contribution in the form of the lunulae necklaces, rendered in amber, besides a number of Type 3 food-vessels from graves. One such food-vessel was accompanied by a number of finely finished arrow-heads, and another, of superb workmanship, was with a double burial with knife-daggers of A-beaker affinity.[81]

Another element is the corded cinerary urns, one of which has a noticeable beaker fabric,[82] which, springing from the corded Mortlake bowls, via Fengate pottery, denote a native strain shown clearly by a few graves containing antler, bone, and tooth artefacts.[83] The Aldbourne, Grape, and Slotted cups, strangely Stonehenge-like, all ceramic types distinctive of the Wessex culture (Fig. 49), may also be from native sources. The former have much in common with Rinyo-Clacton ware,[84] while the knobbed grape-cups resemble the knobbed objects of indeterminate use, thought in instances to copy wooden club-heads, found at Skara Brae[85] and Rinyo.[86] Also some scholars have identified affinities between French Chassey ware[87] and Chassey 'vase-supports'[88] and the Aldbourne cups, and have found later Chassey[89] and Iberian[90] counterparts for the grape-cups.

[81] *PPS*, XXIII, 137.
[82] *PPS*, IV, 91, Fig. 21, 1.
[83] *WAM*, LV, 311–26.
[84] Piggott, 1954, 321–46; *PPS*, XVII, 63.
[85] Childe, 1931, 100, Pl. XXXVII.
[86] *PSAS*, LXXIII, 6–31, LXXXI, 16–42.
[87] *Arch. J.*, LXXXVIII, 52, Pl. III.
[88] Le Rouzic, 1930. See also *BRGK*, XXXVII–XXXVIII, 21, Abb. 8, 19–21, Abb. 9, 10–13.
[89] J. Déchelette, *Manuel D'Archaeologie Préhistorique, Celtique, et Gallo-Romaine*, Paris, 1914, II, 555.
[90] Leisner, 1943, I, Taf. 155.

The exotic elements in the Wessex culture are from the region of Europe most of which is still Germany and from the East Mediterranean. That from the former appears to be in great measure from the Tumulus culture [91] and from the aggrandized and basic Unětice elements which preceded and coexisted with it. From this source come not only a number of imported pins,[92] but the direct inspiration of some of the metal armament. Thus the Bush Barrow dagger blades (Fig. 50) may be based upon such blades as the six-riveted Gaubickelheim [93] daggers and be copied in turn by those from Kladow [94] and Neuenheligen.[95] These last two have hilt and blade cast as one in the manner of the earlier tanged West European daggers. Their solid metal flat hilts are pounced in a manner that near imitates the small nails of the Bush Barrow haft. Such *pointillé* embellishment can only have its origins in the *ornementation pointillée* and *bohrornament* of Mesolithic times,[96] and is clearly a contribution from the native element. The hilts and pommels of the Camerton-Snowshill ogival daggers (Fig. 51) are, on the other hand, in their various media, clearly copies of the metal hilts and pommels of certain of the contemporary Germany *Vollgriffdolche*, as listed and described by Uenze.[97] The lined ogival blades, besides the many blades cited as similar by ApSimon,[98] may owe something, ultimately, to certain Hungarian dirk forms.[99] It is probable that the flanges, and sometimes pointed butts, of characteristic axes in hoards [100] and a number of single discoveries, mostly from south-eastern England, which are generally considered with the Wessex culture, indicate a central European origin for this type also. The axes from the Bohemian Sobochleby [101] hoard illustrate these axes clearly. Undoubted Irish axes and British spear-heads have been exported to middle and northern Europe.[102] In the Wessex Bush Barrow were the remains of what was claimed to have been a shield. The fragments, which are all that remain, could well have been from a composite shield similar to that uncovered in a Tumulus culture grave at Mehrstetten [103] in Bohemia. The Ogmore Down helmets (Fig. 52), although found in a place distant from Wessex, are relevant in this context for their resemblance to the bell-helmet found also about a century ago at Beitzsch,[104] in Saxony, allegedly together with Unětician ingot torques and a triangular dagger. Sheet-metal working was a craft at which the Mid-European smiths were extremely competent, and it is possible that the initial inspiration of sheet-metal products in Wessex and Ireland, in the form of gold ornaments and the first of the superb, distinctively British, shields, which there is good reason to believe may in part belong to the later stages of this period, originates from this source. Indeed boss styles are to be seen early in central and northern Europe on the copper discs from Brześć Kujawski,[105] Hăbăşeşti,[106] and Salten [107] in Denmark.

Many more details underline and emphasize the mid-European contribution to the

[91] Childe, 1929, 296.

[92] *PPS*, IV, 85. See also *Palaeohist.*, V, 73–6.

[93] *Altertümer*, I, II, Taf. 4, 2–5; I, VI, Taf. 26.

[94] *Götze Festschrift*, 93; *PZ*, XVI, 87; Uenze, 1938, 99.

[95] Childe, 1929, Fig. 143.

[96] Clark, 1936, 163, Fig. 57. *Pointillé* ornament in the Bush Barrow style was not unknown in the Northern Bronze Age; cf. Schwantes, 1939, Taf. 37, 411–13.

[97] Uenze, 1938.

[98] *ULIAA Rpt*, X, 62.

[99] Childe, 1929, 422.

[100] *ULIAA Rpt*, X, 62.

[101] Richly, 1893, Taf. XXXIV; *MAGW*, XX, 17.

[102] Irish Axes from Dieskau and Leubingen, *Arch.*, LXXXVI, 303; Müller, 1895, 128, 179.

[103] *Prä. Bl.*, 1906, 50.

[104] *PPS*, XVIII, 36–46.

[105] Childe, 1950, 113, Fig. 87.

[106] *SCIV*, V (1954), 36–54.

[107] C. J. Becker, 'Mosefunde Lerkar, fra yngre Stenalder', *Aarbøger*, 1947, 253, Fig. 54.

Fig. 50. Map showing distribution of Bush Barrow daggers.

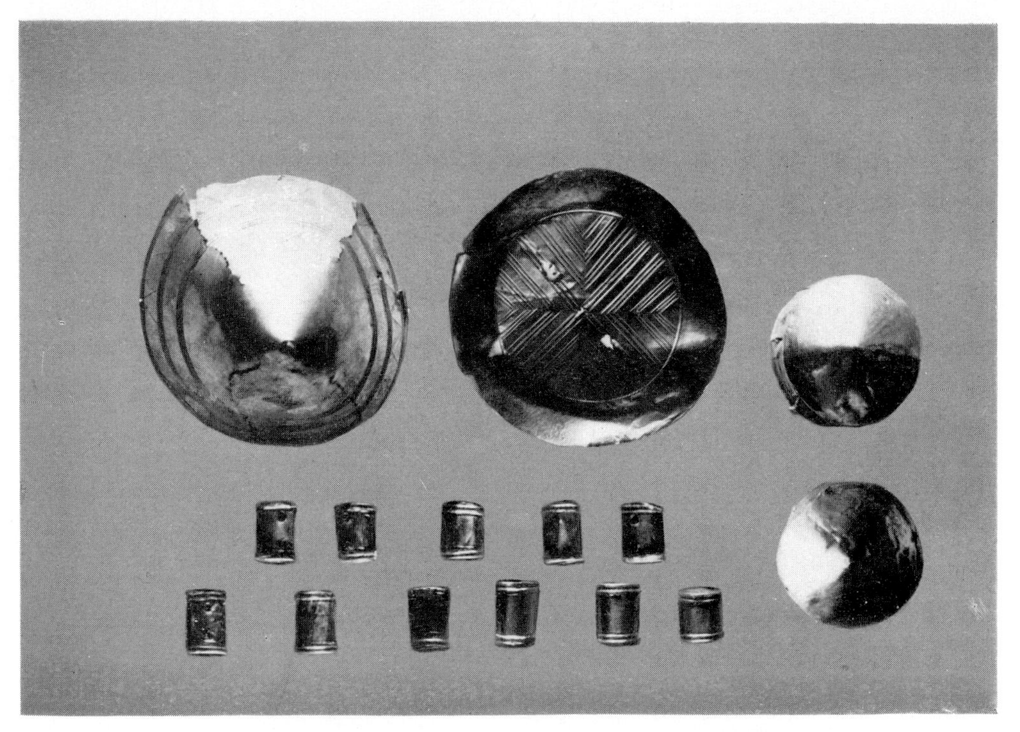

XXVIIa. Sheet-gold casing for a conical shale button, sheet-gold bosses, and gold-cased beads or buttons (1/1), from the Upton Lovell, Wiltshire, 'Gold' barrow.

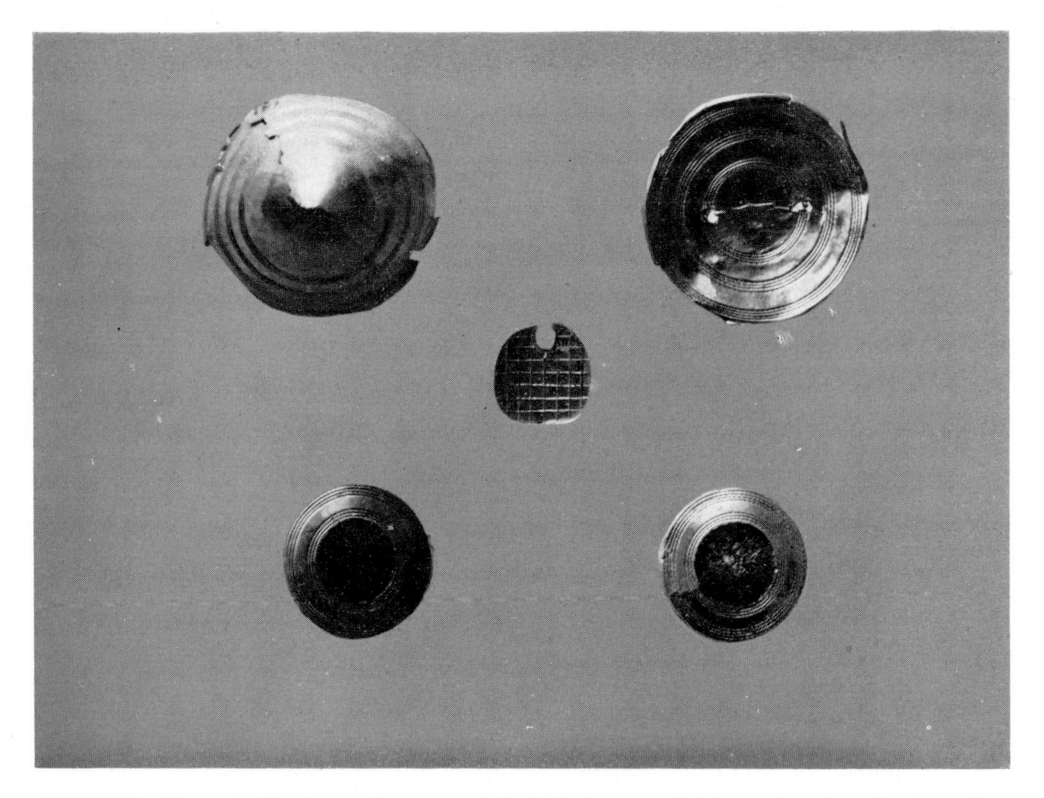

XXVIIb. Sheet-gold casing for conical shale button, gold-bound amber discs, and a gold-cased possible cranial disc (1/1), from Normanton (Barrow H. 155), Wiltshire.

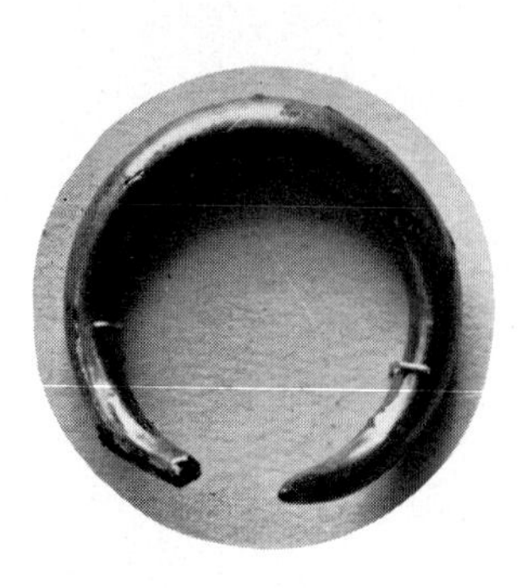

XXVIIIa (ABOVE). The Normanton ingot torque pendant (1/1).

XXVIIIb (RIGHT). The Radewill ingot torque pendant (1/2).

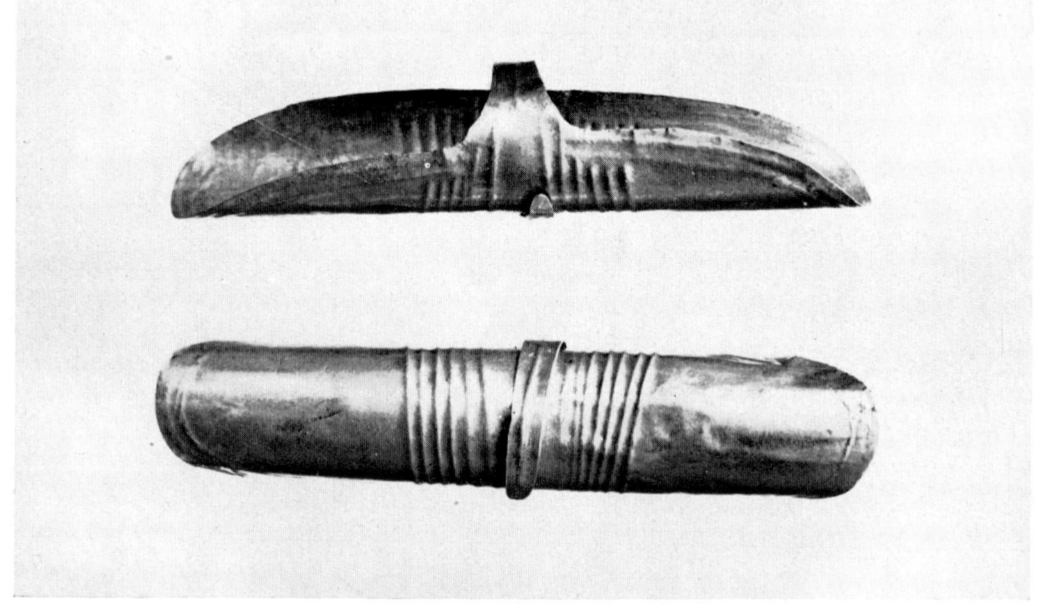

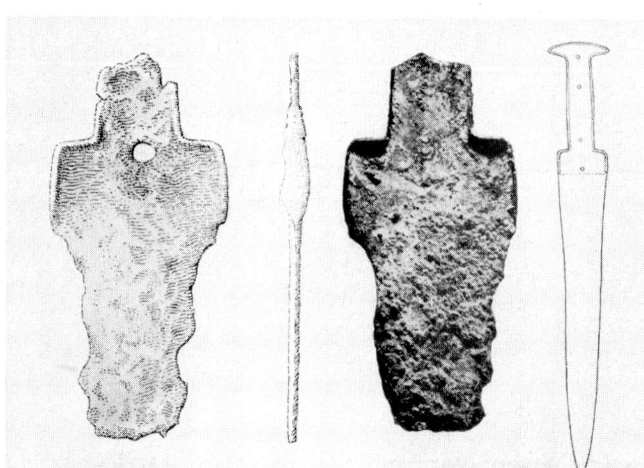

XXVIIIc (ABOVE). The Radley gold ear-rings (2/1).

XXVIIId (LEFT). The Pelynt Mycenaean dagger hilt (1/2).

XXIXa. The Roundway bell beaker; height 6·25 inches (Devizes Museum).

XXIXb. The Bishop's Waltham food vessel; height 9 inches.

XXIXc. Detail of the cord decoration on the Bishop's Waltham food vessel.

XXXa. Stonehenge as it might have appeared in the final phase of its construction. Drawn by Alan Sorrell.

XXXb. Woodhenge in its suggested completed form. Drawn by Alan Sorrell.

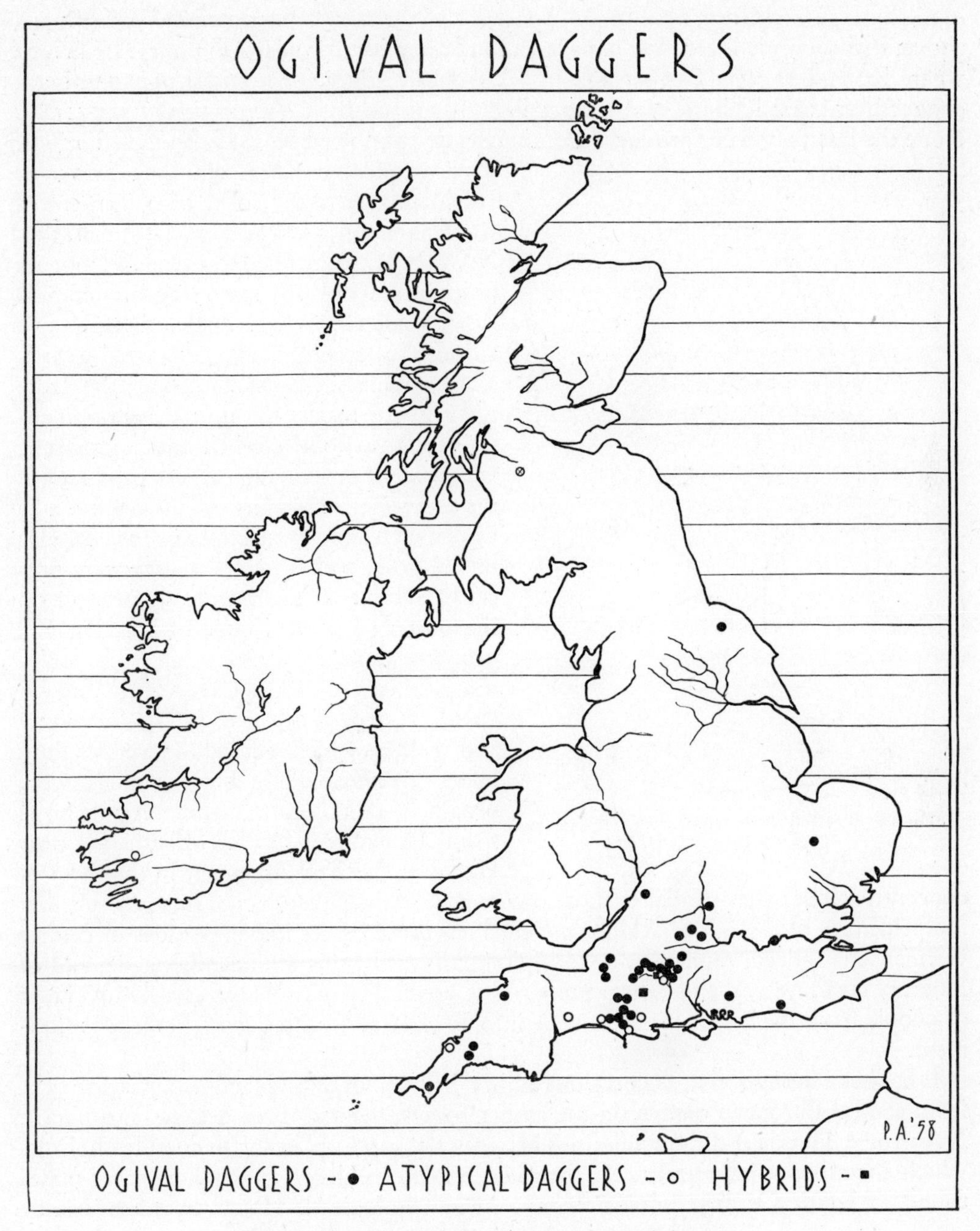

Fig. 51. Map showing distribution of ogival daggers.

Wessex culture. There are the halberd-pendants which copy the metal-shafted halberds of the Saale-Warta Bronze culture.[108] There is also the tantalizing possibility, mentioned above, that such a halberd may have been found in a barrow near Amesbury. In an area where battle-axes were current a central European origin for the idea of mounting a dagger blade as a halberd seems more likely than the Irish one originally suggested. None the less they were produced in numbers and exported by the Irish metallurgists. The torque pendant from the barrow at Normanton has the form of a thin-ended Bohemian torque.[109] A torque-pendant (Pl. XXVIII b), connected by chains from its point of suspension to two ring-headed pins from Radewill,[110] Kr. Halle, resembles it closely. Sheet-gold archers' wrist-guards were popular in central Europe; the Lake wrist-guard recalls the thin strips of sheet-gold found in Bohemian bell-beaker graves,[111] which were one of the earliest products of the sheet-metal craftsmen of the region. The lines which adorn and emphasize the handles of the gold, amber, and shale cups are precisely similar to the handle decoration on the pottery jugs and cups of the Hagenau group of the Tumulus culture.[112] The Rillaton gold cup is a close fellow of that newly found at Fritzdorf near Bonn, the rivets and washers which secured the handles both being lozenges while both handles were ornamented in the same manner. A gold bowl from Gölenkamp,[113] Kr. Bentheim, near Hanover, has base ornament in the form of concentric circles very similar to those on the base of the Rillaton cup. It is possible that the principles of the lidded Aldbourne cups are those of the lidded pyxides of central Germany.[114] Indeed, numerous detailed comparisons of this kind can be made, and of funerary customs, and all of them point to the possibility of, initially, actual movement of people from the continent of Europe into Wessex and subsequent parallel development.

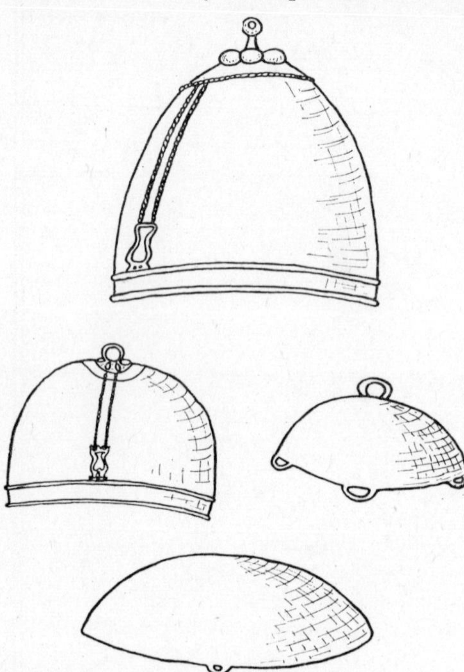

Fig. 52. The Ogmore Down helmets (after *Archaeologia*).

It has been thought that the precious amber, beloved of Wessex women, was brought from central European depots on the amber routes, defined three decades ago by De Navarro.[115] To this end the similarities between the spacer-plates with complex borings which, in amber or jet, regulate the forms of lunulae necklaces, and amber spacer-plates found in south German graves [116] have been emphasized. However, Miss Nancy

[108] *Mannus*, IX, 157; *Arch.*, LXXXVI, 243–4.
[109] *PPS*, IV, Pl. IX, 8.
[110] Ebert, 1924, II, Taf. 192.
[111] Childe, 1929, 191, 193. Compare the sheet-gold encased buttons with the conical 'Bukel', *Germania*, XXXV, 339, Abb. 2, 9–18.
[112] Schaeffer, 1926, I, Fig. 36.
[113] *Mannus-Bibliothek*, No. 12, 19, Taf. XV.
[114] *Mannus-Bibliothek*, No. 9, Abb. 47.
[115] J. M. de Navarro, 'Amber Trade', *Geographical Journal*, LXVI, 482.
[116] *Germania*, XXIV, 99–101; *BVB*, XXII, 1–36.

Sandars [117] has recently observed how the *hessischer Halskragen* is a traditional ornament in the area, and thus such spacer-plates are more probably indigenous. They would seem to be the regional versions of an ornament overwhelmingly popular in the West. It is possible that Wessex amber was derived directly from the North, without an intermediary, along trade-routes hallowed by usage from Mesolithic times.[118] One amongst many sources may have been the workshop at Swartzort [119] on the Baltic, near Memel, in East Prussia. The objects found there included, besides Beaker V-perforated buttons, rings, ring-pendants, and ivy-leaf like pendants, these last possibly destined for the Unětice region, labial or lobal studs precisely similar to those from Wessex. Such studs have also been found in Danish passage-graves,[120] as the precious resin is found also in Jutland.[121] There is also a close correspondence between certain Danish amber beads and British jet fusiform types.[121] Of some relevance is the fact that the only object strikingly like the celebrated Wessex gold-bound amber discs, found north of the Alps, is from Denmark.[122] Thus an amber disc, mounted in bronze and set upon a stave, which has a collar simulating an organic binding, recalls also, as the amber has a cruciform symbol upon it, the sun-discs set upon staves depicted as being borne aloft by figures on northern rock carvings.[123] In addition a partially perforated stone 'pestle' mace, upon which amber beads from Wessex barrows and stone beads from Irish passage-graves must have been modelled, has been found at Tornow, Kr. Prenzlau,[124] in Prussia.

Connections with the east Mediterranean world contemporary with the development and floruit of the Wessex culture may not have been much more than prestige interchange,[125] although there is the possibility of Mycenaean supervision of the sarsen phase of Stonehenge. Thus from this source, as indeed in the graves of more or less contemporary groups in widely distant parts of Europe, are the faience beads.[126] A plain gold-bound amber disc, the only known example of such a disc outside Wessex, and possibly also of Irish gold and northern amber, was found in the Late Minoan II 'Tomb of the Double Axes' at Knossos.[127] The amber spacer-plates from Mycenaean Shaft Grave IV [128] surely denote little more than the general connections between the Aegean and the tribes north of the Alps observable throughout the Bronze Age, rather than specific contacts with Britain, although the crescentic necklace from Kakovatos has spacer-beads with multiple perforations. However, such contacts may be denoted by the bone-mounted discs, reminiscent of Wessex, although within recent years stone discs have come to light in the north [129] but not in Bronze Age graves.

The handled, corrugated, Rillaton golden cup has for a long time been compared with the handled, corrugated, golden cups from Shaft Grave IV,[130] and it cannot be denied that the cups are remarkably alike as is the workmanship, each cup being beaten from an ingot, and the handle secured by rivets. Similarly, the Wessex fondness for

[117] Sandars, 1957, 10.
[118] *PPS*, XV, 63.
[119] Ebert, 1924, XI, Taf. 119.
[120] Childe, 1947 a, Fig. 92.
[121] *Acta Arch.*, XXV, 241–52.
[122] Broholm, 1943–9, II, 191, Fig. 71.
[123] *Mannus-Bibliothek*, No. 9, Abb. 209.
[124] Sprockhoff, 1938, Taf. 65, 3.
[125] J. F. S. Stone, *PPS*, XXII, 59, lists the evidence.
[126] *PPS*, XXII, 54, Fig. 3. C. F. C. Hawkes in *Ampurias*, XIV, 96–9, considers these same matters though more from the Mediterranean and Iberian viewpoint.
[127] *Arch.*, LXV, 42.
[128] *Germania*, XXXIII, 316–18, XXIV, 99–101 (Kakovatos).
[129] *Germania*, XXXI, 233–4.
[130] Karo, 1930, Taf. CIV, 392–3.

sheet-gold work has rightly been compared with that of golden Mycenae. None the less it seems more likely that the cup with its zoned corrugations is an aggrandized beaker, and that the similarities are caused by common origin rather than direct intercourse. Another copy apparently of a beaker in sheet gold, of which only the upper part remains, was found in the Dept Côtes-du-Nord,[131] in northern France. Its surface was apparently unadorned, and while no handle was found, points had been made for handle attachment. It has since been lost. Like these, the Fritzdorf cup seems to have been an aggrandized local drinking vessel.

Unequivocal direct intercourse with the Mycenaean world is attested by the hilt of an actual Late Helladic IIIb dagger (Pl. XXVIII d) dug from a Cornish,[132] not a Wessex, barrow. The double axes, which the traditional stone battle-axes were modified to resemble, emanate from this source[133] also, as may certain bead-mounting techniques. It is conceivable that the construction of the final phases of Stonehenge, surely the Wessex warrior's seat of High-Kingship, were carried out under the supervision of Mycenaean architects. There is a marked resemblance between the preparatory and constructional techniques employed at Stonehenge[134] and those of the architecture of the Lion Gate, and the squared block walls of the Citadel at Mycenae.[135] Some substance is given to this argument by the apparent likeness to a Mycenaean dirk of a dagger representation pecked on a trilithon. Although the possibility exists that this representation of a 'dagger' may be only two superimposed axes, undoubted daggers on a stone of the kerb-ring of the Badbury barrow attest to the practice of such representation. A hint that interchange with the east Mediterranean may be an outcome of the metal trade is provided by the large H-shaped ingot of tin dredged from Falmouth Harbour[136] in the nineteenth century. It recalls the ox-hide ingots used in the copper trade concentrated in Late Minoan and Mycenaean hands.[137]

It will be remembered that besides a dagger there are what appear to be flanged axes, perhaps with pointed butts, carved on a Stonehenge trilithon and other uprights, as they were upon the stone from the Badbury barrow and the cover of a Scottish cist. It is thought that these might be evidence of an axe cult comparable to the Minoan double-axe cult. It is indeed comparable, but it must be remembered that axe cults have a wide European distribution. Representations have been found of apparently sleeved stone axes in the tombs of the SOM culture,[138] and upon Breton megaliths.[139] Later manifestations are to be seen upon a slab of the Kivik tomb[140] in Sweden, and in the *Kultbeile* graven on the rocks or found in bogs of northern Europe.[141] Similarly it must not be forgotten that the apparently Mycenaean hilt of the Stonehenge silhouette could almost equally well be a representation of a local dagger.[142]

Specific types of barrows, and to some extent burial rites and rituals, all discussed in detail in Chapter VII, are to be equated with the cultures defined and analysed in the previous paragraphs. Any surviving low barrows which are apparently merely heaped

[131] *Trésors archaeologiques de l'Amorique occidentale*, Rennes, 1886, Fig. 4, 5; *Mannus-Bibliothek*, No. 12, 51, Taf. XVI.

[132] *PPS*, XVII, 95. See also a dagger of East Mediterranean type from Wessex, *DMC II*, 63.

[133] *ABSA*, XXXVII, 141–59.

[134] Atkinson, 1956, 163.

[135] Mylonas, 1957, Pl. 8.

[136] Evans, 1881, 426, Fig. 514.

[137] Clark, 1952, 258, Figs. 139–40.

[138] Hoernes and Menghin, 1925, 217, 3.

[139] Hoernes and Menghin, 1925, 223, 2.

[140] Hoernes and Menghin, 1925, 239.

[141] Hoernes and Menghin, 1925, 235; Müller, 1895, 154.

[142] *PPS*, XXIII, 158, Pl. XIII, 2.

grave infill are characteristic of the Bell-beaker group. The flat graves, which may have had low barrows or cairns heaped over them, could well be considered characteristic of the Short-Necked Beaker people, although in the Peak group, and in Yorkshire, numbers of Long-Necked Beaker graves, sometimes with Food-Vessel graves, are covered by quite large bowl barrows. This is a feature of the Long-Necked Beaker group in Wessex also. In the north, food-vessels share the burial rites of the necked-beakers; elsewhere there seems to be a tendency for composite, normally bowl, barrows with concealed cairn-rings to be a feature of the Food-Vessel group. The bermed barrows and the pond class, double, treble, and quadruple, and abnormal barrows, termed succinctly by one prehistorian 'fancy barrows',[143] are a distinctive and characteristic feature of the Wessex culture, although bowl barrows covered certain Wessex burials. This is, however, but a general pattern of correspondence; we are ignorant, as yet, of the details.

Certain types of stake circles[144] have been observed in relationship with beakers, food-vessels, and bermed barrows (Fig. 53). Closely spaced single circles have been found encircling bell-beaker burials. Circles that were a compound of two of the elements described in Chapter V encircled a Long-Necked Beaker grave, and both single and concentric circles have enclosed Food-Vessel graves. Widely set circles of posts are a feature of certain bermed barrows, although ogival daggers were associated with concentric circles in one instance.

The influence of the rich Wessex culture was widespread. Relics and monuments in Ireland and the distant Orkneys perhaps point to political intercourse with the builders of the great passage-graves, and a distinctive Bronze culture, probably initiated by immigrants from Wessex, was established in the Breton peninsula.

In Ireland stone mace and pestle beads, with precisely the lineaments of those made of amber from Wessex barrows, have been found in passage-graves.[145] The lozenges loved by the goldsmiths, the ornament of sun-discs, and the bases of Wessex vessels all have their counterparts in the Irish and English passage-grave art repertoire.[146] Of particular note is the anthropomorphic symbolism of upright stones in the Fourknocks (Co. West Meath) and Barclodiad Y Gawres passage-graves. Besides necklaces, both figures bear prominently placed lozenge ornaments recalling the larger sheet-gold plaques from the Bush Barrow burial found 'immediately over the breast of the skeleton'. Masons who had knowledge of the techniques used to square the sarsens of Stonehenge used them on the surfaces of certain stones in the great New Grange passage-grave.[147] A grave at Seskilgreen[148] contained a cremation, accompanied by a battle-axe, with Boyne art designs on stones around it.

Orcadian passage-graves also possess features explicable only in terms of relationships with Wessex. Maeshowe[149] has a berm and an encircling ditch, features almost unknown with chambered tombs, as has the not far distant Ring of Bookan.[150] The Knowes of Trotty,[151] close by, appears to have been a bell barrow, while disc-barrows are also to be seen there. Taiversoe Tuack,[152] another passage-grave, stands on a platform of stones. Much the same type of platform carried the retained cairn of the

[143] Grinsell, 1953, 256.
[144] *Arch. J.*, CXIV, 1–9.
[145] *JCHAS*, LX, 97–127.
[146] Piggott, 1954, 211, Fig. 33.
[147] George Coffey, *New Grange*, 1912, 34, Fig. 61.
[148] *JRSAI*, XLI, 175–9.
[149] *Ant. J.*, XIV, Pl. LV; Piggott, 1954, 243.
[150] *Ant. J.*, XIV; Piggott, 1954.
[151] *PSAS*, III, 195.
[152] *PSAS*, XXXVII, 73, LXXIII, 155.

POST AND STAKE CIRCLES

	BARROW	'B' BEAKER	'A' BEAKER	FOOD VESSEL	WESSEX	CINERARY URN	DEVEREL RIMBURY	NOT KNOWN
CATEGORY A1	BEEDON				◉ I CR			
	POOLE I				◉ P CR			
	SNAILWELL				● I CR			
CATEGORY A2	AMESBURY G61	● I IN CR						
	CAEBETIN			● I CR				
	CANFORD HEATH							● P
	DAVIDSTOW					● P CR		
	LUDFORD MAGNA							●
	SHEEPLAYS 279'					● I CR		
	SIXWELLS 267'					● I		
	SIXWELLS 271'						● I CR	
	SNAIL DOWN XV	● P CR						
	TALBENNY	● P ?IN						
CATEGORY B1	CRICHEL DOWN 2					● I CR		
CATEGORY B2	LETTERSTON I					● P CR		
	LETTERSTON II					● P CR		
CATEGORY C1	ARRETON DOWN				● IN			
	PANT Y DULATH			● CR				
	SHEEPLAYS 293'					● CR		
	TREGULLAND BURROW			● CR				
CATEGORY C2	CALAIS WOLD			◉ I IN				
DISPARATE CONCENTRIC CIRCLES	BLEASDALE					● CR		
	CHIPPENHAM B5		● IN					

● - BOWL BARROW ◉ - BELL BARROW I - INTERNAL CIRCLE P - PERIPHERAL CIRCLE
IN - INHUMATION CR - CREMATION

P.A. '58

Fig. 53. Associations of post and stake circle barrows.

Halangy Down entrance grave [153] on St Mary's, Isles of Scilly, in the far south-west of England. It is not unlikely that these platforms were inspired by the berms of the bermed barrows of Wessex. A hint of a ditch with outer bank has been noticed surrounding the relatively large passage-grave, St Mary's No. 1 [154] on Porth Hellick Down.

Only an early group of Wessex settlers, the warriors being armed with Bush Barrow daggers, might have emigrated to Armorica; there are few battle-axes, although double-axes are known from the region.[155] Their barrows, like those of what must have been a brilliant Cornish Bronze culture,[156] were often cairns covering cists or even corbelled chambers which probably contained timber coffins. The grave-furniture, as in certain Wessex graves, consisted mainly of daggers, axes, and superbly finished barbed and tanged arrow-heads, while one grave contained an archer's amber wrist-guard. Besides amber, exotic imports included a pin of central European origin, silver spiral rings, and a faience bead. Not only do dagger blades resemble those of the earlier Wessex phase, but their wooden hilts, and possibly scabbards, had been embellished with *pointillé* patterns executed with small golden pins in the manner of the Bush Barrow dagger hilt. Biconical urns from the later graves, the function of which is not clear, with two to four handles joining rim and girth, are alleged to have their counterparts in Wessex. The red ware of part of the vessel from a barrow at Winterbourne Stoke has an haematitic appearance, and is quite unlike Bronze Age wares.

Piggott [157] originally explained the Wessex culture by suggesting an invasion from Armorica. Recent re-examinations [158] of the evidence, doubtless influenced by the ring-headed pin, the spirals, one metal-hilted dagger, and the general affinities of the daggers, have suggested an origin in the central European Bronze cultures. More recently Sandars [159] has emphasized the isolation of the Armorican Bronze culture and has pointed to the archaistic metallurgy and its failure to develop. Childe [160] originally reversed Piggott's views and suggested that the evidence would equally well sustain the view that the Armorican Bronze Age originated in Wessex. He later supported [161] the contentions, regarding an ultimate central European origin, of Cogné and Giot,[162] but re-emphasized the dominant British inspiration of the daggers and rightly claimed that for a while Armorica and Wessex were a continuous cultural province. This last view is strengthened by the fact that not only are there close similarities of barrow, content, and rite, but also that in Armorica are found avenues [163] and stone circles [164] in the British tradition. Apart from a possible stone circle in Alsace,[165] long since destroyed, and another at Forrières in Luxembourg,[166] the Armorican avenues and circles are, as far as is known, unique on the European mainland. Thus, as the votive deposits in the Er Lannic [167] stone circle show, affinities with Britain were long-standing, and the development, upon the basis of this colonization, of an aggrandized warrior culture, sitting astride the long-established western trade routes, is not surprising. The failure

[153] Hencken, 1932, 23.
[154] Hencken, 1932, 21.
[155] *Matériaux*, XII (1884), Pl. VI, 8.
[156] *PWCFC*, I, 132–4.
[157] *PPS*, IV, 94.
[158] Hawkes, 1940, 312–14.
[159] Sandars, 1957.
[160] Childe, 1947 b, 143.
[161] Childe, 1957, 320.
[162] *PPS*, XVII, 226; *L'Anthr.*, LV, 442.
[163] James Miln, *Excavations at Carnac: a Record of Archaeological Researches into the Alignments of Kermano*, Edinburgh, 1882.
[104] Le Rouzic, 1930.
[165] R. Forrer, *Heidenmauer von St Odilien*, Strasbourg, 1899, 43; *Antiq.*, XII, 349.
[166] J. B. Geubel, *Annales de la Société pour la Conservation des Monuments Historiques*, Luxembourg, I, 1847–9, 85–96.
[167] Le Rouzic, 1930.

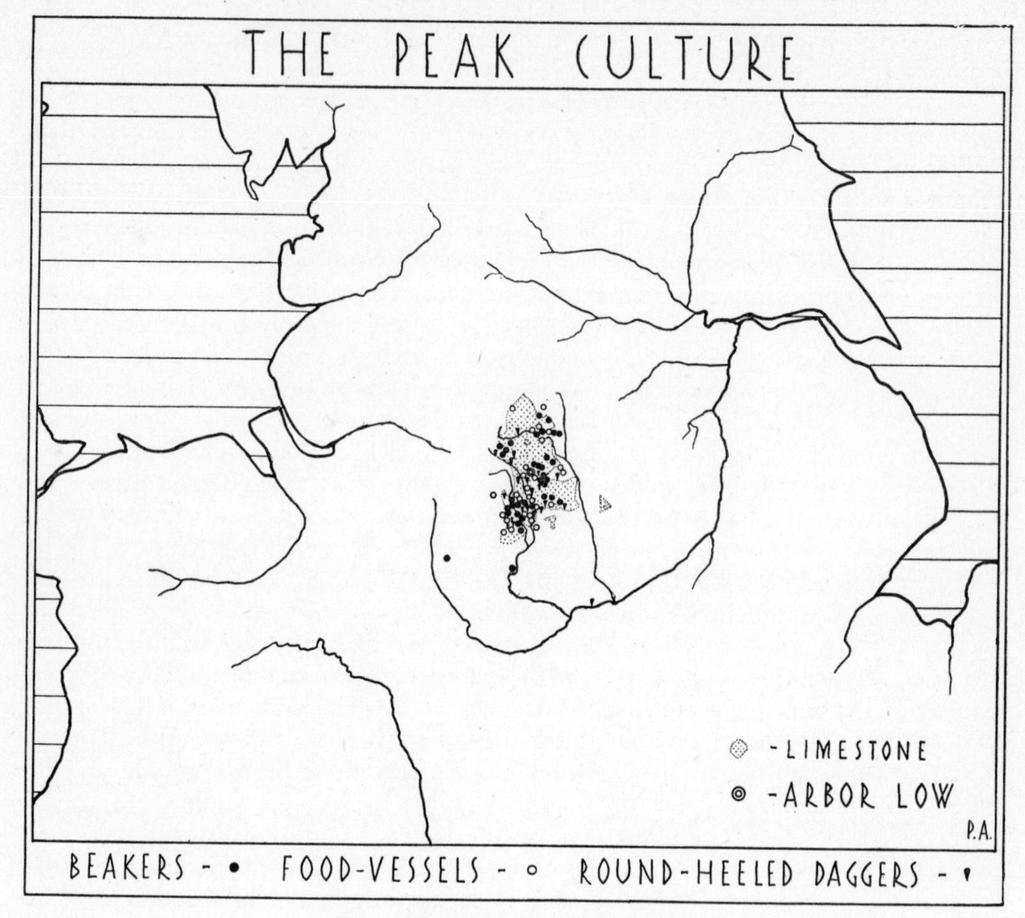

Fig. 54. Barrows of the Peak culture.

to develop might be explained by a decline in the importance of the western routes, as the megalithic Argonauts were absorbed into local Beaker and Battle-axe groups. Following upon this was a rise in the relative importance of brisk metallurgical interchange between Ireland, Britain, and the European mainland that persists throughout the Bronze Age. The Wessex warriors and their heirs were presumably the middlemen!

While these Wessex warriors dominated southern Britain, what of the other parts? Distribution maps of Early Bronze Age antiquities show clearly circumscribed groups in certain areas. There is the possibility that a Cornish Bronze culture of rich warriors' graves, in cists under great barrows and cairns, comparable with that of Armorica, should be considered. On the other hand, the few relics recovered from the region could suggest a south-western extension of the suzerainty of Wessex.[168] Barrows, cairns mostly covering inhumation burials, and probably the political and cultural centre of Arbor Low, in the Peak District of Derbyshire, are the monuments of a clearly definable people. They could justifiably and conveniently be termed the Peak culture (Fig. 54). A recent study [169] has shown that here was a population which maintained itself in

[168] Cf. page 172.

[169] *JDANHS*, LXXV, 66–122.

comparative isolation. It had well-made long-necked beakers, 'Yorkshire Type' food-vessels and bronzes, and one dagger owing much to the earlier Wessex series, but was unable to command exotic imports. This group, it is claimed, resulted from a fusion of local Megalithic, Secondary Neolithic, and Beaker elements in a natural backwater. Rather similar conditions must have obtained on the Yorkshire Wolds and hills, but a slightly wealthier, and infinitely more variegated, group resulted. Secondary Neolithic natives buried their dead beneath round barrows, as in the Peak District. Bell-Beaker immigrants began the process of fusion, followed by Necked-Beaker and Food-Vessel peoples. Two graves may well be of *emigré* Wessex warriors accepted in local society. As yet little understood and undefined in detail are later Corded ware elements [170] from across the North Sea, of which Cord Zone beakers and Willmot's Collared beakers may be but one part, the other being represented by polypod bowls, pyxides, and handled vessels. Since more than three hundred Yorkshire barrows have been dug into, most of which covered more than one burial, some as many as five or six, just over a thousand burials are known, two-thirds of which were inhumations and the remaining third cremations. Only about five per cent of these graves had bronze objects in them, which seems to be the general proportion of metal-accompanied Beaker-graves in Britain. A similar Beaker-based bronze culture spread over East Anglia, although little is known of its barrows. However, bermed barrows and Wessex equipment could point to over-lordship by warriors. Only in Wales do the earlier groups appear to have been relatively free from direct domination. In Scotland dagger graves and great barrows, and necked beakers and food-vessels, indicate another, although not especially numerous, warrior class, perhaps concerned with the control of trade routes. This period in Ireland is defined by Food-Vessel graves and the great passage-graves of the Boyne culture. It seems likely that the remains of dynasties of master metal craftsmen, the men upon whose skill and ingenuity the incredibly rapid technological progress of the European Bronze Age was in part based, were collected in what are mostly impressive and superbly engineered structures.

Everywhere the predominantly Beaker cultures were ultimately superseded by what have been termed the Urn folk. It is difficult to say whether the cinerary urns define a folk, and are not merely a pottery type adapted by a group using what we call 'Secondary Neolithic pottery' for a specific purpose. Few distinctive ornaments are exclusively associated with urns, and indeed the relics that occur with them from time to time are of types more frequently found with necked-beakers and food-vessels. Small flat, narrow knife-daggers were with a few urns, as were oval razors. Barbed and tanged arrow-heads have been found with a number of urns. In the North battle-axes of the Wilsford-Crichie type were allegedly with one or two.

Overhanging-rim urns are, as has been noted above, a part of the Wessex amalgam, having been found in bell- and disc- besides other barrows, all the phases [171] (Fig. 55) being represented therein. The Pond Cairn,[172] in Wales, a composite barrow of a type normally associated with food-vessels, contained an urn, while the cemeteries of overhanging-rim urn burials could be likened to the Beaker cemeteries. At Eynsham [173] a 'Phase I' urn was in a grave which was patently part of such a cemetery, the beakers which accompanied the burials being of the necked type. An urn from Barrow 156 at

[170] Childe, 1957, s.v.
[171] *Arch.*, LXXXIX, 126.
[172] *Arch.*, LXXXVII, 142–66.
[173] *Oxon.*, III, 10–20.

Normanton,[174] it will be remembered, with its zoned decoration and red fabric, is very like a beaker. Sheet-metal beads, identical with those found with a Sussex barrel-beaker, were with horseshoe-ornamented biconical urns in two Dorset graves.[175] At Maiden Castle[176] what could well be the top of a small overhanging-rim urn was found in a layer containing beaker pottery, although the worms had doubtless been active!

Fig. 55. Abercromby Type I urn phases.

A few ornaments do appear to have been more frequently associated with urns than with any other type of vessel. Childe[177] enumerates specific types of faience beads and Scottish bone toggles. To these may be added bone tweezers, which are found more often with urns than with any other ceramic form.

Urns of all types, and the miniature vessels which sometimes accompany them, appear to be the vessels used by the descendants of the Secondary Neolithic groups. That these natives adopted the rites and usages of the intrusive round-barrow people has been shown in preceding chapters. For the overhanging-rim urns the most distant and likely ancestor appears to be the Mortlake bowls, followed by Fengate pottery. Of especial interest is the pot recently found in the West Kennet chamber[178] and now exhibited in Devizes Museum. An exceptionally deep, baggy, Peterborough vessel from Icklington[179] in Suffolk suggests the lineaments of 'Phase III' cinerary urns, as does the Isle of Man's Ronaldsway ware.[180] These Manx vessels, apparently a local devolution which contained in one instance a cremation, were accompanied by miniature vessels, and were buried in 'cemeteries'. An 'overhanging' rim was a feature of one of the Woodhenge rusticated vessels,[181] surely derived from a wooden tub, and a bipartite proto-urn was found at Peterborough itself.[182] Sheep Down urns,[183] with narrow, internally concave rims, are considered to be early versions of the overhanging-rim urn. Some have alternate depressions and lugs around their shoulders, a feature thought to relate them to food-vessels. While northern cordoned urns are an end-product of overhanging-rim urns, it seems likely that encrusted urns derive basically from Rinyo-Clacton ancestors. The decorative techniques are identical with those employed on certain sherds from the Orcadian villages.

[174] Hoare, 1812–19, I, 202.
[175] *Arch.*, LXXXV, 213.
[176] Wheeler, 1943, Fig. 30, 67.
[177] Childe, 1947 b, 155.
[178] *Antiq.*, XXXII, 239.
[179] Piggott, 1954, Pl. X, 2.
[180] *PPS*, XII, 139–69.
[181] Cunnington, 1929, Pl. 37.
[182] *Arch.*, LXII, 340–52.
[183] *Arch. J.*, CVIII, 20.

If this suggested ancestry of overhanging-rim urns be correct, the distribution of the elements enumerated, and of Peterborough pottery, would point to their having evolved in south-eastern England and having spread thence to Wales, the North, Scotland, and Ireland. In Scotland urns were usually of quite a modest size, contrasting markedly with the great, well-finished urns of Wessex and the South. In these places subsequent devolution, the product of which is thought by some to be the cordoned urn, would have taken place. A similar devolution might have taken place in the regional isolation of Cornwall,[184] which, in spite of its affinities with Wessex, preserved individual characteristics deriving perhaps even from central Germany[185] throughout the Bronze Age. Here narrow and broad, internally concave, rimmed urns, with handles, some of the former resembling the Sheep Down class, have apparently following upon them collared urns and bucket urns with narrow rims and collars. The distinctive ribbon-handled urns appear to be a parallel strain, owing much to food-vessels, for which a native origin seems unlikely.

An Urn folk group emigrated across the North Sea and settled in the Low Countries. Urns, directly derivable from British overhanging-rim urns, because of their bevelled rims, cord ornament, and paste, two specimens of which were early identified by Dunning,[186] have been called *Hilversum* urns by Glasbergen.[187] They were interred in barrows, certain of which embodied features peculiar to the Wessex bermed barrows. The distinctive local derivatives of the Hilversum urns have been named *Drakenstein* urns. Cord ornament was no longer used on them, while biconical, bucket, and barrel shapes developed.

Like other groups the Urn folk had intercourse with the mainland of Europe apart from emigration. Childe[188] compared their Scottish bone toggles with a Danish[189] series, identical in every detail. A small blade with a notched butt, found with a Scottish urn,[190] has a mid-rib on one face only. This, and a similar example from Ireland,[191] also found with a cinerary urn, has been compared with daggers from Los Millares and Alcala in the Iberian Peninsula.[192] This points to a continuum of the earlier interchanges attested by beads, ear-rings, lunulae, and pins.

Apart from distinctive funerary vessels, cremation cemeteries and a number of enclosures and the evidence of industry and husbandry therefrom are the main characteristics of the Deverel-Rimbury culture. There is evidence from more than one allied site that particular types of bronzes were used.[193]

It was thought for long that our Deverel-Rimbury pottery was evidence of an invasion. The Urnfield folk (of the German *Urnenfelderzeit*), as a result of their expansion in the latter part of the second millennium B.C., were considered to have encountered Tumulus folk (of the German *Hügelgräberbronzezeit*) in the Upper Rhine region. The result was a hybrid culture considered to be reflected in the funerary practices of the Deverel-Rimbury culture that was ultimately established in Britain. Progenitors of barrel and bucket urns were found in northern France and Flanders,[194] and the distant ancestors of the globular urns were seen in the amphorae of Lausitz and the south-west

[184] *Arch. J.*, CI, 17–49.
[185] *PWCFC*, II, 40.
[186] *Ant. J.*, XVI, 160–4.
[187] Glasbergen, 1954, II, 89.
[188] Childe, 1947 b, 155.
[189] Müller, 1895, 232. But see *PPS*, XXIV, 227.
[190] *PSAS*, XXV, 459.
[191] *JRSAI*, LXXI, 139.
[192] *APL*, IV, 182–4.
[193] *PPS*, I, 32; see also *PPS*, XXV, 155–9.
[194] *Ant. J.*, XIII, 439.

German urnfields.[195] The chronological implications of this belief are clear. The continental urnfields provided a *terminus post quem* for the British Deverel-Rimbury culture. That means the Deverel-Rimbury culture *could not* be earlier than its continental forbears.

In recent years our conceptions of the nature of the Deverel-Rimbury culture have changed considerably. It is no longer necessary to invoke continental urnfields as a source and inspiration for the cremation cemetery mode of burial. The cremation cemeteries, and the barrel and bucket urns, when their decoration and the trick of cruciform base reinforcement are taken into account, have an origin in the Secondary Neolithic groups.[196] The origins of the enclosures might be sought in such native Bronze Age enclosures as Ram's Hill,[197] Berkshire.

It is possible that the globular urns,[198] which have a distribution[199] even more restricted than their fellows, may be an intrusive element. Their hard, relatively thin ware recalls the Western Neolithic. Indeed a baggy pot from a barrow at Kinson[200] is not dissimilar to the Neolithic vessels, termed amphorae, recovered from southern contexts.[201] The decoration of globular urns is distantly reminiscent of the Channelled ware[202] of western France. Of especial note in this context are globular and barrel urns, probably early, judging by their associations, from a Scillonian entrance grave,[203] and a vessel from Woodminton Bowerchalke[204] in Wiltshire, precisely similar to pottery from the passage-grave of La Varde[205] in Guernsey. It should be remembered also that Abercromby[206] drew attention to a series of vessels in south-west France and Spain. Although the Deverel-Rimbury folk used barrow burial, usually with a pit beneath for the pyre ashes, their burial rite was the cremation cemetery. This has its origin in the cremation cemeteries of the Secondary Neolithic groups, and is sometimes used by the Cinerary Urn folk.

The increasing impoverishment of British barrow graves, first apparent in the later Middle Bronze Age, was pointed out at the conclusion of Chapter IX. The metal equipment of Beaker, Food-Vessel, and Wessex cultures is well known because it was regularly deposited in graves. Who, then, could have used the great variety of metal gear, typologically later, not found in graves? It could only have been the Urn folk who, with insular independence, perpetuated the Neolithic principle of burying practically nothing with the dead.

That the later[207] metal products of Irish and British craftsmen are partly based on those of an earlier age is clear. Tanged spear-heads were lengthened into formidable weapons such as the blade from Raphoe,[208] Co. Donegal. Flanged axes were modified into true palstaves. Spear-heads, socketed and looped, were adorned with double non-functional rivet-heads as an ornamentation, perpetuating the Snowshill spear-head, as, indeed, were some socketed axes. Daggers were elongated into rapiers, inspired perhaps by those of Mycenaean Greece, often of astounding length and grace. They could only have been used in conjunction with the bossed and ribbed shields. Swords were introduced and distinctive insular forms were soon evolved. Interchange and

[195] *PZ*, XXI, 161–75; *Zephyrus*, VIII, 195–240.
[196] Piggott, 1954, 276–364; *JRAI*, LXXXVIII, 97–107. See also *PDNHAS*, LXXIX, 104.
[197] *Ant. J.*, XX, 465–80.
[198] *PDNHAS*, LXXX, 146–59.
[199] *PPS*, IV, 185, Fig. 10.
[200] *PDNHAS*, LXXX, 139.
[201] *PPS*, LV, 211, Fig. 3; Wheeler, 1943, 141, 7.
[202] *Arch. J.*, XCV, 126–73.
[203] *Ant. J.*, XXXII, 21–34.
[204] *WAM*, XLIII, 316, Fig. 5, 5.
[205] Kendrick, 1928, 113.
[206] Abercromby, 1912, II, Pl. CVII, 5–13, 20.
[207] H. N. Savory has summarized the Welsh Late Bronze Age material. *Arch. Camb.*, CVII, 3–63.
[208] Evans, 1881, 255, Fig. 323.

intercourse with the mainland of Europe continued, while at about this point distinct industrial regions became apparent in Britain. A Danish palstave was, for some exceptional reason, deposited in a Yorkshire [209] barrow grave. British palstaves reached Denmark,[210] northern and central Germany,[211] and even Hungary.[212] A spear-head with basal loops and leaf-shaped blade reached East Prussia,[213] and others have been found in Holstein [214] and Baden.[215] A spear-head with lunate openings in the blade, dredged from Huelva [216] harbour, allegedly with many other bronzes, attests to the continued but less important western route, as do double-looped palstaves,[217] winged-axes,[218] Breton square-mouthed socketed axes,[219] and Britain and Ireland's distinctive 'Atlantic' cauldrons.[220] Examples of the last reached Denmark and inspired local fashions.[221] The estimated chronological relationships of this metal gear to the cultures defined in this chapter are tabulated in detail in Fig. 56.

The round barrows of Britain, Ireland, and Armorica are only the westernmost of the myriads that still stud the surface of the continent of Europe and beyond. From the higher land of Holland to the steppes of Siberia, from the Alps to Jutland, from the Bosnian Highlands to the Baltic and Scandinavia, heaths and uplands bear barrows. In the enormous area local differences of contents are only to be expected, and their contents contribute to the complexity of cultures that characterize the later Stone and the Bronze Ages of Europe. Like our British barrows, when mapped and described, their siting and types of cemeteries exhibit marked characteristics. Thus in Germany,[222] which is relatively well explored, great barrows lie in rows on heights, or strung out along what must have been prehistoric ways, or singly, or in small groups. In north-west Germany great fields of barrows of moderate size are concentrated into close groups. While the great Saxo-Thuringian barrows [223] stand solitarily, like the Hove barrow in Sussex, Saale-Warta barrows recently explored at Łeki Małe [224] in Poland, comprised a linear cemetery like those of Wessex.

The common denominator beneath and behind the round barrow burying cultures of Bronze Age Europe is the many groups designated the Battle-axe cultures.[225] Almost all groups buried their male dead singly and contracted, in barrow-surmounted graves, accompanied usually by a stone battle-axe and a cord-ornamented pottery beaker. Beads and trinkets were placed with females. The graves are classically shafts, in which the remains of timber linings or, exceptionally, mortuary houses, have been observed. Some barrows were demarcated by a ring of posts. Barrow burial, when practised by Bell-Beaker folk, apparently originated from this source. These warrior bands lie behind our British Necked-Beaker cultures and could only have been the inventors of the halberd. While basic British battle-axes differ markedly from the basic drooping-bladed weapon, the type normally accompanying our beakers is often found in both stone and

[209] *Ant. J.*, III, 370.
[210] Forssander, 1936, 220.
[211] Bohm, 1935, 49, Taf. 9, 13; *BRGK*, XXI, II Teil (at least two categories of German palstave may well be of British origin).
[212] Hampel, 1890, Taf. VIII, 8.
[213] Sturms, 1936, 29.
[214] Forssander, 1936, 195, Taf. XL.
[215] *MZ*, XXIX, 58.
[216] Ebert, 1924, s.v. Huelva.
[217] *Ant. J.*, XIX, 320.
[218] *PPS*, XIV, 155–76.
[219] *PPSEA*, VII, 104, Pl. IX.
[220] *Arch.*, LXXX, 1–36; *Ant J.*, XXXVII, 131–198.
[221] *Acta Arch.*, XX, 265.
[222] *BRGK*, XXXI (II Teil), Abb. 4–7. See also *Aarbøger*, XIX, 1–64; Behrens, 1916, 175, Abb. 16.
[223] *JST*, V, 1–59, 86; Ebert, 1924, VII, 286; *Götze Festschrift*, 84–9.
[224] *Fontes*, IV, 43–76, VII, 116–43.
[225] Childe, 1957, 158–74.

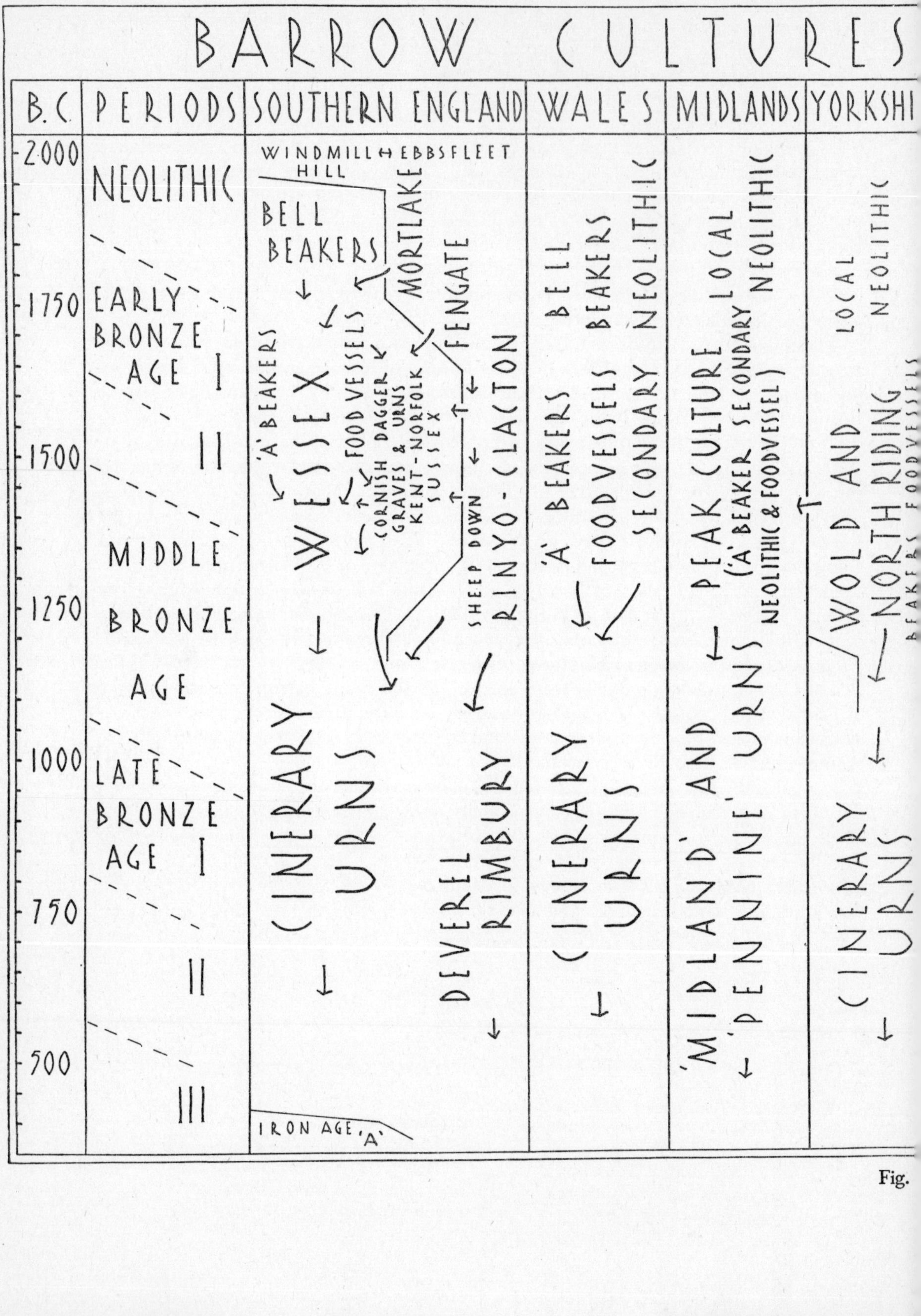

BARROW CULTURES

B.C.	PERIODS	SOUTHERN ENGLAND	WALES	MIDLANDS	YORKSHI
2000	NEOLITHIC	WINDMILL HILL ↔ EBBSFLEET; BELL BEAKERS; MORTLAKE; FENGATE	BELL BEAKERS; NEOLITHIC	LOCAL NEOLITHIC	LOCAL NEOLITHIC
1750	EARLY BRONZE AGE I	'A' BEAKERS; WESSEX; FOOD VESSELS; CORNISH DAGGER GRAVES & URNS; KENT-NORFOLK SUSSEX; RINYO-CLACTON	'A' BEAKERS; FOOD VESSELS; SECONDARY NEOLITHIC	PEAK CULTURE ('A' BEAKER SECONDARY NEOLITHIC & FOODVESSEL)	WOLD AND NORTH RIDING; BEAKERS FOODVESSELS
1500	II	SHEEP DOWN			
1250	MIDDLE BRONZE AGE				
1000	LATE BRONZE AGE I	CINERARY URNS; DEVEREL RIMBURY	CINERARY URNS	'MIDLAND' AND 'PENNINE' URNS	CINERARY URNS
750	II				
500	III	IRON AGE 'A'			

Fig.

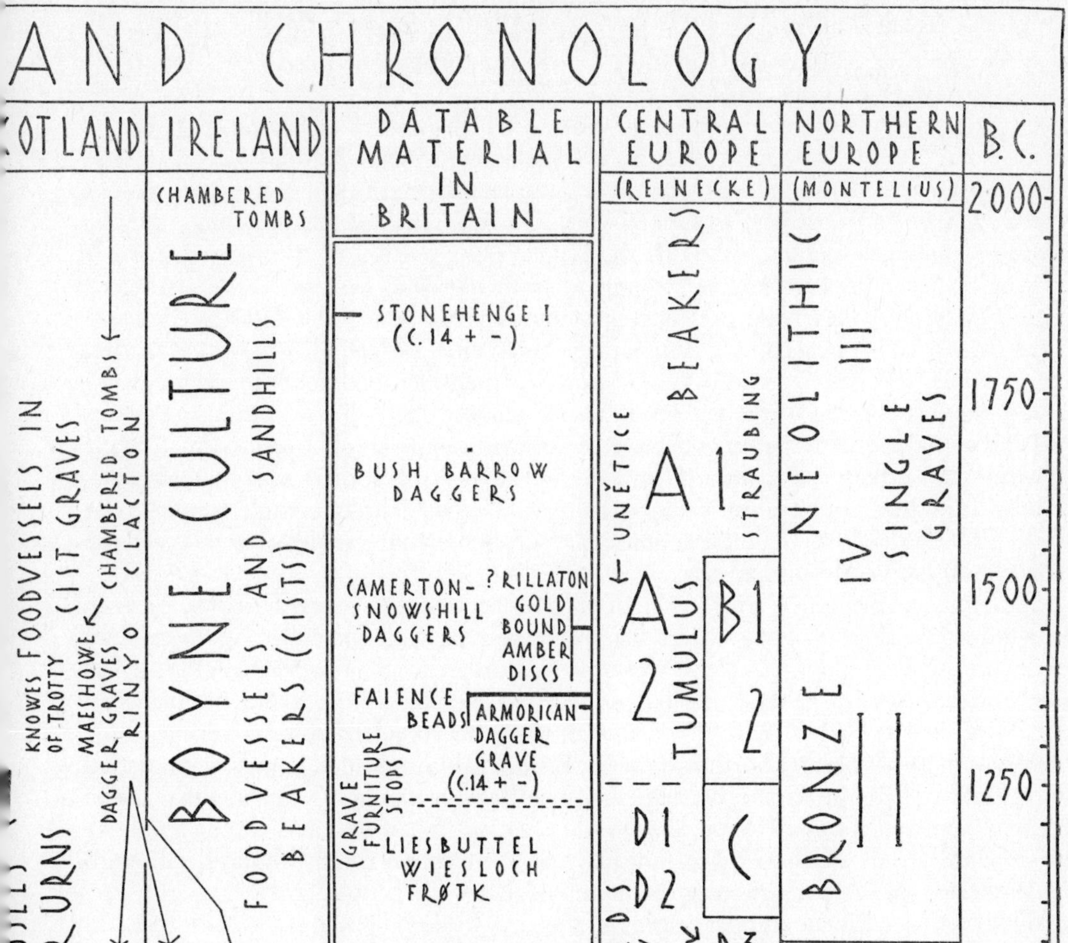

AND CHRONOLOGY

[S]COTLAND	IRELAND	DATABLE MATERIAL IN BRITAIN	CENTRAL EUROPE (REINECKE)	NORTHERN EUROPE (MONTELIUS)	B.C.
KNOWES OF TROTTY; MAESHOWE ← CHAMBERED TOMBS; DAGGER GRAVES RINYO CLACTON; FOODVESSELS IN CIST GRAVES	CHAMBERED TOMBS; BOYNE CULTURE; FOODVESSELS AND BEAKERS (CISTS); FOODVESSELS AND SANDHILLS	STONEHENGE I (C.14 + -)	BEAKERS; A1; ← UNĚTICE; STRAUBING	NEOLITHIC III	2000
		BUSH BARROW DAGGERS		NEOLITHIC IV; SINGLE GRAVES	1750
		CAMERTON-SNOWSHILL DAGGERS; ? RILLATON GOLD BOUND AMBER DISCS	A2; TUMULUS B1		1500
		FAIENCE BEADS; ARMORICAN DAGGER GRAVE (C.14 + -); (GRAVE FURNITURE STOPS)	TUMULUS 2	BRONZE II	
		LIESBUTTEL WIESLOCH FRØTK	D1; D2; URNFIELDS; TUMULUS C	BRONZE II	1250
ENCRUSTED & CORDONED URNS; ENLARGED FOODVESSELS; OHR URNS	ENCRUSTED AND CORDONED URNS; ENLARGED FV'S; OHR URNS	HEMIGKOFEN AND ERBENHEIM SWORDS IN SOUTHERN ENGLAND	D3; E (CHILDE)	III	1000
		BLACKROCK AND THE SUSSEX LOOPS; SUNFLOWER PINS; ADABROCK BOWL	F (CHILDE)	IV; V	750
		HALLSTATT BRONZE SWORDS	H1; H2; LA TENE	VI	500

[Chr]onological Table.

metal in northern and central Europe.[226] The hammer-end of the British Stourton-Loose Howe type is clearly another battle-axe feature.

A battle-axe basis is beneath the rich culture which built the great Saale-Warta [227] barrows, and their fellows in Poland. Similarly the widespread Tumulus culture [228] has a battle-axe nexus, although daggers are here more important than battle-axes. As has been seen from the affinities examined earlier in this chapter, these groups are the European mainland's counterparts of the rich Wessex culture of southern Britain. It must be realized that for peoples moving in from the east, western Europe is a geographic *cul-de-sac*; the established natives cannot retreat into the sea. Thus, particularly in the British Isles, succeeding cultures must be an amalgam of what has gone before, for newcomer and native must, if they want to live together, bed down together. However, if the distribution of the European round barrow single-grave cultures be examined and compared with that of collective chambered tombs, it will be found that, while in certain areas there are 'overlaps' and the newcomers bury their beakers and food-vessels in the graves of the pre-existing culture, they are largely complementary. For single-grave and collective burial peoples must ultimately have amalgamated, as did the former with native Mesolithic stock.

Therefore, in Britain,[229] which is such an overlap area, the round barrows, or as in Scotland [230] the single flat graves, are mainly in the east while the collective chambered tombs are, with exceptions, in the west. In Armorica, another overlap region, it has been noticed how, in general, the barrows of the Bronze culture avoid the principal megalithic centres.[231] In Spain [232] there seem to be no round barrows covering single graves, as there are further north and east in Europe, although such burials were carried out in cists and jars in Argaric settlements. The Beaker population qualified for burial in the chambered tombs. Round barrows are, as far as can be seen, absent from the littoral and islands of the Mediterranean, where collective tombs abound, although battle-axes [233] are known, attesting the march of that virile people.

Whatever the ultimate human origins of the two disparate burial rites, collective and single, that is, impersonal and individual, their spread to Britain followed two clearly differentiated and geographically demarcated routes, the Atlantic and the Northern Coast and Plain, by two equally dissimilar modes of transport. The former people have been called Argonauts, for they ranged the rocky, dark, island-studded seas, in a uniformity of environment which indissolubly links the East Mediterranean world with the *Ultima Thule* of Orkney and Shetland. The latter may be termed Voortrekkers, for they traversed river, steppe, and fen, as they spread westward—finally to settle, consolidate, and evolve their culture on the chalk downs of Wessex. Both routes were already old, having been followed since early Post-Glacial times. Both channelled the courses of invaders, traders, emigrants, saints, and scholars, *back and forth*, down the ages into historic times. Thus do the realities of geography determine the lives of men.

[226] Müller, 1895, 88, 90, 92, 139; R. Schroeder, *Die Nordgruppe der Oderschnurkeramik*, Berlin, 1951, 198, Taf. 30, 1–41; B. Norotný, *Slovensko v mladšej Dobe Kammenej*, Bratislava, 1958, Tab. LIV, 7, LV, 3.

[227] *JST*, V, I–59; Ebert, 1924, VII, 286; *Fontes*, IV, 43–76, VII, 116–43.

[228] Childe, 1929, 296–318.

[229] Fox, 1952, compare Fig. 1 (omit earthen long barrows) with Figs. 2, 20, 21, Pls. IV, VII.

[230] Childe, 1946, compare Fig. 1 with Figs. 10, 15.

[231] *PPS*, IV, 65, XVII, 226–8; *L'Anthr.* LV, 428.

[232] Childe, 1957, 282.

[233] *PPS*, XVI, 52–64.

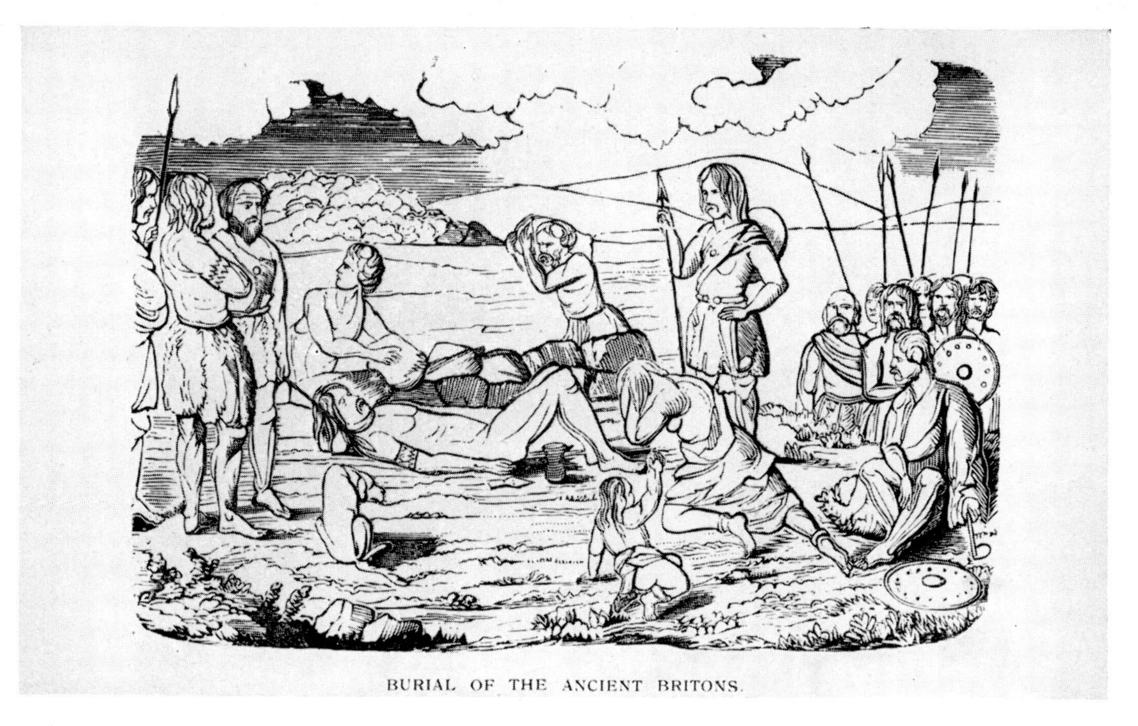

XXXIa. A nineteenth-century conception of the funeral ceremony at a round cairn. Bateman's frontispiece to his *Vestiges of the Antiquities of Derbyshire.*

XXXIb. Alan Sorrell's reconstruction of the rites at the Pond Cairn.

XXXII. A panel (right side) of the Frank's Casket. The murdered hero lies in his barrow while mourning him are female and horse.

CHAPTER XI

CHRONOLOGY

PERSPECTIVE was given to Europe's prehistoric past, more than a century ago, by Thomsen's 'Three Age System'.[1] The next significant step was the formulation of the principles of typology and association for metal gear and a system of type periods, and from these a relative chronology. Montelius [2] recognized six phases (I–VI) in Scandinavia, and later extended his system to the remainder of the mainland of Europe [3] and to Britain.[4] At the same time Flinders Petrie [5] provided a measure of synchronization between Schliemann's Mycenaean and the Aegean, and Egypt, for which last country there was a well-documented chronology. It thus became apparent that any absolute dates for Bronze Age Europe depend ultimately upon the written historical records of the urban civilizations [6] of the Middle East. Thereupon, using Petrie's results, among other things, Montelius [7] propounded systems of absolute chronology for Europe.

The system of Montelius is, with modifications,[8] in current use in northern Europe today. For south Germany, Reinecke [9] devised another sixfold division (A–F). The tendency since has been to extend this to all central Europe, and even to Hungary, using Italy as a starting point.[10]

Britain's Montelian system was passed over by our prehistorians, who preferred a tripartite division. This system of an Early, Middle, and Late Bronze Age, based again upon the typology and association of metal objects, was put forward by Fox [11] in 1923. It clarified and carried forward the penetrating analysis and tabulation of bronzes and their ordering into a tripartite frame, evolved forty years before by Sir John Evans,[12] who also put forward shrewd absolute chronological assessments.

Meanwhile the Montelian principles of typology and association had, with chronological intent, been applied to Britain's Bronze Age pottery by Abercromby.[13] This he ranged against the absolute periods set down for our islands by Montelius. The weaknesses of applying rigid typological principles to a variable substance like pottery have been apparent down the years, yet these have been abandoned only recently.[14] The

[1] C. J. Thomsen, *Ledetraad til Nordisk Oldkyndighed*, Copenhagen, 1836.

[2] *Matériaux*, XIX (1885), 108.

[3] *L'Anthr.*, XII, 609.

[4] *Arch.*, LXI, 97–162.

[5] Flinders Petrie, *Illahun, Kahun, and Gurob*, 1891; *Tell-el-Amarna*, 1894.

[6] Childe, 1952, 1–13.

[7] O. Montelius, *Die Älteren Kulturperioden im Orient und in Europa*, 1903.

[8] Broholm, 1943–9.

[9] *Altertümer*, V, 281 ff., 288 ff., 330 ff., 359 ff., 364 ff., 394 ff.; *Germania*, VIII, 44, XVII, 11.

[10] e.g. Aberg, 1930–5.

[11] Fox, 1923, 50; and *A Handbook of the Prehistoric Archaeology of Britain*, Oxford, 1932, 32.

[12] Evans, 1881, 462–79.

[13] Abercromby, 1912.

[14] 15 March 1952 (C. F. C. Hawkes).

problems that are raised by any attempt to correlate any sequence based on funerary pottery with typological periods defined by bronzes remain with us.

Cultural formulae, used together with the systems of Montelius (and Müller) and Reinecke, which are merely assemblages of types found together in graves and hoards, have rendered chronological considerations complex beyond belief. Childe,[15] in his accounts of European prehistory, used, in an incidental manner, a system of numbered periods in conjunction with dates. For British prehistory[16] he set down a system of dated periods designated I–IX. Such an objective framework of periods and dates, differing from dated periods defined typologically, has the marked merit of allowing cultures and objects to be referred to it impartially. Many have urged[17] revision of our chronological nomenclature in recent years but the response has been disappointing. Thus at present any chronological expression must be made in two or three different modes.

During the past two decades, considerable progress has been made in the application of the natural sciences to the problems of what have been termed para-historic times. Thus in Holland, Waterbolk[18] has set the barrows of a cemetery in relative chronological order, using the determined pollen content of their ancient soils, sods, and silts. Dimbleby[19] has done much the same for a series of Dorset barrows, although from a wider area, using his own particular methods. Cornwall[20] has hinted at the chronological possibilities inherent in the study of barrow soils, their weathering and composition. Recently, Atkinson[21] has propounded the doctrine of differential weathering, the processes of which I have described in Chapter IV (p. 59). He has set the heights of ancient soils beneath monuments of varying ages in their assumed relative chronological order. The importance of the realization of the broad general principles of weathering lies in the possibility that in specific areas the physical height above the modern surface of a sealed ancient soil, unaffected by subsequent weathering, could be indicative of age.

C14 dating, the principles of which are briefly noted below (p. 192), was greeted with jubilation on its introduction, when it seemed to pour forth absolute dates. The inexorable clicks of the Geiger counter from the glowing lead-shielded apparatus were hailed as oracular pronouncements with which the panorama of prehistory was to be reconciled. However, the potential sources of error have proved manifold, and the diffidence of the proffering physicists is only matched by the prudence with which prehistorians accept the dates. None the less, those that are relevant will be brought forward below.

A measure of synchronism for the relative chronologies provided by the type sequences of the principal regions of Europe can be deduced from the progressive modification of tools and weapons in those regions. More precise data is provided by the diffusion of the products of the Britannico-Hibernian bronze-smiths, coupled with the brisk interchange of articles between regions (Fig. 57) which is a feature of the age of metal. However, when the products of Europe are matched with those of regions like Crete, Mesopotamia, and even Egypt, difficulties arise, for there, instead of a relatively rapid evolution and a subsequent multiplicity of types, simple forms were created and

[15] Childe, 1929, 1957.
[16] Childe, 1947 b, 11.
[17] *Man*, LI, 34–7.
[18] *Palaeohist.*, II, 105–25.
[19] *PPS*, XX, 234.
[20] *PPS*, XIX, 129–47.
[21] *Antiq.*, XXXI, 228–33.

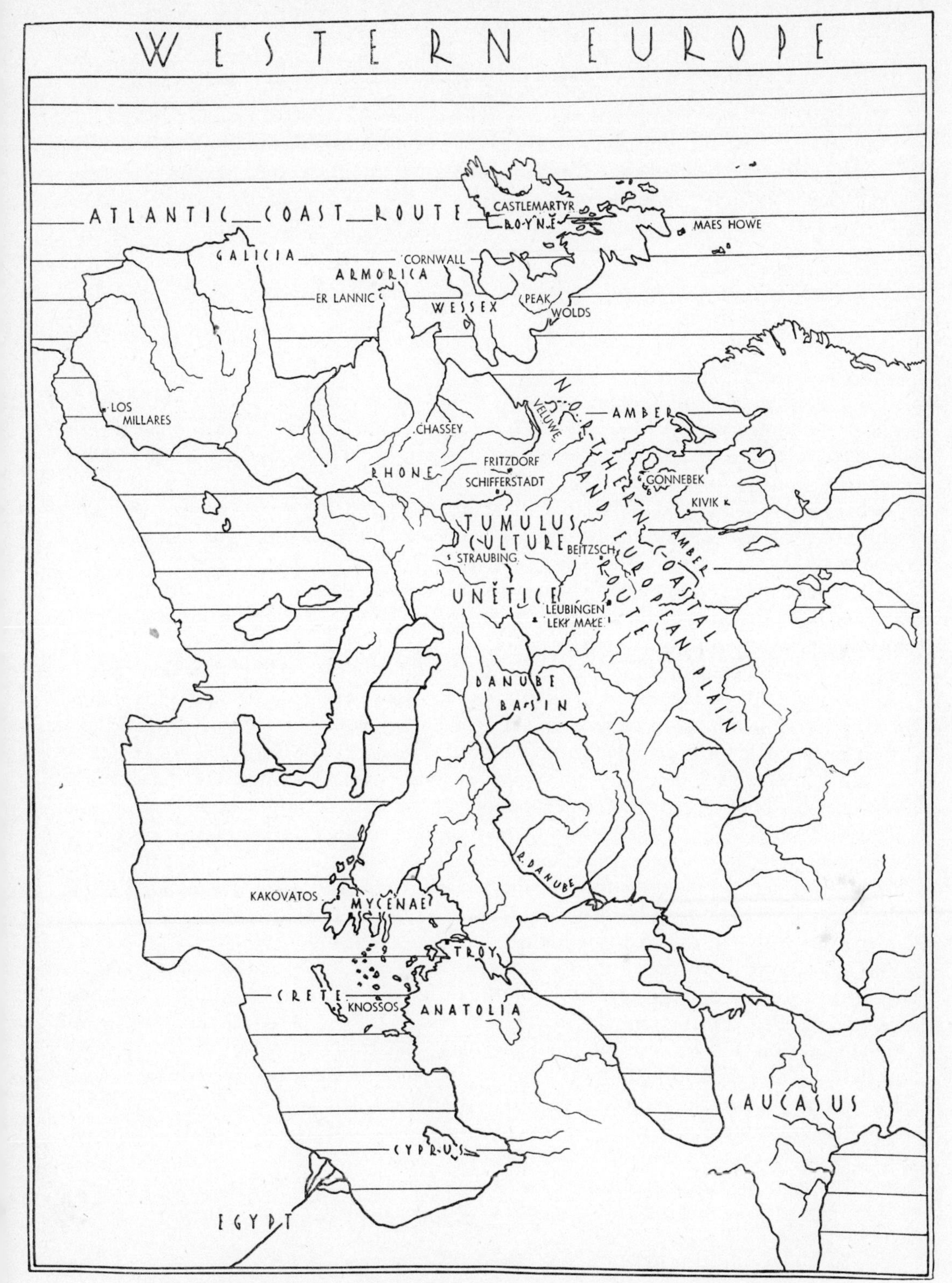

Fig. 57. Map of Europe showing sites, cultures, and routes mentioned in the text.

thereafter retained without material modification. Thus chronologically significant contacts between the technologically capable barbarians of Europe and the urban communities of the Middle East are few and tenuous.

In spite of this, absolute dates in barbarian Europe must depend upon contacts with historic civilizations. Professor Childe [22] has shown that such contacts are expressed to the prehistorian in three main forms:

(*a*) Actual importations of historically datable objects found in chronologically significant contexts.
(*b*) Obvious imitations of such made exceptionally among the barbarians themselves.
(*c*) Datable types adopted and manufactured locally among the illiterate peoples.

He continued by emphasizing that only in the first instance is a synchronism reasonably well established, and then even so it is only reasonably certain if it be bilateral, that is, if appropriate exports turn up in the historic context. The second condition is tied to the first, while in the third the historically datable types are but a *terminus a quo* for the barbarian products. It is only with these premises and principles in mind that any chronological assessment of Britain's barrows and Bronze Age can be embarked upon.

Any assessment of the age of British round barrows and Bronze cultures must also depend upon the dates deducible from the European scene as a whole. For the beginning of European metallurgy, two chronological systems,[23] long and short, have been adduced and defended. Thus with a long chronology the earliest pins and torques appear in Childe's Danubian IV, about 2300 B.C., and with a short chronology about 1700 B.C., while it must be remembered that Asian originals of these early metal objects were fashionable for nearly two thousand years after 3000 B.C. Hence no precise date is possible, and a final judgment must rest on other variables. With all the available evidence before him, plus the determinations of the C14 method, Childe,[24] in his final study of the problem, decided that these were still insufficient for him to be able to decide between the competing systems, but he ventured to conclude that the Stonehenge I date, 1850 B.C. ±, makes extremely long or short estimates for the beginning of the Unětician culture improbable.

In spite of the impressive typological systems, based upon a wealth of hoards and grave-furniture, of northern Europe and central Germany, the less complex system of the British Isles is not only probably more reliable but also has other advantages over its fellows. Here direct contacts with the historically dated East Mediterranean allow of the conversion of relative chronology into absolute better than anywhere else north of the Alps. The general bases of the British sequence have been indicated above while the relevant links and detailed synchronisms for lowland and highland zones were tested and discussed by Childe [25] two decades ago, and were reviewed from a European standpoint in 1948 by himself [26] and Hawkes.[27] Recently [28] he set his period sequence, together with the funerary pottery, against the Bronze Age divisions, but was careful

[22] *Antiq.*, VI, 208.
[23] *AJA*, XLIV, 10–26; Childe, 1947 a, 330–6.
[24] Childe, 1957, 342.
[25] *Amer. Anth.*, XXXIX, 1–22.
[26] *PPS*, XIV, 177–95.
[27] *Council for British Archaeology*, 1948, 32–41; *PPS*, XIV, 196–218.
[28] *APL*, IV, 178.

to emphasize the difficulties inherent in the correlation. It is therefore superfluous in this context to re-examine all the evidence in detail.

Any expression of chronological assessment, which is at the best little more than a reasoned sequence, of British round barrows, their rites and contents, and the cultures, is better made in tabular form prior to examination of the salient features:

Bronze Age	*Bronzes*	*Childe's Period*	*Pottery*	*Burial Rite*	*Barrows*
Early Bronze Age I	West European daggers riveted knife-daggers flat axes	III	bell-beakers necked-beakers & food-vessels	inhumation inhumations & a few cremations	low bowl bowl bermed
Early Bronze Age II	halberds Bush Barrow & ogival daggers flanged axes tanged, & tanged & ferruled spear-heads	IV	necked-beakers & food-vessels Wessex pottery & urns	inhumations & cremations	bermed pond saucer large bowl
Middle Bronze Age	rapiers palstaves basal looped spear-heads	V	urns	cremation	bowl
Late Bronze Age I	later palstaves socketed axes leaf-shaped swords	V & VI	urns	cremation	bowl
Late Bronze Age II	Spear-heads types IV b & V socketed sickles gouges knives winged axes & carp's tongue swords		urns	cremation	bowl
Late Bronze Age III	Hallstatt bronze swords & stray imports		urns	cremation	bowl

Bell-beakers and flange-hilted West European daggers, together with riveted knife-daggers, found with necked-beakers, limit the beginning of the sequence. The former correspond with the ubiquitous European bell-beakers, the latter are typologically parallel to the earliest Unětician, and also found in presumably later Bell-Beaker graves in Bohemia and the Rhineland. In view of this the following C14 dates for typologically early corded Dutch beakers of corded ware ancestry are of some interest: Ede, 2237 B.C. ± 120; Schaarsbergen, 2477 B.C. ± 320.[29] If these dates are reliable a starting point, with bell-beakers at about 1800–1900 B.C., would be possible. ApSimon[30] has insisted upon a division of the succeeding Wessex culture into two phases, based upon a clear separation of the daggers and the possibility that their associations have disparate values in the central European sequences. Thus the Bush-Barrow daggers and their associations

[29] *Palaeohist.*, IV, 9. See *Antiq.*, XXXIV, 16–17, for the most recent statement and further relevant dates.

[30] *ULIAA Rpt*, X, 37–62.

belong to that part of the Early Bronze Age which corresponds to Reinecke's A1 division, while the Camerton-Snowshill ogival daggers, pins, and other artefacts are later because they correspond to Reinecke's A2/B1 division. Battle-axes would mainly belong to the earlier phase, but localized forms continue into the later. It is in this Camerton-Snowshill (or Wessex II) phase that the direct datable contacts with the Mycenaean world are demonstrable; indeed they fulfil the primary conditions set down in a previous paragraph. The gold-bound amber disc, probably from Wessex, found in the Knossian cemetery [31] is from a context dated to about the fifteenth century B.C.[32] Navarro [33] has argued ingeniously in favour of a Mediterranean origin for these discs, and a reduction of Evans's dating for the tomb, but Childe [34] does not accept his contentions. An apparently British crescentic amber necklace, with complexly bored spacer-beads, as found in British amber and jet lunulate necklaces, from Kakovatos,[35] is considered to have reached Greece at about the same time. Thus about 1500 B.C. is a *terminus ante quem* for the later phase of the Wessex Bronze Age. The Mycenaean dagger fragment from the Cornish barrow grave, an import into Britain, is not precisely datable in Greece nor had it associations. It is therefore of no chronological value and serves only to emphasize the direct connections between the regions discussed in Chapter X. Segmented faience beads are the only imports from the historic eastern Mediterranean region which make the chronological connection bilateral. Only a restricted number of such beads of glassy faience, found mostly in Wessex,[36] can be dated. Stone has pointed out that the nearest analogies to those are still those from Egyptian and Palestinian graves, datable to about 1400 B.C., but glassy beads have been found in a context of about 1380–1350 B.C. However, a glassy faience Maltese [37] bead is considered to suggest a date between 1450 and 1350 B.C. Thus it is to be concluded that the main movement to the west of these significant beads must have been after 1450 B.C., which could be accepted as an approximate *terminus post quem*. It should be remembered that these absolute dates are estimates, at the best correct only to approximately ± 350 years! The relative absence of battle-axes from the Armorican Bronze culture's barrows might suggest an advanced date for its establishment in the peninsula, in spite of the typologically early daggers. Such a contention could be supported by a C14 date of 1,350 ± 50 years B.C. obtained from wood taken from the floor of a dagger-grave at Kervingar, Plouarzel, in Finistère.[38]

At about this point associations between funerary pottery and typologically significant bronzes ceases, nor are there further direct contacts between Britain and the historical world. With minor exceptions further chronological considerations are correlations of the typological sequences provided by bronzes. Thus little more can be undertaken in the present state of knowledge than to demonstrate, briefly, how Britain, Central Europe, and the North march together to the end of the Bronze Age (Fig. 56).

Britain's Wessex Bronze Age, to which the distinctive bermed and other atypical barrows belong, coincides with Reinecke's divisions A1 and A2/B1. On a basis of flint and bone copies of metal types current in central Europe at this time, plus a few exchanges with Wessex, this period in the North is the modified Northern Neolithic IV

[31] *Arch.*, LXV, 42, Fig. 56.
[32] *Festschrift für Otto Tschumi*, Frauenfeld, 1948, 70–6.
[33] Fox and Dickens, 1950, 100–2.
[34] *APL*, IV, 179.
[35] *Germania*, XXIV, 99–101.
[36] *PPS*, XXII, 58.
[37] *PPS*, XXII, 58.
[38] *Antiq.*, XXXII, 194.

of Montelius. Control of the trade in precious amber and a monopoly of local flint [39] may well account for the fact that at about this time the North was able to import the products of the Britannico-Hibernian smiths, and those also of smiths producing distinctive wares for the central European market. Early British axes [40] have been found side by side with native derivatives, and a few halberds were also imported. Thus upon this British and central European basis, which in relative chronological terms limits the beginnings of the distinctive Northern sequence, there began a Northern Bronze Age, using perforce imported ores.

A few British palstaves [41] and a basal-looped spear-head,[42] of a type which in the Maentwrog [43] Middle Bronze Age hoard was associated with three developed rapiers, have been found in Northern contexts of Montelius II. A similar spear-head found in an urnfield at Wiesloch [44] in Baden was in a context attributable to Reinecke's C.

The bronze sword of the Late Bronze Age [45] was not a British invention, but was introduced, fully developed, from the Continent. As Cowan [46] has so succinctly argued, our earliest swords must find their counterparts on European soil; and, conversely, sword types that are not represented abroad cannot be the earliest. Imported swords, found by chance in the Thames Valley, belong to two continental types, distinguished by the names *Hemigkofen* and *Erbenheim*, which are considered to belong to Reinecke's Hallstatt A (Childe E)/Montelius IIIb. The development of distinctive British sword types, of which there are considerable numbers, must be *after* this point.

Toggles found with Scottish cinerary urns [47] are precisely similar to toggles found in the North in contexts of Montelius V, as are crooked-necked sunflower pins,[48] one having been found with a sword at Tarves [49] in Scotland. The so-called Sussex loops found in the Blackrock [50] hoard, a pair of which were found in a barrow, together with bronze pins,[51] are thick, heavy versions of elegant wire bracelets current in Reinecke's Hallstatt B (Childe F)/Montelius V. A fragment of a distinctive bronze bowl [52] found with other bronze implements at Adabrock [53] in Lewis, can also be referred to the same horizon. End-winged axes and carp's-tongue swords correspond to Reinecke's Hallstatt B (Childe F) and Montelius V in the North. Britain's Late Bronze Age III, defined by Hallstatt bronze swords and other occasional objects, would seem roughly to approximate to Reinecke's Hallstatt C–D and Montelius VI in the North. The chronological relationships inherent in the material discussed in the previous paragraphs are shown in Fig. 56, and are there set against their parent cultures.

Within recent years efforts have been made to bring the Iberian Peninsula into Europe's chronological fold. Childe [54] has examined the slender evidence, and although there was an interchange with the peninsula throughout the Bronze Age, noted in Chapter X, the articles involved were for the most part scarcely those upon which reliable chronological conclusions could be based.

[39] *Kuml*, I, 23–39.
[40] *Kuml*, V, 36–45.
[41] Forssander, 1936, 220.
[42] *MZ*, XXIX, 56.
[43] *Bronze Age Guide*, 42, Fig. 29.
[44] *MZ*, XXIX, 58.
[45] *Arch.*, LXXIII, 253–65.
[46] *PPS*, XVII, 195–213. See also *PPS*, XVIII, 129 ff., and references to Sprockhoff in *Festschrift zum 75 Geburtstag von Paul Reinecke am 25 September 1947*, Mainz, 1950.
[47] Childe, 1947 b, 155; but see *PPS*, XXIV, 227.
[48] *Arch. J.*, C, 197; *PSAS*, LXXXII, 306.
[49] *Bronze Age Guide*, 101, Fig. 105.
[50] *PPS*, XV, 107–21.
[51] *SAC*, II, 265; *JBAA*, I, 148; Evans, 1881, 368.
[52] Behrens, 1916, 62, Abb. 15.
[53] *PSAS*, XLV, 27.
[54] *APL*, IV, 167–85.

To conclude, the interrelationships of the earlier British barrow-building cultures (Fig. 56) must also be reviewed briefly. Sherds of bell-beaker from the mound of the Giant's Hill, Skendleby,[55] long barrow point to a coexistence of bell-beaker and Western Neolithic elements. Bell- and necked-beakers have often been found contiguous in cemeteries,[56] as hybrids, or as in the Wick Barrow,[57] where a bell-beaker apparently preceded the necked-beakers. Again, beaker pottery frequently occurs with the wares termed Secondary Neolithic in such a manner that separation as cultures is difficult if not impossible. That the Wessex Bronze Age contained a considerable necked-beaker, as well as food-vessel, strain has been shown in detail above. The evidence for the coexistence of the Secondary Neolithic cultures, considered at this point in time as apparently separate cultures, with the Wessex Bronze Age, has been cited in detail by Piggott.[58] Indeed, the Secondary Neolithic axe factories continued in use for the production of battle-axes, while the routes along which their products were distributed must have been taken over by those who brought metal tools and weapons from craftsman to user. Cinerary urns, in the forms which apparently persist until the Iron Age,[59] first occur at about this time. It is difficult to isolate the earliest Deverel-Rimbury urns. Nothing datable has been found with them, although a spear-head and axe fragments from their settlement sites suggests the Late Bronze Age.

[55] *Arch.*, LXXXV, 53.
[56] *Arch.*, XC, 52.
[57] *PSANHS*, LIV, 1–77.
[58] Piggott, 1954, 380.
[59] *PSAS*, V, 312.

CHAPTER XII

BARROWS AND BRONZE AGE SOCIETY

SIR MORTIMER WHEELER, in *Archaeology from the Earth*, said that: 'The archaeological excavator is not digging up things, he is digging up people; however much he may analyse and tabulate and desiccate his discoveries in the laboratory, the ultimate appeal across the ages, whether the time interval be 500 or 500,000 years, is from mind to intelligent mind, from man to sentient man.' With this firmly in mind, the prehistorian must look at the fragments which form an archaeological record, here barrows and their burials and associated monuments, and decide precisely what information he can truly, objectively, and legitimately distil from them. He will find that it falls into three categories: technological, economic, and social.[1] Furthermore he will find that the relative reliability of his account will vary in that order. While technological and economic information can be gleaned directly, or if not directly by the aid of certain specialized techniques, the inferences of social and political structure, and of the ideology that lubricated them, are usually less direct, more subjective, and more difficult matters. Indeed, recently,[2] a timely warning has been sounded, together with a reminder that there may be no logical relationship between human activity in some of its aspects and the evidence left for the prehistorian. To this must be added a further reminder that what, viewed from our vantage point in time, may seem to us simple and logical processes, were not so for an early society, bounded by its contemporary environment, material, and conceptual equipment.

A round barrow, with the burial or burials beneath it, is an expression of the social and political structure that threw it up. Not only the burial rites, but the entire concept of the monument pertains to its ideology. A barrow is a ritual structure for burial of the dead, the outcome of human activity presumably motivated by considerations of the supernatural, though barrows and cairns may have been in the very beginning of man's consciousness functional structures, to deter carrion feeders, besides being houses of the dead. Technological and economic information can be recovered from a study of the articles of grave-furniture, from ritual deposits, and from the structure, but this fact does not detract from the barrow's primary function. As technological, economic, social, political, and ideological data can all be recovered from a single monument, there exists a specific relationship between them. Technology and economy, the means of production within their contemporary environment, may determine the pattern of society, and, indeed, even ultimately produce a concomitant ideology. This ideology will in its turn modulate the roots from which it sprung. Thus a society organically

[1] *Amer. Anth.*, LVI, 155–68.

[2] *ANL*, VI, 1–5.

existent in time is the interaction of these basic elements, all of which are expressed at this period in barrow-building.

Applying sociological interpretations to archaeological evidence is no new thing. In spite of the adventurous Victorian era's preoccupation with progress, certain of its scholars looked beyond the urns and daggers to the men who made them. Although many saw the past as a process of evolution from promiscuity to their age's probity, considering all things they acquitted the 'noble savage' builders of Britain's round barrows rather well (Pl. XXXI a). Greenwell,[3] comparing, subconsciously perhaps, the labour of heaping a barrow with that involved in the production of the florid and substantial funerary monuments then current, thought that 'these mounds must be regarded as the places of sepulture of chiefs of tribes, clans and families, or of other people in authority claiming and being allowed a position of respect, and of those who were nearly connected with them, as wives, children, and personal dependants.' For what he termed 'the mass of the community' burial in flat graves, or small mounds and cairns, without grave-furniture, sufficed. Mortimer[4] merely repeated these remarks and added to them only a comment upon the settled nature of life which he inferred from the Wold barrow groups.

Abercromby,[5] in this century, was of the opinion that Beaker society was matriarchic, that is that kingship was passed on through the female line, selection depending upon the choice of the reigning queen. His evidence for this was that he considered that unusually large barrows had been reared over the graves of some women and even girls. This he thought also applied to what we term the Wessex culture. Not only were there, he claimed, high barrows over women's graves, but also no male burial contained grave-furniture so rich as those of the women.

After Abercromby, attempts to wrest information regarding defined social institutions languished while prehistorians pursued the technological and, lately, the economic[6] aspects of prehistoric societies. It is only recently that Childe[7] has rationalized the sociological implications of prehistory and has summarized the European evidence. It is therefore possible to peer hesitantly beyond the barrows and their relics and glimpse the serried social institutions[8] which should lead, ultimately, to reliable and objective historical interpretation.

In the present context it is not possible to discuss in detail the technological processes, in their various media, of the societies that form Britain's round barrow-building cultures. As yet little is known of the practices of the earlier metal craftsmen, although founders' hoards and a greater availability of metal define the later Bronze Age. Similarly, the study of Irish mining and metallurgy is as yet in its infancy[9] although a useful beginning has been made in the field of spectro-analytical examination of implements, the identification of sources,[10] and the study of moulds.[11] The study of specific objects, however, has revealed much regarding the basic methods and techniques of the Irish smiths.[12]

[3] Greenwell, 1877, 112.
[4] Mortimer, 1905, lxxi.
[5] Abercromby, 1912, II, 110–14.
[6] Clark, 1952; *PBA*, XXXIX, 215–38.
[7] Childe, 1951.
[8] Childe, 1951, 54; Hobhouse, Ginsberg, and Wheeler, 1926.
[9] R. Kane, *The Industrial Resources of Ireland*, Dublin, 1844; *UJA* (Old Series) I, ix, 212; *JRSAI*, XV, 34, XVI, 281; *PSA*, 2nd Series, V, 223; *PRIA*, XXX, 524; *PPS*, III, 365.
[10] *PPS*, XXIII, 91–123.
[11] *UJA*, XVIII, 62–80.
[12] *PRIA*, XLIV, 181–228.

Thurnam,[13] Greenwell,[14] and Mortimer[15] noted and commented upon faunal remains from the large number of barrows that they examined, as did Thomas Bateman.[16] Unfortunately their records do not permit of statistical analysis for comparative purposes. Mortimer notes that of the domestic species the most frequent bones were those of the ox, followed by those of the pig, and then the goat (or sheep), the horse and dog being rare. Greenwell records the same species, putting the ox at the top of his list. While Thurnam notes bones of oxen from a number of barrows in Wessex, he was most impressed by the number of graves which had produced shed antlers, in instances stacked around interments, and the record of animals 'of the chase'. These last were noted in numbers by both Mortimer and Greenwell. Sites of comparable age at which evidence of occupation has been found are Woodhenge,[17] Plantation Farm,[18] and Durrington Walls.[19] At Woodhenge the wild species represented by bones were the wild ox or urus, red deer, roe deer, fox, cat, weasel, water-vole, brown rat, mole, and frog, and the domesticated consisted chiefly of oxen of robust form, and pig, together with scanty remains of sheep or perhaps goat. At Plantation Farm, in the Fens, it was noted how domestic forms predominated over wild forms, a surprising feature in that environment. At Durrington Walls pigs predominated, followed by cattle, and sheep (or goats). Here the bones reflect the choice of joints for food, and many long bones were split for marrow. The occupants appear to have had a preference for hand and leg of pork, and rib and shin of beef.

The remains of cereals have been found in a number of barrows, and grain impressions have been noted upon funerary pottery from others. A wheat grain was recovered from a Devon[20] barrow in the mid-nineteenth century. Mortimer found three wheat grains in a half-baked food-vessel sherd from a Wold barrow[21] and a wheat grain was found with a cremation at Theale[22] in Berkshire. Sir Cyril Fox recovered wheat and a few barley grains from the Pond Cairn,[23] and a barley grain was recognized amongst carbonized matter from one of the Barnby Howes[24] in Yorkshire. Straw had been placed in the Bishop's Waltham[25] timber coffin before the cremation and daggers. The remains of, or the pollen from, weeds of cultivation appropriate to cereals have been noted from a number of barrows where soil conditions have been favourable to preservation.

Although these wheat grains have been found in barrows and burials, the study of grain impressions upon funerary and other pottery of the Bronze Age, undertaken by Jessen and Helbaek[26] just before the last war, led them to believe that the dominant cereal crop of that time was Naked Barley. This study was continued after the war by Helbaek[27] and it is now possible to see that while the cereal of the Neolithic farmers was wheat, the Beaker folk brought a change in agricultural habits to Britain by introducing this barley, the cereal of a more northern clime.

From these fragmentary records of the subsistence economy of the builders of round

[13] *Arch.*, XLIII, 536.
[14] Greenwell, 1877, 109.
[15] Mortimer, 1905, lxix.
[16] Bateman, 1861, 298–9.
[17] Cunnington, 1929, 61–9.
[18] *Ant. J.*, XIII, 278.
[19] *Ant. J.*, XXXIV, 175–7.
[20] *TDA*, IV, 646.
[21] Mortimer, 1905, 111.
[22] *PPS*, IV, 40.
[23] *Arch.*, LXXXVII, 171–2, Pl. LXIII, 2.
[24] *YAJ*, XXXIX, 30.
[25] *PPS*, XXIII, 149.
[26] Knud Jessen and Hans Helbaek, KDVS, *Biologiske Skrifter*, Bind III, Nr. 2, 1944.
[27] *PPS*, XVIII, 194–233.

barrows, a definite pattern emerges. There was mixed farming, that is the raising of cattle, and sheep or goats, coupled with cereal-growing. Of the circumstances and the methods of this, the British archaeological record, apart from the funerary monuments, tells us little or nothing. An enclosure on Ram's Hill [28] in Berkshire could have housed cattle, and partial excavation has revealed what are surely nucleated agricultural communities of the later Bronze Age on the Sussex Downs.[29] Here excavation may have revealed only part of a complex story. Looming large in this economy is the importance of the chase, not only for food but for raw material such as antler, furs, and hides. For antler one can visualize regular collection and conservation. Such a reliance on the chase must have been an inheritance from the native Mesolithic substratum via the Secondary Neolithic, which is the basis of the Bronze Age cultures.

Society's institutions, the products of its technology and economy, have been classified [30] under the headings of government, justice, the family, rank, property, and war. To these Childe [31] has added institutional religion. All overlap, and government and institutional religion frequently coincide.

We can perhaps see in Stonehenge, Avebury, Tara, and other lesser groups of henges and circles, set about with their barrows, mute evidence of the political and religious systems that directed the lives of our Bronze Age ancestors. Indeed, one would like to deduce a unity over much of the British Isles, dominated if not surely ruled by the individual or individuals who caused Stonehenge in its final form to be built, which, if not political, was based upon some affinity of belief. Only such people could have undertaken the prestige exchanges with Europe and the Mycenaean world. Vassals from such centres as Knowlton, Thornborough, and perhaps even Stenness, must have paid tribute, having at appropriate times journeyed to assemblies at Stonehenge, where they indulged in the unlimited feasting, games, music, and verse proper to such an occasion.

It is in this Early Bronze Age funerary record that a pattern of society, which in Europe was to survive for three millennia, can first be seen. This is the so-called 'Heroic' realm of kings and warriors, attested first by great barrows, rich graves, daggers, and battle-axes. Although properly a problem of rank in our classification, this form of society was at one with what has been termed government and institutional religion. Its organic life is difficult to trace as the earlier stages are enshrined in the archaeological record. None the less, impressions can be gleaned from classical sources such as the *Iliad* and the *Odyssey*. More information is to be obtained from Roman writers such as Caesar who came into direct collision with such people, while the Irish Annals, which document the later stages of that land's paganism, contain a wealth of illustration. Romances such as those of Arthur and his Knights, and the epic *Beowulf*, contain much that is pertinent, while the feudal society of the Middle Ages perpetuates the pattern.

A hint of what must have been a festival of Early Bronze Age, and even Neolithic, communities, in Britain at least, is to be seen in the Irish Celtic records of *Samain*.[32] By modern chronology this would fall on the 1st of November,[33] an important season for

[28] *Ant. J.*, XX, 465–80.
[29] *PPS*, I, 16–59.
[30] Hobhouse, Ginsberg, and Wheeler, 1926.
[31] Childe, 1951, 54.
[32] T. G. E. Powell, *The Celts*, Thames & Hudson, 1958, 116.
[33] T. G. E. Powell, *The Celts*, 116.

people with an economy based largely upon cattle. It was at this time that animals not wanted for breeding were slaughtered. Such public occasions would doubtless be conducted according to ancient ritual and would be accompanied by feasting, the reward of the warrior in Heroic society. Archaeological evidence which could convincingly be equated with all this can be seen from the Western Neolithic causewayed camps.[34] Some of these camps which are almost circular incidentally provide forbears for some of the henges. Such a great enclosure as Durrington Walls, a part of that Stonehenge complex to which I have ascribed the primacy of all Britain, has upon excavation provided similar evidence,[35] and while it may have enclosed certain structures it could have been the place of assembly for such rites.

From barrow excavation, there is evidence for a number of actions which may well come into the religious category. Charcoal and burning indicate grave-fumigation. Flint implements, sometimes broken, sherds, piled occupation earth and hearth sweepings in barrows must have some abstract significance. Again, while the grave-furniture of the earlier Bronze Age might suggest a belief in an individualistic after-life to which the deceased went equipped, is the later paucity or absence of such grave-furniture evidence of a change of basic beliefs or has the greed of the heirs overcome their religious scruples? Or was there a change in technology and economy mirrored in the ideology? It seems as if there was a reversion at least to the meagre furniture of Neolithic times, if not to their impersonal rites!

Large numbers of implements, and spectacular bronzes such as shields and cauldrons, of the Middle and Later Bronze Age have been recovered from peat, which suggests that they may have been cast into meres, or from rivers. The numbers are too large, and many of the objects too fine, for them to represent chance losses from boats. Was there at this time a reversion to the aquatic deities, first apparent in immediate post-glacial times and to which in the Iron Age great quantities of gear were given in many parts of Europe? Such vessels as the Caergwrle and Broighter boats may have been connected with such rites.

Even less is known of the rites appropriate to such idols as those from Roos Carr or from the Folkton barrow. Again, we are grossly ignorant of the function of all that is called 'art' and vaguely ascribed to the ideological superstructure, although we discern 'cults' based upon depicted objects such as axes. Furthermore, at what specific rites and functions were such regalia as the Mold cape or the gold, amber, and jet lunulae worn? Were they the regalia of devotees of the deity of the pick-axe face who sometimes wears necklaces? Even more complex would be the reasons for the burial of the infant with cleft skull at the centre of Woodhenge. Could it be a foundation sacrifice comparable to the skeletons set beneath Skara Brae houses? Similarly, with the cremations set in Stonehenge's Aubrey Holes, or within the precincts of Cairnpapple, what determined the place of burial? Why did this late-Neolithic cremation cemetery possess such sanctity for the later barrow-builders? Do such cremations represent the remains of normal people or are they perhaps sacrifices?

Infilled, so-called ritual pits, as well as being a feature of certain henges, are, as it will be remembered, found beneath barrows. In the *Odyssey* a pit appears to be a means of communication with certain cthonic deities.[36] Such *βοθροι* were classically dug with

[34] Piggott, 1954, 28.
[35] *Ant. J.*, XXXIV, 155–77.
[36] *PPS*, XXIII, 160.

a sword. By pouring libations directly, or from such vessels as the Minoan rhytons or, in our province, the Tipperary and Schifferstadt 'hats', vows could be made and the spirits of the departed summoned back for counsel.

Justice as a social institution is unlikely normally to leave any trace in the archaeological record. It is sometimes an expression of the will of the specific society through an individual, and would be in the present circumstances a prerogative of government and institutional religion, applied as a solution to a situation, condition, or circumstance, as much as a system of retribution. There is in the Early Bronze Age and in Neolithic times fairly constant evidence of the trepanning of living subjects, and other head operations. Have we then here evidence of the imposition of society's will to a circumstance of perhaps pathological origin?

It is possible from a study of barrows and their contents to make certain simple deductions regarding the families whose members they cover. Basically, male and female graves are reasonably clear when grave-furniture is present, and critical skeletal anatomy is often of assistance when it is absent, even with cremations. Male graves contain battle-axes or daggers and the like, while female graves are distinguished by a wealth of beads, trinkets, with, perhaps, awls and small knives. However definite the distinction, the archaeological record does not disclose the nature of the relationship of male and female, whether wives were won or purchased. From the furnishing of the burials it would seem that women may have had property, although this might merely be appropriate display by the husband. Abercromby [37] deduced matriarchy from large barrows over women and girls, and it cannot be denied that some of the richest Wessex graves are probably those of females,[38] though pastoral and mixed farmers, and certainly Heroic societies, are with exceptions normally patriarchic.

Double burials,[39] apparently of men and women, are sometimes found in barrows, both burials usually being in close contact. One may ask whether this is evidence of a suttee, wife or concubine being dispatched at the death of her consort and buried with the man? Something similar could be an explanation of satellite burials under barrows. Have wives and dependants or even slaves been dispatched and buried, either by inhumation or cremation, to accompany a master or mistress into eternity?

Barrow cemeteries, linear, nuclear, or dispersed, and composite double, triple, and quadruple barrows, may be evidence of family or clan. Each barrow cemetery, in the vicinity of the henge, or elsewhere, could belong to a certain family. The grave-furniture from the cemetery would then be a sequence illustrating the fortunes of the family over a period of time.

In barrows the differences of grave-furniture can be examined, and there is little doubt that the marked differences are those of rank. The extremes are readily recognizable though intermediate stages are not. There is no point where one can say that an upper class ends and a lower class begins, although royal graves are discernible. Besides grave-furniture, coffins may denote a separate class. Coffins may have been a normal adjunct of Beaker burials, but during Childe's Period IV it is clear that while certain martial individuals were buried in timber coffins others were not, so that an especial class within the warrior hierarchy is to be suspected. In Wessex and other parts of England at this time, distinctive bermed barrows, bell and disc, appear to have

[37] Abercromby, 1912, 110–14.
[38] *ULIAA Rpt*, X, 53.
[39] *PPS*, XXIII, 160.

covered burials of Wessex warriors and their female counterparts respectively, as grave-furniture attests. Who, however, were the persons interred in the distinctive pond barrows?

Barrow size may indicate rank also, for it reflects the labour necessary to build it. However, several of the barrows in Wessex from which gold objects have been recovered were by no means the largest, whereas a number of great mounds covered, as far as is known, merely simple cremations. Yet vast size indicates considerable command of labour, that is, an effort by society to raise a barrow commensurate with the deceased person's rank. Therefore when a great barrow covers a burial richly furnished there can be little doubt of the erstwhile social status of its occupants.

Grave-furniture in the form of weapons, tools, ornaments, and regalia would be the property of the individuals that wore or carried them in life. Property, in the sense of weapons, tools, or even houses belonging to families and individuals, is recognized even amongst the simplest peoples of today. There are proprietary marks upon bones and weapons in Upper Palaeolithic times, and Danubian clay stamps [40] denote a similar principle. While the grave-furniture, and particularly the metal gear, from British barrows has a certain uniformity, the pottery, although conforming to the general specification demanded by society, has sufficient localized individuality, especially in ornamentation, to suggest that such variations may denote families and clans.

The change of custom with regard to grave-furniture in about the Middle Bronze Age has been commented upon above with regard to religious principles.[41] Even in relatively stable societies, that is in cultures that endured for a long time, the wealth of grave-furniture actually declined even though the resources, i.e. the wealth, in our case the availability of metal, of the society were increasing. Thus property that had previously been consigned to the grave accrued to the heirs.

The barrow cemetery, in which a family or clan regularly interred its dead and built its barrows, would certainly be the property of the group. Surmounting stones, and more particularly posts, for which there is evidence, might have been totems. Again, in terms of land, it would seem possible that in certain areas certain groups had the rights of the chase, and that the cattle grazed in specific areas. There is, however, no assured archaeological evidence relevant to the ownership of land until late in the Iron Age.[42]

War in primitive communities can, unlike modern warfare, be a lucrative source of income to the victors. Or it can assume the form of head-hunting for prestige, as in modern savage society, or be a part of the rites of passage. The warriors of Bronze Age society were probably akin to the war-parties of the North American Indians, and in the earlier forms of Heroic society, as in later, various grades, accompanied by the appropriate rites of passage, had to be passed through before full warrior status was conferred.

The difficulties of distinguishing tools from weapons has been commented upon above. It seems almost certain that the battle-axes, as their martial appearance suggests, and the halberds, are weapons primarily intended for war and war-parties, although this does not exclude their use as weapons of the chase, unless their usage was circumscribed by taboos. The great bronze daggers and rapiers, used probably in the

[40] Childe, 1950, 102, Fig. 80.
[41] *Man*, XLV, 13–19.
[42] G. Halt, KDVS, *Historisk-philologiske Meddelelser*, XXVI, No. 6, 1938.

Mycenaean manner with the circular single-grip bucklers and shields, and perhaps even with bell-helmets or their leather equivalents, are again almost certainly martial gear, although the renowned Idaean Hunt Shield [43] depicts lion-hunting with rapier and shield. Again the slashing-swords of the later Bronze Age cannot be other than weapons of war.

However, though weapons in Heroic society have parade uses, and, if of exceptional workmanship, certainly signify rank, their uses may be varied, for the warrior needed to be versatile. Certain Wessex graves contain both dagger and battle-axe, and the bow was current. Some comparison can be made with Mycenaean warriors, who, to judge by the various representations, were skilled in the use of various arms, although rapiers, like daggers in the north, were basic equipment.

It would be impossible from the archaeological evidence to determine the form that conflict took amongst the warriors who lie beneath many of Britain's barrows. The absence of fortifications more substantial than cattle stockades indicates its modest scale. War amongst pastoralists or mixed farmers is normally for prestige, cattle, and slaves. Indeed, the evidence for warfare increases as the importance of stock-breeding increases in the economy and that correlation can hardly be accidental.[44]

As the peoples who built the round barrows of Bronze Age Britain were apparently illiterate, that is, they left no written records, it is impossible objectively to assess the effects of speech as a modulatory and formative element in those societies. Human society is perpetuated through articulate speech, and the social tradition and experience is transmitted through this vehicle, and, furthermore, it is the unitive medium which coalesces society. Thus it is as important as, if not more than, the other elements in the composition of society. Its efficiency as an instrument for abstract technological and scientific ideas may be a vital determining factor in a society's material progress. Indeed, it is probable that the underlying unity and the continuity of European prehistory and history were matched by a lingual unity generally termed Indo-European. This means that our barrow-builders may well have spoken some provincial version of this language group. With a few exceptions, all European languages, including Greek and Latin, as well as Persian and Hindustani, are considered to belong to a single language group, and it has long been the contention of the comparative philologists that these Indo-European [45] languages had a single area of origin and, in the prehistoric past, spread into Europe. However, the location of a homeland for this language, and the identification of its apparent spread with archaeological phenomena, has been a matter of controversy and, indeed, perversion of history since the first formulation of the hypothesis. For example, national feeling and prestige, channelled by Gustaf Kossina,[46] saw the Indo-Europeans as blond *Nordics* peopling the North European plain, where they were as 'Aryans' subsequently deified by the gaseous nonsense of Nazism.

It would be logical for the common lingual basis to be equated with a common cultural denominator. On these grounds, and those of the considerable age of Indo-European language as suggested by the Mycenaean basis of Greek, one is directed to the Battle-Axe cultures, which, as has been briefly indicated above, lie directly behind the cultures of those who built round barrows during the Bronze Age. Thus any search for

[43] *AJA*, LIV, 298, Fig. 13.

[44] *Sociological Review*, XXXIII, 126–38.

[45] V. G. Childe, *The Aryans*, Routledge & Kegan Paul, 1926; *Antiq.*, XV, 50–68.

[46] G. Kossina, *Die Indogermanen*, Würzburg, 1921.

the Indo-European, or, as it is sometimes more succinctly but hesitatingly termed, *Aryan*, homeland, using a combination of linguistic and archaeological indications, would become enmeshed with an inquiry into the origins of the battle-axe. From linguistic study, certain traits, which could be detected in an archaeological record, have been isolated. Indo-Europeans are said to have used battle-axes, horses, wheeled vehicles, and bows and arrows, to have been patriarchic, to have raised cattle and sheep and had a dairy economy, to have buried their dead with battle-axes in separate graves, sometimes under a barrow. As a society they appear to have been essentially of the 'Heroic' type discussed above. However, the problem is one of a vast space and a long time, and it is highly improbable that all traits were current at any one time. Indeed, to postulate the origin of the Indo-Europeans in the single culture in which the greatest number of 'Indo-European' traits have been detected would cause a literal inversion of current chronologies [47] both relative and absolute. From a linguistic point of view it seems likely that there would have been an accruing vocabulary, side by side with material development. Therefore any search for a single culture or for that matter a single race is fruitless.

Most responsible prehistorians and philologists are agreed that the possible region of origin of the Indo-Europeans is a limited one, somewhere between the Danube and the Oxus! Linguistically, the Indo-European speaking area has been divided according to the root word for 'one hundred'. The *centum* has on the whole a western distribution, except in the dead Tocharian language, and the *satem* an oriental. There are certain differences between East and West as well as similarities. The eastern Aryans, who, as is related in the *Rigveda*,[48] clashed with the urban dwellers of Harrapān northern and central India in the second millennium B.C., were armed with chariots and the bow, plus sword or dagger. Cremation was their main funerary rite, although inhumation was not unknown, in circumstances which almost uncannily recall the practices of the post and stake barrows in western Europe.

No such saga as the *Rigveda* documents the earliest spread of the Indo-Europeans into western Europe and to Britain. Although there are metallic-looking stone battle-axes, hinting at distant contacts with the Orient, and inhumation burials under barrows, sometimes with tent-like mortuary houses, followed by cremations, there is no unequivocable evidence in the West regarding the use of horses, let alone wheeled vehicles, at this time. While a few horse bones have been recovered from British barrows and occupation sites, and a horse has been found with two corded beakers under a Dutch barrow,[49] this may only be evidence of the horse as a source of food. The earliest representation of a horsed vehicle, the northern European Kivik [50] chariot, on a slab of the great cist, is Montelius III/Reinecke D-E, about 1000 B.C., although the alleged schematic ox-carts depicted upon a slab of a cist at Züschen,[51] in Hesse, might be earlier. The British and Irish Bronze Age saws, necessary concomitants to carriage building, belong apparently to the Middle Bronze Age.[52]

[47] Childe, 1957, 127; but see *Amer. Anth.*, LVII, Pt 3, Mem. 84.

[48] S. Piggott, *Prehistoric India to 1000 B.C.*, Penguin Books, 1950, 244–89; *Antiq.*, XVII, 1–10.

[49] *PZ*, IV, 368–73.

[50] Schwantes, 1939, Abb. 847; *Antiq*, XVI, 160–174. See *AJA*, LXIII, 53, on this problem of early wheeled vehicles in Europe.

[51] *Mannus*, XXV, 131–2; H. Kühn, *Die Felsbilder Europas*, Stuttgart, 1952, 153–4.

[52] R. E. M. Wheeler, *Prehistoric and Roman Wales*, Oxford University Press, 1925, 161, Fig. 58; *PPS*, XII, 161, Pl. XIII.

However, this is not the place to examine in detail who and what were the Indo-Europeans. One thing seems certain, they did not fall upon the late Neolithic Western Europeans, as they did upon the Harrapāns of the Orient. We should not imagine battle-axe-armed hordes, supported by their horsed vehicles, flooding out of the Pontic Steppe! The battle-axes could still be primarily hunters' weapons, and the carts, if they existed at this early time, adjuncts to a transhumance economy!

The Indo-European contribution to Britain and western Europe was, however, of primary importance although intangible, for the flexibility of their languages, besides other factors, have aided, moulded, and determined the remarkable technological progress of the Bronze Age. The unique feature of their structure was the manner in which a sequence of reasoned conceptual relationships might be expressed by subordinate clauses! With such subtle, delicate, and pervasive aids the development of progressively more abstract ideas, and thence scientific and economic advancement, has been assured.

CHAPTER XIII

IN EARLY LITERATURE

APART FROM a record [1] of the voyage of a nameless Greek mariner to the sacred island Ierne (Ireland) and, perhaps, nearby Albion (Britain), history accords these countries scarcely any mention [2] until almost two millennia after the first round barrows were thrown up. When the territorial ambitions of literate Romans led them to subdue barbarian Western Europe, they found barrow-building still a living practice, but, as would be expected, nowhere did they accord it more than incidental mention.

Barrow-raising and the rite of cremation were also Roman, and before them Greek, customs. Therefore, from the first their lore, literature, history, and topography contained much, all of which is generally applicable, even in Britain, regarding such burials and the procedure attendant upon them.

Beyond the imperial frontiers furnished single-grave barrow burial continued, basically unchanged and ever more rich and elaborate, as the mode of burial for warrior aristocrats and chieftains. These footloose and fluid barbarians finally disrupted the stability imposed by the Roman raj and in the process became themselves literate. Much that was then written would, like the Homeric epics, have been adapted from the detailed and complex oral legends, which had long been current within their pre-, para-, and pene-historic world, giving a picture of the life, adventures, and funerary practices of Heroic society.

These gleanings from a vast area, when supplementing or supplemented by the evidence provided by archaeology, vivify to a surprising degree the bare bones of barrow and grave. The principal relevant sources can be considered for convenience in three categories. First of all there are heroic tales, sometimes in Greek, or garbed in one instance as a sophisticated Latin epic, or set down after singing to haunting euphonious melodies in the smoky halls of the north. Secondly, there are the descriptive works ranging from comprehensive detailed accounts to the laconic incidental in writings ranging from travellers' tales to military memoirs. Finally, there is a miscellany which varies from Christian fulmination against black heathendom to occasional inscriptions.

Homer's *Iliad* describes how Achilles [3] cremates and buries in a barrow his close companion Patroklus. 'First they put out with sparkling wine all parts of the funeral pyre in which the flames had done their work and the ash had fallen deep. Then, with tears on their cheeks, they collected the white bones of their gentle comrade in a golden vase, closed it with a double seal of fat, laid it in his hut, and covered it with a soft linen

[1] Avienus, *Ora Maritima*, 90–112.
[2] Strabo, *Geography*, I, 4, II, 4.
[3] *Iliad*, XXIII, trans. E. V. Rieu, Penguin Classics, 1951.

shroud. Next they designed his barrow by laying down a ring of stone revetments round the pyre. Then they fetched earth and piled it up inside.'

The ignition and combustion of what must have been a large and elaborate pyre, even allowing for heroic embroidery, was accompanied by mourning, libations, and human sacrifice, and games marked the completion of the barrow. This would be of the composite class covering a mortuary house. Some British barrows appear to have had beneath them remains of substantial pyres, while satellite burials may hint at human sacrifices. Yet the mourning, the rites attendant upon libations, and the games are all intangibles irrecoverable by the methods of archaeology!

Infilled pits found under barrows,[4] to which only a 'ritual' function can be ascribed, have been likened, as, indeed, have the peculiar pond barrows,[5] to the βοθροι of the *Odyssey*.[6] These were a means of communication with the underworld of shades and cthonic deities. Odysseus[7] recounts how he went to the kingdom of Persephone to get advice from the dead Tiresias and was to vow an offering for his safe return, upon the instructions of Circe, by digging a pit (βοθρος) and pouring a libation (χοή) to all the dead. Then he took sheep brought for the occasion and cut their throats over the pit. Thereupon the shades gathered around. But Odysseus, sitting sword in hand, kept them at bay until Tiresias should come, drink of the blood, and thus become capable of speech.

Pits loomed quite large in Mediterranean lore and ritual. Philostratus[8] says how 'The cthonic gods welcome trenches and ceremonies done in the hollow earth.' Pausanius,[9] in his guide-books, describes how at Titane, a town in Sicyonia, a priest performed secret rites in four pits to soothe the winds. Each of the four winds dwelt, it would seem, as a cthonic power in a pit. Much the same principle could have been seen in some Italian cities where the *mundus*, a round pit, was dug. In Rome on the Palatine, this was closed with a stone removed thrice a year on the festivals of the powers of the nether world.

Virgil's *Aeneid* gives an account of pyre preparation, cremation, and inurning of the bones when it is related how the dutiful Aeneas buried Misenus under a barrow.[10]

'The Trojans on the beach wept Misenus and to the thankless dust the last duties paid. First they build up a vast pyre fat with pine torches and cleft oak, whose sides they interlace with dark foliage, and set up funeral cypresses before it, and adorn it above with his shining armour. Some prepare warm water in cauldrons bubbling over the flames, and wash and anoint the cold body. A groan is made. Then, the dirge done, they duly lay his limbs upon a couch, and spread over it a crimson cloak, his well-known covering. Some shoulder the huge bier, a melancholy service, and with averted faces, in the manner of their forefathers, thrust in the torch. Gifts of frankincense, food, bowls of poured out oil are piled upon the fire. After the embers sank in and the flames died down, they washed the thirsty ashes with wine and Corynaeus gathered up the bones and covered them with an urn of brass. Then three times he purified his companions with clear water sprinkling them with dew from the bough of the fruitful olive and spoke words of farewell. Then the dutiful Aeneas heaps a huge mass over him for

[4] Glasbergen, 1954, II, 150–1.
[5] *Antiq.*, VIII, 459–61.
[6] βοθρος: literally any hole or pit dug in the ground.
[7] *Odyssey*, XI, 25–50, 97–99.
[8] Philostratus, VI, 11, 18.
[9] Pausanias, II, 12, 1.
[10] *Aeneid*, VI, 212–35.

a tomb and places on it the hero's own arms, an oar and a trumpet, on the mount beneath the sky; which is now called Misenus after him, and keeps the name immortal through the ages.'

About a half-millennium later the Old English heroic epic *Beowulf*[11] describes dramatically how, after Beowulf's defeat of a scaly and irascible dragon, guardian of treasure in what seems to have been a corbelled chambered tomb of an earlier age, the hero was, after his death, cremated and the ashes set beneath a barrow.

'The people of the Geats prepared for Beowulf, as he had asked of them, a splendid pyre hung about with helmets, shields, and shining corslets. Then mourning, the soldiers laid their loved and illustrious prince in the midst. Upon the hill the men-at-arms lit a gigantic funeral fire. Black wood-smoke whirled over the conflagration; the roar of flames mixed with the noise of weeping, until the furious draught subsided and the whitehot body crumbled to pieces. Sadly they complained of their grief and of the death of their king. A Geat woman with braided hair keened a dirge in Beowulf's memory, repeating again and again that she feared bad times were on the way, with bloodshed, terror, captivity, and shame. Heaven swallowed up the smoke.

'Upon the headland the Geats erected a broad, high tumulus, plainly visible to distant seamen. In ten days they completed the building of the hero's beacon. Round his ashes they built the finest vault that the most skilful men could devise. Within the barrow they placed collars, brooches, and all the trappings which they had plundered from the treasure-hoard. They buried the gold and left that princely treasure to the keeping of earth, where it yet remains, as useless to men as it was before.

'Then twelve chieftains, all sons of princes, rode round the barrow lamenting their loss, speaking of their king, reciting an elegy, and acclaiming the hero. They praised his manhood and extolled his heroic deeds.'

A Danish writer of the late twelfth century[12] describes how in the middle of the eighth century A.D. Sigurd Ring, having defeated his uncle, King Harald Hildetand, in battle, 'washed the corpse, placed it on Harald's war-chariot, and buried it in a tumulus which he had formed for the purpose. Harald's horse was also slain and buried with him, with the saddle, so that Harald might either ride to Valhalla, or go in his chariot, as he preferred. Sigurd then gave a great feast, after which he recommended the chiefs present to throw their ornaments and arms into the tumulus in honour of Harald. Finally the tumulus was carefully closed'.

An early Irish manuscript[13] recounts how 'Dearg Damhsa, the Druid, made a capacious yellow-sodded Fert [mound] for Mogh Neid on the plain, and he buried him in it with his arms, and with his clothes, and with his armour'. A suggestion that captives sometimes accompanied heroic Irish warriors to the grave is contained in an extract from the *Book of Ballymote*:[14] 'Now when he had reached Forraidh in Uibh Maccuais, in Meath, Fiachra died of his wounds. His Leacht [grave] was made, and his Fert was raised, and his Cluicht Caintech [perhaps pyre?] were ignited and his Ogham name was written and the hostages which had been brought from the south were

[11] *Beowulf*, trans. D. Wright, Penguin Classics, 1957, Chap. 43; *Medieval Archaeology*, Society for Medieval Archaeology, London, I, 57–77.

[12] Saxo Grammaticus, *Historia Danica*, L, X, chap. XII; C. Engelhardt, 1868, *Guide Illustré du Musée des Antiquités du Nord à Copenhague*.

[13] E. O'Curry, *Manners and Customs of the Ancient Irish*, London, 1873.

[14] Vellum MS., Royal Irish Academy, Lebor na h-Uldhri, 130, col. 1.

buried alive around Fiachra's Fert that it might be a reproach to the Momonians for ever and that it might be a trophy over them.'

The more prosaic and perhaps objective accounts of barrow burials begin with that of Herodotus, the father of history (and indeed of travel and topography), when he describes [15] how a Scythian king was buried. Many of his observations have been corroborated by the excavation of Scythian barrows in which optimum conditions of preservation obtained.[16] If anything, such an account emphasizes not only the bareness of the bones from some of Britain's barrows, but also the importance of careful and sympathetic excavation, particularly of large and potentially important barrows.

Caesar,[17] while for the first time clearly differentiating Gaul from German, notes the relative splendour of the rites leading to the Gallic pyre but is silent regarding those of the austere Germans. However, Tacitus [18] is clear regarding the absence of display at German funerals. He wrote: 'There is no pomp about their funerals. The one rule observed is that the bodies of famous men are burned with special kinds of wood. When they have heaped up the fire they do not throw robes or spices on the top; but only a man's arms, and sometimes his horse, too, are cast into the flames. The tomb is a raised mound of turf. They disdain to show honour by laboriously rearing high monuments of stone; they would only lie heavy on the dead. Weeping and wailing are soon abandoned—sorrow and mourning not so soon.'

Glasbergen [19] has claimed that the simple sod-piled barrows of Holland illustrate the remarks of Tacitus regarding the German barrows. This could equally be said wherever sod-barrows are found! However, one early writer's observations may be relevant to Holland. Ammianus Marcellinus,[20] who wrote a continuation of the history of Tacitus, may, it is thought, have been referring to post-revetted barrows when he mentions how the Alamanni feared the *circumdata retiis busta* of their ancestors.

Stonehenge, that unique structure which is itself indicative of the wealth, power, and social organization of those beneath the barrows about it, may possibly have been the subject of a passage from a lost work quoted by Diodorus Siculus,[21] a contemporary of Caesar's. 'Hecateus and some others [writes Diodorus] tell us that opposite to the land of the Celts there exists in the ocean an island no smaller than Sicily, situated under the constellation of the Bear, inhabited by Hyperboreans [those who lived beyond the North Wind]. . . . The inhabitants honour Apollo more than any other deity. A sacred enclosure is dedicated to him in the island, as well as a magnificent circular temple adorned with many rich offerings. . . .' The Celts would here be the people of France, so that one can say only that the island might have been Britain. As for circular temples, there are none that can deserve the term magnificent except Stonehenge, or its neighbour Avebury. One could incline to the former by seeing the axes, daggers, and figures carved on certain stones as vestiges of the rich offerings adorning the temple.

What may have been an Irish stone circle allegedly adorned with gold, silver, and bronze is described in the Tripartite Life of St Patrick,[22] a ninth-century compilation recording early fifth-century events, which is preserved in an eleventh-century manuscript. It is said that the chief idol of Ireland was richly clad with gold and silver and

[15] Herodotus, IV.

[16] T. Talbot-Rice, *The Scythians*, Thames & Hudson, 1957.

[17] Caesar, VI, 11–20.

[18] Tacitus, *Germania*, 27.

[19] Glasbergen, 1954, II, 10.

[20] Ammianus Marcellinus, XVI, 2, 12; *PZ*, XV, 137.

[21] Diodorus Siculus, II, 47.

[22] W. Stokes, *Tripartite Life of St Patrick*, 1887, 91.

had around it twelve other idols covered with bronze ornaments. Stripped of their ritual embellishment, this description could record a stone circle with a central monolith. This circle, if it was such, was apparently on the Plain of Slecht, near the modern Ballymagauran, in Co. Cavan.[23]

From the archaeological evidence cited earlier (Chaper IV) it would appear reasonably certain that an interval of time elapsed between interment and the raising of the barrow. This custom has been recorded in literature. An Arab, Ahmad bin Fudhlan, who visited a Scandinavian settlement on the Volga early in the tenth century, witnessed the rites attendant upon the burial of a chieftain. He set down an account of this which has been known in Europe since the early nineteenth century.[24] Ten days elapsed while preparations were made for the ceremonies of cremation. The dead chief, completely dressed, was burnt in a boat, together with a maidservant, food, dog, beasts of burden, and weapons.

Lorimer[25] has commented upon the points of resemblance between this chief's cremation and those of Patroklus and other Homeric heroes. Besides food, drink, garments, and weapons, there were burned only the bodies of living things, whose spirits could accompany him into the shades. The barrow built over the pyre and surmounted by a stele is a type of monument alluded to in the *Iliad*.

Although not strictly a literary source, another record of barrow burial of about the same period has survived from northern Britain, where immemorial usages lurked beneath a veneer of literate Christianity. A panel (Pl. XXXII) of the Frank's Casket,[26] one of five in whalebone, depicts a murdered hero within his barrow. Flanking the mound are a mourning female figure and a faithful horse. Above and beneath the Runic inscription, as far as it can be determined, reads, *Here Hos sits on a sorrow-hill in grief and anguish of mind.* This inscription epitomizes the poignant emotion which leavens all but the most impersonal among early written accounts and which is apparent even in the care and planning of barrow burial—that of human bereavement.

[23] *PRIA*, XXXVI, 23.
[24] *PSAS*, IX, Pt. 2, 518–26.
[25] *Antiq.*, VIII, 58.
[26] *Anglo-Saxon Guide*, 96–8, Pl. VIII.

CHAPTER XIV

EXCAVATION AND RECORD

BARROWS were the first field monuments to be dug into for information regarding their origin and purpose, and have suffered accordingly. Early digging methods ranged from the reasonably precise observations and the drawn section of Stukeley[1] and the stratigraphical precision of Thomas Jefferson[2] in the New World, to those of the light-hearted, top-hatted gathering of the local nobility and gentry whose labourers hewed a great gash through a tall Romano-British barrow on a Kentish hillside.[3] The activities of the former are now receiving some recognition, while those of the latter have achieved notoriety.[4] From our vantage point in time we adopt an attitude of righteous indignation when confronted by an account of Colt Hoare's digging methods,[5] and one of horror when we read of how a late start on the fourth barrow convinced Bateman 'of the impolicy of attempting to explore so many barrows in one day'.[6]

It is now a commonplace of British archaeology that General Pitt-Rivers, at the end of the nineteenth century, brought to excavation a precision of detail and record that is surpassed by only a few, even at the present day. The fruits of the General's genius, which was applied to round-barrow excavation besides many other things, have withstood the tests of thirty years' intense critical activity. They can confidently be re-interpreted in the light of contemporary knowledge.[7]

Beginning with Sir Cyril Fox's barrow excavations in the middle of the third decade of the century, total excavation of round barrows has become the accepted standard. Not only are the burials excavated and studied, but also the whole range of internal and peripheral features. For a barrow is normally a single ritual structure for one peculiar end. It is more than a strictly functional structure, or structures, and a series of associated relics; it is also the outcome of human activity presumably motivated by religious considerations. Skilled total excavation, accurate and intelligent recording, and, finally, logical evaluation, can breathe life into the inanimate archaeological record and resuscitate some of the ritual and life of the Bronze Age (Pl. XXXI b).

Excavation is destruction, partial excavation is partial destruction, and total excavation is total destruction. However, the destruction must be orderly and methodical. It must proceed hand in hand with not only accurate and intelligent recording, but with that logical evaluation without which knowledge cannot advance.

[1] S. Piggott, *William Stukeley*, Oxford University Press, 1950, 111, fn. 2.

[2] T. Jefferson, *Notes on Virginia*, 1801, 142–7; Wheeler, 1954, 41–2.

[3] *Gents. Mag.*, Dec. 1852; T. Wright, *Wanderings of an Antiquary*, 1854, 183–8; *Arch. Cant.*, LVIII, 68–72, LXVIII, 1–61.

[4] Wheeler, 1954, 7.

[5] *WAM*, X, 85–6.

[6] Bateman, 1848, 63.

[7] *Arch. J.*, CIV, 27–81.

Not long ago it was customary to look upon excavation as four or five pleasurable weeks spent in the open air digging away a specific barrow, or even barrows. There, it was often thought, the matter ended. A few drawings were made, notebooks were filled, and perhaps some photographs were taken, to aid a report that might be written during the ensuing years. Although such fallacies are now nearly dead, they still linger on, alas!

General Pitt-Rivers and Sir Mortimer Wheeler, the latter constantly and insistently, have said much regarding excavation, and all of it was good. One statement made by the former is of overwhelming importance. 'A discovery dates only from the time of the record of it, and not from the time of its being found in the soil.' This, Sir Mortimer emphasizes, 'proclaims fairly and squarely the ultimate moral and scientific duty of the field archaeologist'.[8] Thus an excavation is but a phase of a project which is in progress from the cutting of the first sod to the day of publication of the journal in which the final report is presented. It does not end when the digging ceases.

Although work in the study may often assume alarming proportions, when compared with the period in the field, it should basically consist of the following: Compilation of a concise and objective narrative, the fine drawing of plans and sections, the selection of photographs, and the study, description, drawing, photography, and tabulation of the relics. If, however, the record, evaluation, and ultimate comprehension of all that is destroyed are not undertaken during the physical process of excavation, the ensuing work may be in vain. In short, if the structure or structures of a barrow are not understood while digging is in progress, they may never be so.

A barrow is such that its sequence of excavation is, broadly, a reversal of the process of its construction. Thus, features which had been erected last are generally examined first.

At the time of writing, two standard types of barrow excavation are current. One is *total* excavation, which entails complete removal of the barrow and any structure which it may cover, the excavation of all graves and pits beneath it, the removal of the pre-barrow soil, and the clearance of the ditch around it. This method, essential to a complete record, was instituted by General Pitt-Rivers and cannot be called in question. The other type is *partial* excavation, improvised in emergency, and invoked as an economy and thought in some quarters to be all that is needed. Partial excavation by means of a diametric trench, or radial trenches, subsequently expanded at the middle of the mound, is undesirable and unjustified save in dire emergency, although better than no record at all.

The record which can be recovered from a partial excavation of this sort comprises a preliminary contour plan and sections, together with details of such features as chance may throw into the excavator's path. These should include a central grave and possibly a pit, mere indications of internal and external ditch magnitude and diameter, and perhaps also of stake, post, or cairn-ring, cairn or kerb arrangements, but little more; and important features are often off-centre in barrows. But this method can hardly ever yield knowledge of whether or not the mound contained secondary or covered satellite burials, of the full character of stake, post, cairn-ring, cairn, or kerb, of the character and circularity or otherwise of the ditch, of whether or not the ditch was continuous or interrupted or, finally, of the details which often reveal the nature of the rites practised when the barrow was built.

[8] Wheeler, 1954, 182.

The general basic principles governing careful, scientific excavation have recently been stressed in a number of publications.[9] Assuming, therefore, the reader's cognizance of and sympathy with such principles it remains for the writer to indicate the general procedures of total round-barrow excavation.

Before excavation, a map or plan should be prepared showing the exact site of the barrow in question. This can be an adaptation of appropriate Ordnance Survey sheets or the results of a special survey of the local terrain. At the time of publication, such a drawing should be presented, together with maps indicating not only the regional topography but also the region in its wider setting. To supplement plans and maps, photographs of the barrow, which excavation will destroy, must be taken. They should show, besides the character of the mound, something of the immediate surroundings.

Before a sod is cut, an accurate contour plan should be made of the mound, and of its ditch and bank if these features are present. For the sake of convenience and clarity such a record should be related to a carefully chosen datum point, which is normally on the zero contour. Plus, and, if necessary, minus, contours can be shown in relation to this. Thus a just appreciation of height and dimension can immediately be gained from the contour plan. It is undesirable to show barrows as vertical continuations of the local Ordnance Survey contours. Much time can be wasted calculating heights when such a complex system is used.

The method of depicting barrows by *hachures*, in the tradition of Heywood Sumner,[10] is still favoured by some.[11] Although decorative, and, in capable hands reasonably accurate in detail, as a system it ultimately relies upon sections for an impression of the convexity of a mound.

A further consideration which can often be decided beforehand, and indeed must be decided during the early stages of a barrow excavation, is the scale to which plans and sections will be drawn. Ideally, plan and section should be to the same scale. At the same time, they should be drawn to a scale chosen to depict, accurately, the smallest relevant detail. This, for the average round barrow, should never be less than 1 inch to 4 feet (1 : 48).

It is not always easy to draw sections to the same scale as the overall plan. When the height of a barrow is small in relation to a considerable diameter, *radial* sections (Fig. 58), to a larger scale than the overall plan, are essential. When height is in a reasonable proportion to diameter a *diametric* section (Fig. 59) is possible. Adjustments of final relative sizes of plans and sections can be made when the finished plans are reduced in size for publication. A common fault in the recording and presentation of barrow excavation, and indeed in that of many other types of excavation, is the selection of inadequate scales for plan and section, which allow of no more than the barest uncritical representation.

Thought should be given to the depiction in drawings of layers and structures. Such structures as internal cairns, cairn-rings, kerbs, and the like should be faithfully represented in section as well as being accurately planned. For layers, two methods are in vogue, the diagrammatic and the naturalistic. A middle way between these extremes is perhaps best.

[9] Atkinson, 1953; Kathleen Kenyon, *Beginning in Archaeology*, Phoenix House, 1952; M. B. Cookson, *Photography for Archaeologists*, Parrish, 1954.

[10] Heywood Sumner, *Ancient Earthworks of Cranbourne Chase*, 1913, etc.

[11] *PCAS*, XLIII, 30–49.

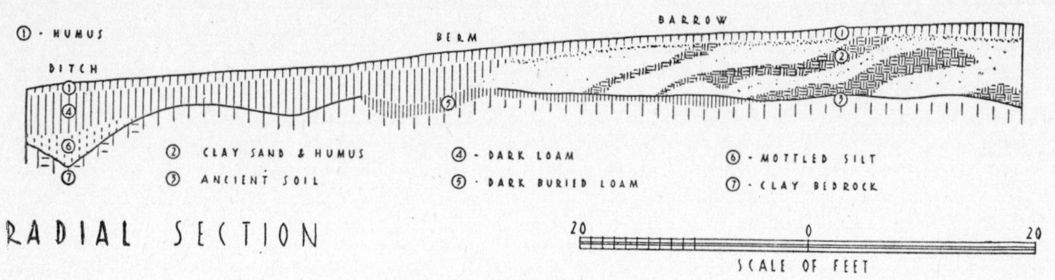

Fig. 58. A radial section.

A photographic record should be made at all stages of the excavation. This should normally embrace all features.

When all these things have been undertaken or considered it remains to decide upon the method to be adopted for the removal of the mound. Two principal methods, which if circumstance demands permit variation, are usual. The first is the *strip*, the second the *quadrant* method.

With the strip method (Fig. 60) the mound is divided into a series of parallel strips, which should be not more than 5 feet in width. In each strip the soil is removed, layer

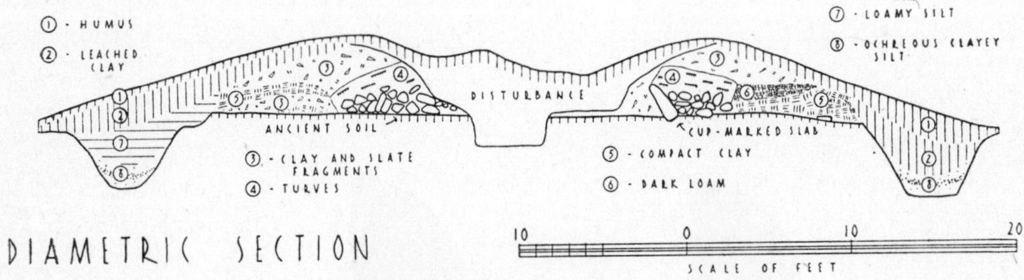

Fig. 59. A diametric section.

by layer, down to the underlying natural subsoil. The merits of the system are ease of record and working, and, no mean thing in a complex structure, a large number of sections. Its demerits are difficulty in exposing without damage any considerable area of the pre-barrow surface, difficulties of tipping unless the director is skilled in the use of plant and organization, and the fact that unless the entire system is altered during an excavation, the sections are exclusively upon a single axis. Sub-barrow features are approached from one direction only and, further, if the system is adopted for speed and the spoil from each strip is dumped into the last to be excavated, the excavator never sees the sub-barrow features of his site as an entity, and thus misses much.

An outstanding example of the use of the strip method was the excavation of the barrow and circle at Ysceifiog in Flintshire[12] by Sir Cyril Fox. A measured section was drawn along every face which revealed any feature of note. Sir Cyril published six parallel sections and one cross-section of this barrow.

[12] *Arch. Camb.*, LXXXI, 48–85.

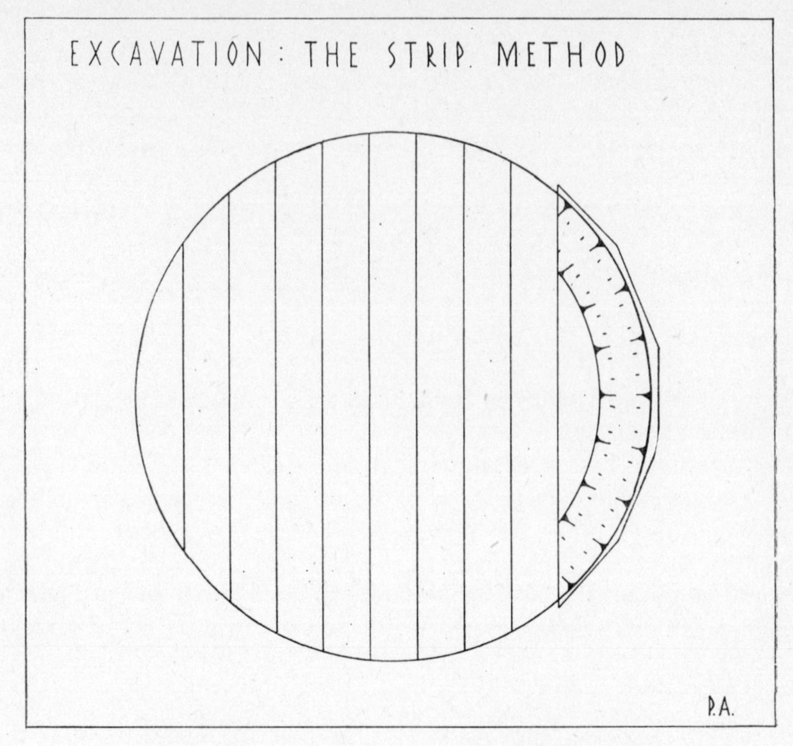

Fig. 60. The excavation of a round barrow by strips.

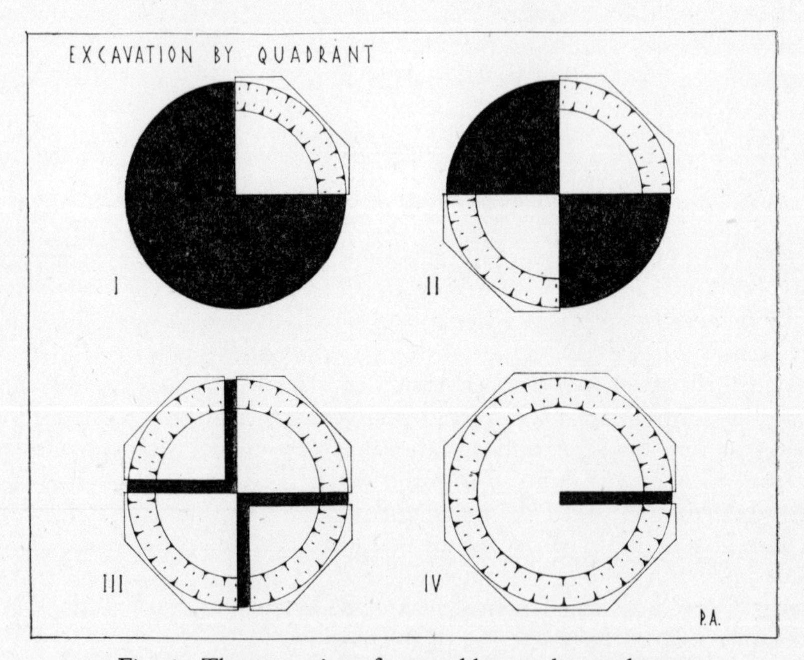

Fig. 61. The excavation of a round barrow by quadrants.

The second, and more usual, method of barrow excavation at the present time is the quadrant method (Fig. 61). The mound is set out, by strings, into quadrants, or octants, etc., if the size so warrants. The quadrants are separated by balks, which should not be less than 3 feet in width. Datum pegs, for three-dimensional recording, should be set on the balks, preferably at horizontal intervals of 5 or 10 feet. The soil is then removed from each quadrant, beginning with opposing quadrants, layer by layer, until only the balks remain to give radial or diametric sections of the mound.

The grid method of excavation normally used for horizontal areas has recently been used on a large barrow [13] with some success. Except for the initial difficulties of setting out an accurate grid on a steep-sided barrow and possible resultant difficulties of record, besides the problems of soil disposal at all stages, the method has much to commend it.

The entire surface of the buried soil beneath a barrow should be exposed as an entity. This often raises problems regarding comfort of digging and soil transport. With experience, and the use of running planks, however, such problems are surmountable, and the dividends of knowledge are great. Stone features such as cairns, cairn-rings, kerbs, etc., should be cleaned up and left *in situ* upon the ancient surface, and one should be continually on the watch for timber structures in the body of the mound. Often, in stake circles or mortuary houses, certain holes did not penetrate into the bedrock, while cremations and burials were often put into shallow graves. Again, pyres and fires were burnt on these buried surfaces, pots were smashed, and men went about the doubtless complex rites of burial on them. It is possible under favourable conditions to recover traces of pre-barrow ploughing, or an exceptionally compact surface might denote trampling or even dancing. For the trouble taken, the excavator sees with his eyes the whole surface upon which the builders of his barrow trod, he can study the tangible evidence of the living ritual as a whole, which is sometimes visible on such a surface, and thus he has not only his progressive record, but also an overall appreciation against which such records can be tested before the evidence is destroyed for ever.

Since, therefore, the stripping of the buried soil from a barrow site follows the removal of the balks, the use of a fixed datum line for the measurement of sections is necessary. Thus posts or stout stakes should be driven in at the appropriate ends of sections, common heights fixed with a surveyor's level, and nails driven in to hold the line or lines. An indication of the levels should be painted on the posts to prevent error, should a nail fall out. It is possible with a surveyor's level to traverse and check a long line for sag far more readily than with any other instrument.

A barrow ditch is not normally excavated until the corresponding part of the mound has been removed. The principles of the natural processes of ditch-silting have been clearly set forth by Pitt-Rivers,[14] and during the third decade of this century by Curwen.[15] Recently, the general procedures to be adopted during the excavation of all ditches have been expounded by Atkinson.[16] Besides silts derived from the sides, the fillings of barrow ditches usually reflect the construction of the barrow that they surround. It is desirable that a barrow ditch be completely emptied, the silts being removed layer by layer. Particular attention should be paid to the problems of confluent or intersecting ditches. Theoretically, it should be possible to determine priorities

[13] *Mound of the Hostages*, Tara, *PPS.*, XXI, Pl. XXII.

[14] Pitt-Rivers, 1887–98, IV, 24.

[15] *Antiq.*, IV, 97–100.

[16] Atkinson, 1953, 63–5.

of construction of such ditches. Every effort should be made to do this, though in practice it is not always possible to do so with any certainty.

Now and again a barrow proves to be a complex structure raised at different times. Thus an excavator should be mentally and physically prepared to deal with not only primary but secondary and even tertiary aspects of it. For example, Sir Cyril Fox was able, in a barrow at Llandow [17] in Glamorganshire, to isolate a Beaker primary structure and a Middle Bronze Age extension. Such structural phases should be shown on plan in vari-colour, while the interrelationships may be shown in section in the same way, or by mere emphasis of line.

So-called *secondary* burials are sometimes met with in barrow mounds. If numerous they should be shown on a separate plan. They should always be recorded in a sectional relationship to the primary structure or to each other where possible. Secondary burials are often confused in excavation reports with what should be more properly termed *satellite* burials (see Chapter IV).

Pits, ritual and otherwise, should be treated similarly to satellite graves. Graves and pits, when excavated, should always be sectioned on two axes.

Stake circles present special problems. It should be observed whether the remains of the stakes, or the holes filled with replacement material, or with worm mould, continue through the buried soil into the body of the mound. Such stake circles, or, as is usually the case, circles of stake or post sockets, should be planned separately if their complexity warrants this. Each hole should be sectioned and its plan noted. Plaster casts, particularly in chalk and some stiff clays from which worm mould can easily be cleared, often make a satisfactory and sometimes substantial additional record. If there is not time for sectioning and making casts, diameters, depths below the buried surface (or the natural soil), and general character should be tabulated. Stake and post circles, cairns, cairn-rings, and kerbs should be photographed as well as being the subjects of plans and sections. Photographs taken from a height are favoured by some, and with care panoramas can be composed.

So much has been written regarding the excavation and recording of graves that it seems almost superfluous to say more. However, certain points should be uppermost in an excavator's mind when faced with the task of excavating a barrow grave, primary, satellite, or secondary. First of all the sides should be located and the filling removed towards the middle in layers about 1 inch in depth. It is almost impossible to excavate a small grave in two parts, although this can sometimes be done in the upper part of the grave. Thus a section has to be completed in parts.

At an early stage in a barrow-grave excavation it should be possible to detect the presence or absence of a coffin of wood, monoxylous, composite, or wicker. Under certain conditions in non-oxygenated soils [18] the remains are often substantial, but more usually they are ephemeral.

Grave-goods should be cleaned up and left *in situ* together with the inhumation or cremation, the latter being often in an urn. Such vessels, together with the visible contents, must also be cleaned up *in situ*. It is desirable to record relics and cremation or inhumation in a grave on one photograph. This should be published side by side with the plan of the grave in question. This should never, except with an unusually large grave, be prepared at a scale of less than one quarter full size. It should be borne in

[17] *Arch.*, LXXXIX, 89–126.

[18] *PPS*, XXI, 104.

mind that small objects, such as sherds and flints, sometimes met with in graves and their fillings, are often not in their original position at the time of excavation owing to the action of earthworms,[19] which also fills up such subterranean cavities as post sockets or the interstices in stone cairns.

In a barrow grave search must be made for the remains, often mere soil stains, of organic materials such as dagger hilts, sheaths, and, sometimes, fabric wrappings, wooden clubs, fabric or bast cremation covers, bags of hide or the like, wooden masks, shields, etc. Indeed, anything unusual and not readily recognizable should be recorded and removed for expert examination. Identification of substance is often illuminating. Natural objects such as echinus and other fossils, flint nodules, iron pyrites, etc., are sometimes found in graves where they were deposited with intent.

Special attention should be paid to beads, which are often only a part of composite objects such as necklaces, or, as has been observed in Scotland, lunulae. They should be planned in detail and photographed separately, in addition to the master plan and photograph of the grave. A method should be devised, for each case upon its merits, of lifting the beads as an entity for further study.

Unurned cremations can sometimes be removed as a block for study in the laboratory, more often they can only be collected and packed for later examination. Urns containing cremations should be removed as a single entity also. Large urns containing cremations are usually fragile and wet. Drying can sometimes be hastened by artificial means, e.g. a blowlamp, but covering with tissue or grease-proof paper and bandaging with plaster of Paris is a solution. Such an encased urn can safely be removed when the plaster is dry. This method may be resorted to, if necessary, for the safe removal of beakers, food-vessels, and all other funerary vessels.

Skeletons should be cleaned up *in situ*.[20] The excavator should possess sufficient knowledge of human skeletal anatomy to identify the principal bones as they appear. Furthermore, it is often only during excavation that it can be observed whether the bones were interred as a body, a mutilated body, or as an assemblage of bones, as sometimes seems to have been the case. Such precise observations are normally possible only in chalk and limestone soils, which afford optimum conditions for the preservation of bone. Besides photographs, a plan at half-size of a skeleton in its grave or on a surface should be prepared if possible. Each bone should be recognizable on the drawing, although this is frequently an impossibility because of the fragmentary nature and lack of characteristics attendant upon decay.

It is normally beyond the competence of most prehistorians authoritatively to describe the bones recovered from inhumation and cremations. Therefore such remains should be submitted for examination by an expert physical anthropologist. When complex problems of deposition are met with, such a person should if possible visit the site and examine the remains *in situ*. His reports should be an appendix to the main excavation report. Animal bones which appear to have been deliberately buried should be treated similarly and should be submitted for expert report.[21]

In acid soils and certain sands and clays, inhumation burials may survive only as

[19] Charles Darwin, *Vegetable Mould and Earthworms*, 1904; Atkinson, *Antiq.*, XXXI, 219–33; *BA*, XV, 165–72.

[20] I. W. Cornwall, *Bones for the Archaeologist*, Phoenix House, 1956.

[21] I. W. Cornwall, *Bones for the Archaeologist*, 1956.

silhouettes. Surface scraping or, in exceptional circumstances, partial three-dimensional clearance, together with photography (colour techniques are useful) and planning is all that can be done.[22] Phosphate tests have been carried out in apparently empty graves in acid soils with some success,[23] and there is some evidence that under certain conditions inhumation burials act as manganese accumulators.[24]

Besides the relics recovered from barrow graves, broken pottery, occupation debris, and flint implements are recovered from barrow mounds. Such material should be scrupulously collected and recorded during excavations. Sherds should be minutely examined to determine whether they were freshly broken or were worn sherds when deposited, while flints and flint industries should be assessed in detail, and statistically [25] if they are numerous.

If barrows are on acid soils their composition has a pollen content, from which ecological information can be extracted in some detail. The technique [26] depends at the present time upon a method of sampling devised by the originator of the process. It can demonstrate the whereabouts of a buried surface when local conditions make it difficult of discernment, and yield evidence of local environment at the time of building, and even a relative date.[27]

Charcoals and carbonized wood samples collected from a barrow body, and from graves, pits, stake holes, etc., can also provide evidence of structure vis-à-vis environment when identified by a botanist.[28] Their chief value, however, lies in their suitability as chronological indicators when submitted to the C14 process.[29] The method is based upon a series of assumptions, one being that a given sample of organic matter has not been contaminated by younger carbon compounds since it was first laid down in an archaeological deposit. Any open site in Britain might well be contaminated by the percolation of humic solutions. However, it should be borne in mind that organic material from primary, and certain satellite, and even secondary graves, beneath and in barrows is suitable for C14 examination, as the depth may often preclude excessive contamination from such sources. There is little point in the submission of samples unless a reasoned archaeological date is possible for the barrow. This is necessary to enable a cross-check with archaeological or palaeobotanical dating to be made.

At least since the war it has been the custom of excavators to collect samples of the soils [30] that they have removed during the clearance of their site. They have hopefully sent them to a soil-scientist experienced in archaeological problems with a label informing the harassed man of nothing more than the fact that they were taken from a specific site. Such an approach is useless. All that the scientist can do in such circumstances is to determine by chemical methods the soil's relative acidity, which could be approximately ascertained by an intelligent scrutiny of the local terrain. In certain circumstances co-operation between a prehistorian and a pedologist can be fruitful. The archaeologist should phrase his inquiry in the form of specific questions; a mere general description

[22] *PPS*, XXIII, 151.

[23] *YAJ*, XXXIX, 27–30; *PSAS*, LXXXVIII, 200–4.

[24] *PPS*, XXIII, 162–3.

[25] *PPS*, XXIII, 162–3.

[26] *PPS*, XX, 231–6.

[27] H. Tj. Waterbolk in Glasbergen, 1954, I (soil samples).

[28] *PDNHAS*, LXXVI, 50.

[29] F. E. Zeuner, 'Archaeological Dating by Radioactive carbon', *SP*, CLIV, 154, 225–38; Zeuner, 1952, 341 ff.; *Germania*, 1957, 102–10; *Antiq.*, XXVI, 35–45, XXXII, 253–63, XXXIII, 289–90.

[30] *PPS*, XIX, 129–47; I. W. Cornwall, *Soils for the Archaeologist*, Phoenix House, 1958.

or exhibition of the site has little value. In particular cases samples of soil can be submitted for laboratory examination if a question of composition, origin, or content is involved.

Similar considerations govern co-operation with a geologist.[31] There are local questions regarding cairns, cairn-rings, kerbs, etc., which a geologist might answer. Pieces of fine-grained rocks, or even celts of similar material, which are met with in barrows, also the gritting of sherds in certain cases, might be submitted for petrological examination.[32]

Much has been written in the past regarding the evidential value as climate indicators of the remains of non-marine molluscs. It would appear that while in specific local circumstances their evidence may be of some value,[33] they have little ubiquitous significance for this purpose.

In general, the esoteric methodology of physical science should be applied only to specific problems which other methods cannot hope to solve. Other than this its merits lie in unique processes such as C14 or the recovery of pollen remains from acid soils.

The presentation of the final report should have been in the mind of the excavator from the beginning of the operation. If the excavation has been carried out along the general lines sketched above, it should present few methodological problems. Such a report should comprise an introduction, a summary of the whole work, an indication of local topography and geology, method of excavation, and as the main body, a concise objective description of the structure, or structures, and the relics. It should be illustrated by plans and sections, general and detailed, drawings, and where necessary photographs of the relics and significant aspects of the site. In general, the illustrations should bear the burden of description rather more, perhaps, than the written word. Finally, an archaeological evaluation should be made of the results of the work; it should be classified and assigned its niche in prehistory. One should remember that while interpretations change, facts remain.

[31] *Antiq.*, XIV, 377–94.
[32] *PPS*, VII, 50, XIII, 47, XVII, 99–158.
[33] Zeuner, 1950, 382–4.

CHAPTER XV

BARROWS, THE FUTURE AND THE STATE

BARROWS, once thought of as mere repositories of relics, are now recognized, at least by prehistorians, as potential sources of a great deal of information regarding our prehistoric past. The last half-century has seen considerable change in both attitude to and method of study of the subject of barrows. Thus lines of inquiry which will have to be pursued in the near future, and the advances likely to be made, must be reviewed.

In spite of the recognition of barrow groups and cemeteries for more than two centuries they are still frequently thought of simply as single mounds. Only within recent years have such cemeteries, besides being listed, been studied as entities. No such cemetery has, as yet, had its barrows set in *reliable* relative chronological order, either by archaeological estimate and inference or by application of the methods of natural science. The potentialities of such a cemetery standing upon acid podsolized soils, as were the barrows in the Dutch 'Eight Beatitudes' set in order by Waterbolk,[1] have been neglected.

With the dwindling of the number of undamaged or unploughed barrows the assessment of such problems as rates of denudation of mounds by weathering, or estimates of time and labour involved in construction, a problem ultimately of social organization, becomes difficult if not impossible since assessment must be based upon the size and structure of the mound. There still remain opportunities of detecting by excavation satellite and secondary burials and their precise relationships, which ploughing destroys. For many of our concepts of association and sequence are based upon excavations of dubious worth by modern standards, undertaken during the formative period of archaeology. Again even the gashes of early barrow excavations are sometimes informative, as will be the completion of many present-day partial excavations.

Future excavation must record all structural features objectively and clearly in plan and section. Our knowledge of such features as post and stake circles, mortuary houses, grave-forms, turf-stacks and mounds, cists, cairns, cairn-rings, and kerbs, as well as complexity and confluence of barrows, is slender. Nor has an area between barrows been cleared to reveal the presence or absence of burials since the days of Pitt-Rivers,[2] as has been done in Holland.[3] At present more than provisional synthesis of such material is difficult or impossible.

There is much more to be learnt by the application of specialized techniques to bones, grave-furniture, and other features revealed by excavation. Only a few of the many and varied scientific approaches to the study of the prehistoric past can be mentioned within

[1] H. Tj. Waterbolk in Glasbergen, 1954, I; *CISPP*, 1950, 130–3.

[2] Pitt-Rivers, 1887–98, IV, 147–57, Pl. 295.

[3] *ASAB*, XI, 240; Glasbergen, 1954, II, 142.

the compass of this chapter. While the scrupulous expert can glean much from cremations,[4] there has recently been opened up a great field of relative physical anthropological study in problems of prehistory, which may give some indication of family relationships. This is the application of the techniques of blood-grouping[5] to the often well-preserved internal tissue of long-bones from inhumation graves of both Neolithic and Bronze Age date, in the chalk and limestone country.

The further petrological study of the distinctive battle-axes is desirable, and the sources must be compared with those exploited by the Secondary Neolithic groups which appear to lie behind our native Bronze Age. Bronze weapon and tool spectro-analysis will, I trust, go on to give more valuable information regarding the sources of metal and clues as to the origins of the first metallurgists. Archaeomagnetism[6] could be applied, with relative and absolute chronology in mind, to the baked earth which, with charcoal, attests fires, perhaps pyres, beneath barrows. Pollen identification and count on material from acid-soil barrows has numerous potentialities. Besides chronological and environmental information, hints as to time and sequence of construction may be given, and the sudden introduction of extraneous species might even suggest such things as funeral garlands. In spite of a decade of brilliant work by Dimbleby, British palynologists have hardly begun to exploit this field, but the richness of results available is not open to doubt. Again the recognition of weather and worms in action under all conditions opens a further reservoir of information. At the same time field archaeology could be revolutionized by a wider and more systematic use of electric resistivity survey and the now infant proton magnetometer.[7] Whole low-ploughed barrow groups, or for that matter the barrows of a region, might be surveyed and their salient subterranean features recorded for comparative purposes. However, without skilled and logical comparative interpretation and synchronism with sequences provided by pottery and metal these processes are only meaningless formalities.

It is clear that only by an extension of the principal and basic modes of research, enumerated in the first chapter, can reasoned study of Bronze Age barrows proceed. However, this must affect the future of the whole of British archaeology.

The last few decades, allegedly the dawning of the age of the common man, have witnessed the passing of the peculiarly British institution of the independent scholar of means, living in the country and owing no allegiance to any particular academic body or institution, and also the decline in the activities, prestige, and influence of the local and county learned societies, often in the past officered by such scholars. The former are almost extinct, while the latter mostly make polite pilgrimages to their castles and churches and are mercifully still able to publish their proceedings, although sometimes intermittently. At the same time, as a result of the growing complexity of a subject which demands acquaintance not only with processes proper to the natural sciences but also with an ever-increasing literature couched in the babel of tongues which is modern Europe, the leadership of archaeological scholarship has become concentrated into the hands of a relatively small number of experienced specialists. There has also been a marked increase in the activities of the departments of the State[8] charged with responsibilities towards the nation's past inherent in its ancient monuments. Archaeology has

[4] Atkinson, Piggott, and Sandars, 1951, 124–7.
[5] *BA*, XIII, No. 50, 91–103; No. 51, 191–204.
[6] *Antiq.*, XXXII, 167–78.
[7] *Archaeometry* (Oxford), I, No. 1, 24–6; *Antiq.*, XXXIII, 205–7.
[8] *Antiq.*, VIII, 414–28.

never known such widespread popular interest as it enjoys at the present time. Through the television screen some of its foremost figures are known in every household, while academic parlour games and dramatic, though none the less accurate, accounts of its achievements are viewed by multitudes. Only one fly blemishes the stimulating balm of this miraculous post-war ointment; archaeology has become popularly synonymous with digging! Thus for various, though not always valid, reasons the soil of Britain is being turned as never before!

The study of information wrested from barrows, their graves and structures, is dependent upon the availability of material. Abercromby's work, like Piggott's, was mainly based upon the great collections of grave-furniture accumulated from nineteenth-century barrow-opening. A classification of post and stake circles[9] has been undertaken, besides other generalizations regarding structure, chiefly as a result of the number of barrows that have been carefully excavated during the past two decades. Further assessments of barrow structure and features will be possible as the number of carefully excavated and lucidly published barrows increases in the future, and with them the use and potentialities of incidental information from such undertakings. Likewise, the Council for British Archaeology's 'Register of Bronze Age Pottery' will, by making available much unpublished material lurking in museums, allow the resolution of many problems of association, distribution, and locality.

However, there are factors peculiar to barrow study which at the present time, and probably even more so in the future, will set limits to it. At present it is no exaggeration to say that their very existence as a coherent group of monuments is threatened mainly from two quarters. First, during the past twenty years there has been in this country an almost insatiable demand for land, which has resulted not only in a more intensive utilization of existent enclosures but also in a major encroachment upon land which was hitherto marginal.[10] Thus, there is a high damage and obliteration incidence, which will worsen with the years. Secondly, the very number of round barrows has encouraged until recently a cavalier attitude towards them by those charged in the nation's name with their protection. As a result of this there was until recently a myopic reluctance to recognize modern deep-ploughing as a destructive agent! The outcome has been the progressive razing of the great barrow cemeteries around Stonehenge, and to a lesser extent Avebury, as well as of barrows elsewhere in the country, a process culminating in the dismal holocaust of Normanton.[11] There is now only one relatively undamaged major barrow cemetery in the immediate vicinity of Stonehenge, that at Winterbourne Crossroads, and this is, at the time of writing, not yet a monument maintained and guarded for, or accessible to, the nation.

While synthesis will continue to be the activity of the specialist, excavation, field survey, and record have been and will increasingly be, therefore, the concern of the state. Naturally, this does not mean that appropriate individuals and organizations will no longer undertake excavation or field studies, but that because of progressive inflation, sufficient money and resources for present-day excavation and fieldwork can usually only be provided from the public purse. Because of their very numbers and rate of destruction, the study of barrows, more than that of any other monument, should be coming increasingly within the orbit of the state's contribution to archaeology.

[9] *Arch. J.*, CXIV, 1–9.
[10] *Ant. J.*, XXIX, 142–3.
[11] *The Times*, London, 23 April–1 May, 1954.

The Ancient Monuments Inspectorate of the Ministry of Works is perhaps the least meagrely endowed official body of its kind. It is chiefly concerned with the conservation and protection of structures which are mostly medieval, via the scheduling system, but when this is either impossible or impracticable, excavation also becomes its concern.

Their sponsored excavation of prehistoric monuments threatened with destruction began, appropriately enough, with a round barrow in 1938.[12] It has continued since then with ever more comprehensiveness and intensity. During the second world war fifty-five excavations [13] were carried out on sites that, owing to the exigencies of that time, had to be destroyed. Of these some fifty or sixty were round barrows in various parts of the country from Cornwall to Caithness. At the present time more excavations have been undertaken in a single year than in the half-decade following the war, and again, many barrows were explored.

Such a large number of excavations has made a signal contribution to knowledge. Indeed, it would be no exaggeration to say that the more intimate appreciation of the complexities of Britain's prehistory which is a feature of this post-war period devolves upon it. Almost all our more accurate knowledge of barrow structure and burials, mortuary houses, post and stake circles, etc., is a result of state-sponsored excavation. Many such excavations have been in inaccessible places far removed from population centres, and thus to some extent from local attention; a searching selection of the country's barrows has now been examined.

This scheme of excavation of threatened sites was piloted throughout the war, and the critical immediate post-war years, by the late B. H. St J. O'Neil, Chief Inspector of Ancient Monuments from 1945 to his untimely death in 1954, championed by the sympathetic Assistant Secretary of the Ministry, Dr F. J. E. Raby, now at Jesus College, Cambridge.

A result of the present spate of officially sponsored and financed excavations has been a vast increase in the number of persons required to carry them out. Sometimes persons have been entrusted with this work mainly because they were available at short notice and in spite of their lack of archaeological acumen. Itinerant *soi-disant* archaeologists, inexperienced and untrained in all but the barest rudiments of their craft and lacking full appreciation of the complexities and comparative material comprising their continent's prehistory, may have done their best, but the consequences of this use of official moneys might have been foreseeable! Besides an increase in the insularity of outlook which seeks to strangle our studies, there have been grotesque claims regarding the character of barrows and other monuments. Another consequence is the lack of any published record of such people's work. It is plausibly argued that any examination of a site about to be destroyed is better than nothing!

The Ministry of Works' lack of promptness in publication has incurred considerable criticism for some time.[14] The present situation with regard to publication is this. First of all, though they are little known, more than half of the war-time excavations, which include reports of round-barrow excavations, have been published [15] or are in the press at the time of writing. These have been compiled by the many eminent archaeologists who undertook officially sponsored excavations in those critical years. Since the war

[12] *Arch.*, LXXXVII, 129–30.

[13] *Ant. J.*, XXVIII, 20–44; *War and Archaeology in Britain*, HMSO, 1949.

[14] R. G. Collingwood, *An Autobiography*, 1944 ed., 86.

[15] *Ant. J.*, XXVIII, 25.

also there has been steady publication of the reports of excavations [16] by individuals trained and versed in their ultimate scientific and moral obligations. Until the recent launching of the Ministry's monographs, volumes which have set high standards for those that are to follow them, excavation reports were published in the established local and national archaeological journals. Grants have been given to the publishing societies when necessary. For reasons of security the official provision of resources was not referred to in wartime, but today this is always acknowledged.

Large numbers of excavations have been undertaken in the past decade, but little or no attempt at definitive publication of these great accumulations of material has been made. So grave is the situation that if the proportionate time for analysis and preparation for the reports, as set down by Pitt-Rivers,[17] were taken, for some it will soon far exceed the expected span of human life! It is unfortunate that professional civil servants who are not archaeologists should have the responsibility of the administration of such a specialized department.

The attitudes of officialdom to publication may well be subconscious products of this age of popular archaeology. Digging and the immediate results thereof have a certain news value and are accorded space in the vehicles of public enlightenment. This popular reporting may seem to some a discharging of their responsibilities. Ultimate, definitive, publication is rarely greeted with such fanfares.

One would like to see in the Ministry of Works a more calculated policy, planning and channelling chance discovery and rescue excavation, under expert guidance and decisive leadership, into a research programme designed to elucidate some of the many outstanding problems of British prehistory. Such a policy would further enhance the reputation of a department of the nation's archaeological activity, which has more than proved its worth in the past two decades.

Many have spoken and written [18] regarding the Ministry's Inspectorate, and it is not the present writer's intent to malign its conscientious and hard-working officials, shackled as they are to unpliable bureaucracy concerned with official expediency.

The Royal Commissions on Ancient and Historical Monuments [19] in England, Wales, and Scotland, and the Northern Ireland Archaeological Survey and the Archaeology Branch of the Ordnance Survey [20] are concerned with inventories and topographical record. Thus Britain's Bronze Age barrows come within their terms of reference. While their responsibilities are no less onerous, they have not the Ministry's grave liability. An error of descriptive recording made by those bodies can be rectified at a later date, if the monument in question has not meanwhile suffered damage or destruction, but excavation is destruction, and lack of appreciation and observation in that process is irreparable.

On the Commissions' staffs are archaeologists who, outside their official duties, have made signal contributions to their subject. The only charge that can be levelled is general inadequacy in the face of the progressive destruction that is all about us. This, coupled with the slow speed of publication of the English and Welsh Commissions' volumes, only four of which have been issued since the war, is a factor surely frustrating for the organization's field-workers as well as perturbing to the country's scholars.

[16] *Antiq.*, XXVI, 147–8.

[17] Pitt-Rivers, 1887–98, IV, 27–8.

[18] *Antiq.*, XXXI, 234–6; *ULIA*, *Occasional Paper*, No. 5, 65–71; *PPS*, XIII, 183–4.

[19] *ANL*, II, 193–5; III, 1–3 (Scotland only).

[20] *ANL*, II, 1–3; *Antiq.*, XXXIII, 195–204.

The Ordnance Survey is by far the senior of the state bodies concerned with antiquities. In its modern form it is already 167 years old, and has been active throughout the formative period of archaeological study. Colt Hoare, aided by his surveyor, Richard Crocker, corrected the sheets recording the barrows and other prehistoric monuments on Salisbury Plain. About a half of the Survey's archaeological activities in this century have been identified with the work of the late O. G. S. Crawford,[21] its Archaeology Officer from 1920 to 1946, who adapted air photography to archaeology and brought method and system to field studies.

Lord Davidson's report of 1935 reviewed and approved of the work of the Archaeology Branch. With the gathering speed of revision after this time, it was seen that the creation of a proper record of the country's archaeological topography was its premier task. The importance of the Archaeological Branch to British archaeology can be readily appreciated, for no other state body has such a mandate, nor can it maintain the running revision which is essential for a living record. In practice the Branch's work is to collect all information on archaeological topography, to organize a record of it, and to present the results in map form.

The Ordnance Survey lists Bronze Age barrows as they should only be listed, in their geographical setting. Antiquities are entered on a complete set of 6-inch maps of the entire country, which are supplemented by Archaeological Name Books in which they are listed in accordance with numbers allotted for the specific sheets. Each site is described, with a list of published references thereto, and illustrated by photographs, from air and ground, or by drawings as necessary. From these sources specialized card indices are in the course of compilation, with the preparation of period maps in view.

The archaeological interests of Eire have much in common with those of Britain, and have suffered accordingly. There the problems of the pace of destruction are perhaps not so acute, so there is correspondingly more opportunity of inspection and record. Though there is a national consciousness of the prehistoric past and its monuments surpassing, perhaps, that of any other European country, these are matters of some urgency. While there have been numerous barrow excavations of an extremely high standard (Appendix III), together with regional studies of barrows (Appendix II), their type and distribution, almost nothing comparable with the work of Grinsell has been undertaken by any individual for any county in modern times. Thus though barrows (often called raths), some not dissimilar to the especial Wessex types, have occasionally been noted, we have no notion of their number and general distribution. While an enlightened Board of Works carries out many excellent projects there are as yet no publications which detail the monuments of the twenty-six counties along the lines envisaged by the percipience of Larcom, and above all by the genius of Petrie.[22] Let Eire rectify the niggardliness which brought the Topographical Memoirs to a halt a century ago, and enumerate its barrows and field monuments while they still stand unaltered, except by time and weather, and untouched by the agencies of unthinking and uncaring man.

In Britain the stage is set for advances in the functions and functioning of the state's

[21] O. G. S. Crawford, *Said and Done*, Weidenfeld & Nicholson, 1955.

[22] W. Stokes, *The Life and Labour in Art and Archaeology of George Petrie*, 1868, 87–109. However, the National Monuments Act, 1930, makes mandatory the reporting of all finds of archaeological objects to the Keeper of Irish Antiquities of the National Museum.

Archaeological Departments. It is only to be hoped that performance is not delayed. The problem is how comprehensive record and safe, satisfactory, preservation can best be ensured.

At risk of reiteration, emphasis must again be laid on the threats to barrows and cairns, which make urgent recording and a reasoned plan of preservation. A man guiding a horse and a relatively light plough did little *immediate* damage. But today, by bulldozing woods, coppices, hedges, banks, boundaries, humps, hillocks, and *barrows*, many hundreds, or even thousands of acres, can be broken for agriculture in a matter of days. Bulldozing followed by deep ploughing will leave a barrow as though it had never been, its only memorial a soil mark and perhaps the stones of cairn, cist, or kerb pushed to the fringe of the area. This is the dismal record of totalitarian agriculture. The same methods are used everywhere to fulfil the insatiable demands for land as subtopia spreads in this overcrowded island. Only the photographs of the last decade's field-workers serve to remind us of our erstwhile wealth of barrows and other prehistoric monuments.

The primary need is protection from damage, or further damage, of groups of barrows and single barrows, especially in Wessex, Cornwall, East Anglia, and Yorkshire. I will say again that there is now left to us only one relatively undamaged cemetery of barrows in the immediate vicinity of Stonehenge. This protection can be given in two ways. First of all there must be determined enforcement and strengthening of the provisions for scheduling contained within the Ancient Monuments Acts [23] and not merely feeble pleas for mercy on them. Failure up to the present to do this is no doubt due to a desire not to interfere unduly with the rights of property enjoyed by landowners, whether private or public, which are archaic in the present circumstances. New conceptions proper to the present are needed. Barrows and other monuments embody the national prehistory and are thus its people's heritage. They should be available for all to see and study, not be regarded as excrescences to be destroyed or damaged, whether in ignorance or deliberately. Representative groups of barrows *must* be taken into guardianship by the Ministry of Works, for preservation. These must by now include not only undamaged, but also partially damaged, and even low-ploughed groups where these possess special features. Posterity, which includes the archaeologists of the future, must be allowed to view and examine, as we and those who have gone before us have done, the great, gaunt, strangely satisfying lines of barrows, striding like lunar-mounts across down and upland. It is also essential that some barrows be preserved for future destruction. Most probably our present-day methods of excavation, record, and study will one day be as outdated and obsolete as those of Merewether and Greenwell seem today. We must not be stampeded into an overt policy of gut and section by all comers in the name of rescue excavation!

Within the existent framework of the records of the Archaeology Branch of the Ordnance Survey there is the machinery for a National Register of Round Barrows. Not only would such a register serve as a basis for special maps, both national and regional, but inventories of areas, similar to the papers and lists of Grinsell (Appendix II), could be published as Professional Papers, an extension of their pre-war series. These would serve as a basis for further work. At the same time our Royal Commission,

[23] *ANL*, III, 121–4, 137–41; Council for British Archaeology, *Memorandum on the Ancient Monuments Acts*, 2nd ed.

guided by such lists, could continue with its more detailed examinations and descriptions. Such a register could be correlated and cross-referenced with the new Register of Bronze Age Pottery, thus forming a basis for the study of ceramics against a background of barrow and cairn type, structure, group, and area, etc. Cards could be published for more important groups and their grave-furniture, embodying all information, on the lines of the international *Inventaria*.

One cannot conclude a chapter upon the state's activities with regard to round barrows without considering our museums. Presumed by some, not without reason, a place of the muses, they are nevertheless the repositories of the portable fragments that are, after the field monuments, the original documents of our prehistory. The two types, regional and national, should fulfil the functions of preserving and exhibiting within these terms of reference this material (and the remainder committed to them). Attenuated funds with the resultant decay and decrepitude has rendered many regional institutions impotent. Where this has not happened the post-war fungoid growth of fashionable museology, plus little more than superficial appreciation of the material, has resulted in exhibitionistic trick and distortion wedded to improbable and, indeed, frequently impossible groupings. Dublin, Edinburgh, and Cardiff have for long housed well maintained collections for the nations of which they are the capital cities. The last is a model example of what such a museum should be. But in London, where one might expect a dynamic power-house of prehistory geared to the proper collection, co-ordination, and conservation of English, and for that matter British, antiquities, one finds only a slender sub-department devotedly striving to show its treasures, most of which have been now for a generation incarcerated in the dust and decay of depository and deep-shelter, against the neo-lilac of Bloomsbury's pantheon. The Trustees, still led by an archaic theopolitical triumvirate, have promised us in an unspecified future better things, among them the elevation of Prehistoric Archaeology to the status of a department. Is this enough? Let us hope that this pitiful sop will not satisfy British public opinion and that Parliament will be moved to constitute a proper and functioning Museum of National Antiquities.*

A realistic and determined scheme for what are the most numerous field monuments of our prehistoric past would entail co-operation, not only between individuals and academic departments, but also between the different departments of state concerned with antiquities. Up to now this has been absent; each fulfilling its own terms of reference, in spite of overlapping, or even conflicting, interests. None the less a policy of unified responsibility could be adopted. A lead is present in the very existence of the Ordnance Survey's Archaeological Name Books. Let action be taken and the *élite* of the country's archaeologically trained minds be attracted to one united archaeological service, all joined by a sense of vocation and purpose. Such a force led by a Queen's Antiquary with adequate powers would ensure the safety of Britain's whole prehistoric past.

* Since writing the foregoing early in 1959 my views on the Royal Commission on Historical Monuments (England) and the British Museum have had a measure of substantiation. For the first see *Antiq.*, XXXIV, 1; for the second see Professor C. F. C. Hawkes's letter in *The Times* (London) of 2 June 1959 and *Antiq.*, XXXIII, 159.

APPENDIX I

PRINCIPAL BRONZE AGE ROUND BARROW LITERATURE: EARLY WORKS AND SPECIAL AREAS

WILLIAM STUKELEY, *Stonehenge: A Temple restored to the British Druids*, 1740; *Abury: A Temple of the British Druids*, 1743. He describes barrows in the vicinity of these monuments.

SIR RICHARD COLT HOARE, *The Ancient History of Wiltshire*, vol. i, 1812, vol. ii, 1819. The results of the excavation of barrows in Wiltshire and north-east Dorset. Knowledge of the Wessex Culture rests largely upon this work.

THOMAS BATEMAN, *Vestiges of the Antiquities of Derbyshire*, 1848, which incorporates the work of William Bateman; and *Ten Years' Diggings in Celtic and Saxon Grave Hills in the counties of Derby, Stafford, and York from 1848 to 1858*, 1861. The Batemans, father and son, together with their friends, Samuel Carrington and James Ruddock, opened well over four hundred barrows.

CHARLES WARNE, *The Celtic Tumuli of Dorset*, 1866. He opened about forty-six barrows besides recording the work of others.

JOHN THURNAM, 'Ancient British Barrows' in *Archaeologia*, XLII and XLIII, 1869–71. Here is a systematic study of the external forms of long and round barrows in relation to their contents. It is based upon almost all the work undertaken up to the time he wrote.

WILLIAM COPELAND BORLASE, *Naenia Cornubiae*, 1872. A book considered below the standards then obtaining. W. C. Borlase and W. C. Lukis: 'Typical Specimens of Cornish Barrows' in *Archaeologia*, XLIX, 1885, supplements this work.

CANON WILLIAM GREENWELL, *British Barrows*, 1877, deals with the opening by the Canon of barrows in Cumberland, Durham, Gloucestershire, Northumberland, Westmorland, and Yorkshire. A paper, 'Recent Researches in Barrows in Yorkshire, Wiltshire, Berkshire, etc.', in *Archaeologia*, LII, 1–72, supplements this work.

G. B. WITTS, *Archaeological Handbook of Gloucestershire*, 1883, lists 126 round barrows in the county.

J. R. MORTIMER, *Forty Years' Researches in British and Saxon Burial Mounds of East Yorkshire*, 1905. Describes the excavation of and the relics from barrows on the Yorkshire Wolds.

LIEUT.-GENERAL PITT-RIVERS, *Excavations in Cranborne Chase*, 1887–1903, Vol. IV. The first satisfactory excavations of round barrows.

REV. E. H. GODDARD, 'A List of Prehistoric, etc., Antiquities in the County of Wilts.', *WAM*, XXXVIII, 153–378, lists and describes most of the round barrows of Wiltshire and notes the relics taken from them by Hoare and others. This work has to a great extent been superseded by the publication of the *Victoria County History of Wiltshire*, Vol. I, Part I.

APPENDIX II

PRINCIPAL MODERN BRONZE AGE ROUND BARROW LITERATURE

(1) TOPOGRAPHICAL: GENERAL AND REGIONAL

BRITAIN

(*a*) O. G. S. Crawford: 'Barrows' in *Antiquity*, I, 419–34, and discussion and ratiocination of the external characteristics of barrows in *Wessex from the Air*, 1928, 13.

(*b*) L. V. Grinsell: General: 'Bell-Barrows' in *PPSEA*, VII, 203–30. 'The Bronze Age Round Barrows of Wessex', *PPS*, VII, 73–113. *The Ancient Burial Mounds of England*, 1936, revised edition, 1953.

County Surveys:

'Berkshire Barrows', *Berks AJ*, XXXIX, 3–23; XL, 20–58; XLII, 102–16; XLIII, 9–21.

Dorset Barrows. Published by the Dorset Natural History and Archaeological Society, Dorchester, 1959.

'Hampshire Barrows', *PHFC*, XIV, 9–40, 195–229, 346–65.

'Isle of Wight Barrows' (with G. A. Sherwin), *PIOWNHAS*, III, 179–222.

Somerset: 'Some Rare types of Round Barrow on Mendip', *PSANHS*, LXXXV, 151–66.

'Surrey Barrows', *Surrey AC*, XL, 56–64; XLII, 26–60.

'Sussex Barrows', *SAC*, LXXV, 216–75; LXXXI, 210–14; LXXXII, 115–23.

Wiltshire Barrows: *Victoria County History of Wiltshire*, Vol. I, Part I.

IRELAND

(*a*) S. P. Ó Ríordáin, 'Burial Mounds', in *Antiquities of the Irish Countryside*, 75–80, 1953.

(*b*) P. McCaffrey, 'The Dukellin Barrow Group, Co. Galway', *JRSAI*, LXXXV, 218–25.

(*c*) M. de Paor and M. P. Ó h-Eochaidhe: 'An Unusual Group of Earthworks at Slieve Breage, Co. Meath', *JRSAI*, LXXXVI, 97–101.

(2) EXCAVATION: ENGLAND AND WALES

C. F. Fox, *Life and Death in the Bronze Age*, 1959; excavations undertaken between 1925–8 and 1938–1943.

APPENDIX III

PROVISIONAL LIST OF PRINCIPAL AUTHENTICALLY EXCAVATED AND DEFINITIVELY PUBLISHED ROUND BARROW EXCAVATIONS

(For Post and Stake Circle Barrows see Appendix IV)

ENGLAND

This is an expansion and revision of a basic list of well authenticated barrow excavations in Wessex, prepared by L. V. Grinsell (*PPS*, VII, 110–13) and containing material up to 1941.

I. EARTHEN BARROWS

Bowl Barrows

Bedfordshire

'The Excavation of Barrows at Dunstable', *Arch. J.*, LXXXVIII, 193–227.

Berkshire

'Round Barrows and Ring Ditches in Berkshire and Oxfordshire', *Oxon.*, I, 7–23.
'Further Excavations in Barrow Hills Field, Radley', *Oxon.*, III, 31–40.
'Excavations in Barrow Hills Field, Radley', *Oxon.*, XIII, 1–17.

Cambridgeshire

'Two Bronze Age Barrows at Chippenham', *PCAS*, XXXVI, 134–55.
'Excavation of the Snailwell Barrows', *PCAS*, XLII, 30–49.

Derbyshire

'The Bronze Age Round Barrow at Swarkston', *JDANHS*, LXXV, 123–39.

Devonshire

'The Excavation of Two Barrows at East Putford', *PDAES*, III, Pt. IV, 156–63.

Dorset

'The Excavation of a Round Barrow on Canford Heath', *PDNHAS*, LXXVI, 39–50.
'The Excavation of Barrows on Crichel Down', *Arch.*, XC, 47–80.
'The Excavation of a Round Barrow on Chick's Hill', *PDNHAS*, LXXX, 146–59.
'The Excavation of two Barrows at Frampton', *PDNHAS*, LXXX, 111–32.
'Excavation of three Barrows at Kinson', *PDNHAS*, LXXX, 133–45.
'Litton Cheyney Excavations', *PDNHAS*, LXXX, 160–77.

Hampshire

'Three Turf Barrows at Hurn, Near Christchurch', *PHFC*, XV, 248–62.
'The Excavation of Fifteen Barrows in the New Forest', *PPS*, IX, 1–27.
'The Excavation of a Barrow on Rockbourne Down', *PHFC*, XVI, 156–62.

Leicestershire

'The Excavation of a Bronze Age Round Barrow at Lockington', *Transactions of the Leicestershire Archaeological and History Society*, XXXI, 17–29.

Oxfordshire

'A Middle Bronze Age Barrow at Cassington', *Oxon.*, XI–XII, 5–26.
'Excavations at Cassington', *Oxon.*, XVI, 1–4.
Excavations at Dorchester, Oxon., Vol. I, Ashmolean Museum, 1951, 60.
'Excavations at Stanton Harcourt', *Oxon.*, VIII–IX, 19–63.
'Excavations at Stanton Harcourt', *Oxon.*, X, 16–41.

Suffolk

'The Excavation of the Beaconhill Barrow', *PCAS*, XXVI, 19.
'Report on the Removal of a Tumulus on Martlesham Heath', *Proceedings of the Suffolk Institute of Archaeology*, XXIV, 36–57.

Bell Barrows

Berkshire

'Excavations in Barrow Hills Field, Radley, 1944–5', *Oxon.*, XVII–XVIII, 14–23.

Dorset

'Excavation of a Barrow at Oakley Down', *PDNHAS*, LXXV, 36–44.
'A Barrow on Black Down, Portesham', *PPS*, XXIII, 124–36.

Hampshire

'The Great Barrow at Bishop's Waltham', *PPS*, 137–66.

Oxfordshire

Dorchester VII. *Excavations at Dorchester, Oxon.*, Vol. I, Ashmolean Museum, 1951, 60.

Pond Barrow

Dorset

'A Pond Barrow at Winterbourne Steepleton', *Arch. J.*, CVIII, 1–24.

II. CAIRNS

Yorkshire

'Excavations on Kildale Moor', *YAJ*, XL, 179–92.

III. COMPOSITE BARROWS

Cornwall

'The Excavation of Tregulland Burrow', *Ant. J.*, XXXVII, 174–96.

Gloucestershire

'The Adlestrop Hill Barrow', *Transactions of the Bristol and Gloucestershire Archaeological Society*, LX, 152–64.
'The Ivy Lodge Round Barrow', *Transactions of the Bristol and Gloucestershire Archaeological Society*, LXIX, 59–77.
'The Marshfield Barrows', *Transactions of the Bristol and Gloucestershire Archaeological Society*, LXXII, 23–44.

Hampshire

'A Round Barrow on Stockbridge Down', *Ant. J.*, XX, 39–51.

Somerset

'Bronze Age Barrows near Chewton Mendip', *PSANHS*, XCIII, 39–67.
'The Excavation of Barrows on Charmy Down and Lansdown', *Ant. J.*, XXX, 34.
'The Tynings Farm Barrow Group', *PBUSS*, VI, 111–73.

Yorkshire

'Barnby Howes', *YAJ*, XXXIX, 9–31.
'Loose Howe: an Early Bronze Age Burial in a Boat-shaped Wooden Coffin', *PPS*, XV, 87–106.
'Quernhow: a Food Vessel Barrow', *Ant. J.*, XXXI, 1–24.

WALES

I. CAIRNS

Flintshire

'Excavation of a Cairn on Cefn-Goleu', *Flint History Society Publications*, XIII, 91–7.
'Excavation of a Cairn on Cefn-Goleu', second report, *Flint History Society Publications*, XV, 112–40.

Pembrokeshire

'Corston Beacon: an Early Bronze Age Cairn', *Arch. Camb.*, LXXXIII, 137–74.

II. COMPOSITE BARROWS

Brecknockshire

'A Stone Circle and Cairn on Mynydd Epynt', *Arch. Camb.*, XCVII, 169–94.

Flintshire

'The Ysceifiog Circle and Barrow', *Arch. Camb.*, LXXXI, 48–75.

Glamorganshire

'Simondston and Pond Cairns', *Arch.*, LXXXVII, 129–80.
'Two Bronze Age Barrows on Fairwood Common', *Arch. Camb.*, XCVIII, 52–63.
'A Barrow on Breach Farm', *PPS*, IV, 107–21.
'A Bronze Age Barrow in Llandow Parish', *Arch.*, LXXXIX, 89–126.

Monmouthshire

'A Middle Bronze Age Barrow at Crick', *Arch. Camb.*, XCV, 169–91.

Pembrokeshire

'A Bronze Age Barrow on Kilpaison Burrows', *Arch. Camb.*, LXXXI, 1–35.

Radnorshire

'A Round Barrow of the Bronze Age near Jacket's Well', *Transactions of the Radnorshire Society*, VII, 23–9.

SCOTLAND

CAIRNS

Kirkcudbrightshire

'A Bronze Age Cairn and Cist with Food Vessel at Mollance', *Transactions of the Dumfriesshire and Galloway Natural History and Archaeological Society*, XXX, 159–65.

Roxburghshire

'Excavation of Kalemouth Cairn', *PSAS*, LXXXVI, 200–1.

West Lothian

'The Excavations at Cairnpapple Hill', *PSAS*, LXXXII, 68–123.

IRELAND
(In part after S. P. Ó Ríordáin)

I. EARTHEN BARROWS

(RB denotes ring barrows, the remainder are bowl barrows.)

Co. Galway

'Two Bronze Age Burials at Carrobeg North (Carrobeg II)', RB, *JGHAS*, XVIII, 121.
'Excavations in the Townland of Pollacorragune, Tuam', RB, *JGHAS*, XVII, 17.

Co. Kildare

'Three Burial Sites at Carbury', *JRSAI*, LXVIII, 130.
'Excavation of some Earthworks on the Curragh', RB, *PRIA*, LIII, 249.

Co. Limerick

'Two Barrows at Ballingoola', RB, *JRSAI*, LXXIX, 139.
'Excavations at Cush (T. II & III)', *PRIA*, XLV, 137.
'Excavation of a Barrow in Cahercorney', *JCHAS*, LIV, 101.
'Excavations at Lissard', RB, *JRSAI*, LXVI, 173.
'Excavation of a Barrow at Rathjordan', RB, *JCHAS*, LII, 1.
'Further Barrows at Rathjordan', RB, *JCHAS*, LIII, 19.

Co. Mayo

'The Tumulus Cemetery of Carrowjames', RB, *JGHAS*, XVIII, 157; XIX, 16.

II. CAIRNS

Co. Antrim

Lyles Hill: The Cairn, Evans, 1953.

Co. Clare

'A Cairn at Poulawack', *JRSAI*, LXIII, 191.

Co. Cork

'Excavation of a Cairn at Moneen', *PRIA*, LIV, 121.

Co. Limerick

'Excavation of a Cairn in Townland of Curraghbinny', *JCHAS*, XXXVIII, 80.

Co. Londonderry

'Two Cairns at Gortacloghan', *UJA*, XI, 54–7.

Co. Mayo

'A Tumulus at Carrowlisdooaun', *JRSAI*, LXV, 75.

Co. Westmeath

'The Cemetery Cairn at Knockast', *PRIA*, XLI, 232.

III. COMPOSITE BARROWS

Co. Dublin

'The Excavation of a Composite Tumulus at Drimnagh', *JRSAI*, LXIX, 190.

Co. Fermanagh

'The Cairn in Castle Archdale Deerpark', *UJA*, IX, 53–7.

Co. Limerick

'Excavations at Cush (T.I.)', *PRIA*, 133.

Co. Mayo

'"Turnincorragh". A Bronze Age Burial Mound', *JGHAS*, XXVI, 72.

APPENDIX IV

PROVISIONAL LIST OF POST AND STAKE CIRCLES BENEATH AND AROUND BARROWS

ENGLAND

Berkshire

Beedon: *Arch. J.*, VII, 66.

Cambridgeshire

Chippenham: *PCAS*, XXXIX, 33–68.
Snailwell: *PCAS*, XLIII, 356.

Cornwall

Davidstow: *ANL*, II, No. 7, 110.
Tregulland Burrow: *Ant. J.*, XXXVIII, 174–96.

Dorset

Canford Heath: *PDNHAS*, LXXVI, 39–50.
Crichel Down: *Arch.*, XC, 64–6.
Poole: *PPS*, XVIII, 150.

Isle of Wight

Arreton Down: *Unpublished information from Mr J. Alexander.* PPS XXVI (1960), 263

Lancashire

Bleasdale: *Ant. J.*, XVIII, 154–71.

Lincolnshire

Ludford Magna: *Ant. J.*, XXVIII, 27.

Wiltshire

Amesbury: *WAM*, LVI, 238 (interim note).
Snail Down: XV: *WAM*, LVI, 144 (interim note).

Yorkshire

Calais Wold: Mortimer, 1905, 153–6.

WALES

Denbigh

Pant-y-Dulath: *P. Hayes to Council for British Archaeology, 11th January 1958.*

Glamorgan

Six Wells 267′: *Ant. J.*, XXI, 118–22.
Six Wells 271′: *Antiq.*, XV, 142–61.
Sheeplays 279′: *Ant. J.*, XXI, 115–18.
Sheeplays 293′: *Ant. J.*, XXI, 98–114.

Montgomery

Caebetin: *Mon. Coll.*, 1932, 176–81.

Pembroke

Letterston: *Arch. Camb.*, C, 67–87.
South Hill, Talbenny: *Arch. J.*, XCIX, 1–32.

APPENDIX V

THE WESSEX CULTURE: PRINCIPAL LITERATURE

Definitive Account

'The Early Bronze Age in Wessex' (lists of graves, etc.), *PPS*, IV, 53–106.

Dagger Graves

'Dagger Graves in the Wessex Bronze Age' (lists of Dagger graves), *ULIAA Rpt*, X, 37–62.

Battle Axes

'The Perforated Axe-Hammers of Britain' (describes associated examples), *Arch.*, LXXV, 77–108.

Halberds

'The Halberd in Bronze Age Europe', *Arch.*, LXXXVI, 195–321.

Flanged Axes

'British Decorated Axes and their Diffusion during the Earlier Part of the Bronze Age', *PPS*, IV, 272–307.

Faience Beads

'Faience Beads of the British Bronze Age', *Arch.*, LXXXV, 203–52.
'A Necklace from a Barrow in North Molton Parish, North Devon', *Ant. J.*, XXXI, 25–31.
'The Use and Distribution of Faience in the Ancient East and Prehistoric Europe' (with revised lists), *PPS*, XXII, 37–84.

Handled Cups of Gold, Amber, and Shale

'Two Shale Cups of the Early Bronze Age and other Similar Cups', *WAM*, XLIV, 111–17.

Gold Ornaments

'The Gold Ornament from Mold, Flintshire, North Wales' (comparison with Wessex sheet gold work), *PPS*, XIX, 161–79.

Timber Coffins

'Pre-Roman Coffin Burials with a Particular Reference to one from a barrow at Fovant', *WAM*, XLIV, 101–5.
See also *PPS*, XV, 101–6.

Distinctive Barrows

For Bell Barrows and Disc Barrows see Appendix II.

Chronology

'Cross-dating in the European Bronze Age', *Festschrift für Otto Tchumi*, Frauenfeld, 1948, 70–6.
'The British Isles and the Northern Early Bronze Age', Fox and Dickens, 1950, 102–5.
'The Wessex Early Bronze Age: A chronological re-assessment', *CISPP*, 225.

General Accounts

'Wessex before the Celts', J. F. S. Stone, London, 1958.
'The Archaeology of Wessex', L. V. Grinsell, London, 1958.

BIBLIOGRAPHY

PERIODICALS

Abbreviations	
Aarbøger	*Aarbøger for Nordisk Oldkyndighed og Historie*, Copenhagen
ABSA	*Annual of the British School at Athens*
Acta Arch.	*Acta Archaeologica*, Copenhagen
Actas	*Actas y Memorias*, Madrid
AJA	*American Journal of Archaeology*, Cambridge, Mass.
Altertümer	*Die Altertümer unserer heidnischen Vorzeit*, ed. L. Lindenschmidt, Römisch-germanisches Museum, Mainz
Altschles.	*Altschlesien* (Schlesische Altertumsverein), Breslau
Amer. Anth.	*American Anthropologist*, Beloit
Anglo-Saxon Guide	*Guide to the Anglo-Saxon and Foreign Teutonic Antiquities*, British Museum, 1923
ANL	*Archaeological Newsletter*
Ant. J.	*Antiquaries' Journal*
Antiq.	*Antiquity*
APL	*Archivo de Prehistoria Levantina*, Valencia
Arch.	*Archaeologia* (Society of Antiquaries), London
Arch. Ael.	*Archaeologia Aeliana*, Newcastle-upon-Tyne
Arch. Camb.	*Archaeologia Cambrensis*, Cardiff
Arch. Cant.	*Archaeologia Cantiana* (Kent Archaeological Society), London
Arch. J.	*Archaeological Journal* (Royal Archaeological Institute), London
ASAB	*Annales de la Société d'Archéologie de Belgique*
BA, *BA*	British Association: *The Advancement of Science*
BBCS	*Bulletin of the Board of Celtic Studies*
Berks AJ	*Berkshire Archaeological Journal*
BH Arch.	*Brighton and Hove Archaeologist*
BRGK	*Berichte der römisch-germanischen Kommission des deutschen Archäologischen Instituts* (des deutschen Reiches), Frankfurt
Bronze Age Guide	*Guide to the Antiquities of the Bronze Age*, British Museum, 2nd edition, 1920
BVB	*Bayerische Vorgeschichte Blätter*, Kommission für bayerische Landesgeschichte, München
CISPP	Congrés International des Sciences Préhistoriques et Protohistoriques, Zürich, 1950
DMC II	*Catalogue of Antiquities in the Museum of the Wiltshire Archaeological and Natural History Society at Devizes*, Part II, 2nd edition, 1934.
Ethnos	*Ethnos, Revista do Instituto portugues de arqueologia, historia e etnografia*, Lisbon
Fontes	*Fontes Archaeologici Posnaniensis*
Gents. Mag.	*A Classified Collection of the Chief Contents of 'The Gentleman's Magazine' from 1731 to 1858*, ed. G. L. Gomme; Archaeology, Vols. I, II, 1886
Germania	*Germania, Anzeiger der römisch-germanischen Kommission des deutschen Archäologischen Instituts* (des deutschen Reiches), Berlin
Götze Festschrift	*Studien zur Vorgeschichtlichen Archäeologie . . . Alfred Götze dagebracht*, Leipzig, 1925

Inv. Arch.	*Inventaria Archaeologica*
IPEK	*Jahrbuch für prähistorische und ethnographische Kunst*, Köln
JBAA	*Journal of the British Archaeological Association*
JCHAS	*Journal of the Cork Historical and Archaeological Society*
JDANHS	*Journal of the Derbyshire Archaeological and Natural History Society*
JGHAS	*Journal of the Galway Historical and Archaeological Society*
JRAI	*Journal of the Royal Anthropological Institute*, London
JRSAI	*Journal of the Royal Society of Antiquaries of Ireland* (formerly the Royal Historical and Archaeological Association), Dublin
JSG	*Jahrbuch der Schweizerischen Gesellschaft für Urgeschichte*, Frauenfeld
JST	*Jahreschrift für die Vorgeschichte der sächsich-thüringische Länder*, Halle
KDVS	Det Kongelige Danske Videnskabernes Selskab, Copenhagen
Kuml	*Kuml, Arbog for Jysk Arkaeologisk Selskab*, Aarhus
L'Anthr.	*L'Anthropologie*, Paris
LPA	*Later Prehistoric Antiquities of the British Isles*, British Museum, 1953
MAGW	*Mitteilungen der anthropologischen Gesellschaft in Wien*
Man	*Man, A Monthly Record of Anthropological Science* (Royal Anthropological Institute), London
Mannus	*Mannus* (Gesellschaft für deutsche Vorgeschichte), Berlin-Leipzig
Matériaux	*Matériaux pour l'histoire primitive et naturelle de l'homme*, Paris
MBV	*Materialhefte zur Bayerischen Vorgeschichte*, Kallmünz
Mon. Coll.	*Montgomeryshire Collections*
MZ	*Mainzer Zeitschrift*, Mainz
NDV	*Nieuwe Drentsche Volksalmanak*, Groningen
Offa	*Offa, Berichte und Mitteilungen des Museums vorgeschichtlicher Altertümer in Kiel*
OMROL (NR, OR)	*Oudheidkundige Mededeelingen uit het Rijksmuseum van Oudheden te Leiden* (Niewe Reeks, Oude Reeks)
Oxon.	*Oxoniensia*
Palaeohist.	*Palaeohistoria*, Groningen
PBA	*Proceedings of the British Academy*
PBNSS	*Proceedings of the Bournemouth Natural Science Society*
PBUSS	*Proceedings of the Bristol University Spelaeological Society*
PCAS	*Proceedings of the Cambridge Antiquarian Society*
PDAES	*Proceedings of the Devonshire Archaeological Exploration Society*
PDNHAS	*Proceedings of the Dorset Natural History and Archaeological Society*
PFIC	*Proceedings of the First International Congress of Prehistoric and Protohistoric Sciences, 1932*, Oxford, 1934
PHFCAS	*Proceedings of the Hampshire Field Club and Archaeological Society*
PIOWNHAS	*Proceedings of the Isle of Wight Natural History Society*
PPS	*Proceedings of the Prehistoric Society*, Cambridge
PPSEA	*Proceedings of the Prehistoric Society of East Anglia*
Prä. Bl.	*Prähistorische Blätter*, München
PRIA	*Proceedings of the Royal Irish Academy*, Dublin
PSA	*Proceedings of the Society of Antiquaries of London*
PSANHS	*Proceedings of the Somersetshire Archaeological and Natural History Society*
PSAS	*Proceedings of the Society of Antiquaries of Scotland*, Edinburgh
PWCFC	*Proceedings of the West Cornwall Field Club*
PZ	*Prehistorische Zeitschrift*, Berlin
RCHM	Royal Commission on Historical Monuments
Reliquary	*The Reliquary and Illustrated Archaeologist*
SAC	*Sussex Archaeological Collections*
SCIV	*Studii si Cercetări de Istorie Veche*, Bucharest
SP	*Science Progress*
Stourhead Cat.	*Catalogue of Antiquities in the Museum of the Wiltshire Archaeological and Natural History Society*, Part I, *The Stourhead Collection*, Devizes, 1896

Surrey AC	*Surrey Archaeological Collections*
TAASDN	*Transactions of the Architectural and Archaeological Society of Durham and Northumberland*
TCWAAS	*Transactions of the Cumberland and Westmorland Antiquarian Society*
TDA	*Transactions of the Devonshire Association*
TNDFC	*Transactions of the Newbury District Field Club*
UJA	*Ulster Journal of Archaeology*, new series, 1937 ff.
ULIA (A Rpt)	*University of London Institute of Archaeology (Annual Report)*
VCH	*Victoria County History*
WAM	*Wiltshire Archaeological Magazine*, Devizes
YAJ	*Yorkshire Archaeological Journal*
Zephyrus	*Zephyrus* (Seminario de Arquelogia de la Universidad de Salamanca)

BOOKS

ABERCROMBY, J., 1912, *The Bronze Age Pottery of Great Britain and Ireland*, 2 vols., Oxford University Press.

ABERG, N., 1930–5, *Bronzezeitliche und Früheisenzeitliche Chronologie*, Stockholm.

ALLCROFT, A. HADRIAN, 1908, *The Earthwork of England*, Macmillan.

ANDERSON, W., 1886, *Scotland in Pagan Times (Stone and Bronze)*.

ARMSTRONG, E. C. R., 1933, *Catalogue of Irish Gold Ornaments in the Collections of the Royal Irish Academy*.

ATKINSON, R. J. C., 1953, *Field Archaeology*, 2nd revised edition, Methuen.
1956, *Stonehenge*, Hamish Hamilton.

ATKINSON, R. J. C., PIGGOTT, C. M., and SANDARS, N. K., 1951, *Excavations at Dorchester, Oxon*. Vol. I, Ashmolean Museum, Oxford.

BATEMAN, THOMAS, 1848, *Vestiges of the Antiquities of Derbyshire*.
1861, *Ten Years' Diggings in Celtic and Saxon Grave Hills in the Counties of Derby, Stafford, and York from 1848 to 1858*.

BEHRENS, G., 1916, *Bronzezeit Süddeutschlands*. (Catalogue des römischen-germanischen Central-museums, Mainz).

BLEGAN, C. W., 1950, *Troy*, Oxford University Press.

BOHM, WALDTRAUT, 1935, *Die ältere Bronzezeit in der Mark Brandenburg*, Berlin.

BORLASE, W. C., 1872, *Naenia Cornubiae*.

BROHOLM, H. C., 1943–9, *Danmarks Bronzealder*, 4 vols., Copenhagen.

BROOKS, C. E. P., 1949, *Climate through the Ages*, revised edition, Benn.

BURSCH, F. C., 1933, *Die Becherkultur in den Niederlanden*, Marburg.

BUSHE-FOX, J. P., 1915, *Excavations at Hengistbury Head, 1911–12*. Third report of the Research Committee of the Society of Antiquaries of London.

CASTILLO, YURRITA A., 1928, *La Cultura del Vaso campaniforme*, Barcelona.

CHILDE, V. G., 1929, *The Danube in Prehistory*, Oxford University Press.
1930, *The Bronze Age*, Cambridge University Press.
1931, *Skara Brae, A Pictish Village in Orkney*, Routledge & Kegan Paul.
1935, *The Prehistory of Scotland*, Routledge & Kegan Paul.
1946, *Scotland Before the Scots*, Methuen.
1947 a, *The Dawn of European Civilization*, 4th edition, Routledge & Kegan Paul.
1947 b, *Prehistoric Communities of the British Isles*, revised edition, Chambers.
1950, *Prehistoric Migrations in Europe*, Oslo.
1951, *Social Evolution*, Watts.
1952, *New Light on the Most Ancient East*, revised edition, Routledge & Kegan Paul.
1956, *Piecing Together the Past*, Routledge & Kegan Paul.
1957, *The Dawn of European Civilization*, 6th edition, Routledge & Kegan Paul.

Clark, J. G. D., 1936, *The Mesolithic Settlement of Northern Europe*, Cambridge University Press.
1947, *Archaeology and Society*, revised edition, Methuen.
1952, *Prehistoric Europe; the Economic Basis*, Methuen.
Council for British Archaeology, 1948, *A Survey and Policy of Field Research in the Archaeology of Great Britain.*
Crawford, O. G. S., 1925, *The Long Barrows of the Cotswolds*, Bellows, Gloucester.
1939, *Luftbild und Vorgeschichte*, Berlin.
1953, *Archaeology in the Field*, Phoenix House.
1957, *The Eye Goddess*, Phoenix House.
Crawford, O. G. S., and Keiller, A., 1928, *Wessex from the Air*, Oxford University Press.
Cunnington, M. E., 1929, *Woodhenge*, Simpson, Devizes.
Curwen, E. C., 1954, *The Archaeology of Sussex*, 2nd edition, Methuen.
Dobson, D. P., 1931, *The Archaeology of Somerset*, Methuen.
Ebert, M. (ed.), 1924, *Reallexikon der Vorgeschichte*, Berlin.
Elgee, F., 1930, *Early Man in North-East Yorkshire*, Bellows, Gloucester.
Elgee, F. and H. W., 1933, *The Archaeology of Yorkshire*, Methuen.
Evans, E. E., 1953, *Lyles Hill, a late Neolithic Site in Co. Antrim*, H.M.S.O., Belfast.
Evans, J., 1881, *The Ancient Bronze Implements of Great Britain.*
1897, *The Ancient Stone Implements of Great Britain.*
Fergusson, J., 1872, *Rude Stone Monuments in all Countries.*
Forssander, J. E., 1936, *Der Ostskandinavische Norden während der Ältesten Metallzeit Europas*, Lund.
Fox, C. F. (Sir Cyril), 1923, *The Archaeology of the Cambridge Region*, Cambridge University Press.
1952, *The Personality of Britain*, 4th edition, National Museum of Wales, Cardiff.
1959, *Life and Death in the Bronze Age*, Routledge & Kegan Paul.
Fox, C. F., and Dickens, Bruce (eds.), 1950, *The Early Cultures of North-West Europe* (Chadwick Memorial volume), Cambridge University Press.
Glasbergen, W., 1954, 'Barrow Excavations in the Eight Beatitudes', *Palaeohistoria*, II, III.
Greenwell, William, 1877, *British Barrows: a record of the examination of sepulchral mounds in various parts of England, together with a description of figures of skulls and general remarks on prehistoric crania by George Rolleston.*
Grimes, W. F., 1939, *Guide to the Collection illustrating the Prehistory of Wales*, National Museum of Wales.
(ed.), 1951, *Aspects of Archaeology in Britain and Beyond: Essays Presented to O. G. S. Crawford*, Edwards.
Grinsell, L. V., 1953, *The Ancient Burial Mounds of England*, 2nd edition, Methuen.
Hampel, J., 1890, *Altertümer der Bronzezeit in Ungarn*, Budapest.
Hawkes, C. F. C., 1940, *The Prehistoric Foundations of Europe to the Mycenaen Age*, Methuen.
Heathcote, J. P., 1947, *Birchover: its Prehistoric and Druidical Remains*, printed by W. Edmunds Ltd, Chesterfield.
Hencken, H., 1932, *The Archaeology of Cornwall and Scilly*, Methuen.
Hoare, Sir Richard Colt, 1812–19, *The Ancient History of Wiltshire*, Vol. I, *South Wiltshire*; Vol. II, *North Wiltshire.*
Hobhouse, L. T., Ginsberg, M., and Wheeler, G. C., 1926, *The Material Culture and Social Institutions of Simple Peoples*, Chapman & Hall.
Hoernes, M., and Menghin, O., 1925, *Urgeschichte der bildenden Kunst in Europa*, 3rd edition, Vienna.
Howarth, E., 1899, *Catalogue of the Bateman Collection of Antiquities in the Sheffield Public Museum.*
Karo, G., 1930, *Die Schachtgräber von Mykenai*, Munich.
Kendrick, T. D., 1928, *The Archaeology of the Channel Islands*, Vol. I, Methuen.
1950, *British Antiquity*, Methuen.
Kendrick, T. D., and Hawkes, C. F. C., 1932, *Archaeology in England and Wales, 1914–1931*, Methuen.
Kersten, K., 1936, *Zur älteren nordischen Bronzezeit*, Neumunster.
Kramer, Werner (ed.), 1958, *Neue Ausgrabungen in Deutschland*, Römisch-Germanische Kommission, Berlin.

Le Rouzic, Z., 1930, *Les Cromlechs de Er-Lannic*, Vannes.
Leisner, G. and V., 1943, *Die Megalithgräber der iberischen Halbinsel*, Vol. I, *Der Süden*, Berlin.
Macalister, R. A. S., 1931, *Tara, A Pagan Sanctuary of Ancient Ireland*, Scribners.
MacWhite, E., 1951, *Estudios sobre las Relaciones Atlanticos de la Peninsula Hispanica en la Edad del Bronce*, Madrid.
Mortimer, J. R., 1905, *Forty Years' Researches in British and Saxon Burial Mounds of East Yorkshire.*
Movius, H. L., 1942, *The Irish Stone Age*, Cambridge University Press.
Müller, S., 1895, *Ordning of Danmarks Oldsager.*
Munro, R., 1899, *Prehistoric Scotland.*
Mylonas, G. E., 1957, *Ancient Mycenae*, Routledge & Kegan Paul.
Ó Ríordáin, S. P., 1953, *Antiquities of the Irish Countryside*, 3rd revised edition, Methuen.
1954, *Tara, the Monuments on the Hill*, Dundalgan Press, Dundalk.
Piggott, S., 1954, *The Neolithic Cultures of the British Isles*, Cambridge University Press.
Pitt-Rivers, L. F., 1887–98, *Excavations in Cranborne Chase*, 4 vols.
Raftery, J., 1951, *Prehistoric Ireland*, Batsford.
Richly, H., 1893, *Die Bronzezeit in Böhmen*, Prague.
Sandars, N. K., 1957, *Bronze Age Cultures in France*, Cambridge University Press.
Schaeffer, F. A., 1926, *Les Tertres funéraires préhistoriques dans la Forêt de Haganau*, Vol. I, Hagenau.
Schliemann, H., 1880, *Ilios: the City and Country of the Trojans.*
Schrickel, W., 1957, *Westeuropäische Elemente im Neolithikum und in der frühen Bronzezeit Mitteldeutschlands*, Leipzig.
Schultz, A., 1939, *Vor- und Frühgeschichte Mitteldeutschlands*, Halle.
Schwantes, G., 1939, *Die Vorgeschichte Schleswig Holsteins.*
Smith, R. A., 1931, *The Sturge Collection of Flints: Britain.*
Sprockhoff, E., 1938, *Die Nordische Megalithkultur*, Handbücher der Urgeschichte Deutschlands, Berlin.
Stukeley, William, 1723, *Itinerarium Curiosum*, Vol. I; Vol. II, 1776 (post.).
1740, *Stonehenge: a Temple Restored to the British Druids.*
1743, *Abury, a Temple of the British Druids.*
Sturms, E., 1936, *Die ältere Bronzezeit im Ostbaltikum*, Berlin.
Sumner, A. Heywood, 1931, *Local Papers, Archaeological and Topographical, Hampshire, Dorset, and Wiltshire*, Chiswick Press.
Uenze, O., 1938, *Die Frühbronzezeitlichen Triangulären Vollgriffdolche*, Berlin.
Van Giffen, A. E., 1930, *Die Bauart der Einzelgräber*, Vol. I, Mannus-Bibliothek, Nr. 44, Leipzig.
Wheeler, R. E. M. (Sir Mortimer), 1943, *Maiden Castle, Twelfth Report of the Research Committee of the Society of Antiquaries.*
1954, *Archaeology from the Earth*, Oxford University Press.
Williams-Freeman, J. P., 1915, *Field Archaeology as illustrated by Hampshire*, Macmillan.
Zeuner, F. E., 1950, *Dating the Past*, 2nd edition, Methuen.
1952, *Dating the Past*, 3rd edition, Methuen.

INDEX